Reading 1922

Reading 1922

A Return to the Scene
of the Modern

MICHAEL NORTH

New York   Oxford

Oxford University Press

1999

Oxford University Press

Oxford   New York

Athens   Auckland   Bangkok   Bogotá   Buenos Aires   Calcutta
Cape Town   Chennai   Dar es Salaam   Delhi   Florence   Hong Kong   Istanbul
Karachi   Kuala Lumpur   Madrid   Melbourne   Mexico City   Mumbai
Nairobi   Paris   São Paulo   Singapore   Taipei   Tokyo   Toronto   Warsaw

and associated companies in
Berlin   Ibadan

Copyright © 1999 by Michael North

Published by Oxford University Press, Inc.
198 Madison Avenue, New York, New York 10016

Oxford is a registered trademark of Oxford University Press.

Library of Congress Cataloging-in-Publication Data
North, Michael, 1951–
Reading 1922 : a return to the scene of the modern / Michael North.
p.   cm.
Includes bibliographical references and index.
ISBN 0-19-512720-X
1. English literature—20th century—History and criticism.   2. Modernism (Literature)—Great Britain.
3. Literature and society—Great Britain—History—20th century.   4. Literature and society—
United States—History—20th century.   5. American literature—20th century—History and criticism.
6. Eliot, T. S. (Thomas Stearns), 1888–1965.   Waste land.   7. Books and reading—
History—20th century.   8. Modernism (Literature)—United States.
9. Joyce, James, 1882–1941.   Ulysses.   10. Nineteen twenty-two, A.D.   I. Title.
PR478.M6N67   1999
820.9'112—dc21   98-40366

1 3 5 7 9 8 6 4 2
Printed in the United States of America
on acid-free paper

102699-3080 R

Preface

ANYONE WHO WRITES about or teaches modern literature spends a good deal of time in 1922. In fact, a very plausible account of modern literature in English can be based on the work of a very few months extending from the publication of *Ulysses* in February 1922 to the publications of *Cane*, *Harmonium*, and *Spring and All* in the fall of 1923. After offering such an account for a few years, I began to imagine myself in a bookstore of the time, browsing among tables containing both *The Waste Land* and Willa Cather's *One of Ours*, or *Babbitt* next to *Jacob's Room*. And though this would certainly have been possible at the time, it is now a little disorienting to think about, because our way of looking at modern literature so thoroughly insulates such works from one another. Modern British literature is generally taught and interpreted quite separately from modern American literature, which is itself subdivided so that possible connections between Eliot and Toomer or Eliot and Cather can hardly be imagined. Of course, this conjectural bookstore would also have had newspapers and magazines, not to mention popular novels like Zane Grey's *The Wanderer of the Wasteland*, which a reader could have taken home along with Eliot to get a different perspective on wandering in the desert. So far is most literary criticism from examining such materials that their very existence is usually an astonishment.

Dissatisfied with this situation, I decided to turn myself into the ideal reader of 1922, with an insomnia so ideal it would be adequate not just to *Ulysses* but to anything else published in the same year. I wanted to approach the written materials of this single, important year without a priori distinctions and hierarchies, though I was well aware that I could hardly approach them without preconceptions. I did not, in other words, start with the two most prominent works of the year, *Ulysses* and *The Waste Land*, and then read so as to reconstruct a context for them. I read everything I could get my hands on, assuming that sooner or later it would probably bring me back to those works, quite possibly from a new and unexpected direction.

In the end, I think the experiment was worth performing. In the course of it, I largely satisfied my desire for a more comprehensive understanding of how the masterworks of literary modernism fit into the discursive framework of their time. But I also said a good deal less about *Ulysses* and *The Waste Land* than about other works, some of them almost entirely unknown, and I think it only fair to warn readers of that at the outset. I have not tried to provide what I never intended to produce—another comprehensive reading of those two great works—confident that readers wanting such a thing will not have far to look. I comment, sometimes at length, on works quite well known outside literary studies, and I am well aware of the dangers of such intellectual poaching, though I know of no protection against it except exceptional care. I can only hope that in my case it has been enough. I also permit one major omission, or one that I am most aware of among the many, and that is any considerable analysis of the major African American works of 1922, Claude McKay's *Harlem Shadows* and James Weldon Johnson's *Book of American Negro Poetry*. The reason for this is simply that I have already written in a previous book what I would have written on those works had I considered them here. Perhaps readers interested in that material could simply annex chapters 4 and 5 of that book, *The Dialect of Modernism*, to this one to help repair my omission.

Inevitably, there are many other omissions less easy to repair. Pursuing certain aspects of my inquiry led me away from some works by major authors, such as Fitzgerald's *The Beautiful and Damned* or Woolf's *Jacob's Room*, and toward other works less obviously situated in my year, such as *The Great Gatsby*, which is set in 1922, or *Mrs. Dalloway*, which was begun in that year. Sadly, I was never able to say anything very useful about certain works, chief among them Elizabeth von Arnim's *Enchanted April*, that made me feel from time to time as if 1922 were filled with unexpected literary riches. Nor was I finally able to comment in any satisfactory way on a great many works that convinced me this was a time of unparalleled linguistic futility. What is surprising to me now, however, looking back over the whole project, is not that I was forced to omit such a large number of the things I read but that I was finally able to include so many, and the sense of waste that comes over me as I recall so many hours spent with such little success is modified by the satisfaction of having read so many unexpected things I would never have discovered otherwise.

Astute readers will also notice a few instances in which I stretched the strict

limits of 1922 so as to include examples that might otherwise have been omit-
ted. In particular, it has proven difficult not to pursue controversies, news stories, or literary careers into 1923, but there are other instances in which the desire to provide context or make a point has led me far away from my particular
year. Of such lapses I can only say that a year is a peculiar unit of time to write
about. The simultaneity it seems to offer is almost always specious, and there
is far too much chronology within a year to ignore it altogether. The simple
fact that very few literary works are conceived, written, and published in a single year makes it impossible to seal 1922 off from the years around it. In the
end, I had to be guided by my original motives in attempting this study, which
were to take 1922 as a limited test case in investigating the relationship between literary modernism and the public world of which it was a part. I did
not have any very elaborate historiographical ambitions, but I did hope to
learn something more about modern literature by considering at least a little
of it in a dramatically enlarged context. If there are still so many omissions
and biases even in an account of so short a period of time, as it is only inevitable there should be, these must be attributed to my desire to make a particular contribution to the study of modern literature, even if that left certain
aspects of my chosen year unregarded.

I have had some bibliographical help in my work, for which I want to thank
Louis Chude-Sokei and Alison Chin. I would also like to thank Erin Temple-
ton for her help in compiling the index. In those times when the viability, if
not in fact the sanity, of this project have seemed to me in doubt, I have been
thankful to know two other scholars, Richard Stein and Tom Harrison, who
have successfully completed similar projects. In the time in which I have been
at work on this year, several other years have been given similar treatment,
and, in a way, I have been pleased to see the method validated. I have also noticed, however, that no scholar who has mastered a single year has ever chosen to do another, and this seems to me both revealing and a little sobering.

Los Angeles, California   M. N.
July 1998

Contents

Reading 1922

Introduction

Accordbing to Ezra Pound, the Christian era ended on October 30, 1921, when James Joyce wrote the final words of *Ulysses*. Actually, Pound had proclaimed the end of the Christian era at least once before, but this time he was serious enough also to propose a new calendar, in which 1922 became year 1 of a new era.[1] For better or for worse, the new calendar never saw much use outside the pages of the *Little Review*, in which it was first proposed; but Pound did succeed, nonetheless, in making people think of 1922 as a year in which something definitively new had happened. By helping to bring both *Ulysses* and *The Waste Land* into print, Pound had introduced to the public the two works that would constitute, in the words of Gilbert Seldes, "a complete expression of the spirit which will be 'modern' for the next generation."[2] Ever since, the coincidental publication of these two works in 1922 has been taken as signifying a definitive break in literary history.[3]

This dramatic advent of a new literature was at least part of what Willa Cather had in mind when she complained, "The world broke in two in 1922 or thereabouts." Although Cather won the Pulitzer Prize in 1922 and achieved her greatest financial success in that year, her work had been rendered obsolete by *Ulysses*, according to a harsh review published by Edmund Wilson in October, and the bewildered resentment she felt at this separation of the avant-garde from the "backward" was still fresh years later.[4] But literary controversy was only part of the break that Cather felt in 1922. There was a larger, more general separation of the avant-garde from the backward, one that younger observers sensed and celebrated just as strongly as Cather lamented it. Searching, in a retrospective essay, for the definitive moment of the Jazz Age, F. Scott Fitzgerald asked, "May one offer in exhibit the year 1922!" The year that seemed catastrophic to Cather was for Fitzgerald "the peak of the younger generation."[5]

The two writers were looking from different sides of a generational divide at a collection of social changes that seemed to culminate in the year of *Ulysses* and *The Waste Land*. When Fitzgerald set *The Great Gatsby* in the summer of 1922, he apparently intended to link it to these changes, some of which he symbolized by direct reference to Eliot's poem. The geographical center of the novel, the site at which the plot lines quite literally collide, is Wilson's garage, "a small block of yellow brick sitting on the edge of the waste land, a sort of compact Main Street ministering to it and contiguous to absolutely nothing."[6] *The Great Gatsby* is concentrated—geographically, temporally, and stylistically—on this spot, where *Main Street* meets *The Waste Land*, where the small-town lives of the Gatz family meet modernity head-on, where an older realist literature meets the new literary modernism. Though modernist works like *The Waste Land* may have presented a stylistic challenge to the realism of Sinclair Lewis and Willa Cather, it was not simply literary change that Fitzgerald tried to register, but rather a new social and cultural world of which the new works were merely a part.

When Cather and Fitzgerald looked back to 1922, each may have remembered it as a generational dividing line, because it was in fact a time of open generational conflict. A good deal of this conflict was merely rhetorical, stirred up by Harold Stearns in works like *America and the Young Intellectuals* and *Civilization in the United States*, a collection that was dedicated to proving its title an oxymoron. Stearns was determined to show that Main Street *was* the waste land, and his efforts were rewarded with a host of disapproving reviews and editorials, many of them with titles like "The 'Young Intellectuals' Versus American Civilization."[7] At the same time, generational conflict of a more mundane sort—involving jazz, gin, and late hours—became a staple of popular fiction. Next to Wilson's disapproving review of her new novel in *Vanity Fair*, Cather might have found advertisements for Fitzgerald's *Tales of the Jazz Age* and Stephen Vincent Benet's *Young People's Pride*, a novel that promised to answer the burning question of the day: are all our young people really "flappers and shifters"?[8] Many works came forward in this year either to appease or to aggravate such anxieties, and some of them took the threat of drastic social change quite seriously indeed. The word "revolt" appears in book titles from old-fashioned liberals like Brander Matthews and from bitter nativists like Lothrop Stoddard.[9] Perhaps only Daniel Chauncey Brewer would have answered in the affirmative the question posed by his book *The Peril of the Republic: Are We Facing Revolution in the United States?*, but the notion was not so outlandish as to prevent the book from receiving considerable attention in the reviews.[10]

In England a similar question was being asked. It was posed in a sensational way by novelists like "Sapper," whose wildly popular hero Bulldog Drummond thwarts a revolutionary conspiracy of petty criminals, Jewish malcontents, disgruntled workers, and foreign agitators in this year.[11] In his best-seller *The Middle of the Road*, Phillip Gibbs seems to mock such alarmism, since those who are obsessed with the idea of a workers' revolt are those who know the least about work or workers. In fact, the chief alarmist, the protagonist's wealthy mother-in-law, travels around England giving lectures that connect "the revolutionary spirit which they found in the world around them" with "the tradition of Satan worship." But the protagonist is not himself entirely free from such apocalyptic fears: "Other forces were at work, biological, evolutionary, and mysterious forces, which no man could understand or govern. There was a new restlessness in the soul of humanity. Some great change was happening, or about to happen. The old checks and balances had become unhinged, in the minds of men, in the spirit of peoples, in great races."[12] The very title of the novel, in fact, symbolizes the position of England: indecisively poised between alternatives and balanced at a moment of historical crisis.

As the *Daily Mail* noted in its year-end wrap-up, 1922 was for England the first real postwar year, when "signs of, and restrictions connected with, the Great War were finally abolished," a return to normalcy that seemed to be symbolized in the press by the wedding of Princess Mary.[13] The definitive end of the war was marked in a more substantial way by the fall of Lloyd George and the election of a new Tory government under Bonar Law. And yet general reaction to the new world is probably best summarized by the blunt title of C. E. Montague's *Disenchantment*, the first instance of what was to become a new genre, the postwar reassessment. A. G. Gardiner might have introduced all these books when he introduced George A. Greenwood's *England To-Day* by saying, "'England To-day' is an England in an unprecedented moment of transition."[14] According to C. F. G. Masterman, the changes facing England in 1922 are greater than any seen since 1066: "Here, then, is a complete and startling transformation of values; not slowly changing from one to another, but suddenly and almost brutally forced upon the life of millions by causes altogether outside their own control."[15] Fear of revolution was, in other words, a displaced recognition of social changes that had already taken place, but so swiftly and completely that they baffled the understanding. The *Encyclopedia Britannica*, which had published its famous eleventh edition just before the war, issued a three-volume supplement in 1922 recognizing that its greatest and most comprehensive compilation of knowledge had already been rendered obsolete.

Though Great Britain and the United States shared the metaphor of revolution, the two countries applied it to somewhat different social changes. The deep pessimism evident in Montague, Greenwood, Masterman, and Gibbs reflects the very serious economic difficulties facing England after the war.[16]

The threat descried by Brewer, Stoddard, and Matthews comes less from decline and more from complacency. Their polemic seeks to awaken an American public that is perhaps too secure and successful on the one hand and ir-
responsibly exuberant on the other. But these very different economic states
did not prevent the two countries from being equally affected by what turned
out to be the most ominous developments of 1922. The reparations bill dictated by the Versailles treaty had been finally computed and delivered to the
German government on May 5, 1921, and international affairs in the following year were dominated by the diplomatic and economic consequences.[17]
Despite the efforts of John Maynard Keynes, who dedicated tremendous energy to a revision of the treaty,[18] despite international controversy at Genoa
and Rapallo, the ensuing conflicts were resolved only by another war.

Although the Christian era did not quite come to an end in 1922, a considerable number of observers besides Ezra Pound felt the world breaking in
two in that year, and the changes they sensed seemed to go well beyond stylistic innovation in poetry and the novel. Of course, observers living at many
different points in the twentieth century have felt the earth heaving beneath
them, and historians have rarely proposed 1922 as being uniquely troubled or
troubling. Virginia Woolf dated the definitive break in her century to 1910,
though it is worth mentioning in this context that she first started writing
about this break in 1922.[19] And according to D. H. Lawrence, "It was in 1915
the old world ended"; but he also wrote this in 1922.[20] Even in the case of literary history, it might be argued, however, that 1922 is so late a date as to mark
not the beginning but rather the end of a process, one that might be traced
back into the 1880s or even beyond.[21]

Even if literary modernism is traced back, as it often is, to its first dim
inklings in the poetry of Baudelaire, it arrived as a commonly accepted public fact, at least where English speakers are concerned, in 1922, and when it arrived it was surrounded by a social milieu full of conflict and change. To writers as different as Pound, Cather, and Fitzgerald, the new literature seemed
part of that social milieu, and yet the connections between them are rarely
explored. The "matrix of modernism," to take the title of one very accomplished study, is generally constructed in temporal terms, as a genealogy, and
is restricted to literature and perhaps philosophy.[22] Such a study produces, as
a necessary effect of its interpretive method, a modernism disconnected
from all other varieties of historical crisis, a modernism that lives primarily in
the deepest imaginings of its most radical perpetrators.[23] But what of modernism as a social fact, as part of the lived experience of a reader of *The Waste
Land* or *Ulysses*, who also lived in the world of incipient revolt described by
Gibbs and Brewer? What connections might have been made in the mind of
such a reader between literary modernism and the other innovations of the
same year?

As it turns out, 1922 might have been named as year one on any number of
calendars besides the one Ezra Pound suggested in the *Little Review*. The diplo-

matic calendar included a number of important conferences, including the Washington Naval Conference, which, according to Charles Beard, ratified the end of the naval supremacy Great Britain had enjoyed since the Armada, with the United States taking its place.[24] Another important conference, at Genoa, saw the first diplomatic appearance of the Soviet Union on an international stage, an event that attracted a ravenous press corps, including the young Ernest Hemingway.[25] And while in Italy, Hemingway was able to examine more or less firsthand another new political phenomenon that drew a good deal of press attention: the Fascisti. By the time Mussolini's regime took power in November, the world had duly recognized and acknowledged the three forces that would determine global events until 1945.

Other political calendars began at the same time. This year marked the birth—after many years of disappointment and agitation—of the Irish Free State. By itself, as the first alteration in the boundaries of Great Britain since 1801, this event would have been significant enough, but coupled with the self-determination accorded to Egypt in the same year, it looks like the beginning of the postcolonial era. At the very least there was a decisive shift in the rationale behind the British Empire and a new need to enunciate its reasons for being, both of which are evident in Lord Lugard's *The Dual Mandate in British Tropical Africa*. Lugard, born in the year of the Indian Mutiny, had helped to establish both the Kenya Colony and Nigeria, and, on his retirement as governor-general of Nigeria in 1919, he set out to preserve by writing what he had established by force. *The Dual Mandate* became the "authoritative justification" for continued colonial administration at a time when radicals like Gandhi were calling for an end to the Empire.[26]

Lugard was among those colonial officials who felt that their administration might benefit from the knowledge provided by fieldwork anthropology. Indeed, in his retirement he carried on a friendly correspondence with Bronsilaw Malinowski, who had also published an influential book in 1922, *Argonauts of the Western Pacific*.[27] Malinowski self-consciously and somewhat self-righteously promoted his book as the first instance of an entirely new anthropological method, one based on immersion in the language and culture of the people under study. His book coincided in 1922 with another, rather similar, work, *The Andaman Islanders* by A. R. Radcliffe-Brown. Between them, these two works make 1922 the annus mirabilis of modern anthropology, the year in which the fieldwork method decisively replaced all earlier modes of research.[28] The ascendancy of the new generation in this year is also marked by the death of W. H. R. Rivers, who had in fact inaugurated the fieldwork method with the Cambridge expedition to the Torres Straits in the 1890s.

The last book Rivers saw into publication before his death, *Essays on the Depopulation of Melanesia*, became itself a minor anthropological classic, and there were a number of posthumous publications as well that in their variety exemplified the range of Rivers' interests. One of these interests was linguistics, which had been the more particular study of a very unorthodox Cambridge acquaintance of his named Ludwig Wittgenstein. In 1922, when Wittgenstein was teaching school in Austria, a number of other Cantabrigians collaborated to publish for him the first authoritative version of the *Tractatus Logico-Philosophicus*, the book that is now held to have inaugurated the "linguistic turn" in modern philosophy.[29] The advent of this idea—that the dissolution, if not the solution, to philosophical problems is to be found in the study of language—coincides in space and time with the development of a new method of literary study pioneered by a young man who attained his first regular teaching post in 1922, I. A. Richards. In the same year, Richards published his first collaboration with C. K. Ogden, *The Foundations of Aesthetics*,[30] a book now very much forgotten, though it paved the way for the influential works the two writers were to produce in the next few years.

The method that Richards invented was, of course, to find its appropriate subject matter in the new literature introduced at the same time, in the form of *Ulysses* and *The Waste Land*. But other new literatures were introduced the same year, among them a very ambitious one located in Harlem. The year of *The Waste Land* was also the year of Claude McKay's *Harlem Shadows* and James Weldon Johnson's *Book of American Negro Poetry*, which were commonly reviewed together as the first instances of a new African American spirit.[31] That spirit was evident in other areas as well—in Carter Woodson's *The Negro in Our History*, on stage in *Shuffle Along*, and in the visual arts with the establishment of Albert Barnes' collection of African art—so that 1922 has also been called the annus mirabilis of the Harlem Renaissance.[32] At the same time, 1922 marks the indictment of Marcus Garvey and thus the beginning of the collapse of his movement in Harlem. This, along with the proposal and ultimate defeat of the Dyer Anti-Lynching Bill, might make 1922 look more like the end than the beginning of an African American renaissance.[33]

The renaissance was, for better or for worse, a development in popular entertainment as well as literature, but it was not the only such development in 1922. A new meaning for the word "broadcast" had come into being the year before, along with a tremendous boom in amateur radio activity in England and the United States. In England at this time there was only one station capable of broadcasting music with any regularity, but this lack was addressed by the postmaster general, who instituted a "regular broadcasting service, consisting of eight stations controlled by a broadcasting company," which was to become the BBC.[34] Though there was no such formal nationwide network, the United States was ahead of Great Britain in other ways, having already aired the first radio commercial.[35] To this "first" might be added other, equally dubious achievements, including the first movie biography and the first use of the term "public relations."[36]

As the list grows, it seems more eccentric and disparate, and yet there is a small number of important developments, coincidental with the publication of *Ulysses* and *The Waste Land*, that clearly helped to establish a very different cultural and intellectual world from that existing before 1922. The connections among these developments and between them and literary modernism suggest that the "matrix of modernism" might be expanded and complicated in a number of significant ways. For example, the fact that both philosophy and anthropology date their current methodological regimes from this year does not seem a trivial coincidence, especially considering the fact that both Wittgenstein and Malinowski were passing their work of this year through the hands of C. K. Ogden, who was simultaneously collaborating with I. A. Richards on *The Meaning of Meaning*.[37] For Ogden, at any rate, the links between linguistics, literary study, philosophy, anthropology, psychology, and politics were all quite clear, or at least the strength of those links was obvious, if not their precise nature. Ogden represented these links in the eclectic publication list of the International Library of Psychology, Philosophy, and Scientific Method, which he founded in this year and in which he published works by Moore, Rivers, Russell, and many others besides Wittgenstein and himself.

The indirect and rather unexpected relationship between Wittgenstein and Malinowski might offer a model for relationships linking other seemingly distant disciplines and activities. What effect might it have on current belief in the resolutely anticommercial bias of early modernism to know that Edward Bernays, founder of the discipline of public relations, perfected his techniques in association with Horace Liveright, "the principal publisher of modernism"?[38] How might it change current notions of a "great divide" between popular culture and modern literature to know more about the campaign on behalf of popular culture carried on by Gilbert Seldes, who first published *The Waste Land* in *The Dial*, or to see the long list of literary figures with whom Charlie Chaplin started or renewed acquaintance during the transatlantic tour he called *My Trip Abroad*? One of these acquaintances was Claude McKay, whose poem "The Tropics in New York" offers Chaplin a moment of escape from the pressures of celebrity and civilization. As it happens, this poem had first been published by C. K. Ogden in the *Cambridge Magazine*, which brings us back, somehow, to the intellectual birthplace of Wittgenstein's *Tractatus*.[39] In fact, the difficulty in making such connections is getting them to stop somewhere—and it soon becomes clear, after concerted study of a very concentrated time span, that this is what conventional disciplinary boundaries are for. They filter out the noise, so that the seemingly irrelevant fact that Ogden was involved in a distant way with African American literature cannot trouble accounts of his dealings with Wittgenstein. In protecting us from such irrelevance, however, disciplinary boundaries also impoverish our sense of a period, and this seems to be an especially acute problem when it comes to relations between literary modernism and other aspects of modern culture.

This is not to say, of course, that such connections have never been considered. Hugh Kenner, the scholar who so influentially named the new post-Christian era after Ezra Pound himself, also linked the new literary work to a Poundian assemblage of cultural particulars. Certain pages of *The Pound Era* clearly aspire to the condition of *The Cantos*, juxtaposing, for example, Henry

James' trip to America, *The Great Train Robbery*, Poincaré's principle of relativity, and Teddy Roosevelt's meeting with Ernest Fenollosa, all of which converge on 1904, the year in which *Ulysses* is set.[40] Yet such a list is not truly exemplary of Kenner's method, which concentrates far more heavily on technology than on politics or popular culture.[41] This interest in science and technology made it possible for Kenner to link modernist literature with other disciplines advanced by experiment, but at the same time made it relatively more difficult to consider other kinds of innovation, especially those in the popular arts. And this tendency accentuates the ignorance of African American literature and literature by Anglo-American women that Kenner shares with most of those who came to interpret modernism in the immediate postwar period.

The result—a canonized version of modernism that could not accommodate Claude McKay, Willa Cather, or even, under some circumstances, Virginia Woolf[42]—was ripe for the repudiation it received from postmodernism, feminism, and African American literary studies. Since postmodernism defined itself in large part by its greater eclecticism and stylistic openness, it required as foil a modernism as exclusive as possible. Thus, the rivalry between postmodernism and modernism was read back into history, quite openly, as an antipathy between modernism and mass culture, one whose existence has always seemed more a matter of theoretical necessity than of empirical fact. The most widely influential formulation of this view, that of Andreas Huyssen, offers no specific discussion of conditions in the United States or Great Britain, and yet its conclusions are routinely repeated as if they were as applicable to Eliot as to Wagner.[43] Thus, modernism has been transformed in the general estimation from Hugh Kenner's brilliant young technocrat into a doddering old paranoiac possessed by "an anxiety of contamination by its other: an increasingly consuming and engulfing mass culture,"[44] a life history that seems to match that of Howard Hughes better than that of Eliot or Joyce.

At the same time, the repair work necessary to bring African American literature and literature by Anglo-American women back into the canon had to begin with the demolition of a certain view of modernism. Houston Baker insisted in *Modernism and the Harlem Renaissance* that "the very *histories* that are assumed in the chronologies of British, Anglo-American, and Irish modernism are radically opposed to any adequate and accurate account of Afro-American modernism."[45] It now seems that Baker's emphasis was very justly placed, for it was the histories of modernism that were so thoroughly insulated and not Anglo-American modernism itself, which, as a number of studies have shown, had a tense and complicated relationship with African American literature.[46] Similarly, the project of *No Man's Land*, Sandra Gilbert and Susan Gubar's multivolume study of women's writing in the twentieth century, had to begin by addressing a version of twentieth-century literature in which there were virtually no women. For them, this absence is the result of the misogyny of the most influential male modernists, who made their reputations in part by offering other men an antidote to a popular literature increasingly written by and for women. In this view, which has been closely associated with that of Huyssen, "a reaction formation against the rise of literary women became not just a theme in modernist writing but a motive for modernism."[47] And though it seems from the work of scholars like Wayne Koestenbaum that the gender identity of even the most misogynist of male modernists may be as complicated as their racial identity,[48] the influence of feminist scholarship has helped to produce a modernism defined by its dichotomies. Though the prestige of Eliot and Pound, if not of Joyce, has been considerably diminished since the days in which the whole of the literature could be named after one man, what used to be called modernism has not been expanded or even changed very much; rather, it lives on, in a mummified state to provide a determinate negation for its successor.

In short, most of the scholarship that has challenged Kenner's formulation of modernism as the Pound Era has not tried to change his view but rather has begun from it. The result has been the preservation of something called "modernism" in intellectual amber, something whose purported insulation from the cultural world into which it was introduced is now retrospectively accomplished by critical consensus. Modernism has so thoroughly come to mean that which rejects everything progressive and challenging in the early twentieth century that another term is needed, such as "avant-garde" or even "postmodern," for those writers and artists friendly to change.[49] This simply locks the modern in a tautological box, where it is what it is by definition and not by demonstration.

A different view, one that keeps its distance from old orthodoxy and new, is promised in the posthumous collection of papers by Raymond Williams called *The Politics of Modernism*. Williams apparently hoped to provide a coherent analysis of modernism as a social formation, the key to which would have been geographical mobility: "It is a very striking feature of many Modernist and avant-garde movements that they were not only located in the great metropolitan centres but that so many of their members were immigrants into these centres, where in some new ways all were strangers."[50]

Williams' analysis provides a useful way of looking at a wide variety of literary and cultural figures. Consider three "English writers" who covered significant distances in 1922: Chaplin, McKay, and Lawrence. D. H. Lawrence spent virtually his entire year in transit, leaving Italy at Mabel Dodge's invitation to travel to New Mexico, which he did by going eastward via Ceylon and Australia. His novels of the year are set in Italy and Australia, and his chief critical work is *Studies in Classic American Literature*. Lawrence was clearly hoping to find somewhere a deep-seated reason not to return home at all, an organic community to which he might belong instead of simply existing in England. The odd assumption that one might go and find such a community and then simply elect to join it has its ironic outcome in the constant disappoint-

ment that drove him all the way around the world, so that the only place he
finally belonged was in transit.

Claude McKay, a British subject born in Jamaica, is usually considered a
part of the Harlem Renaissance even though he left New York in 1922 for a
twelve-year trip that neatly spanned the time period in which the renaissance
had its greatest influence. McKay originally left the United States to attend an
international labor conference in the Soviet Union, and though he was widely
lionized while there, his credentials were challenged by the American delega-
tion.[51] This might be considered the quintessential experience of McKay's
life, for his credentials were always being questioned, and he spent a fair
amount of the ensuing decade quite literally without a country, unwilling to
live in England or Jamaica yet wary of returning to the United States on a
British passport. When he did return, he was often homeless, and he died a
pauper in the late 1940s.

Charlie Chaplin's account of his first trip home to England after a ten-year
absence was entitled *My Trip Abroad*. Actually, Chaplin's British publisher, apparently embarrassed to use such an unfilial title, used *My Wonderful Trip* instead, but the difference itself is telling. When Chaplin arrived in England, he
felt sadly estranged, having become very much an American, and at the same
time unpleasantly at home, for his own movies had preceded him, changing
the very places he wanted to revisit. On one hand, then, he is utterly deraci-
nated; on the other hand, it is impossible for someone so universally known
to go "abroad." He was known just as well, or just as little, in Berlin as in London or Hollywood. The only place he felt truly comfortable was in the middle of the Atlantic Ocean—three thousand miles from Hollywood, three
thousand from Europe, belonging to neither.[52]

What these three very different people have in common is obviously not
British citizenship but, rather, a shared experience of restless travel so relentless that citizenship ceases to have any meaning, as does the difference between home and abroad. They offer three instances of the social formation
Williams associates with modernism, but this kind of mobility was not limited
to expatriate modernists, nor was it concentrated exclusively on the metropolitan centers that figure so largely in Williams' analysis. As James Clifford
has recently argued, global migration is a much older and more widespread
phenomenon than we tend to assume.[53] Evidence of this is abundant in the
writing of 1922.

For example, *South Sea Reminiscences* by T. R. St.-Johnston, one of the dozens
of memoirs by current and former colonial officials published in this year, describes a contingent of Tongan and Fijian stevedores that St.-Johnston accompanied to the front during the war: "What a motley crowd we found all
round that district: Egyptians, Fijians, Chinese, Colonial troops, and—a few
—Indians, while not many miles away were the 'Cape boys,' whose special job
was wagon-driving. Altogether a most annoying reminder to the German (who
frequently came over us to spy out the land) of the widespread influence of

the British Empire." But the Empire does as much in this way to undermine British certainties as it does German ones. St.-Johnston chuckles over the difficulties anthropologists will have in sorting out a population formed by intermarriage among Chinese, Indian, Samoan, and Fijian laborers, and he describes how difficult it is to speak to such a group, in which there may be as many rival pidgins as native languages.[54] If accounts like this are taken seriously, then it seems that the social system in which "all were strangers" was already global and not exclusively metropolitan in 1922, and the linguistic effect on which Williams puts much emphasis, "the elements of strangeness and distance, indeed of alienation" imported into language, was not in any way limited to expatriate writers.[55]

Even at this early date, global migration was a disparate social formation with a number of distinct parts. It included the movement of colonial subjects, present and former, into the imperial center, as in the cases of Eliot, Pound, and McKay. There was also a movement in the same direction on the part of Europeans, some of them, like Conrad and Malinowski, to take up work made possible by the Empire, others, like Wittgenstein, simply to follow certain intellectual currents. At the same time, British citizens left for the colonies or for other far-flung countries to study the strange and foreign. Some of Rivers' works of this year came from such trips, as did Bertrand Russell's *The Problem of China*. There was also immigration from Europe to the United States, which brought such different personalities as Chaplin and Bernays. There was as well American expatriation in postwar Europe, which became the subject of so much literature later in the 1920s, and emigration within the United States, principally that from south to north, which is the unspoken central subject of Jean Toomer's *Cane*. One or the other of these movements can account for a great deal of what was distinctive in the literature of 1922.

The intellectual results of these social movements can be glimpsed even in the most obtuse examples. One of the most frightening documents of 1922 is the diary kept by Alfred Viscount Northcliffe on an extended Far Eastern tour that was meant to recruit his failing health. Though Northcliffe controlled a vast publishing empire that included the *Times* and the *Daily Mail*, he appears in his diary to have been a remarkably insular personality. For example, at one point during his tour of Australia he records this troubled observation: "I went to the hospital, which had mostly black patients. It is curious to see a lot of black people in bed."[56] But Northcliffe is also capable of reflecting on such experiences and on the feelings they cause in him, and he is not always able to take these for granted. Though he has strong preconceptions about foreigners and foreign countries, he is capable of being genuinely surprised when these are not met. In fact, the idea that "things are always different from that which one expected" becomes almost a refrain.[57] Rather more significantly, Northcliffe becomes aware of the fact that he is himself an object of curiosity. "Orientals like looking,"[58] he complains at one point, blithely unaware of the odd light this testiness sheds on his own project of foreign inspection. And yet, being looked at does enable him to turn the project of inspection at least partly around so that it focuses on himself: "It is good to see ourselves as others see us."[59]

Here Northcliffe shares in a common anthropological experience, one that Rivers recounts in a number of different works.[60] It is rendered humorously in the same year in a short story by Frank Worthington, secretary for Native Affairs in Rhodesia. In this story, a young colonial official, who may or may not bear a significant resemblance to Worthington himself, is aghast to find an African house decorated with a disjunct collection of European paraphernalia including a toilet seat, female underwear, a teakettle, and an egg cup. Challenged to explain herself, the woman of the house responds: "Do you not like the things my people use? For myself, I like the things the white people use. You put the black man's things in your house. I put the white man's things in my house. We are two friends who have the same thoughts."[61] Worthington's protagonist is thus forced to look at his own house, which is filled with African artifacts, in a new light. It would be too much to suggest that he also looks at colonial administration in a new light, but even a slight shift of perspective is remarkable under these circumstances.

Worthington's protagonist begins to see that a practice he had taken completely for granted, as if it required no explanation or justification, might, under other circumstances, seem nonsensical. Another collection of short stories from this year, also with a colonial theme, is entitled *As Others See Us*, and this title, which coincidentally echoes Northcliffe, might be applied to a significant segment of the colonial writing of this time, even that by the most committed servants of the Empire.[62] As Simon Gikandi suggests, the meaning of world travel changes for English-speaking writers as the imperial hold over distant places begins to slip: "the imperial spaces can no longer be conceived—or represented—as spaces that secure English identity."[63] The irony of Empire, in such cases, is that it exposes the British perspective as partial and local in the very act of asserting its universality. The same irony appears when the fieldwork anthropologist sets himself up like a human recording station in the midst of some unfamiliar society, only to find, as Malinowski did most notoriously, that he is himself the object of scrutiny.[64]

The goal of philosophy, according to Wittgenstein, is to produce this self-reflexive experience without all the trouble of actual travel, to approach one's own language games as if they were the practices of a strange and unfamiliar society.[65] For Wittgenstein, this was a fairly arduous practice, since it is so difficult not to take one's own language for granted; but for Walter Lippmann, who published his most influential book in the same year as the *Tractatus*, this sort of displacement seemed all too easy to achieve. Since, as Lippmann put it, "our opinions cover a bigger space, a longer reach of time, a greater number of things, than we can directly observe,"[66] human beings in the twentieth century are in a state of perpetual travel, and their opinions are always a size too small and a shade too parochial. Lippmann's work implies that one of Malinowski's dearest goals, to "bring anthropology home," was already being accomplished and that the result was not a greater objectivity but rather a self-consciousness about the power of point of view so great that it undermined the notion of objectivity itself. Thus Lippmann enunciates what has become one of the few certainties of twentieth-century thought: "The accepted types, the current patterns, the standard versions, intercept information on its way to consciousness."[67] On this, even a notorious stay-at-home like Wallace Stevens would agree. "Things seen," he says in the *Adagia*, "are things as seen."[68]

One limitation of Williams' analysis of modernism may be, then, that it takes the idea of travel a bit too literally, missing the effects that global mobility had as they percolated throughout anthropology, philosophy, psychology, and political science. The multiplicity and incompatibility of human points of view were never more unavoidably obvious than in the early twentieth century, when the Great War focused for the first time nearly the whole of human consciousness on a single event,[69] an odious squabble the purpose of which almost no one could enunciate. The unity and the disunity of the modern world appear together, as effects of one another, for the parochialism of the particular point of view could never have appeared until it had been qualified by exposure to a more cosmopolitan experience. This relation, which is too tightly contradictory even to be called ironic, is one of the chief characteristics of the twentieth century, which feels itself to be too unified and too various at once, too rational and too darkly unconscious.

As Anthony Giddens has argued, "The local and the global . . . have become inextricably intertwined," but this is not simply because "even the smallest of neighborhood stores . . . probably obtains its goods from all over the world."[70] It is also because any point of view, any perception, can now seem simultaneously local and global, as individuals respond to the world around them and then note and contextualize their responses in relation to some other, putatively larger point of view. Since no such point of view is ever final, it is easy to confuse this situation with a relative subjectivity, but it might make just as much sense to see it as relentlessly objective, since any individual point of view is inevitably found to be partial. Modernity is, as Giddens has also said, fundamentally reflexive, and a major engine of this reflexivity is the oscillation between local and global points of view.

Another possible limitation of Williams' analysis appears when he asserts that the only community open to the polyglot expatriates of the modern metropolis was "a community of the medium: of their own practices."[71] In this analysis, formalist experimentation becomes its own international language and the medium, of paint or of letters, an alternate homeland quite separate from any real country or community. But there was another international community just coming into existence along with the modernist works of 1922. When network broadcasting began, with the creation of the BBC, a new sort of community was established, one that linked different localities and

Radio broadcasting in 1922 (*Illustrated London News*, April 29, 1922).

even different countries with a simultaneity that made physical travel seem antediluvian by comparison.

There was almost nothing actually to listen to in 1922: the full program available to the family grouped around the gigantic speaker cone in the *Illustrated London News* for April 29 seems to have consisted of an afternoon concert from the Eiffel Tower, the Tuesday evening concert from the Marconi works at Chelmsford, Thursday evening concerts from the Hague, and the Sunday afternoon "Dutch concert."[72] To range this far afield was a necessity at the time, but it was also part of the romance of early radio, the possibilities of which were explored in a linked series of "wireless romances" published in this year by the mystery writer William Le Queux.[73] The power to speak and even to act at a distance, to be in two places at once, to defeat many of the seemingly eternal limitations of bodily materiality was extremely attractive to Le Queux, as it was to Northcliffe, who was amazed to see how easily American officials in Manila could communicate with Washington.[74]

No one was quite so fulsome about these possibilities as Edward Van Zile, who declared rhapsodically, "The disappearance of the last frontier, the solving of Earth's ancient mysteries, the coming of the wireless and the Esperanto of the Tongue and of the Eye seem to presage some new revelation to the soul of Man that shall remove forever from the entrance to the Garden of Eden that angel with the flaming sword."[75] In this vision, the wireless, the Esperanto of the Tongue, joins the movies, Esperanto of the Eye, to reverse the Fall itself, removing all the boundaries of material existence by removing the boundaries between languages. Van Zile is extrapolating wildly from the conditions of 1922, the year of *Nanook of the North*, in which travel films were so popular that entrepreneurs like Martin Johnson ended up flooding the market with them.[76] Many of these seemed to reopen the Garden of Eden almost literally, since they showed human beings still living in the state of nature. Such films seemed to conquer both time and space, to show humankind in its temporal and spatial entirety, and though this was obviously an illusion, it was a necessary illusion around which a real human totality, the mass audience, was constituted.

My Trip Abroad, Chaplin's unassuming little travelogue, is such an important document of this time because it registers some of the key ironies of this new human community. In the book, Chaplin offers his own worldwide popularity as a prime example of the freedom with which film could ignore international boundaries. Seeing a sign for a movie theater in a small Belgian town, he exclaims, "It is universal, this sign. Here is a movie in this tiny village. What a wonderful medium, to reach such an obscure town."[77] As Chaplin may have known, movies had reached towns even more remote from Hollywood. In 1922 there were about 100 movie theaters in China, 168 in India, and 250 in Java.[78] And though Chaplin himself may not have been visible in all these theaters, it was plausibly suggested at this time that because of the worldwide distribution of his movies he was the first human being to be truly world famous.[79]

Chaplin is, in other words, foreign to no one, and yet *My Trip Abroad* is full of scenes in which he seems foreign to himself. He is impressed, on his return to England, by how American he has become, how alien he seems even to his cousin Aubrey and old friends in Lambeth. And yet, even though the very prose of his account distances the English, who are always "they," it cannot completely assimilate Chaplin to America: "They seem to talk from their souls. . . . I think of Americans and myself. Our speech is hard, monotonous, except where excitement makes it more noisy."[80] In the division between them and us, Chaplin seems strangely alone, apart from new countrymen as well as old. Pride in his worldwide fame is thus always undercut by this melancholy sense of isolation, for it is not really Chaplin himself who is famous but rather the Tramp. The difference between the two is at the heart of the strangely ambivalent adulation that Chaplin receives from crowds that seem to want with equal intensity to see the "real" Chaplin and at the same time to see the Tramp in person. The structural impossibility of satisfying such demands torments Chaplin and turns some of the audience's adulation into hostility.

Chaplin discovers on his trip, then, that the very process that makes him at home everywhere depends on a more fundamental alienation of the reproducible image from its unique source that makes him feel uncomfortably dissociated even at home. And yet this very dissociation seems to be part of his popularity. The same crowd that clamors for Chaplin to take a few turns as the Tramp responds to his refusal with the crushing truth that "they could see Charlie Chaplin at any time for a nickel."[81] Thus the naiveté that demands a look at the "real" Charlie Chaplin, as if he were a precious rarity, coexists quite easily with the ironic awareness that "Charlie Chaplin" is a manufactured image whose infinite reproducibility has made it intrinsically worthless.

If film and radio were making the world into one grand unity, then, it was by importing into the very heart of things an entirely new kind of estrangement. It was in part to decry this situation that Walter Lippmann wrote *Public Opinion*, one of the most enduringly influential books of 1922. Lippmann was terrified of a world in which the difference between Charlie Chaplin and the Charlie Chaplin one could have any time for a nickel would disappear. Lippmann was perhaps only the most visible of many discoverers of what G. K. Chesterton called, in an article on the fame of Einstein, a new and even more relative theory of relativity. Einstein was discussed, Chesterton complained, by people who hadn't a prayer of understanding his theories because science was promoted in the public mind by the same processes that promoted soap. In this way, the theory of relativity, by becoming a mere shibboleth, illustrated another kind of relativity even more influential in the modern era, according to which even the validity of science was dependent upon the influence of cultural fashions over public opinion.[82]

For Lippmann, as for many others at this time, there was a definite connection between the global mobility that displaced so many people and the new arts that were reorganizing them into audiences. It was not just that, in the United States at least, early film and radio were controlled by recent immigrants. As Lippmann put it, "We are all of us immigrants in the industrial world, and we have no authority to lean upon. . . . The evidence is everywhere: the amusements of the city; the jokes that pass for jokes; the blare that stands for beauty, the folklore of Broadway, the feeble and apologetic pulpits, the cruel standards of success, raucous purity."[83] According to this, the new popular arts are expressions of the raw juvenility of the modern, a juvenility from which Lippmann fastidiously distances himself even as he seems to confess its ubiquity. It seems, however, that the real connection between migration and the media is that both contribute to a greater sophistication, even to cynicism. Though Lippmann and Chesterton are both violently disturbed by the capability they see in the new media for subterfuge, they are themselves evidence of the fact that newer and more powerful media simply make audiences more aware than ever of the fact of mediation. In so doing, they accomplish for a vast public what philosophy, anthropology, and psychology were accomplishing for an intellectual elite.

To rewrite Williams, then, the newly mobile populations of the modern period find their community in a new medium, one that does not counteract but rather reflects and exaggerates the effects of global travel. As Arjun Appadurai says, "Those who wish to move, those who have moved, those who wish to return, and those who choose to stay rarely formulate their plans outside the sphere of radio and television, cassettes and videos, newsprint and telephone. For migrants, both the politics of adaptation to new environments and the stimulus to move or return are deeply affected by a mass-mediated imaginary that frequently transcends national space."[84] But even the sedentary might be mobilized, because, as Appadurai says, "both viewers and images are in simultaneous circulation. Neither images nor viewers fit into circuits or audiences that are easily bound within local, national, or regional spaces."[85] If worldwide globalization makes even the patron of the neighborhood store familiar with the concept of action-at-a-distance, if it puts even the most parochial experience in resonance with some slightly more global perspective and in so doing "disembeds" it, to use Giddens' terminology, then mediation has become an ordinary, inescapable fact of existence. What we call "the media" formalizes a more general and more prevalent mediation of which it is in fact only a part.[86]

According to Appadurai, "it is only in the past two decades or so that media and migration have become so massively globalized, that is to say, active across such large and irregular transnational terrains."[87] But it is possible to trace these changes much further back, perhaps as far as the 1860s, when telegraph cable first linked Great Britain with North America and India. By 1924 King George V could send himself a telegram that circumnavigated the globe in eighty seconds.[88] Two years earlier, the first modern media network, the BBC, had been established, and that same year also witnessed what might be considered the first truly modern media event, which occurred the very month *The Waste Land* reached the bookstores. This event began on November 26, 1922, when Howard Carter first peered through the small opening he had made into what proved to be King Tutankhamen's tomb. The troubled history of the ensuing excavation exemplifies the conjunction of migration and media and the changes this conjunction was to make in everything from literature to fashions in clothes.

The excavation was, on one level, an exercise in modern geopolitics. Forced to defend in advance the possible abstraction of so many foreign antiquities, Carter, the excavation's leader, offered the same sort of justification proposed by Lugard for British imperialism in general. Carter translates from original papyrus an elaborate story about official grave robbing, the point of which is that Egyptians have never been trustworthy where their own treasures are concerned: "One moral we can draw from this episode, and we commend it to the critics who call us Vandals for taking objects from the tombs. By removing antiquities to museums we are really assuring their safety; left *in situ* they would inevitably, sooner or later, become the prey of thieves, and that, for all practical purposes, would be the end of them."[89] British science, that is to say, must represent Egypt against itself, serving for a time as a sort of stand-in for the mature political entity that has yet to develop.

In this very familiar way, Great Britain interposes itself between modern Egypt and its own ancient history, offering itself as rightful heir and inheritor of all the glory of the past, no matter where it might have occurred. But the day is late, even in 1922, for this imposture, for almost at the very moment

of Carter's discovery, a nationalist government comes to power in Egypt that
will eventually bar him from the very tomb he discovered. The first volume of
Carter's account of the tomb is written in a very literal state of suspense, for
he left the lid of the sarcophagus hanging in mid-air and refilled the mouth
of the tomb with rubble until negotiations with the Egyptian government
clarified his right to proceed. These developments, which stall Carter inches
from his objective, are more than mere administrative changes. Between the
time the tomb entrance was discovered and when the lid of the first sarcophagus was lifted, the idea behind archaeological and anthropological collection—that the world exists to be brought to unity within the mind of Europe—was called into question. Carter's utter inability to comprehend this
change unnecessarily exacerbated his dispute with the new Egyptian government. He was unable to see that locking and barring the tomb against Egyptian visitors would seem a gratuitous insult because he was incapable of regarding modern Egyptians as anything other than potential grave robbers. As
Thomas Hoving puts it, Carter and his colleagues "were locked into positions
rooted in pre–World War I attitudes, based upon outmoded concepts of colonialism, elitism, and a misguided sense of scientific privilege."[90]

If the oddly incomplete status of Carter's first volume represents this tran-
sitional moment in what has come to be called geopolitics, it also represents
a shift in the organization of time, in the relationship between the old, the
new, and the news. Carter himself provided the best account of the way that
his discovery seemed to collapse the old and the new into one:

> I suppose most excavators would confess to a feeling of awe—embarrassment al-
> most—when they break into a chamber closed and sealed by pious hands so many
> centuries ago. For the moment, time as a factor in human life has lost its meaning.
> Three thousand, four thousand years maybe, have passed and gone since human
> feet last trod the floor on which you stand, and yet, as you note the signs of recent
> life around you—the half-filled bowl of mortar for the door, the blackened lamp,
> the finger-mark upon the freshly painted surface, the farewell garland dropped
> upon the threshold—you feel it might have been but yesterday. The very air you
> breathe, unchanged throughout the centuries, you share with those who laid the
> mummy to its rest. Time is annihilated by little intimate details such as these, and
> you feel an intruder.[91]

The shamefaced awe with which Carter confronts his own discovery must
come at least in part from the realization that the new newness of the old is
horribly temporary; that it will begin to age again, in physical actuality and in
human perception, almost instantly; that these artifacts that seem so ancient
and yet so fresh have not been preserved by discovery but instead have been
made perishable by it.

Carter was aware that his discoveries were perishable in another, less physical, sense as well. As soon as he was certain of his find, he sent a quick report to the *Times*, whose story caused such intense international press interest that he had to take extraordinary measures to prevent its interference with

the excavation. Even so, every step was dogged by reporters and photographers: Carter noted that one perfectly unimportant piece of mummy cloth was photographed eight times as it was carried from the tomb to his field lab.[92] Through the end of 1922, photographable evidence of this extraordinary find was so scarce that the *Illustrated London News* was forced to run baldly synthetic mockups of "What the Great 'Find' in Egypt May Bring," using artifacts already in British museums.[93] The various ironies attending the "news" are already visible in these pathetic picture spreads, whose haste implies that another week or two of waiting, tacked on to the three or four thousand years the world has already lived without these treasures, is simply too much to endure. But the publishers of the *News* simply responded to the reality that, having become news, the Tut artifacts now ran the risk of becoming not just old but passé. To avoid this eventuality, the *News* compromises with its name in another way, by providing manufactured representations instead of information. The requirement that news be fresh and up-to-date seems, in this instance at least, very much at odds with the requirement that it be true.

One reason the *News* was forced to use such transparent expedients was that Lord Carnarvon, sponsor of the excavations, had signed an exclusive contract with the *Times*, whose attitude of proprietary ownership over news about the tomb became as dangerous an irritant as Carter's similar attitude about the tomb itself. Once again, Carter utterly misunderstood the moment, assuming that transmitting news through the *Times* somehow certified it as scientific and noncommercial. What Carter failed to understand was that, for most of the world, news *was* the treasure and possession of it was just as contentious an issue as possession of the actual artifacts. He and Carnarvon were accused of having set up "Tutankhamun Ltd." to rob the world of its information rights, just as they were robbing the Egyptians of their archeological rights. As Hoving points out, this misstep in public relations, though it had nothing actually to do with the discovery or the excavation itself, played just as strong a role as Egyptian politics in the disagreements that forced Carter out of the tomb he had discovered.[94]

Carter simply did not realize that, along with the gold and jewels, he had discovered another treasure, insubstantial and yet even more valuable.[95] Unseemly though it may have been, the haste with which the *News* cobbled together its coverage of the discovery of Tut was barely sufficient to the Egyptomania that raged through Europe and America at the end of 1922. In part, the discovery had such a strong impact because it coincided with the crest of a preexisting fad for Egyptian things. Grauman's Egyptian Theater opened in Hollywood in 1922, but it was simply continuing a fashion established by the Louxor in Paris the year before. Ernst Lubitsch's *Das Weib des Pharaohs* was released in the United States in 1922, but it had been running in Europe for a year.[96] Thus, when Carter's discovery was announced, the effect was a bit like adding gasoline to a fire. One day the *Times* representative remarked of a pair

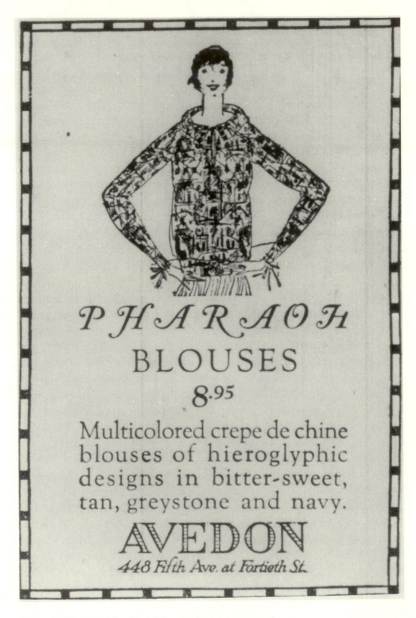

Pharoah Blouses (*New York Times*, February 25, 1923).

of royal sandals, "Probably we shall see our smartest ladies wearing footgear more or less resembling and absolutely inspired by these wonderful things," and within days Carter received dozens of requests for the rights to such designs.[97] Edward Bernays was but one of a number of enterprising entrepreneurs who decided to base new fashions on motifs from the tomb: there were

Shoe Craftsmanship as Old as the Sandals of Tut-Ankh-Amen Himself. King Tut
footwear (*New York Times*, February 25, 1923).

fabrics, sandals, blouses, and "the Luxora Frock." There were even "King Tut
Lemons."[98] In fact, the rage for Tut was so intense that by the time Bernays'
designer returned from Egypt, it had burned itself out, and the public was so
sick of Tut that the project was dropped.[99] But Bernays was not the only
clever businessman to be caught in this way. William P. S. Earle's film *Tutankhamen*, scheduled for release in 1923, had to be reworked and retitled *The
Dancer of the Nile* because interest in Tut had collapsed so suddenly and so
completely.[100]

Still, the fad was strong enough to establish an identifiable style, Egyptian
art deco, that influenced design throughout the 1920s, appearing in theaters,

steamship interiors, furniture, and ladies' fashions. A very particular kind of popular modernism, Egyptian art deco makes almost graphic the ironic convergence of migration and the media at this moment in time. The common use of Egyptian motifs for movie theaters suggested an association between a real and an imaginative imperialism, between travel in space and the aesthetic transposition of film. The ease with which the new media could bring ancient Egypt to Seattle or Los Angeles made everyone a potential world traveler in a world of manufactured representations. If space and time had both collapsed, they were succeeded by another kind of distance, a distance between reality and representation that Bernays or the *Illustrated London News* were unable and probably unwilling to close.

In one way, Egyptian sacred objects appealed to a contemporary Euro-American audience by supplying the aura progressively stripped from the art of Europe. The Tut treasures were ideal for this purpose, since they were quite literally untouched. But it is also obvious that the aura thus preserved to them was consumed in the very process of celebration, that the unique, the traditional, the sacred, the old very quickly became the new, the secular, and the manufactured—so quickly, in fact, that interest in them was almost immediately exhausted. At the same time, however, another kind of aura, a kind of prestige almost diametrically opposed to the one Benjamin defines, was produced in the process. The Egyptian handbag introduced at the end of 1922 was valuable primarily as a reference, an allusion. It marked its user as one who knew. And the Tut treasures themselves became valuable because they could be known, discussed, and reproduced, literally as well as figuratively. Thus, the ultimate auratic paradox governing the Tut phenomenon was that the new, the secret, the hermetic had to be hurriedly exploited before it became too common, and yet common knowledge of it was itself the value being mined.

What relationship might there be between this sort of popular modernism, exemplified in all its crassness by Bernays, and the literary modernism that arrived in bookstores just as Carter was opening Tut's tomb? There are some rather close practical connections, for Bernays had worked very closely with Horace Liveright in 1919 and 1920, so the strategies Boni and Liveright used to make *The Waste Land* the poetic equivalent of a best-seller were not so very different from those Bernays was using at the same time to exploit ancient Egypt.[101] But there are intrinsic resemblances as well. Franco Moretti calls *The Waste Land* and *Ulysses* "world texts" because of "the supranational dimension of the represented space" in these works.[102] This supranational dimension can hardly count as an aesthetic innovation if an ordinary consumer in a place like De Kalb, Illinois, could buy dry goods decorated with motifs from King Tut's tomb. The world text, with its crazy mixture of Greece, Germany, India, and Rome, exists within a world economy where the mixtures are, if anything, even more indiscriminate.

The world text also makes connections across time. This feature, the "continuously manipulated parallel" between the present and a mythological past,

Bedell

AT ALL THREE STORES
West 34th Street—Thru to 35th St.

NEWARK:
BROAD ST. cor. W. PARK

BROOKLYN:
FULTON ST. near HOYT

Sponsors the Tut-ankh-Amen Influence in Silhouette and Embellishment in Spring Apparel

Capricious Fashion, ever in quest of the New, delves into the realms of the Pharaohs for inspiration—bringing forth new creations for the idealistic woman who appreciates art in dress.

Bedell, always responsive to the newest and over changing trends in fashion, takes the initiative in presenting the Tut-ankh-Amen silhouette, colorings and artful embellishment—exquisite and fantastic embroideries, colorful and artistic prints—inspired by the delicately wrought Egyptian carvings of three thousand years ago.

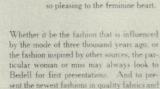

Just as the ancient tombs are resplendent with their rare works of art, so the Bedell Salons disclose a magnificent ensemble of brilliant attire for Springtime. As each treasure has its own particular beauty, so is there a treasured beauty in Bedell Apparel—each with an individuality so pleasing to the feminine heart.

Whether it be the fashion that is influenced by the mode of three thousand years ago, or the fashion inspired by other sources, the particular woman or miss may always look to Bedell for first presentations. And to present the newest fashions in quality fabrics and at moderate prices has at all times been the ideal and achievement of the Bedell shops.

Spring Coats
Wraps that tie on the side have the straight, clinging silhouette. Sports coats in swagger new modes.

Sports Modes
$25—$35—$55
Costume Wraps
$45 to $275

Suit Costumes
Contrasting silks and soutache braids, in all-over Egyptian motifs with side-tie paletots.

Sports Modes
$29.75 to $150
Costume Types
$34.75 to $175

Spring Frocks
Egyptian motifs, Paisleys, Renaissance designed silks in paneled patterns and all-over prints. Drapes extend from ornate Egyptian buckles in front.
$25 to $75

Trig Skirts
Delightfully fashioned of blocked and checked Camel's hair and rich Printed Crepes in knife-plaited types.
$8.98 to $18

New Sweaters
A smart adjunct to the Spring wardrobe. Fashioned of Silk, Fibre and Worsted in Slip-on and Golf Coat models.
$5 to $49.75

Sports Frocks of knitted Silks and Wools
up to $75

The Tut-ankh-Amen Influence in . . . Spring Apparel (*New York Times*, February 25, 1923).

is one of the most heavily advertised innovations of *Ulysses* and *The Waste Land*. But it is also a banality of the time, something every moviegoer could experience in the local version of Grauman's Egyptian Theater. When Carter first opened Tut's tomb, many of the pieces he saw struck him as "extraordinarily modern-looking."[103] In this, he repeats and is probably influenced by the primitivism that had been a feature of "modern" art from the Pre-Raphaelites on. The furniture and artifacts deposited in the tomb looked modern because modern art had been mining the archaic for nearly seventy-five years. But they also looked modern for the far more banal reason that they *were* modern, since Carter's discovery took place in the midst of a vogue for Egyptiana that had already had an effect on modern architecture and decoration. And they would look even more modern as the months passed and Egyptian motifs came to define a certain kind of chic. In fact, within a year Le Corbusier would use this convergence to define modern design, manipulating within the pages of *Vers une architecture* a continuous parallel between ancient architecture and ordinary American consumer items.[104]

In the traditional reading, Eliot's use of the past differs from that of Edward Bernays or Sid Grauman because it is self-consciously and ironically allusive. But surely the appeal of an Egyptian handbag depends on allusion just as much as *The Waste Land* does. The bag exists to advertise the wearer's knowing relationship with a prominent news event; like any fashionable item, it primarily signifies the possessor's awareness and compliments that of any observer chic enough to notice the reference. Clearly Bernays does not rush his designer off to Egypt because he is astonished by the intrinsic beauty of Egyptian designs, since these had been available quite literally for millennia. What he hopes to capture in fabric is the notoriety of the newly opened tomb, and once that notoriety wears off the fabric is of little value to him. Such a use of allusion is, if anything, vastly more self-conscious and ironic than Eliot's. In *The Waste Land* there is always some doubt about the actual relationship between the present and the past, but in the handbag it is plain that the past is nothing more than a magazine of references, useful only in that ironically infinitesimal moment when their past obscurity is perfectly balanced against their coming banality.

Aesthetic modernism may very well be, as Jeffrey Weiss has argued in regard to Picasso and Duchamp, an irony based on such ironies, a mockery and a mimicry of strategies of *publicité* and *réclame* perfected by modern salesmanship.[105] Such a possibility seems perfectly likely in the case of Joyce, who bases *Ulysses* on parallels between a Greek hero and a modern ad man, but not so likely in the case of Eliot, who has long been the personification of aesthetic modernism's resistance to modern commodification. An allusion to the Shakespearean Rag can, in such readings, only be dismissively distancing. But Eliot's reference is also archly self-referential, for Clive Bell had published in September 1921 an elaborate denunciation of jazz in which both Eliot and Joyce are accused of being "ragtime" artists. Thus Eliot had before him as he worked on this part of *The Waste Land* the charge that he was "playing the devil with the instrument of Shakespeare and Milton" and that Joyce's work "rags the literary instrument."[106] When Eliot alludes to the Shakespearean Rag in the second section of *The Waste Land*, then, he is alluding to an actual popular song and to the common modern process it exemplifies of mining the past for current fashions as well as using a designation that had recently been applied to his own work. Even if he is not ragging the literary instrument himself, he is most certainly ragging Bell, playing his own level of private irony over the public irony of the Shakespearean Rag. In this way, he both mocks and confirms Bell, who would no doubt have been equally offended to learn that tourists in the Luxor hotels were at this very moment dancing to the Tutankhamen Rag.[107]

The existence of something like the Tutankhamen Rag, with all that it implies about the convergence of colonialism and metropolitan fashion, modern science and modern marketing, shows how complex and how quickly changing was the modernity into which Joyce and Eliot introduced their works. The status of modernity itself had already been rendered ambiguous by the turn of modern European scientific and artistic attention outward in space and backward in time, so that every innovation in knowledge or art seemed to involve modernity more thoroughly with its opposite. When this involvement reaches the level of fashion, the whole notion of the new becomes ironic. That ancient Egyptian designs might become the latest fashion seems a contradiction in terms, and yet it is a contradiction that the twentieth century has staged over and over, as newness races to exceed the very familiarity it feeds on. The technical power of the twentieth century to record, transmit, and reproduce has meant that any present moment can be fixed and perpetuated, so we can quite literally seize the day; but this also means that each succeeding moment of the present is surrounded by a richer and more complex complement from the past so powerful in its presence that actual repetition of it seems not so much inevitable as unnecessary. Modernity creates for itself its own version of Tutankhamen's tomb, mummifying itself on film and tape, so that Carter's awed discovery of a perfectly preserved past that has somehow cheated death is, paradoxically, a quintessentially modern experience, and the fad that brings together ancient Egypt with movie theaters and ragtime expresses some fundamental association between modern media and the past.[108]

Joyce suggests something like this in *Ulysses* when Leopold Bloom fondly imagines a graveyard fitted with recording machines so that the bereaved might hear the voices of their loved ones.[109] It seems an idiosyncratic fancy, but in 1922 the Darbycord company actually marketed its phonographs with this very purpose in mind. Advertisements in the *Illustrated London News* promised that an ordinary consumer might accumulate an Egyptian necropolis in wax: "By means of the 'Darbycord' the songs and sayings of the little ones, the precious gems of fleeting childhood, and the memories of the 'Golden

Let Darbycord Photograph Your Voice (*Illustrated London News*, April 29, 1922).

Age' can be preserved."[110] At the climax of *Ulysses*, however, Stephen Dedalus is driven into a violent rage when he imagines that his mother's voice is coming from a pianola. When he raises his ashplant to smash that voice into silence, he is repudiating history, and with it the filial piety that is so strong a part of Bloom's personality, but he is also rejecting modernity, whose technical power to fix and reproduce the present has made it an ironic echo of the past.

Conventional separation of literary modernism from its popular analogues can thus be challenged on anecdotal grounds, because writers like Eliot and Joyce were so obviously linked to the world of the Tutankhamen Rag. Historical criticism has been able to show, especially for Joyce, that these writers lived in the same world of film, music, advertising, and promotion that is still around us, and that, like most denizens of the twentieth century, they had various and not entirely negative reactions to it.[111] But this separation can be challenged in a more fundamental way as well. For one thing, Eliot and Joyce, like many other modern writers, were clearly subject to the process of global migration that, as Giddens, Appadurai, and Williams have argued, has been an imaginative as well as a political fact of great importance to this century. The inevitable mediation of experience has also become inescapably obvious, so much so that self-consciousness about it has to be considered as a sociopolitical fact. Most human communities are now more thoroughly constituted by representations than by identity or mere contiguity in space, and this fact is also clear to those communities. The result, as Appadurai puts it, is that "many lives are now inextricably linked with representations."[112] What is in some ways the central pun of *Ulysses*, when Martha Clifford confuses "word" and "world," is not so much a bit of clever wordplay as it is a reflection of common experience: Appadurai says that the subject matter of cultural studies is to be "the relationship between the word and the world."[113] That relationship was a slippery one for Joyce's characters in part because it was slippery for Joyce himself, first as an artist and second as a language teacher living in various polyglot communities of Europe, and in part because it was a slippery one for the public at large at a time when the world and the word were beginning to converge in disorienting ways.

The common dichotomies by which the literary modernism of 1922 is distinguished from the larger culture of the time cannot be maintained against the evidence that the very terms those dichotomies depend on were being redefined by literature and culture in concert. The modern itself is obviously an unstable category when the new, in literature and in fashion, comes into being in such close association with the ancient. In a cultural phenomenon like Egyptomania, for instance, the old and the new are not opposite but codependent. The similar distinction between convention and revolt is dissolved by such fashions—by fashion itself, in fact, which moves forward on a delicate balance of conformity and distinction. At the same time, the contrast between the private and the public, the particular and the common, was being ironized by a form of publicity that fed on individual desires for distinction. These dichotomies cannot be used to divide modernism, for their ironic interdependence defines the modern, which displayed itself all across the scene of 1922, from an Egyptian-style handbag to the latest thing in literary innovation.

The purpose of the following chapters is to read the cultural works of that year, those of acknowledged importance like the *Tractatus* and those of apparent triviality like *My Trip Abroad*, including certain pictorial works that promised, by appealing directly to the sense of sight, to make reading unnecessary. By concentrating on the year in which *Ulysses* and *The Waste Land* were published, and not on the long years during which they were contemplated, planned, and executed, this study clearly intends to shift the analytical emphasis from the production to the reception of literary modernism, and very frequently in the following pages it will matter less what a particular author says than what particular readers felt about what he or she was thought to have said. In some ways, then, this is a study in reception theory, and it owes an obvious debt to Hans-Robert Jauss' notion of a "horizon of expectation" that would form a particular reader's reaction to a particular literary work. The "horizon of expectation" is, as Wlad Godzich paraphrases it, "the sum total of reactions, prejudgments, verbal and other behavior that greet a work on its appearance."[114] But the focus of this work is also somewhat broader, since its purpose is not to reconstruct a contemporary reading of either *Ulysses* or *The Waste Land* but rather to reconstruct, insofar as it may be possible, the larger public world into which those works were introduced. To some extent, this means trying to recapture the period's own sense of its "reactions, prejudgments, verbal and other behavior," and to some extent it means trying to interpret a historic moment in which the whole notion of "prejudgments" was making a considerable impact on various different disciplines in the human sciences. That every human being brings to every experience a "horizon of expectation" was, perhaps paradoxically, the unifying perception of the time. The ways in which the different media of the time alternately reinforced that sense and promised to reduce it will provide a good many of the examples to follow.

1

Translation, Mistranslation, and the *Tractatus*

FOR THE *TIMES LITERARY SUPPLEMENT*, one of the notable intellectual events of 1922 was the hundredth anniversary of the science of comparative philology. In early April the *TLS* commemorated the publication of Jakob Grimm's *Deutsche Grammatik*, which introduced the theory of consonantal shift that came to be known as Grimm's Law, and also took advantage of the date to review a few contemporary works on language. According to the anonymous reviewer, these betrayed "a certain barrenness in modern linguistics."[1] The works under review, which included Otto Jespersen's *Language*, did not, in the opinion of this reviewer, count for much in comparison to the great ambitions of early philology for an all-inclusive science of language. If it had waited just a few months, however, the *TLS* might have included in its survey two works that were to make the modern study of language every bit as fruitful as nineteenth-century philology, if in an entirely different way. Ludwig Wittgenstein's *Tractatus Logico-Philosophicus*, which appeared in November, began the famous "linguistic turn," which has made the study of language the centerpiece of contemporary philosophy, and Bronislaw Malinowski's *Argonauts of the Western Pacific*, reviewed by the *TLS* in July, focused attention on the context of speech in a way that was to be crucial for ordinary language philosophers such as Firth and Austin.[2]

Since they are not often mentioned together, it is somewhat surprising to see how closely associated these two works were in the Cambridge of 1922. C. K. Ogden, who masterminded the translation and publication of the *Trac-

tatus during the winter of 1921–1922, met Malinowski at about the same time and solicited from him a supplement to *The Meaning of Meaning*, which Ogden and I. A. Richards were to bring out in book form early in 1923. While Ogden was working with the text and proofs of the *Tractatus*, going over these quite extensively with Wittgenstein by mail, Malinowski was reading the proofs of *The Meaning of Meaning* and preparing his supplement.[3] Since *The Meaning of Meaning* itself had a substantial effect on the study of language, if not directly then certainly through the influence of Richards on English studies, the projects passing through Ogden's hands at this time represent a remarkable concentration of new and influential linguistic theory.

Nonetheless, a look at *The Meaning of Meaning* shows that the distance between these men and their works began to grow from the very beginning. The references to the *Tractatus* that Malinowski might have seen while examining Ogden's proofs were actually quite disparaging. At one point, in fact, Ogden and Richards draw a direct contrast between the work of "ethnologists" and that of logicians like Russell and Wittgenstein, whose belief that there should be a specifiable and consistent relationship between words and things "has been a chief hindrance to ethnologists in their study of primitive speech."[4] At the same time, Russell was openly scoffing at the notion that ethnologists had anything to teach philosophers of language, especially if their methods involved some approximation of their subjects' point of view:

> when a savage shows that he is muddle-headed as to the muddle in his head, it is assumed that we ought to learn to be equally muddle-headed, and that no clear account of his muddle is possible. This favouritism seems to indicate a bias in favour of muddle. . . . Savages are muddled as to what is going on, whether inside them or outside them, and their account is not to be accepted.[5]

From this evidence it seems safe to say that as of 1922 Malinowski and Wittgenstein seemed in utter contrast to one another in their approach to language, one attempting, along with Russell, to perfect it as an apparatus for conveying thought and the other studying it in practice as an instrument of social action.

At some point in his later life, however, Wittgenstein began to acquire the very point of view at which Russell had scoffed so loftily and along with it a philosophical method that looked a great deal like armchair anthropology. He called it the "anthropologische Betrachtungsweise" or "ethnologische Betrachtungsweise," which might be translated as "anthropological perspective" or "anthropological point-of-view."[6] In either case, it resembles, both as a phrase and as a method, the "Ethnographer's perspective" that Malinowski proclaimed the only one "relevant and real for the formation of fundamental linguistic conceptions" in his supplement to *The Meaning of Meaning*.[7] In fact, a careful examination of that supplement shows a theory of linguistic meaning as use far closer to Wittgenstein's later philosophy than was the *Tractatus* itself.

To some extent this unexpected convergence can be explained by showing that Wittgenstein had long-standing connections with Cambridge anthropology, connections that have not been extensively explored but that may have had just as significant an effect on his philosophy as his far more celebrated relationship with Russell. But the resemblance between these two very different men and the different disciplines they were to found may also be explained by reference to the experience that Malinowski and Wittgenstein shared, the experience of living and working in an alien environment, an experience that was to give new form to influential sciences in part because it was so typical in the twentieth century. Wittgenstein and Malinowski came to England to participate in a project of universalized reason even wider in scope than that imagined by comparative philology: Malinowski to found a science of human society applicable all over the world, Wittgenstein to formulate a method of communication unmediated by any particularity whatever. And yet they became so influential because they suffered from cultural misunderstanding, from mistranslation, which became in its way just as central to the human sciences of the twentieth century as the great philological project of universal translation was for their predecessors.

The Translation of the *Tractatus*

The *Tractatus*, more or less complete by 1919, had appeared in German in *Annalen der Naturphilosophie* by the middle of 1921, but in a form so inaccurate and so unsatisfactory to Wittgenstein that he always considered the Routledge edition of 1922 its first real appearance in print.[8] His feelings about this might have pleased the *TLS*, which was a little testy about "the army of German and other Continental scholars" commonly supposed to have dominated the science of philology.[9] But the most remarkable, and the least commonly remarked, effect of this shift in priority is that it means this seminal work on language was originally published in two languages simultaneously, for the Routledge edition was in English with the German en face, or in German with the English en face, depending on your point of view.

Over the years, a good deal of attention has been focused on the relationship between the German and English texts, all of it taking for granted the notion, first offered in C. K. Ogden's opening note to the Routledge edition, that the German is the "original" and the English a "translation."[10] In fact, assigning responsibility for this act of translation has been notoriously difficult. Ogden and Bertrand Russell, who was instrumental in both the English and German publications of the *Tractatus*, separately reported to Wittgenstein that the translation was being done by "translator*s*" (my emphasis), though only one has ever been identified. And though it has generally been assumed that that one, Frank Ramsey, bears primary responsibility for the translation, even the most recent and most authoritative accounts continue to refer to Ogden as "*the* translator" (my emphasis).[11]

Wittgenstein's own role in the translation has been equally confused and far more controversial. G. E. M. Anscombe's offhand comment in her *Introduction to Wittgenstein's Tractatus* to the effect that Ogden's "very bad" translation had not been checked by Wittgenstein himself started an argument that was not settled for twenty years.[12] Although publication of the correspondence between Ogden and Wittgenstein established that there had in fact been very close consultation between them, a new translation was produced that achieved, according to some experts, a closer approximation to the meaning of the original, even without the cooperation that was possible while Wittgenstein was alive.[13]

These confusions and controversies about relatively limited issues seem to have obscured the larger implications of the "translation" of the *Tractatus*. The separation of a German "original" from an English "translation," like the separation of the philosopher's original words from the poor approximations of his amanuenses, applies a rather primitive notion of translation, not to say of language itself, to one of the most radical linguistic documents of the century. Lost in the academic tug-of-war is the possibility that the most radical implications of the *Tractatus* are located somewhere in the gap between German and English, not in the explicit doctrines of a work Wittgenstein himself hoped to supersede, but rather in the very difficulties that newer, more "accurate" translations are meant to avoid.

Though opinions differ widely on Wittgenstein's command of English, there is no doubt that his philosophy took shape through a process of bilingual conversation.[14] From the very beginning, from the "Notes on Logic" dictated to Russell in 1913, Wittgenstein formulated his thoughts by speaking them aloud—sometimes in English, sometimes in German, sometimes in a mixture of the two—to English transcribers. After the "Notes on Logic" the next step toward the *Tractatus* itself was taken in a series of propositions dictated to the exasperated G. E. Moore, and the propositions that ultimately formed *Philosophical Investigations* passed back and forth between English and German as Wittgenstein dictated them to his students at Cambridge and then translated their transcriptions into German for further work.[15]

The whole notion of translation as proceeding from an original in one language to a more or less authoritative version in another is inadequate to describe these works, which had their genesis and have their being in two languages at once. Yet even the original collaborators in the publication and translation of the *Tractatus*, including Wittgenstein himself, tended to treat the difference between German and English as a mechanical inconvenience and not as a substantial feature of the work itself. Wittgenstein was acutely conscious, of course, of the difficulty of finding equivalents for the expressions of one country in the language of another.[16] But his letters to Ogden also show that, at least in practice, he believed in a "sense" that could be conveyed independent of the actual wording.[17] Of course, it is this very notion of a "sense" behind the words, one that undergirds debates about the veracity of translations, that Wittgenstein most vigorously disputed in his later work: "The fact that in two different languages the thought expressed by a sentence is the same does not mean that one may go looking for the thought conveyed by them."[18] At the time of the *Tractatus*, however, concentration on the relationship between words and things made the relationship between German and English seem trivial indeed.

As Russell explains it in the first paragraph of his introduction to the *Tractatus*, the positive aspect of Wittgenstein's project is to establish "the relations which are necessary between words and things in any language," and its negative aspect is to expose the problems and solutions of traditional philosophy as misconceptions arising from "misuse of language."[19] The easy glide from "any language" to "language" is symptomatic of a philosophy that saw itself dealing with matters so fundamental they concerned all human utterance. Russell quite naturally sees the *Tractatus* as a continuation of Frege's search for a "'concept-script' (*Begriffsschrift*)," a logically perfect system of notation that would at once expose and clarify the logical incoherence of the natural languages.[20] Thus Russell refers in his introduction to the goal of "an ideal language" and "a logically perfect language." Wittgenstein himself invokes both Frege and Russell when he says in the text that dispelling the confusions of philosophy requires a "symbolism . . . which obeys the rules of *logical* grammar" (*T*, 3.325). Given such a symbolism, the problem of translation simply disappears: "Every correct symbolism must be translatable into every other" (*T*, 3.343).[21] Philosophy, in fact, becomes the activity of translating not one natural language into another but any natural language into the logically consistent counterpart that underlies all languages.[22]

In principle, then, differences between the natural languages, like the even more trivial differences within them, count for nothing in the formulation of a logical grammar that must underlie any language. Accordingly, the text of the *Tractatus* assumes the existence of a standard European speaker, an English "We" that speaks essentially the same language as the German "Wir" across the page. But the scrambling about that took place between the two versions, in the gutter as it were, tells a very different story. For example, proposition 3.325 describes the necessary characteristics of a logically consistent grammar: it must not apply "the same sign in different symbols" or apply "signs in the same way which signify in different ways." This seems to be as straightforward as it is dogmatic, but Wittgenstein and Ogden had a difficult time coming up with an adequate English equivalent for the German *Zeichensprache*: "sign language" and "symbolism," the two candidates, both have usages and connotations that interfere with the meaning of the proposition. In fact, in his epistolary comments about the translation of proposition 4.011, Wittgenstein brackets the two possibilities, one above the other, so that the very system that is to exclude linguistic duplicity turns out to have two equally inconvenient names.[23]

The same irony attends many of the comments Wittgenstein made on the first English version of the *Tractatus*. The text claims, "If I know the meaning of an English and a synonymous German word, it is impossible for me not to know that they are synonymous, it is impossible for me not to be able to translate them into one another" (*T*, 4.243). But the correspondence about the text seems to unravel this certainty, starting from the end: being unable to translate one term into another calls into question the whole notion of a "meaning" so separable from the words themselves that English and German might share it and then beyond that the whole notion of a logic that might exist quite independent of any of the natural languages.

It is not simply the case that these translational difficulties surreptitiously and retrospectively ironize the text of the *Tractatus*; at times the gap between German and English seems to open on possibilities Wittgenstein was only to realize explicitly in much later work. One of the sturdiest translational controversies has arisen around propositions 5.6–5.62, in some sense the core of the *Tractatus*. Proposition 5.6 reads in both the 1922 edition and the Pears/McGuinness translation: "*The limits of my language* mean the limits of my world." The first paraphrase of this difficult proposition is provided by Wittgenstein himself in 5.62: "The limits of my language (*the* language which I understand) mean the limits of *my* world." As so often happens, the gloss simply introduced more confusion, "der Sprache (der Sprache, die allein ich verstehe)" having been taken as a statement about a private language, a language that *I alone understand* and not a language that *alone I understand*.[24] The 1922 translation avoids this difficulty in part by applying more italics: "(*the* language which I understand)" (*T*, 5.62). Pears and McGuinness retain the word order and a bit of the ambiguity of the original: "that language which alone I understand."[25] Russell provides perhaps the nicest English version in *his* gloss, which appears in his introduction: "the only language I understand" (*T*, p. 18).

Perhaps these difficulties in translating what is a fairly simple phrase can shed some light on the philosophical difficulties it has caused. If anything is clear from the varying attempts of these competent English speakers it is that "the limits of my language" do not enclose anything nearly so unitary or so sharply delimited as Wittgenstein seems to describe. In their attempts to adjust one language to another, the translators test and stretch the boundaries of both languages, and they gain perspective on one language, discovering difficulties and possibilities within it, from the perspective afforded by the other. But translation is simply a special instance of the more general process by which any speaker tests and expands the limits of his or her language every day as it comes in contact with other languages and idiolects. In the text of the *Tractatus* itself, Wittgenstein is not concerned with language at this empirical level,[26] but in the correspondence concerning it he often explores the limits of his own language in a very empirical way: of a suggested emendation for proposition 5.61 he says, "I would have put it that way but I don't know if it's English."[27] In such situations, outside the boundaries of the text, the *Tractatus* creates a linguistic situation much like the one Wittgenstein was to describe in his later work, where the notion of a single language within its impermeable boundary gives way to a set of language games in constant befuddled negotiation with one another.

A good deal of this difference can be glimpsed in the different possible translations of a single word, the word "limit" itself, in some sense perhaps the most important single word in the *Tractatus*, which seems to have caused translators no difficulty at all. The importance of this word is signified by the number of times Wittgenstein uses it in his own preface, which contains the rather audacious claim that the text to follow will "draw a limit to thinking" (*T*, p. 27). Wherever the German *Grenze* appears, both editions of the *Tractatus* translate it as "limit," but *Grenze* can also be rendered into English as "boundary" or even "frontier," and when Wittgenstein spoke in English of the limits of language in later life, he tended to use the former: "The similarity between new and old uses of a word is like that between an exact and a blurred boundary"; "We never arrive at fundamental propositions in the course of our investigations; we get to the boundary of language which stops us from asking further questions."[28] Perhaps G. E. M. Anscombe is influenced by Wittgenstein's own practice when she translates *Grenze* as "boundary" or even "boundary line" in her English version of *Philosophical Investigations*:

> To say "this combination of words makes no sense" excludes it from the sphere of language and thereby bounds [*umgrenzt*] the domain of language. But when one draws a boundary [*Grenze*] it may be for various kinds of reason. If I surround an area with a fence or a line or otherwise, the purpose may be to prevent someone from getting in or out; but it may also be part of a game and the players be supposed, say, to jump over the boundary [*Grenze*]; or it may shew where the property of one man ends and that of another begins; and so on. So if I draw a boundary line [*Grenze*] that is not yet to say what I am drawing it for.[29]

Wittgenstein's metaphor makes clear the difference between a limit and a boundary: there is nothing beyond a limit, but a boundary has another side. In fact, the playful picture of people jumping over the boundary of language seems almost a purposeful revision of the stern and audacious claim of the *Tractatus* to have drawn a limit beyond which human thought cannot go.

The very word that Wittgenstein chose to represent the unity and impermeability of language thus turns out to have within it possibilities that would not emerge explicitly in his work until many years later. "Limit" is unitary and metaphysical; "boundary" is multiple and empirical. The language contained by a limit is not to be confused with any natural language, much less with a dialect or idiolect; the language within a boundary is almost by definition national. And this difference appears only along its own boundary, the boundary between English and German or, to be more precise, the various boundaries between Wittgenstein's German and his English, between the German of his disciples and their English versions of his German as influenced by his English lectures. The very text that claimed to set a limit to thinking bore down its middle the visual representation of an internal boundary, an empirical one between two natural languages, which the text could no more avoid than it could print the German on top of the English.

What this suggests is that the difficulties attending the translation of the *Tractatus* are not confusions to be dispelled but rather opportunities to be exploited. Often the tensions between different readings illuminate Wittgenstein's thought in a way that individual readings cannot approximate. The Routledge version of 4.002, for example, gives a very loose approximation of the German "stillschweigenden Abmachungen": "The silent adjustments to understand colloquial language are enormously complicated." Pears and McGuinness give a very different and seemingly more accurate version: "The tacit conventions on which the understanding of everyday language depends are enormously complicated." The Routledge translators, on one hand, apparently read this proposition in light of the general understanding of the *Tractatus* in and around Cambridge in 1922. "Silent adjustments" implies something faulty in colloquial language, something very much like the "bad grammar" that Russell's introduction condemned as the source of most conventional philosophical issues. And, in fact, this reading seems very close to the sense of the whole section, which complains about the difficulty of gathering the logic of language, and leads into the famous declaration "All philosophy is 'Critique of language'" (*T*, 4.0031). Pears and McGuinness, on the other hand, read the proposition in light of the later Wittgenstein, for whom "tacit conventions" are not diversions or obfuscations to be "adjusted" away in the search for a perfect logical language but rather the very stuff of human understanding. But the whole point of the comparison is that the "tacit conventions" that govern each reading do not appear until they clash, requiring from the reader "silent adjustments." If there were no confusion, no "bad grammar," no need for "adjustments," then the conventions would remain "tacit," and one would be tempted to read the passage as a relatively simplified version of itself.

The difference in the translations dramatizes a tension in the situation of the *Tractatus* itself. Explicitly, the *Tractatus* announces a program of philosophical ascesis: "Philosophy should make clear and delimit [*abgrenzen*] sharply the thoughts which otherwise are, as it were, opaque and blurred" (*T*, 4.112). And yet implicitly, in its bilingual status on the page, in the differences between the German and the English and between various ways of getting from one to the other, it blurs the very boundaries it was so concerned to establish, or rather it demonstrates that any boundaries that can be drawn are empirical and provisional rather than necessary and permanent. At the same time, the shift in the meaning of this word has a certain political and cultural significance, for the whole notion that there is but one limit to human reason is imperial in its pretensions, while the realization that there are many boundaries within it implies the relative independence of particular types of local knowledge.

In its desire to say clearly once and for all everything that can be said, the *Tractatus* seems to express a project far wider in the scope of its pretensions than comparative philology. It is in some ways the finest and most extreme expression of what Jeffrey Alexander calls "the dream of reason," the ambition to lift thought free of all specificity, all contingency.[30] Other expressions of the same project coincided with Wittgenstein's in 1922, among them the program for a purely geometric architecture announced in articles by Le Corbusier and the supposedly clean and straightforward language just being put into stories by Ernest Hemingway.[31] According to Alexander, it was the First World War that most seriously threatened this project by convincing many modern thinkers, among them Wittgenstein, that neutral reason is at best a figment of the imagination. But the situation of the *Tractatus* suggests that the inversion of modernity's "dream of reason" was always inherent within it, that the very attempt to postulate a neutral container for human thought would expose its ineluctably contingent character. In fact, the irreducible foreignness of language could not have appeared without this attempt to tame it into universal familiarity.

Something like this is suggested in Wittgenstein's later philosophy, in which misunderstanding and mistranslation are given the central place once accorded to clarity and neutrality of expression. In fact, Wittgenstein's later method suggests that understanding is brought most successfully to the level of reflection *by* misunderstanding. The philosopher who had claimed "everything that can be said can be said clearly" (*T*, 4.116) began to show an almost inordinate interest in what was unclearly said, in fact to base his work on it: "Often my writing is nothing but 'stuttering.'"[32] Poor translation, far from being an annoyance or a difficulty, became the core of a philosophical method. In this way he brought his work back to the science with which it had been so nearly associated in 1922.

The Anthropological Method

Sometime in the 1930s, Wittgenstein began to assume what he called an "anthropologische Betrachtungsweise" or an "ethnologische Betrachtungsweise," a phrase that might, of course, be variously translated but that Rush Rhees has rendered as "anthropological method."[33] In brief, this method involves imagining a foreign language that fails to observe what a speaker of English or German might consider a linguistic fact of life. The anthropological focus of these thought-experiments is not, however, the mythical language or its nonexistent speakers, but rather the English or German linguistic habit thrown into high relief by the contrast. As Wittgenstein says of the method in *Culture and Value*, "we are taking up a position right outside so as to be able to see things *more objectively*."[34]

The spatial metaphor itself suggests how radically this method differs from the delimitation project carried on in the *Tractatus*. As Rhees puts it: "We are no longer comparing different ways of saying the same thing (as in the *Tractatus*). We are comparing different ways of speaking or carrying on discourse with one another, and in this sense different languages. And the point is not to see what is common to them all; very often it is just the opposite: to see that there need be nothing common to them all."[35] The anthropological method is, therefore, one of the key features that distinguishes Wittgenstein's later philosophy from his earlier, and thus it is usually considered to have developed only in the 1930s. Wittgenstein himself attributed it to his conversations of that time with the Marxist economist Piero Sraffa.[36] But it is possible that there are earlier antecedents as well, ones that predate but also crucially center on the year of the *Tractatus*.

Despite his long residence in England, Wittgenstein always harbored an uneasy sense of himself as a foreign speaker of English. As he wrote to Frank Ramsey sometime in the late 1920s: "What a statement seems to imply to me it doesn't to you. If you should ever live amongst foreign people for any length of time & be dependent upon them you will understand my difficulty."[37] In letters to Russell and Keynes he agonized about "my beastly English jargon."[38] Frequently he would switch back and forth between German and English, complaining about the difficulty of communicating in both. After one such set of vacillations, however, he seemed to take studious interest in his own ineptitude: "I thought when I began to write that I should write this letter altogether in German but, extraordinarily enough, it has proved more natural for me to write to you in broken English than in correct German."[39]

This statement represents the essence, if not quite the genesis, of the anthropological method, which involved a purposeful projection of the philosopher across the limits of the natural to a situation in which all language is broken. Over and over, in his work and in his life, Wittgenstein purposely distanced himself from the familiar so as to observe it as if it were foreign:

> Two people are laughing together, say at a joke. One of them has used certain somewhat unusual words and now they both break out into a sort of bleating. That might appear very extraordinary to a visitor coming from quite a different environment. Whereas we find it completely reasonable. (I recently witnessed this scene on a bus and was able to think myself into the position of someone to whom this would be unfamiliar. From that point of view it struck me as quite irrational, like the responses of an outlandish animal.)[40]

In his work as well, Wittgenstein frequently thought himself into this position, working on a philosophical problem by imagining someone who could not comprehend the most ordinary social usages: "It's as though there were a custom amongst certain people for one person to throw another a ball which he is supposed to catch and throw back; but some people, instead of throwing it back, put it in their pocket."[41] In fact, this sense of incomprehen-

sion, of estrangement, of foreignness becomes almost synonymous with philosophy itself: "A philosophical problem has the form: 'I don't know my way
about'" (*PI*, 123).

What Wittgenstein is apparently trying to do in such thought-experiments
is to outwit the process that makes language so familiar it becomes invisible.
He speaks in the *Philosophical Investigations* of the "enormously familiar" aspect
that language assumes "like well-known faces" (*PI*, 167). As the eye passes
over print it moves "without being held up . . . it doesn't *skid*" (*PI*, 168). "How
hard I find it to see," he complains, "what is *right in front of my eyes!*"[42] The goal
of philosophy then becomes to make the eye "skid" by presenting the familiar as if it were something utterly unexpected and foreign.

One of Wittgenstein's favorite tactics of estrangement is to imagine "a
tribe" whose language or customs confound some basic assumption of bourgeois European life.[43] He used this tactic throughout the lectures he delivered
at Cambridge in the 1930s, in the *Investigations*, and in the fragmentary notes
collected at the end of his life.[44] In these strategic fantasies, the philosopher's
common role is naturally that of the anthropologist, the "explorer" who first
comes into an unknown country (*PI*, 243), but certain of these instances make
it clear that Wittgenstein is simply extrapolating his own experience of having
come to England: "One human being can be a complete enigma to another.
We learn this when we come into a strange country with entirely strange traditions; and, what is more, even given a mastery of the country's language. We
do not *understand* the people. (And not because of not knowing what they are
saying to themselves.) We cannot find our feet with them" (*PI*, p. 223e).[45]

Perhaps for this reason the anthropologist's role is a curiously unstable one.
It proves quite easy for the philosopher to become identified not with the anthropologist but with his subjects: "When we do philosophy we are like savages, primitive people, who hear the expressions of civilized men, put a false
interpretation on them, and then draw the queerest conclusions from it" (*PI*,
194). With this shift accomplished, the familiar truly does become the foreign
and the customary the exceptional: "Couldn't a member of a tribe of colour-
blind people get the idea of imagining a strange sort of human being (whom
we would call 'normally sighted')?"[46] This seems to mark the goal of the
method, when the philosopher is so thoroughly estranged that he can imagine
imagining his normal, everyday life as if it were the life of some remote tribe.

The sort of incomprehension that Wittgenstein laboriously arrives at is, of
course, exactly the sort that translators labor to dispel. The whole philosophical project of translation that goes on in and around the *Tractatus*, what Rhees
calls "comparing ways of saying the same thing," gives way to a project of
purposeful mistranslation; instead of all language reduced to a universal notation, individual languages proliferate incommensurably. It is for this reason
that the process of translating and mistranslating the *Tractatus* is, in some ways,
more significant to Wittgenstein's later work than the text itself. There are certainly moments in the later work when it seems that such experiences of

translation must have had this sort of significance for Wittgenstein: "Our knowledge of different languages prevents us from really taking seriously the philosophy laid down in the forms of each of them. But at the same time we are blind to our own strong prejudices for, as against, certain forms of expression; to the fact that just this piling up of several languages results in a special picture. That, so to speak, it is not optional for us which form we cover up with which."[47] Possibly, all the evidence produced in the controversy of the 1960s and 1970s over this translation, the letters to Ogden, the conversations with Ramsey, the discussions with Russell and Moore should have had exactly the opposite effect that it did have: instead of laying to rest questions about the authority of the Routledge edition, they should have demonstrated the process by which the authority of the *Tractatus* itself was qualified in the mind of its author.

If this is true, if the translation of the *Tractatus* is in some sense the first important mistranslation of Wittgenstein's life, if the "anthropological method" grows out of the experience of 1922, then it may also be "anthropological" in more than a metaphorical sense. For 1922 was also notable as the year in which anthropology established itself in its currently practiced form, a form remarkably like the thought-experiments Wittgenstein spent his life conducting. The circumstances of that seminal year in the history of anthropology suggest that the connection may be more than coincidental.

By 1923 anthropology was sufficiently institutionalized in England to be available as a course of instruction at eleven universities.[48] But it was still so closely associated with Cambridge that its entire history might have been discerned there in the events of a single year. The beginnings of the discipline were commemorated in 1922 by the inauguration of an annual lecture series honoring Sir James Frazer, who was still alive and active in university politics.[49] Yet the end of the era of his successors, who took anthropology out of the study and into the field, was simultaneously visible in the untimely death of W. H. R. Rivers. At his death, Rivers was president of the Folk-Lore Society and the Royal Anthropological Institute and a Labour candidate for Parliament.[50] Rivers' life had been so various that his death was a serious shock to many outside the discipline of anthropology, including Robert Graves and Bertrand Russell. It also made possible the almost uncannily synchronized ascendance of the next generation, which arrived with the first books of Bronislaw Malinowski and A. R. Radcliffe-Brown.[51] These books, *Argonauts of the Western Pacific* and *The Andaman Islanders*, make 1922 "the *annus mirabilis*" of modern anthropology.[52]

Wittgenstein, who was teaching school in Austria in 1922, could have had no direct connection with any of these events, and, considering the isolation of his life at this time, he was probably unaware of them. Nonetheless, some inkling would have come to him along with the Routledge edition of the *Tractatus*. Ogden published this work as one of the first in his International Library of Psychology, Philosophy and Scientific Method, which also included

Rivers' *Conflict and Dream*.[53] He also advertised from the beginning his own work in the series, *The Meaning of Meaning*, which, when it appeared early in 1923, made much of the research of Malinowski and included his essay "The Problem of Meaning in Primitive Languages" as a supplement. Wittgenstein read the copy of *The Meaning of Meaning* that Ogden sent to him, but grudgingly and without apparent effect on his own work.[54] Yet it was in that supplement that Malinowski made his most direct and impassioned claim for "the Ethnographer's perspective" as the only one "relevant and real for the formation of fundamental linguistic conceptions."[55] And if "Ethnographer's perspective" is not precisely the same as the "ethnologische Betrachtungsweise"[56] that Wittgenstein came to advocate, it is close enough to prompt a suggestive inquiry into the particular concatenation of philosophy and anthropology in the year that changed both disciplines for good.

Wittgenstein had in fact long since experienced a much more direct contact with Cambridge anthropology, one that may go part way toward explaining a significant convergence of his work of 1922 and that of Malinowski and Radcliffe-Brown. Wittgenstein had, of course, been educated at Cambridge —if the term *educated* can be used for the rigorous process of scrutiny to which he subjected his instructors. On the Moral Sciences Board at Trinity College when Wittgenstein arrived in 1912 there was, along with Russell, McTaggart, and Keynes, one Charles S. Myers, with whom Wittgenstein was to work for a brief time almost as closely as he did with Russell.[57] Even in 1912 Myers was best known as a psychologist, but his original training had been at Cambridge at a time when psychologists, such as his teacher W. H. R. Rivers, were inventing fieldwork anthropology. In fact, Myers had been a participant in the 1898 Cambridge expedition to the Torres Straits, from which all anthropological fieldwork dates its inception.[58]

Myers' particular interest then and in 1912 was music. He particularly wanted to investigate the possibility that people in different cultures experience musical elements such as tone and rhythm differently.[59] He therefore carried out a series of studies in which tones or rhythms were subtly altered so as to measure the sensitivity of the subject. For reasons that are now obscure, Wittgenstein became something between an assistant and a collaborator and spent "many hours" in 1912 and 1913 carrying out these experiments and discussing them with Myers and David Pinsent, the friend to whom the *Tractatus* is dedicated.[60] Though Myers was still publishing the results of such experiments as late as 1922, by which time he had moved from Cambridge to London and founded the Institute of Social Psychology,[61] they yielded relatively little in the way of significant results and seem to have played a very minor role in Wittgenstein's intellectual development at Cambridge.[62] However, they did bring him into suggestive proximity with an "anthropological method" that was arriving at a crucial moment in its history.

There were a number of developments in Cambridge anthropology during 1912–1913 of which Wittgenstein might have gathered some inkling. Mali-

nowski and Radcliffe-Brown both published early studies on Australian abo-
rigines, and Radcliffe-Brown completed his fieldwork in the Andamans and
returned to Cambridge, where Myers had been his teacher.[63] Volume 4 of the
massive report of the Torres Straits expedition was published in 1912, with
contributions from Rivers, Myers, and A. C. Haddon. Though Wittgenstein
may not have seen the whole volume, he must have known of Myers' contribution on primitive music, which was also the subject of a talk Myers gave in
February.[64] It also seems possible that Wittgenstein saw the *British Journal of
Psychology*, edited by Myers and Rivers, which contained a notice in its November 1912 number of the experiments Wittgenstein and Myers had performed. In these years the *British Journal of Psychology* also carried reports and
essays of an anthropological nature, such as "The 'Psychological Interpretation of Language,'" by A. M. Hocart, a colleague of Rivers', which appeared
in this same November issue.[65]

Of all these developments, Wittgenstein seems most certain to have
known of the most significant, the 1912 revision of *Notes and Queries on Anthropology*. *Notes and Queries* had served since 1874 as a guidebook for the amateur ethnological investigators on whom the discipline had depended. Its revision in 1912 is usually considered "the first clear statement of what later
came to be identified as the procedural and theoretical basis of British Social
Anthropology."[66] In fact, there is a direct connection between the 1912 *Notes
and Queries* and the 1922 works of Radcliffe-Brown and Malinowski, who depended heavily on it for guidance. George Stocking calls these later works the
"enactment" of the program of investigation laid out in *Notes and Queries*.[67]

Rivers and Myers were both on the editorial committee that prepared the
1912 revision, to which Rivers also contributed articles on sociology, social organization, economics, games, and natural science and Myers articles on psychology and music. It is, of course, this last that Wittgenstein is most likely to
have seen, especially Myers' extensive directions in the use of such elaborate
field instruments as the rhythmograph.[68] It is possibly this very machine that
Wittgenstein demonstrated at the opening of Myers' new psychological lab-
oratory in March 1913, on which he delivered the "most absurd paper on
rhythms" before the British Psychological Society at Cambridge in July 1912.
As McGuinness points out, Wittgenstein, recently lapsed from a career as an
engineer and fanatically devoted to mechanical tinkering, was more likely to
have been interested in the gadgets than in Myers' psychological theories.[69]

Until the very end of his life, however, Wittgenstein spoke as if he had
been trained by Rivers and Myers in the methods of *Notes and Queries*. When
he writes in a manuscript book kept in 1950, "Can't we imagine certain people
having a different geometry of colour than we do?" he is, in effect, continuing the investigations that Rivers began at the turn of the century, the results
of which appeared in articles such as "The Colour Vision of the Eskimo,"
"The Colour Vision of the Natives of Upper Egypt," and "Primitive Colour
Vision," all of which Rivers published in 1901.[70] Myers had done similar work

during the Torres Straits expedition, as reported in articles such as "A Study of Papuan Hearing," and "The Visual Acuity of the Natives of Sarawak." The basic question behind an article like "The Taste Names of Primitive Peoples," which Myers published in the *British Journal of Psychology* in 1904, reappears almost fifty years later when Wittgenstein muses, "Suppose we were acquainted with a people that had a quite different form of colour attribution from ours."[71] Though the actual hearing experiments that Wittgenstein carried out with Myers in 1912 seem trivial in the extreme, they were, in fact, part of an organized program posing the key question of Wittgenstein's later philosophy: "What, that is, would a society be like, that never played a lot of our ordinary language-games?"[72]

If the "ethnologische Betrachtungsweise" behind such questions resembles the "Ethnographer's perspective" behind Malinowski's work, it may be because both stemmed, in some sense, from the anthropological "method" that Rivers outlined in *Notes and Queries*. The 1912 revision represents such a watershed in the history of anthropology because it offers the first sustained definition of an entirely new kind of investigation, distinguished from the casual collecting and armchair philosophizing of the past. Such a method requires not just a grasp of the language of the people under investigation— which is, of course, the very first practical necessity that Rivers mentions —but also the ability to recognize the "differences of category" that so often render what Rivers nicely calls "European Questions and Native Answers" incommensurable with one another.[73] As Rivers says, it is very often the case that "there are many native terms which have no English equivalent," so premature translation will lead not just to linguistic inaccuracy but also to complete anthropological misunderstanding.[74] *Notes and Queries* thus counsels its readers against attempting one-to-one translations into European terms, and this is much more than a practical precaution. It amounts to a new definition of the meaning of social practices, which are no longer to be referred to some independent standard for interpretation and evaluation but are instead to be understood in relation to the peculiar social matrix in which they exist. An individual rite, according to R. R. Marett in his chapter on religion, is to be "taken in its concrete entirety," amid "the whole complex of conditions" in which it is performed and experienced. Only by attending to all such conditions is it possible for the observer "to become a faithful interpreter of that inward meaning which the rite has for the savage mind."[75]

It is tempting, therefore, to see *Notes and Queries* as the ancestor of Wittgenstein's anthropological method, perhaps even to diagram the arc of his career as a curve away from Russell's Cambridge, with its massively reified notion of language, and toward Rivers' Cambridge, with its consciousness of the multiplicity of incommensurable language games. Cambridge anthropology could hardly have *caused* the celebrated shift in Wittgenstein's thinking, but it may have provided a useful model when that shift occurred. Of course, Rivers, no less than Russell, believed in the ultimate goal of successful translation: *Notes and Queries* emphasized consistency of method precisely to bring order to the otherwise bewildering variety of linguistic practices to be found in the field. In practice, however, in the first works of the original practitioners of the Cambridge method, it often turns out that misunderstanding and mistranslation are not merely disruptive but actually constitutive of anthropological understanding. It is because this is so that there is such a suggestive affinity between their works and those of Wittgenstein.

Works of the Annus Mirabilis

Argonauts of the Western Pacific and *The Andaman Islanders* are important in the history of anthropology because they applied and thus helped to popularize the methods of the 1912 *Notes and Queries*. In doing so, they helped to establish a new basis for the authority of the anthropologist.[76] Because the meaning of social customs is to be found only as they are related to one another in a "whole system of institutions, customs and beliefs," the anthropologist needs to immerse himself in the culture, to build up over an extended period of time a "general impression" that will guide him in the interpretation of any particular. As Radcliffe-Brown puts it, in an uncharacteristically defensive passage in *The Andaman Islanders*: "Living, as he must, in daily contact with the people he is studying, the field ethnologist comes gradually to 'understand' them, if we may use the term. He acquires a series of multitudinous impressions, each slight and often vague, that guide him in his dealings with them. . . . This general impression it is impossible to analyse, and so to record and convey to others. Yet it may be of the greatest service when it comes to interpreting the beliefs and practices of a primitive society."[77]

Just how extensive this "understanding" must sometimes be is illustrated by Radcliffe-Brown's discussion of the word *hot*, whose significance in Andaman culture is so multivalent its full elucidation requires over forty pages. These forty pages constitute his most crushing rejoinder to the previous work of E. H. Man, a colonial official who had in fact spent far more time in the Andamans and made a more extensive study of the language there than had Radcliffe-Brown. But Man had assumed "that when an Andaman Islander says 'hot' he means by the word only what we mean, whereas he really means a great deal more."[78] And when Radcliffe-Brown is done showing what that "more" involves, he has also shown how difficult it is to avoid the mistake of Mr. Man, which is "to interpret the beliefs of a native people not by a reference to *their* mental life but by reference to his own."[79]

On the surface, then, Radcliffe-Brown shows in practice the truth of one of the basic dogmas of *Notes and Queries*: "There are many native terms which have no English equivalent." And he is also demonstrating the massively difficult anthropological practice of translating such terms by recreating around them, like a Potemkin village, a simulacrum of their original context. Yet the relationship between the mental life of the "native people" as thus recreated and that of the European observer is a good deal more complex than Radcliffe-Brown's simple dichotomy suggests.

At first glance, there seems to be an agreement between the point of view of the field anthropologist and that of the Andaman Islanders so complete as to be a little suspicious. Just as field anthropology finds meaning in the contextual relationships of social practices and derives its authority from the observance of them, Andaman society finds meaning in social cohesion itself and bases its religion on propitiation of "that power on the interaction of the different manifestations of which the well-being of the society depends."[80] The twist in this net of relative clauses exposes the fact that the "power" so revered is not an entity at all but rather a relation, that it is, in fact, interaction itself. This is so much the case that evil in the Andamans is, by definition, an absence of or a removal from social context: "Every condition in which the individual is withdrawn from full participation in active social life is regarded as dangerous for him."[81] Taking the word "hot" out of context is, in one respect, a methodological error and in another a wicked and dangerous act.

Yet there is also a very great difference between the point of view of the anthropologist and that of his subjects, because they cannot possibly know, as he does, that context is their god. In part, this is due simply to a difference in mental equipment. The Andaman Islanders themselves are "quite incapable of expressing these beliefs in words" and, in fact, "not . . . capable of thinking about [their] own sentiments."[82] But it is also fairly obvious that if, by some miracle, an Andaman were able to raise these beliefs to the level of consciousness, that act would in itself destroy them and him, driving a fissure through the unapparent social cohesion previously all around. The more the anthropologist raises these beliefs to the level of consciousness, then, the less like his subjects he becomes and the more distant he is from their point of view. The Andamans themselves are, it turns out, pretty bad anthropologists, since they show conspicuous disdain for the sort of cohesion that Radcliffe-Brown feels is so important. In fact, they pursue the very form of anthropology that *The Andaman Islanders* is meant to dethrone forever, the simple collection of uncoordinated facts. Like the anthropologist who studies "one isolated custom" after another, the Andamans "regard each little story as independent, and do not consciously compare one with another."[83] This is just as well, of course, because to be a methodologically self-conscious anthropologist in a society in which withdrawal "from full participation in active social life is regarded as dangerous" is to be in a very parlous state indeed.

The idea that the anthropologist works by sloughing off his own point of view and acquiring that of his subjects needs, therefore, to be severely qualified. In fact, it might be more accurate to say that the subject doesn't even have a point of view until the anthropologist *mis*understands it: "Being impelled to certain actions by mental dispositions of whose origin and real nature he is unaware, he seeks to formulate reasons for his conduct, or even if he does not so when left to himself he is compelled to when the enquiring ethnologist attacks him with questions."[84] Left to themselves, the Andamans would hardly bother to formulate the kinds of questions the anthropologist asks, so that in an odd reversal of what seemed the original mirror imagery between his methodology and their beliefs, his incomprehension, his difference, turns out to be a constitutive fact of Andaman culture.

This paradox in the position of the anthropologist, and of anthropology, is even more acutely obvious in the works of Malinowski, in part because he dramatized the anthropologist's role so much more vividly than did Radcliffe-Brown. Like his colleague, Malinowski begins by insisting on the importance of contextual interrelationships in the interpretation of cultures: "One of the first conditions of acceptable Ethnographic work certainly is that it should deal with the totality of all social, cultural and psychological aspects of the community, for they are so interwoven that not one can be understood without taking into consideration all the others."[85] The Kula ring, the circular trade in certain shell necklaces that Malinowski felt was the very heart of Trobriand society, became, not just in Malinowski's work but in functionalist anthropology in general, the classic expression of this interdependence. For the Kula objects have absolutely no value in themselves, not sacred, financial, aesthetic, or practical. "Yet this simple action—this passing from hand to hand of two meaningless and quite useless objects—has somehow succeeded in becoming the foundation of a big inter-tribal institution, in being associated with ever so many other activities" (*AWP*, p. 86).

Malinowski works his most bewitching ethnographer's magic not on a word, as did Radcliffe-Brown, but on these objects, which appear to European eyes as "a few dirty, greasy, and insignificant looking native trinkets, each of them a string of flat, partly discoloured, partly raspberry-pink or brick-red discs, threaded one behind the other into a long, cylindrical roll." "In the eyes of the natives, however," these unprepossessing objects receive an impress of meaning "from the social forces of tradition and custom, which give the imprint of value to these objects, and surround them with a halo of romance" (*AWP*, p. 351). In fact, Malinowski is so concerned to combat what he feels are fallacious views about "Primitive Economic Man" that he insists these and other objects in the Trobriands become valuable precisely because they are of no use, "too good, too big, too frail, or too overcharged with ornament to be used, yet just because of that, highly valued" (*AWP*, p. 173). For Malinowski, social good inheres so entirely in social relations that the actual concrete existence of the objects embodying it is almost an embarrassment, as if it would have been better had the Trobrianders somehow managed to carry on trade without actually exchanging anything at all.

Malinowski also goes beyond Radcliffe-Brown in making explicit the role of language in this theory of culture.[86] In the opening pages of *Argonauts of the Western Pacific* he dramatizes one of the basic tenets of *Notes and Queries* by recounting how he gradually began to work more and more in the Kiriwinian language as he became familiar with it and how this made possible a much deeper understanding of the culture he was studying (*AWP*, pp. 23–24). Learning the language and learning the culture obviously go together, for words, like the Kula objects, have their meaning only in the context of "various associated ideas and customs" (*AWP*, p. 435). In fact, he begins to speak of having "words to exchange" as if they were objects very much like those intrinsically unremarkable beads that make the Kula ring what it is simply by remaining in circulation.[87] The meaning of words, like that of the beads, is not to be found outside the cycle of circulation, nor is their purpose to be found in anything but the maintenance of that cycle. Language, he says in the supplement to *The Meaning of Meaning*, does not, for the most part, serve the rather specialized functions of conveying ideas or communicating thought. Its more prominent role in most societies is simply to maintain society, since "it is the one indispensable instrument for creating the ties of the moment without which unified social action is impossible."[88] Thus he disputes the idea that words need have any important relationship either with things or with the structures of logic. Language, he says in several slightly different ways in different parts of his supplement, is "a mode of action and not an instrument of reflection," and its meaning is therefore to be found in the uses to which it is put in specific social situations.[89]

In other words, Malinowski offers a fairly well-developed definition of meaning as use, for many the keynote of *Philosophical Investigations*, at a time when Wittgenstein is just publishing the *Tractatus*, with its very different picture theory of language.[90] And the anthropological method that gives rise to this definition of language very strongly resembles the one Wittgenstein was to pursue in the later decades of his life. Yet Wittgenstein's later philosophy also illuminates something hidden and apparently unconscious in *Argonauts of the Western Pacific*, for it pushes to its limit a paradoxical interdependence of understanding and misunderstanding of which Malinowski seems only fitfully aware.

For Malinowski, as for Radcliffe-Brown, as for the authors of *Notes and Queries*, the great difficulty is to disentangle the "innermost native mind" (*AWP*, p. 107) from the anthropologist's own European preconceptions. Learning the language is the key to the accomplishment of this difficult feat, for only by learning the language can the anthropologist "grasp the native's point of view, his relation to life, to realise *his* vision of *his* world" (*AWP*, p. 25). Much of the polemical force of *Argonauts* comes from the claim that its author can accomplish this difficult translation, and much of its impact as a literary work derives from the techniques Malinowski used to put his readers where he had himself ostensibly lived: in the heart and mind of Trobriand society.[91] In fact, Malinowski congratulates himself on enjoying the sort of "Slavonic nature [that] is more plastic and more naturally savage than that of Western Europeans" and thus more capable of "joining in" as the anthropologist must, if he is to get adequate results (*AWP*, p. 21).

Yet Malinowski also emphasizes the importance of getting to work early in one's acquaintance with another society, before understanding has had a chance to set in. First impressions are vitally important because "certain subtle peculiarities, which make an impression as long as they are novel, cease to be noticed as soon as they become familiar" (*AWP*, p. 21). Thus it may be necessary, once the anthropologist really begins to participate in earnest, to forget what he knows, "forgetting for a moment that he knows and understands the structure of this ceremony," so as to be able to take it for granted, as its other participants do (*AWP*, p. 21). Here, Malinowski confronts the same contradiction that appeared in *The Andaman Islanders*, for, like Radcliffe-Brown, he believes that the people themselves do not and cannot comprehend their culture as the anthropologist does: they are "in it, and cannot see the whole from the outside" (*AWP*, p. 83). This is the essential dichotomy of the participant-observer, who must "join in" so as to share the point of view of the society under investigation and yet also remain outside so as to grasp it in a way that a participant never can.

It did not take long for the contradictions in this project to appear.[92] In fact, Malinowski might have read before the year was out a vulgarized version of his program and its contradictions in a popular novel, Charles Beadle's *Witch-Doctors*. Beadle's anthropologist, an American named Birnier, who is on a trip to Central Africa sponsored by the American Museum of Natural History, does such a good job of entering into the point of view of his subjects that he becomes their new King-God. He willingly endures the painful and humiliating ritual that initiates the new deity, "lured by the expectation of the secrets he was about to learn," but he is continually frustrated by the inability of these subjects to articulate their beliefs, which appear more disorderly and ad hoc the deeper he penetrates their mysteries. Tempted in this way, he is drawn deeper and deeper into this African society, finally to be carried about in a litter of state, "endeavouring to endure a perpetual bath of sweat in the sacred cause, peeking professorial eyes through the interstices, scribbling in a notebook."[93] Having become the very center of the society he has come to study, the anthropologist peeks out to observe his own worship, to look at himself, as it were, through the eyes of his subjects. But the person of the King-God is so sacred it must be isolated from all profane contact, so that having achieved the most complete penetration of and identification with this society possible, the anthropologist can learn nothing about it at all.

With his notebook at the ready even as he is elevated to godhead, Birnier represents a complete, if very early, satire on the celebrated contradiction between the two roles of the participant-observer, between experience and interpretation as sources of ethnographic authority. But Beadle's novel also demonstrates that there was a deep contradiction within the contemporary notion of ethnographic experience itself. For the more completely the anthropologist experiences a society as its members do, the less there actually is to experience. The events of life come to be constituted *as* experiences only through the intervention of the outsider; they appear only against the background of his incomprehension. And this contradiction appears just as vividly in *Argonauts of the Western Pacific*, perhaps because Malinowski tried so hard to give his ethnography the experiential vividness of a novel.

It is easy to see the essential dramatic technique of *Argonauts*, which is to invite the reader to experience a particular event. "Imagine yourself" is Malinowski's favorite opening gambit. Yet it is a little more difficult to notice and thus respect the full peculiarity of the experience that Malinowski invites his readers to imagine. He does not expect these readers to imagine the experiences of the Trobrianders themselves; though this is the program of his anthropology and the goal of his research, it is apparently beyond the scope of the average reader. Instead, he asks the reader to imagine the experiences of the anthropologist: "Imagine yourself suddenly set down surrounded by all your gear, alone on a tropical beach close to a native village, while the launch or dinghy which has brought you sails away out of sight" (*AWP*, p. 4). What is clearly being dramatized here is not the collective sense of Trobriand society but rather the isolation of the anthropologist, seemingly "alone" though he is also "close to a native village."

Of course, Malinowski is romanticizing his own position as a wayfaring explorer and allowing his readers a little exotic escapism along with their anthropology lesson. But this technique, by which a collective European audience is assembled in the shoes of the solitary European anthropologist, does result in some uncomfortable rhetorical moments, some of them uncannily like those in Beadle's novel. "Let us imagine," he says early in *Argonauts*, "that we are sailing along the South coast of New Guinea towards its Eastern end" (*AWP*, p. 33). Here the collective pronoun manages deftly to conflate European reader and Trobriand sailor, while also merging the individual reader with the anthropologist and his subjects. But a little later the same technique works a good deal less well: "Let us listen to some such conversations, and try to steep ourselves in the atmosphere surrounding this handful of natives" (*AWP*, p. 233). Here the invitation to eavesdrop dramatizes not just the distance between the audience and the "natives" but also that between the audience and the anthropologist, who was capable of unobtrusively observing precisely because he was alone.

Malinowski defends this whole practice at one point by claiming that "frequent references to the scenery have not been given only to enliven the narrative, or even to enable the reader to visualise the setting of the native customs. I have attempted to show how the scene of his actions appears actually to the native, to describe his impressions and feelings with regard to it" (*AWP*, p. 298). But this is clearly not the case, as most of these bits of scene setting actually attempt to show how the scene appeared to the anthropologist. Yet the anthropologist is not just a romantic role tossed in for the sake of liveliness: it is a conceptual necessity, for it is only because of the intervening presence of the anthropologist that there is anything to experience at all. Only by his presence are the episodes of Trobriander life rendered *as* experience. In fact, this is the great danger of anthropology: as soon as the anthropologist begins to talk about something, the native informant is impelled to think about it in a way that is utterly foreign, and thus "his outlook would be warped by our own ideas having been poured into it" (*AWP*, p. 396). The injunction to "imagine" does not connect but in fact radically separates European reader and Trobriand subject, since the Trobriander cannot imagine and must be carefully prevented from imagining. And the anthropologist is less the medium joining the two than the impermeable membrane that keeps them apart, taking to himself the European category of experience so that it can enlighten his readers without polluting his subjects.

Beadle is clearly on to something when he makes his anthropologist the sacred center of the culture he has come to study. By synchronizing his account of the Trobriands with the circulation of the Kula ring, Malinowski does in a way make himself and his book into Kula objects themselves. But here another contradiction emerges, for the Kula object, and by extension any social fact, derives its meaning and its value from context and only from context. Out of context it is absolutely nothing. But the account of the anthropologist has value and meaning precisely insofar as it escapes context. In practical terms, Malinowski makes it clear right at the outset that good fieldwork means "cutting oneself off from the company of other white men" (*AWP*, p. 6). Ostensibly, this makes real integration with the subject society more feasible, but Malinowski actually describes isolation as a kind of precaution to defeat the natural propensity of the anthropologist to "hanker after the company of [his] own kind" and abandon those for whom he is not "the natural companion" (*AWP*, p. 7). And this isolation does not diminish with time, but rather it becomes, as Stocking says, "the *sine qua non* of ethnographic knowledge."[94] At the very end of *Argonauts*, Malinowski reinvokes the Kula object as if it were the Golden Fleece of anthropology and then poses himself as the greatest Argonaut: "In the roamings over human history, and over the surface of the earth, it is the possibility of seeing life and the world from various angles, peculiar to each culture, that has always charmed me most, and inspired me with real desire to penetrate other cultures, to understand other types of life" (*AWP*, p. 517). As a kind of Kula object himself, the anthropologist endlessly circulates; but unlike those objects, his value and his meaning is to be found in the way he moves from context to context with a freedom that is the very antithesis of the social embeddedness of the social facts he studies. These are the two dramatic images with which Malinowski ends his book—the endless circulation of the Kula object and the lonely wanderings of the anthropologist—and though they are in utter contradiction, it is also clear that they each serve to constitute the other. Together they constitute the project of anthropology, which was already showing the strains of its contradictions at the very moment of its inauguration in 1922.

The Depopulation of Melanesia
and the Disillusionment of Europe

With his constant injunction to "imagine," Malinowski invites his European readers to perform a Wittgensteinian thought-experiment, to ask themselves the question Wittgenstein was always asking: "What would a society be like, that never played a lot of our ordinary language-games?" But he insists in *Argonauts* that the most important reason for doing so is not merely to give Europeans vicarious experience of faraway exotica, but rather by investigating the foreign to shed light on the familiar: "Perhaps through realising human nature in a shape very distant and foreign to us, we shall have some light shed on our own. In this, and in this case only, we shall be justified in feeling that it has been worth our while to understand these natives, their institutions and their customs, and that we have gathered some profit from the Kula" (*AWP*, p. 25). At the very end of his book, Malinowski returns to the same suggestive metaphor: "Our final goal is to enrich and deepen our own world's vision, to understand and to make it finer, intellectually and artistically" (*AWP*, pp. 517–518). The closed cycle of the Kula ring, in which riches never settle on anyone for long, opens toward Europe, which takes its earnings in self-knowledge.

This is, of course, an utterly conventional justification for the anthropological project, one that Beadle's fictional anthropologist was voicing in almost exactly the same words at the same time: "Yet what had been Birnier's object in undertaking all these pains and penalties but to study mankind in the making, the black microcosm of a white macrocosm; to aid them to a better understanding of themselves and each other?"[95] Yet it rests rather obviously on the assumption that there is at least one very fundamental *difference* between European society and those it studies. "The difference is," as Malinowski rather bluntly puts it, "that, in our society, every institution has its intelligent members, its historians, and its archives and documents, whereas in native society there are none of these" (*AWP*, pp. 11–12). There is no real use for anthropological knowledge in the Trobriands because there is no one to use it; using it and Trobriander society are in fact mutually exclusive of one another. But what could self-conscious, intelligent Europe possibly learn about itself from such a generally benighted society? As it turns out, European society is also generally governed by what Malinowski calls "the inertia of custom." But this governs only the "average member" of that society, the "man-in-the-street," whose behavior is governed by the same sorts of rules, though not, of course, by the same rules, as the "present-day savage" (*AWP*, p. 326). Though anthropology may be able to explain the life of the average European, it cannot hope to enrich it any more than it can enrich the lives of the Trobrianders themselves. What travels to Europe, then, is not merely ethnographic knowledge but also the whole conundrum of the participant-observer, which is played out again as anthropology tries to apply its lessons and its methods at home.

In fact, it seemed as early as 1922 that intellectual commerce between Europe and places like the Trobriands was impoverishing the experience of both. *The Andaman Islanders* and *Argonauts of the Western Pacific* are both heavy with regret, for the societies they are studying as models of social cohesion and unity are in fact well along in a process of decay. Though the whole structure of his book depends on social integration as a value in itself, Radcliffe-Brown observes very early on that in the Andamans "local organisation has largely broken down."[96] The foreword to *Argonauts* begins with this famous lament: "Just now, when the methods and aims of scientific field ethnology have taken shape, when men fully trained for the work have begun to travel into savage countries and study their inhabitants—these die away under our very eyes" (*AWP*, p. xv). The whole project then moves forward under this cloud of irony. Much of Malinowski's account of Trobriand society turns out to be implicitly retrospective, its frequent appeals to "the olden days" amounting, as Harry Payne has shown, to a structure of regret.[97]

Fear of the decline and even disappearance of societies just touched by European knowledge gave early anthropology a good deal of its urgency, not just because the subject matter was about to vanish but also because it was thought that anthropology might halt or slow down the process. This is the rationale behind another signal work of 1922, apparently the last actually seen into print by W. H. R. Rivers, *Essays on the Depopulation of Melanesia*. After allowing for disease and outright brutality, Sir Everard Im Thurm's preface to the collection places the blame for the decline in population squarely on "want of understanding by us of the islanders and failure to grasp the immense difference which lay between their culture and ours."[98] The colonial prohibition of certain integral pastimes, including headhunting, which Im Thurm calls "an interesting sport," and the prescription of kinds of dress and food inappropriate to the tropics has, according to this analysis, led to demoralization and disease. The remedy is the greater understanding that anthropology can offer, so that missionaries, traders, and colonial officials can have accurate knowledge of "the habits, customs, and ideas natural to the Melanesians."[99]

Yet there are also suggestions in these essays that mere exposure to European society has had a profoundly negative effect on Melanesian solidarity. As Dr. Felix Speiser puts it in his contribution, "A native race soon becomes aware of the weakness of its civilisation." Forced "to compare their organisations with those of the superior people," they feel "consequent contempt for their own."[100] Malinowski is not so smug about the superiority of European civilization, but he makes much the same point in *Argonauts*, where he suggests that merely breaching the smooth surface of a way of life is enough to kill off its practitioners: "If you remove a man from his social milieu, you *eo ipso* deprive him of almost all his stimuli to moral steadfastness and economic efficiency and even of interest in life" (*AWP*, p. 157). Here he echoes what was to become the most famous and influential theory offered in *De-*

population: Rivers' notion that the Melanesians were dying because they had simply lost interest in life.[101] While Rivers tends to point to specific prohibitions that have prevented certain activities (such as warfare) that had once given these societies their shape and purpose, Malinowski generalizes, claiming that physical death is the necessary result of the cultural death that occurs when the solidarity of a society is broken from outside: "A general loss of interest in life, of the *joie de vivre*, the cutting of all the bonds of intense interest, which bind members of a human community to existence, will result in their giving up the desire to live altogether, and . . . therefore they will fall an easy prey to any disease, as well as fail to multiply" (*AWP*, p. 466).[102]

The prescription offered by Malinowski and by the contributors to *Depopulation* is the same: greater anthropological knowledge, which will prevent the unnecessary alteration or the wanton prohibition of cultural practices that are necessary to the continued existence of a people. But the very analysis of the disease offered in these works suggests that the Melanesians may already have been dying *of* anthropological knowledge. Both Speiser and Malinowski suggest, at any rate, that mere knowledge of other cultural practices, especially if these are backed by greater practical power, can so qualify faith in one's own society as to destroy it. Since it is in fact the integration of various cultural practices into a whole,[103] and not the intrinsic value of any one in isolation, that gives them their social value, simply qualifying that unity may be enough to bring the entire structure down. And, though this contradiction threatens to undermine the whole rationale for anthropological work abroad, as it is offered in inaugural works like *Argonauts* and *Depopulation*, it has far more dangerous implications for Malinowski's ultimate project of bringing anthropological knowledge to bear on Europe. If the mere knowledge of another culture, the mere opening of the closed cycle of cultural integration, can mean cultural and perhaps even biological death, what good can anthropological knowledge possibly do? If Speiser can comfort himself with the idea that European society is not under threat, since it cannot possibly be impressed by the cultural practices of a "weaker" society, Malinowski, one of the early champions of cultural relativism, cannot. It was, in any case, a common practice of early anthropology to observe that certain cultural rituals such as golf, cricket, football, or fox hunting would look just as silly to a Trobriander as the Kula ring might to a European. Malinowski, using his position as the ultimate globetrotting outsider, suggests that these practices look just as silly to *him*, "a member of the Polish Intelligencia."[104] If *this* is the result of greater anthropological understanding, it is hard to see how it can fail, by the lights of early anthropology itself, to have any less deleterious an effect in Europe than it had already had in Melanesia.

The depopulation of the tropics, and the death of primitive society in the tropics, turns out to be one of the abiding European preoccupations of 1922, spreading well beyond the professional limits of early anthropology even be-

fore Rivers' collection could have been widely read.[105] From Lord Lugard's
The Dual Mandate in British Tropical Africa, which was to become the bible of
British colonial administration, to popular travel accounts like Martin Johnson's *Cannibal-Land,* the idea that tropical peoples were dying out through
sheer lack of interest in life was spread and repeated.[106] One of the more va-
pidly uninformed of these travel books, W. F. Adler's *The Isle of Vanishing Men,*
took its title from the syndrome and gives an account that differs very little,
in substance at any rate, from that offered by Rivers: "The poor devils within
reach of the punishing whites have nothing for which to live. They are a race
without ambition, lacking zest of life, and seek excitement in excesses that take
toll of hundreds when the roasting-pot claimed but a comparative few."[107] So
prominent was this belief, in fact, that it had already been satirized before *Depopulation in Melanesia* appeared. George S. Chappell's ponderous send-up *The
Cruise of the Kawa* assembles and mocks all the clichés of tropical exploration,
not excepting even epidemic, which in this case turns out to be an epidemic of
prickly heat: "Disease! You know . . . how the other islands . . . Marquesas . . .
Solomons . . . Tongas . . . dying, all dying."[108]

Only one of these echoes of Rivers has been remembered, however, and it
is perhaps the most revealing of them all. In the December 1922 issue of the
Dial, at a time when he had just published a new poem to instant acclaim and
had just begun a new literary journal with comfortable backing, T. S. Eliot
published a most lugubrious essay on the death of Marie Lloyd. For Eliot the
death of this music hall singer signified the death of an entire popular culture,
a death that threatened England with the fate that Rivers foresaw for the
Melanesians: "They are dying from pure boredom."[109] Eliot's association of
cultural health with a unified popular culture is hardly idiosyncratic: it is the
centerpiece of so lurid a novel as Beadle's *Witch-Doctors,* which even uses the
term "dissociation" to describe what happens when cultures cease to be comfortably unified.[110] What is different, amid all this hand wringing about demoralization and depopulation in the tropics, is the openness with which Eliot
applies the lesson to Europe.

Henrika Kuklick has claimed that the fully integrated society that British
social anthropology took as its norm was in fact a kind of wish fulfillment, a
projection onto the tropics of an idealized rural society increasingly impossible to find in the urban Great Britain of the early twentieth century.[111] It was
Europe that had lost its "joy of life," as Bertrand Russell insisted in *The Problem of China,* his contribution to the anthropology of 1922. And though Russell's China, where "the average Chinaman, even if he is miserably poor, is
happier than the average Englishman," is an especially exaggerated example,
it is nonetheless typical of the way in which foreign societies served, often
quite overtly, as negative images of Europe.[112]

Yet the very closeness of Russell's terminology to that used in and around
Rivers' collection demonstrates another possibility: that it is not, as in Eliot's
essay, Melanesian disenchantment and depopulation that evoke European

analogues, but just the opposite. Certainly, disease, forced labor, and other European importations had decreased the population in several parts of the tropics, but there is still controversy as to whether there was any decline in the birthrate in any of these areas, and even more about whether such a decline, if it existed, could be ascribed to "loss of interest in life."[113] There was, however, significant depopulation in Western Europe, well beyond that to be ascribed to the casualties of the war. In fact, one of the other widespread items of belief current in 1922 was that "the dominant white races, dwindling in number, or outswarmed by others, will occupy but a tiny fragment of a territory crowded with Jews and Chinamen and Indians, and the various races at present deemed 'uncivilised.'"[114] And this was not merely the opinion of racist demagogues; it was shared even by a certain Labour candidate for Parliament, one Bertrand Russell, who worried aloud that England was in such a parlous state that it might leave "to negroes and Papuans the future destinies of mankind."[115]

It seems at least possible, therefore, that widespread interest in the supposed depopulation of the tropics was actually a complex projection of fears about Europe, a redirection of anxiety toward those who were in fact its indirect cause. Certainly, if there were any Melanesians who had in fact been demoralised by contact with the superior and more confident civilization of Europe, a quick trip there could have served as an effective cure. "Loss of interest in life" was not just the leitmotif of Eliot's poem, which begins, of course, with the Sibyl's haggard "I want to die," but of much social commentary of the time. The mere title of C. E. Montague's *Disenchantment* serves as summary of a time when "most people believe so little now in anything or anyone."[116] C. F. G. Masterman's *England After War* pictures much the same situation, "a complete and startling transformation of values."[117] George Greenwood's *England To-Day* summarizes the national mood as one of "uncertainty and discontent."[118] Indeed, Rivers' shift from active anthropology and psychology to politics was motivated in part by the same concerns, suggesting that for him as well the real demoralization was to be found at home and not in Melanesia.[119]

There were, of course, a number of distinct material reasons for this slump in confidence, especially in England. By 1922 England had lost both its commercial and its military supremacy to the United States.[120] More immediately, there was a deep financial slump in 1921–1922, one that reached beyond the usual victims among the laboring classes and hit the middle classes hard. Both Masterman and Greenwood speak of the disruption of the stability and confidence of the middle class as the end of a way of life.[121] That this was perceived as a general psychological crisis as well as an industrial and financial one is signified by the inauguration of the National Institute of Industrial Psychology, established in London in 1922 by none other than Wittgenstein's old teacher and associate, Charles S. Myers. Myers' move from Cambridge to London demonstrates how the anthropological and psychological ideas he shared with Rivers had shifted their sphere of application from the Torres Straits to the battlefields of World War I and then to the workplaces of Great Britain. It also suggests that industrial unrest was such a serious problem by 1922 that businesses were willing to enlist psychologists in their attempts to control it.[122]

Myers told his clients that industrial unrest began, in general, when "the social community of management and workers" was strained or even broken. He found, in other words, exactly the situation to which Rivers was ascribing the decline of the Melanesians. And the similarity may in fact be due to another psychological tendency that Myers noted for his clients: "Disturbed individuals would cope with their problems by projecting their own deficiencies onto others."[123] That is to say, Melanesia may serve merely as a convenient screen on which to project Britain's anxieties about itself. But it may also be the case, on a more fundamental level, that the mere fact that the same analysis can be applied to Melanesia and to Great Britain is itself the source of trouble for both. For if, as Rivers and Myers and Radcliffe-Brown and Malinowski were insisting, a society needed cohesion and solidarity in order to remain healthy, then the very fact that Melanesia and Great Britain opened onto one another was bound to make both sick. The British were suffering, according to Greenwood, from the fact that "their fortunes and their very lives were bound up in the nation's relations with foreign countries."[124] Having helped to knit the globe together, Britain was suffering the consequences, the confrontation with other societies, other standards, other systems of value, a confrontation that John Dewey felt gave this period of time its character: "War, commerce, travel, communication, contact with the thoughts and desires of other classes, new inventions in productive industry, disturb the settled distribution of customs. Congealed habits thaw out, and a flood mixes things once separated. . . . Nations and races face one another, each with its own immutable standards."[125] In other words, the experience that Wittgenstein studied with Myers back in 1912, the experience of confronting a perceptual system drastically different from one's own, the experience that Malinowski wanted to make general in Europe, already was general in Europe, the very conditions that brought men like Wittgenstein and Malinowski to England having spread it beyond their power to affect or control.

Babel and Debabelization

The first discussion of literary modernism in relation to these global shifts appeared only a month or two before *The Waste Land* itself. Under the blunt and yet ultimately ambiguous title of *Babel*, it was issued by Boni and Liveright in September 1922 as one of a series of novels vaguely disguising the life of John Cournos, whose poetry had appeared in *Des Imagistes*, the first imagist anthology. Born in Russia, Cournos traveled back and forth between London and New York, becoming acquainted in the process with most of the avant-garde writers of the time, many of whom appear under false names in his novel. Ezra Pound, Wyndham Lewis, Henri Gaudier-Brzeska, H.D. and Richard Aldington, T. E. Hulme, W. B. Yeats, Gordon Craig, and even H. G. Wells appear to act out some of the seminal moments in the history of literary modernism, including the founding of *The Egoist*, the publication of *Blast*, Hulme's lectures on Bergson, and the meeting of Pound and Gaudier-Brzeska, which Cournos arranged.

What most impresses Gombarov, Cournos' autobiographical stand-in, is the international nature of the group in which he moves:

> Before James and Whistler and Conrad, England and her arts had been, to all intents and purposes, English, or produced by Englishmen, but at the time Gombarov came to London, individuals of alien blood were making serious depredations on the native arts, and, in that sense, England had ceased being insular.[126]

At first, Gombarov marvels that he, a Ukrainian Jew and naturalized American citizen, should meet in London a Franco-Pole like Maczishek (Gaudier-Brzeska), an American like Tobias Bagg (Pound), and an Irishman like Raftery (Yeats), but soon he comes to see this artistic concentration as part of the general industrial concentration of the world into "one machine, one Empire" (*B*, p. 350). His rooming house contains lodgers from Calcutta, Kiev, Llandudno, Dublin, Chicago, Marseilles, and Genoa because London is the "heart and core" (*B*, p. 153) of an energy drawing the world closer and closer to concentration on a single point.[127]

Such a concentration produces, and indeed requires, a universal medium of exchange. According to Cournos' first chapter, the modern world has not one but several such media: science, machinery, international finance, and finally modern art. The art produced in London by the polyglot crew of avant-gardistes that Gombarov meets is just as universal, just as standardized, as machinery and machine-made artifacts. As one of the young painters puts it, "We no longer speak in local dialects. We are trying to create a language which the whole world will understand" (*B*, p. 33). Thus the "Universal Speech of Money" and the "Universal Speech of Inanimate Objects" are joined and echoed by the "Universal Speech of Art." In painting this means a rather extreme kind of primitivism, in music it means jazz, and in literature it means English deprived of most of its syntax. But Cournos does not give speech itself much attention. Amid all these metaphorical languages, language itself is taken more or less for granted.

Nonetheless, Cournos identifies in this drive toward a universal speech one of the main connections between transatlantic modernism and the human sciences as practiced by Wittgenstein and Malinowski. Wittgenstein's desire to find the logic at the heart of language itself was expressed in a more mundane and practical way by Ogden, who went on to become the formulator and chief propagandist for Basic English, one of the more successful of the many failed attempts to provide a workable universal speech for the

twentieth century. Basic English began as a method of teaching English to immigrants like Cournos coming to England and the United States and evolved
into a project for greater international understanding and amity. Thus Basic
English brings down to earth Wittgenstein's project for a method of unmediated communication. In the early thirties Ogden began to call this project "debabelization," a term that Pound was willing to commend.[128]

Indeed, Ogden's project for a universal speech echoes the aesthetic campaign on behalf of "complete clarity and simplicity" that Pound had been
pursuing since his own arrival in London.[129] As Kenner puts it in a discussion
that draws direct parallels between the modernist works of 1922 and Jespersen's *Language* of the same year, "We are not to think of babelized languages but of Language."[130] The final term in this process of debabelization
is for Kenner the syllable *DA*, which appears at the end of *The Waste Land*.
The Sanskrit root appears as the simple, unitary source of all language and
thus perhaps of all wisdom. Placing this irreducible phoneme at the very end
of his poem is perhaps Eliot's way of defining the boundary between what
can and cannot be said: beyond it lies "the peace which passeth understanding" and which cannot be put into words.[131] Thus *The Waste Land* ends as the
Tractatus does. Having delimited for good that which can be clearly expressed
in language, Wittgenstein enjoins silence: "What we cannot speak about we
must pass over in silence" (*T*, 7). That silence is in a sense the ultimate goal of
debabelization.

In *Babel*, however, Cournos ironizes this project almost before it can get off
the ground. The universal speech of the artists is anticipated and overwhelmed
by the universal speech of money and manufactured objects, which bring
along with their clarity a deadening conformity. In fact, what truly energizes
the art world of the time is not universality at all but its polar opposite, not debabelization but babel itself. Back in New York, Gombarov attends a gathering in a salon clearly modeled on that of Mabel Dodge, where "every nationality and race was represented . . . and English was spoken in a variety of
accents and intonations" (*B*, p. 375). The focus of this international gathering is a dadaistic poem that seems to have been adapted from the work of
Mina Loy, and though Gombarov is bewildered and even repelled, he is able
to see the relationship between what seems linguistic chaos and the universal
speech all around it: "One thing struck him as being extraordinary: that at a
time when articles of utility and commerce were being standardised there
should be a growing anarchy, a steady effort towards individualisation, in the
fine and the vulgar arts" (*B*, p. 89). Modern art, like modern entertainment, is
at one and the same time an expression of and a reaction against the increasing concentration and standardization of life epitomized by the American and
British capitals.

In fact, Cournos seems to have chosen the story of Babel as his gathering
metaphor because it expresses this dialectic so economically. The term
"Babel" is, on one level, a synonym for "Babylon," and in this sense is used to

designate the original tower of Genesis 11 and after it every grandiose project of human centralization: "And out of the living womb of the new chosen there came forth men on ships to conquer the earth, to establish their speech and new universal laws, and to proclaim London the new and more glorious Babel; for men have always loved Babel, and their aspiration has ever been towards Babel" (*B*, p. 86).[132] But "Babel" also designates the failure and aftermath of that project, the "babble" that God visits on his proud children and that topples the tower and dissevers them from one another. Babel is thus both the tower and the fall of the tower, the desire for unity, concentration, and universality and also its inevitable defeat and fall into disunity and chaos. In fact, the original linguistic disunity of Genesis 11 seems precisely designed to humble a basic human desire for concentration and uniformity: the tower is built, according to its planners, "lest we be scattered upon the face of the whole earth" (Genesis 11:4), which is precisely what God does to them when he afflicts their language.

Cournos adapts this originary fable to the conditions of 1922: "There is a tower in the soul of man . . . and this tower often becomes a reality, whether it be in the form of a pagoda, a pyramid, a skyscraper, . . . or a play by Shakespeare. That tower topples in the end, surely; always to be rebuilt in a new form. . . . All things and all aspirations seem to come to this toppling point, to perish when our brain has become filled with human knowledge and we have become old men and realised the folly of being gods without eternity" (*B*, pp. 365–366). The tower and its demise are in a sense synonymous; Babylon and babble are simply phases of one another. But in more specific terms, the story of Babel expresses what Gombarov learns in London and New York, that without the imperial project of concentration and universalization the incredible variety of human culture and language could never have appeared. As long as Calcutta, Kiev, Llandudno, Dublin, Chicago, Marseilles, and Genoa live apart, each of their respective cultures and languages can seem universal. But once they are brought together in London, their mutual relativity is apparent. What Gombarov discovers in the great Babylon is, therefore, nothing like the universal speech he imagines at the beginning of his stay, but rather it is "a complex, many-tongued civilisation, . . . a million persons [with] a million different opinions" (*B*, p. 124).

It is in this ironically dual sense that Babel provides an apt metaphor for the linguistic situation that includes the *Tractatus*, *Argonauts of the Western Pacific*, the projects of Ogden and Richards, and the classics of modernist literature. The *Tractatus*, in some ways the ultimate debabelization project, is humbled by the very diversity that brings it into print. It is a monument both to international philosophical cooperation and to the irreducible differences between German and English. Wittgenstein's later emphasis on the philosophical utility of being mistaken seems to make a method out of the experience of Babel, and the writings that follow the *Tractatus* seem determined to reenact that primal drama of misunderstanding over and over, in a perpetual process of *re*babelization designed, like the original act of God, to humble human understanding.

Kenner sees *The Waste Land* and *Ulysses* as works of comparative philology, part of a "Romantic quest for purity" that tracks the strands of etymology back to chthonic roots, and this they certainly are.[133] But the philological project for overcoming Babel is only one phase of these works, which come to depend on misunderstanding as much as Wittgenstein and Malinowski. The first break in the smooth stylistic surface of *The Waste Land* comes with a foreign voice: "Bin gar keine Russin, stamm' aus Litauen, echt deutsch" (*WL*, l.12). This correction presupposes a mistake, one concerning nationality, which the speaker's words actually do very little to clear up. The pathetic way in which this speaker dismantles the very boundaries she tries so hard to erect also imperils the notion of true or correct speech: how can "echt Deutsch" exist in Lithuania, a country only very recently distinguishable from Russia? What is dismantled here is the whole notion of *echtheit* in the world of 1922 and in the poem itself. This is true even of the Sanskrit that ends the poem. Sounds so far from any living European speech may seem the very roots of a common European language, or they may seem simple gibberish or "foreign babble," as Calvin Bedient puts it.[134] Surely the immediate reaction of most English and American readers is one of incomprehension, and Bedient is not the only reader to feel that the author "intends us to get lost in translation." Thus, the poem that began with a linguistic mistake ends with an even larger one, as the simple, unitary *DA* of the thunder is broken up, first into the three Sanskrit commands and then into more or less inaccurate English translations.

Ulysses, as Kenner points out, contains an entire chapter devoted to philology, a chapter in which there is a definite tidal pull back to the chthonic origins of language. But there is also, even in the same chapter, a good deal of emphasis on random linguistic deviation, on mistakes that seem to make the language nonsensical. "Nother dying come home father" seemed such an obvious mistake it was corrected in all editions of the novel until Hans Gabler's corrected text was published. But in Joyce mistakes are functional and revelatory.[135] Here, death, in the form of a careless telegraph operator, makes mother into a faceless other with a mere flick of the wrist. Later, Martha Clifford will close the vast distance between the word and the world with another slip of the pen.

Ulysses is, on one level, an anthology of such mistakes, which begin to build up among themselves a parallel universe, peopled by characters like the nonexistent Mr. McIntosh, who is brought into being by a misunderstood word. Joyce provides the most appropriate name for this process in "Nestor" when he refers to the "mummery" of the numerals and letters dancing across the homework of an uncomprehending schoolboy (*U*, p. 23). "Mummery" is masquerade, deception, but it is also motherhood, as Gogarty suggests in the first chapter when he slides from "Our mighty mother" to "a lovely mummer" (*U*, p. 5). When Stephen's own language begins to disintegrate under the influence of drink in "Oxen of the Sun," he remembers his father's fateful telegram as "Mummer's wire" (*U*, p. 347), a piece of mummery itself that merges telegraph line and navel cord, motherhood and the vagaries of mistyping. But "mummer" is also a quintessential example of babble, the prattling syllables associated with savages and children. Out of this sort of random, nonsensical play with the lips, Joyce suggests, come entire orders of being undreamed of in the actual world.

Most of these mistakes seem merely adventitious, but *Ulysses* opens with one that has a particular historical and political character. When Haines, the British lodger, speaks Irish to the old milkwoman in "Telemachus," she takes it for French. The ironies are fairly obvious: having expunged Irish almost literally from the linguistic map, the English now return to chide their colonial subjects for not speaking an authentic tongue. "He's English, Buck Mulligan said," with exquisite irony, "and he thinks we ought to speak Irish in Ireland" (*U*, p. 12). Thus *Ulysses* begins with much the same gesture as *The Waste Land*, ironizing the idea of "echt deutsch," which has become faintly ludicrous in a time when great empires alter national boundaries almost at will. And yet there is also a rather particular political pathos in the old milkwoman's taking her own language for French, for Irish could only become a political cause through alienation and rediscovery. The Irish only come to notice their own language and to value it as a form of national expression once it is imperiled by English. What the old milkwoman accomplishes when she misperceives her own language as foreign is a bit of Wittgensteinian anthropology, which Joyce seems to suggest was not so much a specialized science as an everyday experience.

Bringing these writers together, as Cournos does, under the sign of Babel, is to suggest that they were part of a great project that had turned itself inside out. The project of universal understanding, universal comprehension, "the dream of reason," as Alexander calls it, gave birth to its opposite, a sense of contextual particularity so strong it would seem to make intersubjective understanding into a kind of miracle. It is altogether appropriate, then, that in his supplement to *The Meaning of Meaning*, Malinowski delivers the obituary of the science that the *TLS* had just commemorated. He establishes his own discipline on the ashes of philology—almost literally, for he sees philology as dealing "only with remnants of dead languages," while ethnography "has to rely on the living reality of spoken language *in fluxu*."[136] What he means by enthroning the ethnographer in the place of the philologist is that language, and by extension human culture itself, can no longer be conceived as growing from a single unified root and that it is no longer practical to imagine translating all human utterance into a single set of original terms. Well before Wittgenstein, Malinowski replaces the greatest reification of all, Language, with language games, language in use, and in so doing puts anthropology at the center of the linguistic sciences.

To establish his new science, Malinowski enunciates one of the twentieth century's most influential beliefs, that understanding is bounded by specific social practices, that knowledge is not eternal and fundamental but situated in a context. And yet the very terms in which that belief is first enunciated expose the fact that such social contexts can only be perceived from outside, from some imagined elsewhere. Language games and the social situations they both support and depend on appear only in the sidelights of misunderstanding, and this helps to explain the intimate connection between the notion of context and that other modern preoccupation, the feeling of social rootlessness and anomie. What appears in the works of 1922 is a relation between these two so close as to go beyond cause and effect, compensation and projection. Just as the anthropologist in his loneliness and the anthropological artifact in its social embeddedness define one another, just as the language game is defined, delimited, only by the one who cannot understand it, the concept of the socially determined can only come into existence when there are enough free-floating individuals to discover it.

As Marjorie Perloff says of Wittgenstein, "Only someone who is not fully at home in the world will talk as much as Wittgenstein does about 'the language-game which is [one's] original home.'"[137] This peculiar cultural astigmatism, this discovery of one's own language games in the very process of stepping outside them, was relatively common in 1922, even among those who hadn't traveled. Other new sciences just making their mark on the public in this year were also making the known and familiar seem foreign, even untranslatable. And the sense of the uncanny thus imported into the heart of everyday life would have all sorts of significance in activities ranging from advertising to politics.

2

The Public Unconscious

At the beginning of *Psychoanalysis and the Unconscious*, the first of two psychological tracts he published in 1921 and 1922, D. H. Lawrence sarcastically declared Freudian psychoanalysis to be "a public danger."[1] Lawrence meant in part that widespread acceptance of Freudian tenets seemed to threaten a certain kind of conventional morality, and in that belief he was hardly alone. At about the same time, Dr. Leon Gorodiche denounced Freudianism as "a pretext for licentious mental intercourse," and several metropolitan dailies in the United States blamed Freud for an increase in suicides, supposedly due to excessive introspection.[2] Certain bizarre scandals, including the one surrounding a so-called "psychic tea" held in New York in April, guaranteed that whatever danger psychoanalysis might pose would quickly be made public.[3] But Lawrence, hardly a proponent of conventional morality himself, was more concerned that apparent license was simply concealing a different kind of conformity: "The mob was on the alert. The Oedipus complex was a household word, the incest motive became a commonplace of tea-table chat. Amateur analysis became the vogue."[4] Psychoanalysis had become, in the words of the *New York Evening World*, "our most popular science,"[5] a development that was, to Lawrence at least, offensively paradoxical. The science that seemed to put so much emphasis on the inner workings of the individual had become the focus of intense public attention, and the unconscious had become, mainly by virtue of its supposed inaccessibility, almost ubiquitous.

Malinowski found the appropriately ironic term for this sort of popularity when he criticized psychoanalysis as "the popular craze of the day."[6] And, indeed, the enthusiasm for things psychological was so extreme, both in the United States and in Great Britain, that it might quite reasonably have seemed a psychological symptom itself. In both countries there seemed to be a generalized anxiety about anxiety, which produced a number of odd how-to books like *Outwitting Our Nerves*, with advice on "How to Free Yourself from the Shackles of Repressed Instincts," and a host of products like Genasprin, which promised to control "Stage-Fright and other forms of nervousness" in addition to preventing colds and headaches.[7] There was also the more positive route promised by Emile Coué, the major apostle of "positive thinking," who made triumphant tours of both the United States and Great Britain in the course of 1922.[8] Coué worked by autosuggestion, but even relatively orthodox Freudians might promise the same sort of results, as James Oppenheim did in a series of newspaper articles ultimately published as *Your Hidden Powers*.[9]

There was, of course, a good deal of more responsible commentary at this time as well. A. A. Brill issued a new edition of his comprehensive guide to psychoanalysis in this year, and Smith Ely Jelliffe published *Psychoanalysis and the Drama*. Both were practicing analysts with a number of patients and friends in literary and artistic circles. Brill had analyzed Max Eastman and Mabel Dodge, and Jelliffe had treated Eastman, Dodge, and Eugene O'Neill.[10] To this number might be added the name of Walter Lippmann, who, though he was not an analyst himself, had Freud's approval for the application he was making of psychoanalysis to public life.[11] Brill, Jelliffe, Lippmann, and his associate Alfred Kuttner, among others, provided authoritative translations of Freudian ideas for a general readership, as well as applications of Freudian analysis to literature, art, and politics.

In England the same role was taken up at this time by Bloomsbury. James Strachey, Lytton Strachey's younger brother, published his English translation of *Group Psychology and the Analysis of the Ego* with the International Psychoanalytical Press in 1922, after having undergone a training analysis with Freud in Vienna. Subsequent translations by James and his wife, Alix, were published by Hogarth Press, though the chief impetus in this came not from Virginia Woolf but from Leonard, who had in fact written "the first nontechnical piece on Freud to appear in England."[12] Virginia Woolf's brother, Adrian Stephen, was also in analysis in 1922, preparatory to becoming, along with his wife, Karin, influential in the British Psycho-Analytical Society.[13] Psychoanalysis filtered into and influenced the writing of other members of the group, positively in the case of Lytton Strachey and negatively in the case of Clive Bell and Roger Fry, both of whom wrote polemical pamphlets at this time against Freudian interpretations of art.[14]

However responsible such discussion may have been, it could hardly escape the implications of the "craze": by 1922 the practice of psychology had itself become a factor in group psychology, and widespread self-consciousness about psychological matters had begun to redound upon itself and upon the science in ways that it could not have foreseen and perhaps could not explain. Like the "anthropological method," psychoanalysis made the familiar look foreign, and it vastly increased everyday self-consciousness about mental presuppositions and dispositions. But psychoanalysis also increased what Anthony Giddens calls "the institutional reflexivity of modernity" whereby sciences that seek to describe and explain social processes also become part of the very social world they study.[15] Once psychoanalysis became a fad, it began to affect, if not entirely produce, the behavior it sought to explain, to such an extent, Joel Pfister has suggested, that it became socially obligatory to develop complexes.[16] At the very least, psychoanalysis produced in the public a generalized self-consciousness about the irrational that simply had not existed in earlier times, and this self-consciousness itself became a widely recognized psychosocial fact.

At a time when Freud himself was turning to social questions, the practice of psychological analysis was beginning to change the way that Western societies imagined their public life. This change is reflected in one of the most influential books of 1922, Walter Lippmann's *Public Opinion*. When *Public Opinion* was first published, the title meant, and was taken to mean, almost the exact opposite of what it had meant to traditional liberals. In the view of traditional liberalism, the free and independent reason that Wittgenstein and Malinowski did so much to dethrone had a collective counterpart in politics: this was called public opinion. Though the individual might be ever so biased, public opinion could be counted on to even that bias out by subjecting it to reasoned scrutiny and reasonable debate.[17] Under the influence of modern psychology, however, Lippmann had come to believe that public opinion is not a check against prejudice but rather the source of it. Like Wittgenstein and Malinowski in their respective spheres, he had come to see human reason as embedded in and conditioned by particular social contexts. His book is all the more significant, however, in that, unlike the *Tractatus* or *Argonauts of the Western Pacific*, it was *not* groundbreaking or original, but rather it enunciated in an influential way ideas that were already widely accepted in 1922. By its very existence, then, *Public Opinion* poses a question crucial to twentieth century politics and political theory: what sort of public sphere is possible when the public is generally convinced of its own irrationality and bias? Once the irrational became the subject of public debate and even political controversy, reason and unreason became mutually implicated in ways that neither political theory nor psychoanalysis could altogether unravel.

Modern literature is implicated in this situation as well, in part because it helped to popularize the unconscious. According to Jelliffe, this was the purpose of great literature, which could provide inestimable benefits by "awaking interest in this deep underlying emotional territory, where our mentality is founded, and in revealing its hidden meanings and the yearning and strivings which arise out of these, for moreover ignorance and lack of control of these is the cause of psychic disturbance."[18] Thus, the celebrated inwardness and self-consciousness of modern literature could become its most public-spirited feature: it was certainly one of the most popular. The fact that "stream of consciousness" has become such a catchword signifies the widespread appeal of the subconscious. This popularity meant, however, that literature was to be enlisted not just in the movement that psychoanalysis had started but also in the fad, that it would take part not just in therapy but also in salesmanship. Public opinion as Lippmann conceived it was especially vulnerable to publicity, which was just beginning at this time to make use of the findings of psychoanalysis and of general public interest in the unconscious. Even the earliest practitioners of the art of publicity realized that they did not have to use psychoanalytic principles surreptitiously in order to use them effectively. In fact, even quite blatant appeals to unconscious motivations could have the perverse effect of flattering the audience, which knew as well as the advertiser that they could not be reached in any other way. Modern literature helped to make, and it also began to reflect, this odd new public sphere criss-crossed with self-conscious complicity, which means that it was also implicated in the political controversies stirred up around the public unconscious in the course of this year.

Public Opinion

Psychoanalysis taught its adherents, among many other things, that perception is not spontaneous and voluntary but conditioned and that bias is therefore not incidental but intrinsic to human consciousness. As Lippmann puts it: "In the great blooming, buzzing confusion of the outer world we pick out what our culture has already defined for us, and we tend to perceive that which we have picked out in the form stereotyped for us by our culture."[19] In *Beyond the Pleasure Principle*, Freud offers an admittedly fanciful biological explanation for this situation: organisms grow a kind of shield to protect themselves from the rain of phenomena; the senses exist not to transmit but merely to sample stimuli, sending on mere selections to the really sensitive layers near the heart of the organism.[20] For Freud, the principle of selection is, in general, neither historically nor culturally determined, but he also acknowledged the power of "deep-rooted internal prejudices, into whose hands our speculation unwittingly plays."[21] *Group Psychology and the Analysis of the Ego*, another work of this time, and one heavily indebted to crowd psychologist Gustave LeBon, reaches a similar conclusion: "We are reminded . . . of how much every individual is ruled by those attitudes of the group mind which exhibit themselves in such forms as racial characteristics, class prejudices, public opinion, etc."[22]

Freud's was only one contribution to the general sense that human perception is inevitably tinged and human action inevitably affected by presuppositions over which the individual has little control. A. A. Brill, Freud's first American translator and for a time the only trained analyst in the United States, used the venerable metaphor of the stereotype, "plates or models, as it were, which are the result of mental impressions produced by the parents during childhood."[23] Charles Platt, a non-Freudian psychologist, used much the same metaphor in his investigation of mental "patterns."[24] There was, as Nathan G. Hale says in his definitive study of the popularity of Freudian ideas in the United States, a general sense that reason matters for rather little in human conduct.[25]

Of course, every age in human history has been impressed, in its own way, with the power of bias and irrationality, but modern democracies still derive much of their legitimacy from the Enlightenment ideal of a public sphere in which individual bias is checked and corrected by public discussion. By the turn of the century, however, psychologists could demonstrate that greater numbers were no protection against bias and error, since large groups of people could be just as subjective in their impressions as a single individual.[26] And some psychologists, following the analysis of Le Bon, were suggesting that people in the mass were, if anything, to be trusted less than if they were alone. Gradually, the special case of the mob or the crowd became generalized, so that even an individual minding his or her own business at home might be considered a mere component of the group mind.[27] If, as Freud suggests, "public opinion" is itself a chief source of the irrational, if it is not opposed to but rather synonymous with prejudice and stereotype, then there seems to be very little possibility of neutral or unbiased thought. How could unreasonable ideas or impulses even be perceived as such if perception itself is determined by patterns or stereotypes?

In England, the problem of shell shock had given psychological questions of this kind a great deal of their popular urgency. Rivers, who spent the war investigating and treating shell shock, tended to explain it as the persistence of certain instincts in times and places where they had become not just inappropriate but almost suicidal.[28] The same syndrome, Rivers believed, might appear more generally, even in times of peace. Social behavior, he believed, "is determined much less by reason and much more by deeply seated systems of preferences and prejudices for the explanation of which we have to go far back in the history of the mind."[29] The power of these prejudices over the individual mind means that "human behaviour is much less influenced by ideas than was formerly supposed, but responds rather to appeals made in the symbolic manner by which the subconscious or unconscious levels of the mind seem to be so greatly influenced."[30] The relevance of this kind of thinking to politics was so obvious it made Rivers a candidate for Parliament in 1922. In fact, Rivers had been influenced in this direction not just by his own work in psychology and anthropology but also by the political ideas of Graham Wallas, whose books *Human Nature in Politics* and *The Great Society* also had a strong

impact on Lippmann and the *New Republic*.[31] According to Wallas, people
make their judgments "not by a judicious weighing of facts and their probable consequences, but . . . through instinct, prejudice and habit."[32]

There is a momentous shift here in liberal thought, brought about in part
by Freudian psychoanalysis and other movements in modern psychology, in
part by professional anthropology, and in part by a long-term shift in liberalism itself away from strict individualism and laissez-faire economics.[33] No
longer is the public sphere conceived as a neutral ground wherein individual impulses and emotions might be checked and harmonized. The public
sphere is now a web of partially articulated presuppositions, received ideas,
beliefs, and prejudices from which there is essentially no appeal, because
there is no space outside from which they might be perceived. Once a court
in which prejudice and bias might be tried and exposed, the public sphere is
now itself the very source of prejudice and bias. The private self is already
thoroughly public, but in a negative sense now that the public has lost its aura
of impartiality.[34]

This shift put a number of distinctive twists into the public discourse of
the time, all of which can be observed in three nearly simultaneous but very
different works with the phrase "public opinion" in their titles. The most conservative of these, in nearly every way, is A. Lawrence Lowell's *Public Opinion
in War and Peace*. Lowell, a political scientist who was also president of Harvard
at this time, first presented his book as the Godwin Lectures at Rice University in April of 1922. Throughout, Lowell keeps his distance from newfan-
gled notions such as those made popular by Wallas: "In reading some recent
discussions one would almost gather that human beings hold no opinions
and perform no acts by means of reasoning faculties."[35] To others weary of
this fashion, Lowell's book would have come as quite a relief, for he proceeds to limit his discussion to those matters of opinion "where there is a
conscious choice between possible conclusions evident to the mind of the
person who makes it."[36] Not surprisingly, then, he comes to a conception of
public opinion and of the public sphere utterly faithful to the Enlightenment
ideal wherein, as Habermas puts it, the word "public" purifies the word "opinion" of any taint of the subjective: "The hope of democracy lies in reconcil-
ing conflicting interests by independent opinion strong enough to compel
mutual concessions for the mutual benefit."[37]

For anyone inspired by the classical purity of this vision, it comes as quite
a disappointment to realize that Lowell, who was vice president of the Immigration Restriction League, was taking steps at the very moment he delivered
these lectures to restrict Jewish admission to Harvard and to prohibit the
transfer of Jewish students from other universities.[38] If the traditional public
sphere had fallen into disrepute, one reason was certainly the suspicion that
it was not truly public because access to it was restricted.[39] This Lowell
seemed determined to prove anew. And there is a good deal in *Public Opinion
in War and Peace* that seems inconsistent with the Enlightenment ideal on more

explicit and intrinsic grounds. For Lowell does not believe that reason can be brought to bear on *every* issue that arises in a free society: "A community can form a new opinion only on one question, or a very few questions, at a time, and for the rest must assume the acceptance of a common custom, that is a tradition, so deeply ingrained that substantially everyone acts in accord therewith."[40] For the most part, then, society is ruled by tradition, which is to say by authority, to which submission must be unconscious and unquestioning if chaos is to be avoided.[41]

There is obviously a delicate balance, in Lowell's argument and in society as he envisions it, between that which must be submitted to reason and that which cannot be exposed to it. What this inconsistency might reveal, beyond Lowell's own self-interested incoherence, is the fact that the traditional public sphere could no longer justify itself through appeals to reason, which had itself become just another opinion. Or worse, for it seems fairly clear that in Lowell's analysis the ultimate rule of reason is itself one of those central traditions that cannot be called into question. It becomes a prejudice, to be defended primarily by those who harbor other prejudices.

In England it is Hilaire Belloc who mounts this defense: "I know very well what is called 'modern thought' gives to the unconscious part of man a large place and reduces, as much as it can, the field of reason. I cannot agree with it. It seems to me that man is essentially rational; and his political relations can be arranged consonantly with his conscious morals and his conscious logic."[42] This might also seem a refreshing throwback to the ideals of the Enlightenment, were it not taken from what is perhaps the most closely reasoned work of anti-Semitic propaganda in a year rife with it. Belloc is perfectly willing to admit that much anti-Semitism is unreasoning and unreasonable, and yet he is willing to be tolerant in these cases: even "exaggerated or ill-informed affection or repulsion" should be taken into consideration where it concerns the Jews.[43] It seems rather clearer in this case where the fine line between reason and prejudice is to be drawn: reason lives inside prejudice, as it were, since it can exist only within a context of mutual agreement and likeness. Reason, to put it bluntly, is for Gentiles, who keep this free space open for themselves by consciously deploying what they know to be a prejudice.

As he prepared his own book, Lowell had before him another on the same subject with which he had a rather complicated relationship, Lippmann's *Public Opinion*. Lippmann was Jewish, and, it will be seen in more detail below, he had become embroiled in the controversy over Lowell's proposal to restrict admission to Harvard. He was something of a modernist, a sometime fellow traveler of the avant-garde who frequented Mabel Dodge's salon before the war and helped, along with John Reed, Margaret Sanger, Lincoln Steffens, and others, to put on the Paterson Strike Pageant in 1913. He was, moreover, one of the most literate and influential of the Freudian popularizers, in print and in person, having introduced A. A. Brill into the Dodge salon.[44] Freud himself considered Lippmann's *A Preface to Politics* the first practical attempt to apply Freudian principles to political theory.[45]

By the time he published *Public Opinion* in 1922, Lippmann had become thoroughly skeptical about the power of the ordinary individual to think independently about the important issues of the day, or, for that matter, about much of anything. "Few facts in consciousness," he says in a chapter on stereotypes, "seem to be merely given. Most facts in consciousness seem to be partly made."[46] In fact, it is hard to see how consciousness could even exist without the "stereotyped shapes" given to experience by "our moral codes and our social philosophies and our political agitations" (*PO*, p. 84). For Lippmann, political opinion or philosophical conviction are no longer the results of observation and thought but rather impediments to both. The individual observer cannot witness and then conclude because conclusions are already built into perception. As Lippmann uses it, then, the term "public opinion" has come to mean the exact opposite of what it meant when it first came to currency in the Enlightenment. Though there were, as Habermas has shown, differences of emphasis in England, France, and Germany, "public opinion" was in all three countries a disinterested, impersonal force that checked the influence of "imaginary notions and prejudices."[47] For Lippmann, whose usage simply registers a general shift in the meaning of the term, public opinion is not antithetical to but rather synonymous with prejudice.[48]

Part of this general shift is certainly attributable to the influence of psychoanalysis, which made it far more difficult to believe in a freely reflective, rational consciousness. In *Public Opinion*, however, Lippmann sees psychoanalysis as partial and half-blind, ignoring as it does the sociological context that encloses the individual.[49] The sheer size and complexity of that context poses insurmountable problems even for a perfectly adjusted individual: "The world we have to deal with politically is out of reach, out of sight, out of mind. It has to be explored, reported, and imagined" (*PO*, p. 29). Since the individual cannot personally check on any more than a tiny segment of this world, he or she is utterly at the mercy of representations, the accuracy of which can be verified only by reference to other representations. That all knowledge is mediated in this way is bad enough, but to this passive and automatic distortion must be added the active efforts of all sorts of interested parties to shape information as it passes to individuals. Events, he says, "must be given a shape by somebody, and since in the daily routine reporters cannot give a shape to facts, and since there is little disinterested organization of intelligence, the need for some formulation is being met by the interested parties" (*PO*, p. 345). What Lippmann puts in the place of traditional public opinion is something very like a public unconscious, an open arena in which drives and phobias, prejudices and impressions combine, complicate, and magnify one another. In short, the public sphere, originally conceived as the expression of a free and independent reason, is reconstituted on a psychoanalytic model.

For a traditional liberal like Lippmann this is a catastrophic state of affairs.

What makes Lippmann at once so odd and so typical is that his utter lack of belief in the existence of traditional public opinion does not undermine his faith in it as a norm. That an enlightened public does not and cannot exist does not change his conviction that it ought to exist. Therefore, Lippmann proposes to reconstruct a traditional public sphere within the sham public of the contemporary world. This reconstructed public sphere will be inhabited by a being Lippmann calls "the social scientist" or sometimes "the expert" (*PO*, p. 371). Insulated from policy and thus, apparently, from self-interest, the social scientist will construct "a machinery of knowledge," the results of which will percolate through society, slowly qualifying, though never entirely removing, the ill effects of propaganda and prejudice.

That Lippmann's solution now seems so deeply sinister simply indicates how idealistic it once was. He is himself perfectly aware that there is little reason to believe that "social scientists" can manage to be different from all other human beings, and he is painfully embarrassed by the contradictory necessity of basing his last-minute appeal to reason entirely on faith. Since he cannot suggest that social scientists and other experts will disperse prejudice by showing it to be ill-founded, he must rather desperately assert that the public will discover a certain "zest in objective method" once they see it in practice (*PO*, p. 409). But to hope that reason can somehow be made to seem sexy is not at all the same as hoping that people can someday be made rational. It is, in fact, precisely the opposite, since it admits that even reason can only appear within contemporary public opinion as a picture of itself, dolled up to compete with its more attractive opponents.

This last difficulty goes to the heart of *Public Opinion*, which has apparently been making its appeal all along to a public capable of recognizing a prejudice when one is called to its attention. *Public Opinion* is one of those books that could not exist if its thesis were true, since a society entirely ruled by self-interested prejudice could not produce a Walter Lippmann. The real problem for Lippmann and for the potential Lippmannites to whom he writes is not to recognize prejudice, since that has already been accomplished, and not how to defeat prejudice, because that is impossible, but how to act, what to do with the rational powers that one incontestably has if one is capable of reading and understanding *Public Opinion*, once it is generally accepted that all thought is governed by prejudice. At the very end of *Public Opinion*, Lippmann wistfully suggests that it might be possible to foment "a hearty prejudice" against "hatred, intolerance, suspicion, bigotry, secrecy, fear, and lying," but whether this would mark the triumph of reason or its final dissolution among the other prejudices he does not hazard to say (*PO*, p. 417).

A rather ironic answer to these questions is proposed in the third book of this time to use the phrase "public opinion" in its title. In Lippmann's view, the "development of the publicity man" is one of the direst indications of the decay of public opinion (*PO*, p. 345). And yet, Edward Bernays, who may have been the very publicity man Lippmann had in mind, cheerfully appropriates many of Lippmann's ideas and even Lippmann's title for his own book, *Crystallizing Public Opinion*. The irony of their association begins, in fact, with this title, which Bernays chose because Lippmann's book had given the phrase "public opinion" a certain popular currency.[50] Thus the very phrase that once designated the enlightened public sphere becomes a kind of trademark, a sales device in a campaign that seems on the surface to make a travesty of everything Lippmann hopes to accomplish.

For Bernays presents as a solution to the problem of public ignorance and prejudice precisely what Lippmann identifies as the source of the problem itself. What Lippmann disdains as the "publicity man" Bernays transforms into the "public relations counsel," who is his perverse inversion of the neutral social scientist Lippmann envisions at the end of *Public Opinion*. The public relations counsel, as Bernays explains it, mediates between public opinion and private clients, helping to make the public "cumulatively more and more articulate and therefore more important to industrial life as a whole."[51] Bernays thus contends that the public relations counsel helps the public to put pressure on companies and even on government. The other possibility, that the public relations counsel might help powerful interests to manipulate the public, appears only inadvertently, as when Bernays describes a campaign on behalf of the subways, which strove "to create a feeling of submissiveness toward inconveniences which are more or less unavoidable" (*CPO*, p. 43).

What is most consistently remarkable about Bernays' book, however, is the relative artlessness with which he reveals the more sinister side of public relations and the unself-consciousness with which he calls on Lippmann to support conclusions that should have made Lippmann writhe. He takes from Lippmann, for example, the phrase "the art of creating consent" as if "art" in this context were entirely honorific (*CPO*, p. 38). He repeats Lippmann's description of the vastness and complexity of the human environment and then makes the resultant need for mediation seem like a happy necessity for the press agent (*CPO*, p. 55). He cites Lippmann to the effect that stereotypes determine what people believe, but only to make the use and manipulation of stereotypes into one of the chief devices of the public relations counsel (*CPO*, p. 107). Though Bernays knows that he is supposed to present the public relations counsel as a disinterested public servant and a responsible agent of reason and enlightenment, pride in his profession continually betrays him into revealing the truth: "The counsel on public relations not only knows what news value is, but knowing it, he is in a position to *make news happen*. He is a creator of events" (*CPO*, p. 197). That this makes truth into a purely functional category is something that Bernays is quite willing to accept: "The only difference between 'propaganda' and 'education,' really, is in the point of view. The advocacy of what we believe in is education. The advocacy of what we don't believe in is propaganda" (*CPO*, p. 212).

The only question left, once the very notion of truth has been so thoroughly dismissed, is why a book should have been written to publicize this point of view. The very title of that book, *Crystallizing Public Opinion*, with its blithely insidious metaphor, seems to confirm all the arguments against public relations and the modern market economy that it serves. In *The Structural Transformation of the Public Sphere*, Jürgen Habermas takes the title of a later Bernays book, *The Engineering of Consent*, to epitomize the false, manipulative nature of the modern public sphere. But Habermas seems to ignore the fact that Bernays is quite unself-consciously positive about both his titles and about the activity they seem to betray. For Habermas, public relations "must absolutely not be recognizable as the self-presentation of a private interest," and the targets of manipulation must be convinced that they are in fact still using their reason to arrive at legitimate public consensus.[52] But all of Bernays' efforts were meant to make people more aware of the workings of public relations among them and, moreover, to convince them that reason has in fact very little role to play in public affairs. Psychological manipulation according to Bernays' rules is at once more open and more insidious than Habermas assumes, since it requires a widespread popular awareness, critical and yet impotent at the same time, of the extension of the irrational into every corner of human affairs. Bernays did everything in his power to publicize Lippmann's ideas because it was necessary to his project that the public accept its own irrationality as an inescapable given.[53] In fact, it is part of Bernays' project to make the irrational interesting, even glamorous, so that the public might be entranced by the forms of publicity even if it is not convinced by any of its specific messages.[54]

These three works thus sketch out three different yet mutually implicated responses to a basic modern dilemma. Having determined that human perception is not unmediated and that human relations are therefore contingent on all sorts of uncontrollable conditions, students of human behavior are faced with epistemological and moral problems that have never been satisfactorily resolved. As Lippmann fitfully realizes, the thesis of *Public Opinion* puts his own authority as a neutral analyst and public polemicist in jeopardy. By a process that Clifford Geertz has called Mannheim's Paradox, the science of ideology devours itself, since there can be no science if the science of ideology is sound.[55] At the same time, there is no defensible reason to lament this result, since the neutrality of science has been shown to be just another prejudice among the prejudices. In fact, the general acceptance of the power of prejudice makes it difficult to rationally oppose any particular prejudice. Only Bernays accepts and even welcomes this situation, and for this reason he seems the most comfortably modern of the three. In comparison, Lippmann's nostalgia for the liberal public sphere seems as outmoded and reactionary as Lowell's nostalgia for a world of traditional authority.

In fact, as these three men were writing, the intellectual dilemma they shared was being handily resolved in practice. Bernays exemplifies a moment in which irrationality is not just rationalized but institutionalized. Within a few months of the publication of *Crystallizing Public Opinion*, Charles S. Myers,

Wittgenstein's old collaborator, established the Institute of Industrial Psychology in London and Henry S. Link established the ominously named Psychological Corporation in the United States.[56] Both of these organizations were intended to make known to businesses the findings of psychologists, which were supposed to be useful both in pacifying the industrial workforce and in selling the products they made. In 1923 Daniel Starch published *Principles of Advertising*, "one of the first [books] by a psychologist to discuss the significance of psychographic research as an element of marketing."[57] The effect of these changes must have registered even at the most mundane level. Even Jimmy Martin, the brash press-agent hero of *Fresh Every Hour*, a novel published by Boni and Liveright in 1922, believes that he is a kind of "psychotherapist."[58] The unreflective practicality of such projects, which in general sought to do nothing more than observe and manipulate regularities of behavior, protected them from the agonies of Mannheim's Paradox. The scientists who set up shop in institutions like the Psychological Corporation never doubted that they were engaged in a reasonable endeavor whose intellectual validity remained unsullied by the bias and irrationality they studied.[59] Yet the contradictory nature of such activities, and of the popularization and institutionalization of the psychological in general, still haunted the politics of 1922. The fickle insubstantiality of public opinion had become one of those ruling ideas the strength of which Lippmann had warned against in *Public Opinion*, and the resulting knot was too much even for him to untie.

Modernism, Publicity, and the Public Unconscious

Aesthetic modernism, which has come to be defined by its supposed antipathy to the public and to publicity, is supposed to have very little to do with this situation.[60] As Jeffrey Weiss has recently shown, however, modern art was, in its very earliest stages, very closely identified with the new public sphere that caused Lippmann so much dismay. In fact, Weiss maintains that, in France at least, "modernism as an enterprise seems to have been conceived . . . as part of a larger modern cultural phenomenon: advertising."[61] The prewar avant-garde's desire to shock, to surprise, even to bluff was often associated with the growing industry invented to promote newness in products and entertainment. As Weiss puts it:

> When critics came to perceive and discuss avant-gardism as promotionalism, the terms of advertising were close at hand; conversely, the audacity of contemporary advertising must have conditioned spectators to identify the startling character of new painting with the larger cultural phenomenon of unchecked commercial bluff.[62]

This was a common charge where the other arts were concerned as well: the group of composers known as Les Six was accused of being a "'commercial firm,' a publicity stunt."[63] In response, the avant-garde often accepted the association of artistic with commercial promotionalism and purposely exaggerated its own tendency to commercial bluff in order to annoy. This tactic may be traced back to the futurists, whose manifestos sometimes took the form of mock product advertisements, and it was obvious in 1922 in the work of Berlin dada, where the word *Réklame* was often given satiric prominence.[64]

If the examples that Weiss provides are at all representative, however, the prewar hard-sell was positively charming in its restraint and decorum. The billboards he reproduces as examples of "graphic assault" are simple signboards portraying a product label or even just a name, and the paintings, from artists such as Picasso and Delaunay, that take these billboards as models also focus on unadorned typography.[65] The notion that advertising might do something more than simply notify the public of the availability of a product had clearly not occurred either to advertisers or artists. In short, advertising and art had yet to discover psychology.[66] When they did, the relationship between the two would become not just closer but much more complex, as the two disciplines helped to create and were in turn formed by the public unconscious.

Emblematic of this new relationship is *Crystallizing Public Opinion*, originally published by the small firm of Boni and Liveright, which had distinguished itself primarily by publishing adventurous works of modern literature such as *The Waste Land*. Though Bernays' work might seem out of place on the Liveright list, he was in some ways more intimately connected with it than any other author. In fact, one of the first things Horace Liveright did when he took effective control of the new publishing firm of Boni and Liveright was to retain Bernays, who was himself beginning a new phase in his career as public relations counsel.[67] Their association lasted barely a year, from 1919 to 1920, and yet it was particularly significant for each man and, as it turned out, for modern culture in general. Liveright went on to become "the principal publisher of modernism," responsible for early important works by Eliot, Hemingway, Faulkner, Toomer, Cummings, Pound, Barnes, and many others.[68] At an extraordinary dinner held in Paris in the first days of 1922, he was offered a virtual monopoly on this new growth stock by Ezra Pound, who hoped to form a kind of consortium with his friends James Joyce and T. S. Eliot, with Liveright as their joint publisher.[69] Though this plan did not work out quite as Pound had hoped, Liveright did become more closely associated with literary modernism than any other American publisher of the time.

Bernays, for his part, came to be almost synonymous with the practice he was apparently the first to call "public relations." Before meeting Liveright, Bernays had represented a wide variety of clients in a number of different ways. For clients that ranged from Caruso and the Russian ballet to the nascent states of Czechoslovakia and Lithuania, Bernays provided comprehensive publicity campaigns. He transformed Flores Revalles, an attractive but indistinct member of Diaghilev's company, into an international star by drap-

ing her lavishly and suggestively in the coils of a huge snake, and he advised
Jan Masaryk to declare his country's independence on a Sunday to take advantage of a slack news day.[70] Stunts like this had, of course, been pulled for
decades, if not for centuries, but Bernays has been widely credited, first by
himself, with transforming a loose collection of improvisational techniques
into a coherent, consistent practice with a name, "public relations," which it
acquired just as Liveright was meeting with his trio of modernists.[71]

The two events are not so unrelated as they may seem. Bernays was always
to date the transformation of his profession from mere press agentry into the
science of public relations from his association with Liveright, which continued for a number of years after their formal contract had expired. Though
Bernays was to maintain that the difference is not simply semantic, it seems
clear from all his accounts that press agentry becomes public relations primarily by having better public relations.[72] When the press agent ceases to be
a devious provocateur whose machinations are frustrated whenever they are
exposed and becomes an acknowledged and even respected part of every
business enterprise, then public relations is born. Bernays effected this change
by mounting a public relations campaign on behalf of public relations, a key
element of which was *Crystallizing Public Opinion*. In their plans for this book,
which they developed together in the course of 1922, Bernays and Liveright
exchanged roles: Bernays became an author and added the prestige of au-
thorship to the recipe that makes public relations out of press agentry; and
Liveright became a public relations counsel, conducting a market research
campaign to see if there was a demand for such a book.[73]

This association, so close as to become emulation, existed because each
man derived distinct benefits from it. Bernays became an author and added
his name to a list that included not just aesthetic innovators like Eliot and
Pound but also well-known crusaders like Dreiser and Mencken. And Liveright acquired a new and powerful means of selling books. As Bernays put it
in his autobiography: "We discussed applying the new publicity direction to
book publishing, a hitherto untried approach. Book publishing was dominated by stuffy old firms who treated the business as if it were the practice of
a sacred rite. . . . Books were handled in the same way they had been published—for a select audience and not for a larger public. Book publishing was
static in the content of its books and in its promotion when it should have
been, of course, vibrant with ideas. But Liveright was to change all that."[74]
Liveright effected this change by giving Bernays free reign to apply his techniques in a new and untried arena: "I was eager to try out our strategies and
tactics on books. Books should respond more quickly to our techniques than
almost any other commodity. . . . Liveright and I agreed that a number of
books should receive the dynamic treatment the entrepreneurs give a new
drama, opera or sporting event."[75] As Tom Dardis puts it in his biography of
Liveright, he and Bernays revolutionized the publishing trade by assuming
that "books might be marketed *in the same way as any other product*: by aggressive

promotion in the press and a thorough backup operation of constant advertising."[76] Among the books singled out for such treatment were Waldo Frank's
Our America, Pound's *Instigations*, and John Reed's *The Sweep of the Russian Revolution*. But the influence of Bernays on Liveright's business practices was permanent; he was always known for the flamboyance of his sales copy and the
dash with which he seized promotional opportunities.[77]

If this association seems incongruous, and its results even a bit unseemly,
it is perhaps because it is hard for us to associate the movement represented
by Joyce, Eliot, and Pound with the seemingly very different developments
represented by Bernays. The notion that books might be marketed like "any
other commodity" seems starkly incompatible with the widely accepted notion that "Modernism is among other things a strategy whereby the work of
art resists commodification, holds out by the skin of its teeth against those social forces which would degrade it to an exchangeable object."[78] That modernism not only resists but defines itself against an encroaching "consumerism" has been an article of belief almost from the very beginning, featuring
as largely in the early defenses of Leavis and Richards as it now does in the
critiques of Andreas Huyssen and Terry Eagleton.[79] Of course, publishers
have always wanted to sell books, and the fact that a modernist publisher is
no different should not perhaps come as much of a surprise. And it cannot
be said that Liveright's practices were universally admired within the modernist consortium that Pound hoped to establish. John Quinn, the New York
lawyer who functioned as a kind of American representative for the group,
was disgusted by Liveright's flair for publicity, which fit quite neatly into an
anti-Semitic stereotype he shared with Eliot.[80] But Pound, for one at least, was
originally drawn to Liveright precisely because of his marketing flair, a trait
that Pound shared. As Lawrence Rainey has shown, Pound had a keen sense
of literary modernism's "interaction with market conditions," and Liveright's
letters to him crowing about the publicity *The Waste Land* was receiving were
clearly written to a kindred spirit.[81]

In the end, the fact that some of Liveright's writers shared his taste for
publicity and others despised it does not seem so significant as the social fact
that literary modernism and modern public relations emerge before the public at precisely the same time and in close association with one another. Bernays and Liveright recapitulate, in a much more self-conscious and systematic
way, the association Weiss describes between push, promotion, novelty, and
aesthetic innovation.[82] To this mixture they bring a new element, one that was
to play a central role both in public relations and in literary modernism. For
Liveright was also one of Freud's American publishers, and the *General Introduction to Psychoanalysis* was one of his more popular titles, selling 20,000 copies
in the course of the twenties. The book had been brought to him by Bernays,
who was Freud's nephew and one of several representatives in the English-
speaking world attempting to gain a wider audience for his theories.[83] With
Liveright, Bernays attempted to mount a number of other efforts on Freud's

behalf, including a lecture tour of the United States. Freud himself sensed that his nephew represented certain possibilities for popularizing psycho-analysis, possibilities he attempted to realize by suggesting a series of short ar-ticles to be called "Scraps of Popular Psychoanalysis."[84] Freud never wrote these articles, though he did produce some brief encyclopedia entries on psy-choanalysis at this time, but it might be said that in a way his nephew produced the series for him. Bernays felt a very strong connection between his cam-paign on behalf of public relations and his uncle's struggles to gain accep-tance for psychoanalysis. Part of his public relations campaign on behalf of public relations involved making the public recognize and accept what might be called psychological manipulation. Public relations *used* "the elementary laws of psychology" to achieve its effects, but it was also very largely *about* those laws.[85] Thus one of Bernays' brainstorms on behalf of the Liveright list involved the redaction of a number of short and lively articles from Frank's *Our America* psychoanalyzing different regions of the United States. Bernays was convinced that Frank's book "foreshadowed the lively interest psycho-analysis would arouse in this country," and through it he was able to advance his own cause, Freud's, and Liveright's simultaneously.[86]

This happy conjunction of interests is highly suggestive. For one thing it suggests the extent to which the introspective bent of modernist literature was also a popular preoccupation. Psychological self-consciousness was some-thing that could be marketed to a large popular audience. The techniques by which it could be marketed were themselves dependent on what Bernays called "the elementary laws of psychology," though in two rather different ways. Bernays' brand of public relations certainly attempted to exploit human curiosity, gullibility, and bias as relentlessly and as surreptitiously as the most degraded of press agents. But Bernays also relied on an explicit awareness in his audience of the very laws that were being used to move them. Thus psy-choanalysis and public relations legitimate one another, as Bernays calls upon Freud to help make his audience not simply aware of but actively interested in its own manipulation. As the literature on Liveright's list sharpened the au-dience's attention to psychological matters, it served Bernays' interests and Freud's as well.

What Judith Ryan has called "the simultaneous emergence of modern psy-chology and modernist literature"[87] also necessarily involves a third term, modern publicity. On one hand, certain modern writers helped to create the category of "the psychological," which advertising was then able to offer as a compensation for the increasing impersonality of modern life. Joel Pfister has suggested this in his analysis of Eugene O'Neill, but it might also be applica-ble even to such a relentlessly anticommercial artist as Lawrence.[88] Indeed, Lawrence's complaint that psychoanalysis had become a "public danger" is in part an attempt to wrest what he calls the "true, pristine unconscious" free of the kind of exploitation that Freudian popularization had made possible.[89] On the other hand, however, psychology, literature, and publicity all powerfully dispute the very existence of a "pristine" individual consciousness, which can hardly exist in splendid isolation if all of its perceptions are governed by instincts, presuppositions, and prejudices. And "the psychological" can hardly be offered as an alternative to a debased public sphere if that public sphere is itself modeled on psychological lines. The relationship between psychology, literature, and publicity is such a complex one precisely because the psychological is not distinct from the seemingly impersonal world of politics, commerce, and manufacturing.

Any number of works from Liveright's 1922 list might be instanced to illustrate this relationship. Liveright was, for example, O'Neill's publisher at this time, and it is O'Neill's works more than any others that Joel Pfister has identified as glamorizing the notion of psychological depth for a large middle-class public.[90] Perhaps even *The Waste Land* originally appealed to Liveright for similar reasons, for, as Ronald Bush has shown, the poem appeared to its earliest readers as "nothing more or less than a most distressingly moving account of Eliot's own agonized state of mind during the years which preceded his nervous breakdown."[91] Given the current popularity of psychoanalysis, the new poem might have been a good deal more appealing under this interpretation, as a portrait of psychological extremity, than under the far more intellectual interpretation that would later be offered. Liveright would not have been the only participant in the complex *Waste Land* negotiations to have had a particular interest in this kind of material: Scofield Thayer, co-publisher of *The Dial*, carried on his part of the business from Berlin, where he was undergoing analysis with Freud. This analysis had in fact been arranged by Bernays.[92]

Of course, it can hardly seem surprising to find a concern for psychological depth in any postromantic literature, but it may be a new and peculiar development of the time that such concerns are often mixed with a lively awareness of the psychological powers of publicity. Such an awareness is visible even in a novelist usually considered the most inward of all modern British writers: Virginia Woolf. When Woolf began *Mrs. Dalloway* in November 1922, she was still impressed by what the *Daily Mail* called "the greatest single development in outdoor advertising":[93]

> The sound of an aeroplane bored ominously into the ears of the crowd. There it was coming over the trees, letting out white smoke from behind, which curled and twisted, actually writing something! making letters in the sky![94]

Woolf uses double exclamation points to register the inarticulate astonishment of the crowd, which lacks a name for this amazing activity because it is in fact unprecedented. Derby Day 1922 was the occasion of the first demonstration of skywriting, which the *Daily Mail* was eager to report because the words spelled out in the sky, words that Woolf's characters cannot quite interpret, were in fact "Daily Mail." This was widely recognized as a tremendous public relations coup, even by a competitor like the *Illustrated London News*,

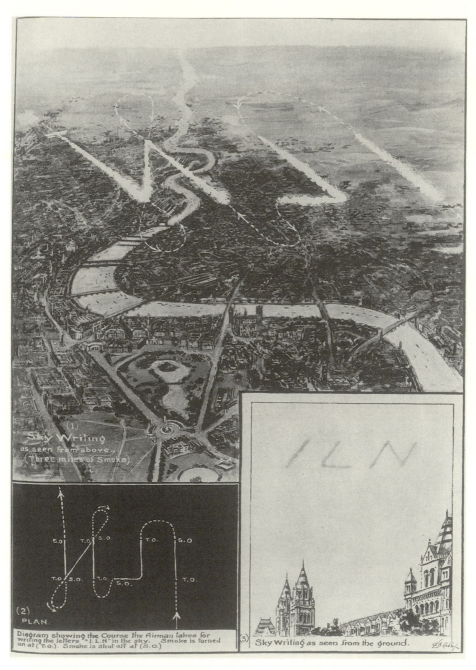

Sky Writing
as seen from above,
(Three miles of Smoke)

(2)
PLAN.

Diagram showing the Course the Airman takes for
writing the letters "I.L.N" in the sky. Smoke is turned
on at (T.O.). Smoke is shut off at (S.O.).

(3) Sky Writing as seen from the ground.

An Aeroplane as "Pen"; the Air as "Paper": The New Advertising. The introduction of sky-writing (*Illustrated London News*, June 10, 1922).

which congratulated "our enterprising contemporary" and then rewrote history with a drawing showing the letters ILN suspended in smoke over the Houses of Parliament.[95] Thus the *News* contends with one of the elementary features of modern public relations, one in which Bernays took inordinate pride, that it effaces the distinction between news and advertisement.

According to the *Daily Mail*, "Sky-writing fulfils a very necessary function in the general sphere of advertising—that of impressing large numbers of people simultaneously with the trademark or slogan to be advertised. In its impression value, sky-writing holds pride of place."[96] This particular advertising claim is, for once, perfectly true, for in a time before broadcasting of any kind existed, there was no other way to reach a large audience simultaneously. And simultaneity is important for a number of reasons, not least because it allows the "reader" to see others in the audience "reading" at the same time and so makes the whole process of reception self-consciously social. The *Daily Mail* claimed that "everyone within an area of a hundred square miles—and there were millions—gazed spellbound at this fascinating sight, and there was a general chorus of 'Daily Mail' as soon as the aeroplane had finished the first word and had just commenced upon the second."[97] Here the desire to excel, to be the first to interpret the mysterious words, meets and merges with the need to conform, to read as everyone else is reading. These responses from the crowd are not mere responses, however; they are, as the *Daily Mail* report makes clear, part of the advertisement itself, the words "Daily Mail" produced first as smoke and then as sound, once by the advertisement and then once more by the crowd of potential consumers.

In her account Woolf lampoons the *Daily Mail*'s pretensions even more mercilessly than had its direct competitors:

> Dropping dead down the aeroplane soared straight up, curved in a loop, raced, sank, rose, and whatever it did, wherever it went, out fluttered behind it a thick ruffled bar of white smoke which curled and wreathed upon the sky in letters. But what letters? A C was it? an E, then an L? Only for a moment did they lie still; then they moved and melted and were rubbed out up in the sky, and the aeroplane shot further away and again, in a fresh space of sky, began writing a K, an E, a Y perhaps? (*D*, p. 20)

Mrs. Coates reads "Glaxo," while Mrs. Bletchley reads "Kreemo," and Mr. Bowley decides "It's toffee," and Clarissa Dalloway looks out her front door and wonders, "What are they looking at?" (*D*, pp. 20–21, 29). Not only does Woolf erase the *Daily Mail* itself from the site of its great triumph, but she also demolishes the unanimity and simultaneity on which skywriting staked its extravagant claims. What we see in Woolf's account is the ineluctable subjectivity and idiosyncrasy of the individual, for whom even the most public language can have a purely personal significance, as these letters have for Septimus Smith, who decides that they are secret signal in a language private to himself.

However, this episode is not brought into the beginning of *Mrs. Dalloway* simply to be dismissed. The public constituted by advertising is finally not so very different from the intersubjective public that is coterminous with the novel itself. Skywriting is in fact but one of a number of devices deployed in the opening pages of the novel to knit together subjectivities. A mysterious car, which may or may not contain the prime minister or the Prince of Wales or the Queen, links together for the first time Mrs. Dalloway, who hears one of its tires burst, and Septimus Smith, who is entirely unknown to her, as she is to him. Later, the stroke of Big Ben will link them again within the "leaden circles" of its ringing. These symbols of the public seem only accidentally to contain the very different subjectivities of Mrs. Dalloway and Septimus Smith, and yet it is the purpose of the novel to show that these are not distinct, since the suicide of Septimus Smith does in some occult way become an episode in the life of Clarissa Dalloway.

As Jennifer Wicke puts it, consciousness in Woolf's writing is "social consciousness, in the sense that absolute privacy of consciousness is unobtainable, and the thoughts, images, and refrains of consciousness take collective forms."[98] The central mystery of the novel, the occult sympathy of Smith and Dalloway, is built up out of the coincidences of public life, the "leaden circles" that enclose many apparently separate minds. Mrs. Dalloway sees this herself from the top of an omnibus:

> But she said, sitting on the bus going up Shaftesbury Avenue, she felt herself everywhere; not 'here, here, here'; and she tapped the back of the seat; but everywhere. She waved her hand, going up Shaftesbury Avenue. She was all that. (*D*, pp. 152–153)

Though Woolf is intensely interested in the interior worlds of her individual characters, those worlds are always connected by various threads to the many others who make up the outer world, so much so that those others become part of the individual self: "So that to know her, or any one, one must seek out the people who completed them; even the places" (*D*, p. 153). Part of the mingled tragedy and exaltation of the end of *Mrs. Dalloway* comes, however, from the fact that people are never actually complete, because the threads of acquaintance and intimacy connect each individual to a wider group that is always changing and expanding, often in unexpected and inexplicable ways. From the very beginning, *Mrs. Dalloway* also suggests what any sentient citizen of the twentieth century knows, that these threads of commonalty are often made up out of public materials, even commercial ones, so that even the most blatant advertising scheme can provide the point of contact for disparate individuals. As Wicke suggests, Woolf's novels are full of "objects of consciousness . . . that are at the same time objects of consumption,"[99] and the very fact that they are objects of consumption enables them to link one consciousness and another.

Psychology studies such "objects of consciousness," but it is also such an object itself, and an object of consumption as well. Smith and Dalloway both see the skywriting, as they both hear the mysterious car and the ringing of Big Ben, and they both see Sir William Bradshaw, whose overbearing advice helps to precipitate Smith's suicide. In fact, it seems entirely possible that Clarissa Dalloway has "seen" Bradshaw in his professional capacity, for she takes an hour's rest after luncheon every day "because a doctor had ordered it once" (*D*, p. 129), just as Bradshaw orders rest for Smith. The coincidental appearance of Bradshaw in both these lives is an accident, even a violation, as Clarissa Dalloway feels it when Bradshaw brings news of Smith's suicide to her party at the end of the novel. But the coincidence also suggests that psychiatry, by making the inner workings of the mind subject to organized study and public discussion, has actually opened one mind to another and helped to make the private more public. The whole notion of the unconscious, Shoshana Felman points out, imports into the self something foreign and unknown, and analysis suggests that it is only by probing that other in an intersubjective process of investigation that the self can even approximately be known.[100] In a way, Septimus Smith is that other, and *Mrs. Dalloway* is about the process of analysis by which Clarissa Dalloway comes to know herself through him.

Woolf was, of course, anything but sympathetic to the kind of psychiatry represented by Sir William Bradshaw. Nor was she notably more positive about Freudian psychoanalysis, with which she had a good deal of incidental and involuntary acquaintance in the years in which she was planning and writing *Mrs. Dalloway*. She was apparently cynically impatient with the analysis that her brother Adrian was undergoing in 1922, and she was more sympathetic toward the attack on Freud mounted by Roger Fry than she was toward the Freudian texts that Hogarth Press began to publish at the same time.[101] In the last years of her life, however, Woolf undertook a concerted reading of Freud's social texts, including *Group Psychology and the Analysis of the Ego*, on which she took detailed reading notes. According to Hermione Lee, Woolf was both upset and impressed by Freud's image of human society ruled by unconscious drives and instincts.[102] The fact that this part of Freud's work had such a profound effect on her was due, no doubt, to the onset of World War II, but there may also have been some belated recognition of the affinity between this work and the one she began in the same year. For Woolf depicts in *Mrs. Dalloway* a public sphere modeled not on the prototype of the rational intelligence but rather on that of the unconscious. But the novel, in which a psychiatrist plays the role of psychological go-between, also seems aware of the way in which this public sphere has been constituted by the science that claims only to describe it. The intense self-consciousness abetted by psychoanalytic knowledge is one of the conditions that links Clarissa Dalloway and Septimus Smith, so that, ironically, what makes them most isolated from the outside world is also what links them to one another. In this they are but a special example of the sort of linkage created every day by psychologically adept practitioners of the advertising art, whose works, both Woolf and Bernays suggest, are not so utterly distinct from those of the great modernists as they may appear.

Intelligence, Immigration, and the Unconscious

As Felman argues, Freud contributes to the general reflexivity of modern life by making what seemed most familiar, the human mind, into something foreign and incomprehensible. Communication with the unconscious is in Freud's view dogged by the same problems of translation and interpretation that afflict communication between different cultures. For Lacan, in fact, the unconscious is the untranslatable, to be surprised out of hiding only by exploiting slips and mistranslations that make the uncanny apparent in the heart of the known and familiar.[103] Some version of this insight was apparent even in the popular psychology of 1922, which extended to everyday domestic life the increased reflexivity that Wittgenstein and Malinowski were to bring to intellectual life through philosophy and anthropology. But psychology was also a political factor in 1922, and the sense it gave of something foreign and untranslatable within the most familiar experience merged in unexpected ways with practical attitudes to the foreign, which took, in the United States at least, a definitively negative turn in this year.[104]

Even as early as 1922, the practice of psychology was influential enough and the habit of psychological self-consciousness pervasive enough to influence public policy and inspire public controversy. Implicit within these controversies were two questions the new public sphere was inherently ill-equipped to answer: of what value is intellectual attainment and distinction if reason has little influence in public affairs, and how can the liberal values of tolerance and fairness be upheld once prejudice is considered to be both universal and inescapable? In short, to what extent and in what ways will the traditional liberal notion of independent reason persist in a public sphere reconstituted on a psychoanalytic model? For obvious reasons, Lippmann was intimately involved in these controversies, which provide a kind of public counterpoint to the arguments of *Public Opinion*, but he did not always take obvious or simple positions on the issues. In fact, Lippmann often turns out to agree, either explicitly or implicitly, with those to whom he seems opposed, and it is these unexpected or implicit agreements, and not the controversies themselves, that tell the most about the actual state of the public unconscious.

At the center of these controversies was the issue of intelligence testing. Robert A. Yerkes, president of the American Psychological Association at the outbreak of the war, had managed to persuade the U.S. Army, much against its better judgment, to administer basic intelligence tests to a certain percentage of its new recruits.[105] The results had been published shortly after the war in a massive volume under the general editorship of Yerkes, and they had begun to excite a good deal of anxious interest, since they seemed to show that the average level of intelligence in the American populace was rather low. The army tests had already become something of a fixture in debates on immigration when Carl Brigham, who had played a small role in the original testing program, published *A Study of American Intelligence*. This book made explicit, in what seemed to be an authoritative scientific context, the implications of the army tests, which showed, according to Brigham, that the low intelligence scores were largely due to the immigration into the United States of inferior stock from southern and eastern Europe: "The results of the psychological tests of foreign born individuals classified according to length of residence, taken as typical of the foreign born population as a whole, indicate definitely that the average intelligence of succeeding waves of immigration has become progressively lower."[106] Brigham's book became the "most influential piece of writing on the social implications" of the army tests, contributing directly to the massive restriction of immigration enacted in 1925.[107]

Brigham was ultimately to recant, and the army tests were restudied and the variations in intelligence they reported were found to correlate, unsurprisingly, with education and fluency in English.[108] But in 1922 there was considerable controversy about the tests and their implications for public policy. There were, in fact, two overlapping controversies, one about intelligence, which gave rise by itself to a large number of books, articles, and speeches, and another about intelligence and immigration, which percolated throughout American society until 1925.[109] Perhaps the most distinguished intervention in these controversies was the series of articles published by Lippmann in the *New Republic* in October and November 1922.

The purpose of the series was, as the editors described it in a general headnote, to "discuss the claim that psychologists test intelligence which is fixed by heredity, and is therefore more or less impervious to education and environment."[110] Lippmann himself attacked the pseudo-science just then growing up around the concept of IQ, questioning the foundational assumption that intelligence is a unitary quality amenable to measurement.[111] But he also spent a good deal of time interrogating the tests in their own terms, demolishing in the process the most widely quoted fallacy emerging from discussion of the tests, that the mental age of the average adult American is only fourteen years. He then went on to attack the use made of the test results, particularly that of anti-immigration agitators such as Lothrop Stoddard. "One has only to read around in the literature of the subject," he says, "to see how easily the intelligence test can be turned into an engine of cruelty, how easily in the hands of blundering or prejudiced men it could turn into a method of stamping a permanent sense of inferiority upon the soul of a child."[112] Finally, he decries the antidemocratic implications inherent in the notion of hereditary intelligence, which could "lead to an intellectual caste system in which the task of education had given way to the doctrine of predestination and infant damnation. If the intelligence test really measured the unchangeable hereditary capacity of

human beings, as so many assert, it would inevitably evolve from an administrative convenience into a basis for hereditary caste."[113]

Lippmann received support from Alvin Johnson, who published a withering review of Stoddard's *Revolt Against Civilization* in the *New Republic*, and he
was attacked by William McDougall, professor of psychology at Harvard and
prominent anti-immigrant alarmist, and by Lewis Terman, the man chiefly responsible for the army tests.[114] If the controversy seems unusually intense and
its tone unaccountably harsh, it should be remembered how much was at
stake. Terman, who became head of the Stanford University Department of
Psychology and the American Psychological Association in 1922, was busily
building up the intellectual infrastructure that would make intelligence tests an
accepted part of American pedagogy. Through World Book he marketed a
National Intelligence Test that was given to over half a million children between April 1922 and April 1923. World Book was also to publish a series of
scientific monographs by Terman and associates, supporting and extending
the arguments originally made for the army tests. There was actually a good
deal of resistance to these plans from schoolteachers and educational experts, to which Terman responded with virulent ad hominem attacks, and yet
he was also shrewd enough to realize the value of any publicity, however negative. Thus, he purposely protracted the exchange with Lippmann in the
hopes of making him a laughingstock and thus increasing World Book's
sales.[115] In the first, at least, he did not succeed, as Lippmann seemed to have
a far surer grasp of all the issues, even the mathematical ones, than Terman
himself. But neither could Lippmann succeed against so thoroughly institutionalized an influence as Terman's, and so intelligence tests became an established fact in American society, though Lippmann's arguments have been
made against them again and again since 1922.[116]

The controversy had more immediate and perhaps more serious implications in the area of immigration. Brigham's *A Study of American Intelligence* had
in fact been suggested by Charles W. Gould, whose *America: A Family Matter*
was one of the basic anti-immigration tracts of the time. According to Brigham, Gould had been such a keen collaborator in *A Study of American Intelligence*
that he should be considered "mainly responsible for the whole work," which
might be read simply as a companion to Gould's own book.[117] Given this genealogy, somewhat odd considering Gould's utter lack of educational or psychological credentials, it is not surprising that Brigham's research leads to this
conclusion: "Immigration should not only be restrictive but highly selective.
. . . The really important steps are those looking toward the prevention of the
continued propagation of defective strains in the present population."[118]

The danger posed by these "defective strains" was a constant theme in the
anti-immigration writing of 1922, from Kenneth Roberts' hyperactive series
in the *Saturday Evening Post*, published in book form as *Why Europe Leaves
Home*, to Stoddard's *Revolt Against Civilization*. To Roberts, the mindless de-
pravity of the new immigrants was so apparent in their faces that no other ev-

idence was required,[119] but Stoddard and most others relied heavily on Brigham's redaction from the army tests. Stoddard told his readers that the tests showed that "intelligence is to-day being steadily *bred out of* the American population."[120] Cornelia James Cannon asked the readers of the *Atlantic Monthly*, "What prospect of success is there here in America, with the average of intelligence of the citizens already so much lower than we could have expected, and with an unceasing influx of potential citizens who are destined to bring the average still lower?"[121] George P. Cutten quoted the army tests to the audience at his inauguration as president of Colgate University: "With . . . 25 per cent. unable to comprehend the significance of the ballot, democracy is out of the question."[122]

Brigham's book became one of the key exhibits in the congressional testimony that led to new immigration restrictions in 1925.[123] But such measures hardly seemed sufficient in face of the deterioration that already seemed to have occurred in the American intelligence, so Cannon suggested an additional limitation on suffrage: "Indeed, we may have to admit that the lower-grade man is material unusable in a democracy, and to eliminate him from the electorate, as we have the criminal, the insane, the idiot, and the alien."[124] Edwin Grant Conklin, professor of Biology at Princeton, seemed quite eager to get on with it: "Let us have finger-prints, but before everything else let us have a mental classification of all children of school age. When once this has been done perhaps the least intelligent group can ultimately be denied the suffrage as are imbeciles, insane, and criminals at present."[125] Of course, even these measures would saddle the country with a vast army of ill-equipped defectives who would continue to lower the general level of intelligence by breeding indiscriminately. The logical solution to this problem was urged by Margaret Sanger and the American Birth Control League, citing the army tests as evidence: "Moreover, when we realize that each feeble-minded person is a potential source of an endless progeny of defect, we prefer the policy of immediate sterilization, of making sure that parenthood is absolutely prohibited to the feeble-minded."[126] Of all the possible solutions, it seems that only the final one was not suggested by some zealot obsessed with a decline in American intelligence, which Lippmann had quite efficiently shown to be nothing more than a mathematical artifact of the tests.

In fact, the whole controversy seems a crystal-clear demonstration of the thesis of *Public Opinion*, with the possible exception that here prejudicial bias is at work not within the crowd but within those, including professors at places like Princeton and Stanford, who despise the crowd. At the same time, however, the controversy illustrates an ironic effect of psychological self-consciousness on public debate no less damaging to Lippmann than to his opponents. For the debate about intelligence self-reflexively illustrated its own pointlessness: though the debate was all about the role of intelligence in a democracy, neither side really believed that the debate itself would be decided on intellectual grounds. Equally convinced of the validity of modern psychology, each side quietly ceded to the irrational the very ground they were overtly defending in the name of intelligence.

The contradiction is more readily apparent in Lippmann's opponents, who tend not to argue but rather to psychoanalyze. Or, rather, Terman first accuses Lippmann of psychoanalyzing *him* so that he can then retaliate in kind. His response to Lippmann's series in the *New Republic* is entitled "The Great Conspiracy: The Impulse Imperious of Intelligence Testers, Psychoanalyzed and Exposed by Mr. Lippmann," and it contains, among others, this clever sally: "Clearly, something has hit the bull's-eye of one of Mr. Lippmann's complexes."[127] Implicit in Terman's feeble witticism is the belief that people come to hold the views they do not by intellectual reflection but at the prompting of "complexes," instincts, biases, and prejudices. Equally implicit in this letter, in the way that Terman turns the attention of psychoanalysis away from himself and back toward Lippmann, is the fact that Terman does not extend this explanation to himself. Both sides, in fact, pose as lonely bastions of reason under attack from the dark forces below. McDougall contends that Lippmann's rejection of the idea of hereditary intelligence implies the rejection of all modern science, to which Lippmann retorts that McDougall is simply "airing his impressions and his prejudices."[128]

In short, the debate about intelligence shows that something has already happened to American democratic discourse, and it has happened not because of immigrants or mental defectives but because of men like Lippmann and Terman. For all the careful reasoning of his series on the army tests, Lippmann has, if anything, a lower opinion of the rational intelligence of the American public than do Terman and Stoddard. At one point, in response to the charge that he is defending a "naive theory of democracy," he says, "All that I can say to that is that I have written a book of over four hundred pages devoted to arguing the fallacy of the naive democratic theory."[129] The fallacy in question, of course, is that most people are capable of making reasoned decisions, and Lippmann wrote against it quite eloquently throughout the 1920s. There is a certain element of confession in the statement, included in *The Phantom Public*, that "the discovery of prejudice in all particular men gave the liberal a shock from which he never recovered."[130] Lippmann never recovered from this discovery, which came to him first through Freud, nor did liberal discourse in general, which was forced thereafter to go forward in bad faith using rational methods in which it no longer believed.[131]

The position of the conservatives in the debate is no less insecure. The importance of intelligence in a democracy is such an unexamined article of faith in the anti-immigrant movement that no one needs to explain or justify it, but it is quite difficult to determine, given the conservative political views of men like Terman and Stoddard, just what intelligence is *for*. Both men tended to explain social deviance, a concept that could stretch from actual crime to mere unconformity, in terms of low intelligence.[132] Brigham implicitly defines intelligence as the ability to adapt and conform: "It is natural to expect that individuals of superior intelligence will adjust themselves more easily to their physical and social environment, and that they will endow their children not only with material goods, but with the ability to adjust themselves to the same or a more complex environment."[133] But it is hard to see why such a result could not be accomplished just as successfully and with far less fuss by sheer stupidity. If people are simply to mimic what already exists, then intelligence just seems so much unnecessary baggage.

Terman admits as much in an unintentionally hilarious article of this time entitled "Adventures in Stupidity." The subject is a Stanford undergraduate who intrigues Terman by his inexplicable dullness. After subjecting the docile student to a battery of sophisticated tests, Terman concludes that he is hopelessly stupid: "Why honesty is the best policy, why women and children should be saved first in a shipwreck, why marriage licenses are necessary, involve issues too subtle for him to grasp." Here Terman implicitly admits that "intelligence" is for him nothing more than the ability to recognize and conform to commonplace morality, and yet he despises his poor subject because he can never rise above mere conformity: "He is about as likely to be a moral reformer as to be a philosopher or poet or inventor or scientist."[134] What a moral reformer, a philosopher, a poet, or an inventor might do in a society in which no one ever asked why honesty is the best policy is a question that simply does not appear on Terman's intelligence test.

The whole debate, in other words, is about a quality in which neither side retains any real belief. In this particular struggle between reason and prejudice, both sides portray themselves as the agents of reason, and yet widespread acceptance of the power of prejudice in the public sphere has left Lippmann, at least, in an untenable position. Terman obviously lives in a more conveniently stratified universe, in which the findings of psychology pose no reflexive threat to his own scientistic project. For Terman, it seems, the unconscious rules only outside academia and below a certain social line, a line that may be the function of the IQ tests to draw. And yet this careful sequestration of reason from the social unconscious makes it even more difficult to specify what most ordinary people would do with intelligence if they could somehow be injected with it.

Just how much Lippmann shares with those he seems to be opposing is exposed in a different, but closely related, controversy of the same year. In 1922 A. Lawrence Lowell began to receive inquiries, apparently not entirely spontaneous ones, about the size of Harvard's Jewish student body, which was about 21 percent of the whole. Lowell, who was himself concerned about the issue, began to cast around for a way to limit what was to him an unwelcome increase. An expedient that had been tried at Columbia and New York University was, ironically, the intelligence test, which appeared in this context quite frankly as a test of cultural conformity. Columbia managed to reduce the Jewish percentage of its student body by half with such a test because, as one official explained, "most Jews, especially those of the more objectionable type, have not had the same experiences which enable them to pass these tests as successfully as the average native American boy."[135] Lowell favored a more direct approach, and so he began to establish simple quotas, first on scholarships, then on transfers, and finally on admissions, the model for these being the restriction on immigration then working its way through Congress.[136]

In the controversy that followed, Lippmann, who was fighting so diligently against anti-immigration forces in the case of intelligence tests, supported Lowell and his quotas. He accepted, apparently quite sincerely, Lowell's reasoning that too large a percentage of Jews prevented their even dispersal throughout the student body, and the resulting concentration caused racial ill-feeling that would not otherwise have existed.[137] Thus Lippmann put himself in association not just with intelligence testers and anti-immigrationists but with a scholar, Lowell, whose notion of public opinion was almost diametrically opposed to his own.

Why did Lippmann take such a position, implicitly supporting the very forces he was opposing in the pages of the *New Republic*? First of all, Lippmann's positions in these two controversies may be less inconsistent than they seem on the surface. One of the reasons Lippmann deplored the notion of hereditary intelligence is that it solidified and perpetuated ethnic difference. A conspicuous Jewish presence at Harvard might, he feared, lead to the same result, by preventing the "even dispersion" of Jewish students into the rest of the student body. Lippmann strongly favored "dispersion" for any minority bearing "some striking cultural peculiarity" because he feared the disintegrative force of such differences in a democracy.[138] On one level, then, Lippmann is defending a traditional "melting pot" notion against its detractors, nativists like Stoddard, McDougall, and Roberts, for whom the melting pot meant mongrelization. Supporting quotas at Harvard may have been a strategy designed to keep ethnic distinctions inconspicuous enough so that they might one day disappear.

On the other hand, however, Lippmann did not believe in such a vision any more than did Stoddard. In fact, immigrants play almost as ominous a role in his social philosophy as they did in that of the nativists. For Lippmann, the basic problem facing a modern democracy is the "wide and unpredictable environment" in which its citizens must live. Insofar as democracy depends on an involved and informed electorate, it also depends on "protected boundaries" around the experience of that electorate. But a modern electorate is constantly exposed to that which is "distinctly alien," and therefore it can never get a grasp of the conditions in which it exists: "Modern society is not visible to anybody, nor intelligible continuously and as a whole."[139] Far more openly than Lowell, Lippmann admits that reason is only relative, that it works only within certain boundaries, and that the qualification of those boundaries in a diverse and constantly changing society leaves it helpless. As he said in a letter to Judge Learned Hand, one of those who felt that *Public Opinion* had allowed too little to reason: "In a sealed and more or less enclosed community, such as the Greeks took for their premise, I should not find it difficult to maintain such a faith [in human reason]. Science is power if you can fence off the area in which it operates long enough. But as I said in the last chapter, the rate at which science expands is much slower than the pace of politics. If there is no way of slowing up the invasion (by birth and by immigration) I think the Hearsts will overwhelm us before they are tamed."[140] Starting from different premises and motivated by completely different political beliefs, Lippmann arrives at precisely the same place as Stoddard, McDougall, and Brigham: immigrants present a threat to the rule of intelligence in the United States.

The argument of *Public Opinion* is, on this score at least, identical to that of a wild-eyed alarmist tract like Daniel Chauncey Brewer's *The Peril of the Republic: Are We Facing Revolution in the United States?* Brewer, who could not have read Lippmann's book before publishing his own, offers the same fearful analysis: "The greatest change wrought in a free nation like the United States is brought about by the shift from concerns which are within the grasp of humanity to a bigness which is beyond the comprehension of its finite mind."[141] Thus, a system founded on a presumption of fundamental likeness and like-mindedness is placed under extraordinary stress in a time in which "shades of thought are as numerous as the coteries that give them birth, and these are without number."[142] Of course, Brewer, who sees Bolshevik conspiracies not just under the bed but practically between the sheets, would not have welcomed Lippmann's agreement had he known of it, since his fear of revolution is, like most such fears at this time, explicitly anti-Semitic.

What makes this rather remarkable agreement between such different political thinkers possible is the common reconstitution of the public sphere on a psychoanalytic model. Behind this lies the ancient analogy between the well-balanced individual and a harmonious society, one that was being influentially restated for liberal society at this time by John Dewey: "The good society was, like the good self, a diverse yet harmonious, growing yet unified whole."[143] It proves fairly easy to adapt this model to include the new findings of psychoanalysis. Once the group mind is imagined to have, like the individual mind as mapped by Freudian psychology, different levels or faculties or agencies, the opaqueness of the individual mind to itself, the fact that its most powerful sections are somehow occulted from the rest, seems to offer a persuasive model for social incoherence and misunderstanding. The idea that social problems might have psychological causes becomes, by extension and generalization, the idea that society itself may have a psychology.

The idea that social problems might be analogous to psychological problems, that they might be analyzed and perhaps even cured by the same means, was both widespread and authoritative at this time. To a liberal academic analyst like James Mickel Williams, writing from a point of view influenced by Dewey and Wallas, social conflicts are the result of "a suppression of impulses throughout the social organization. When an impulse is suppressed, there is resentment, which may express itself in unconscious reflexes, or in the margin of consciousness, or in the intense consciousness of baffled rage or depression."[144] The same message was delivered in a slightly livelier way in popular works like William Fielding's *The Caveman Within Us*, which ascribes race riots, pogroms, and prejudice in general to the sudden release of unconscious impulses.[145]

Williams and Fielding were both, like Lippmann and Rivers, good-natured liberals who felt that there was a persuasive analogy between psychological suppression and political repression. Like Dewey, and perhaps in part because of him, they tended to see a direct relationship between successful personal integration of reason and impulse and a benign democratic pluralism. None of these writers was influenced by his psychological interests to ignore the material causes of social unrest, and even Fielding, who wrote a sensationalized account for a popular audience, took issue with the prejudicial use being made at this time of the army tests.[146] In fact, the idea that crowds are ruled by their least intelligent members, who betray the whole to its social unconscious, is a commonplace of crowd psychology that was at the heart of the prejudicial reasoning that Lippmann was fighting so hard in the controversy over the army tests. And yet the psychological model itself, understood as liberally as it may have been, betrays his position. Once it is understood on the model of the individual mind, where the parts are obscured from and in conflict with one another, social diversity can never be seen as anything other than neurotic. And it is desperately difficult to avoid associating the unconscious, that foreign principle at the heart of the self, with the actual foreigners who were at this time such a contentious issue in American political life.

The psychoanalytic model of the public sphere thus leads both liberal and conservative into seeing diversity and social change as if they were psychosocial illnesses. For a liberal like Alfred Kuttner, who had originally introduced Lippmann to the work of Freud, the chief psychological interest of the time lay in the neurotic relations of immigrant and "native aristocrat." His article on "Nerves" in Harold Stearns' compilation *Civilization in the United States* seems to hold out only two possibilities to the arriving immigrant: neurotic dissociation or neurotic conformity. In either case, the "immigrant's neurosis" is matched by the "state of tension" in which the Anglo-Saxon lives once he can no longer take his own society for granted.[147] Despite the many differences between Kuttner, a longtime associate of Lippmann, and Stoddard, this image of society in a state of psychic distress is quite similar to that in *The Revolt Against Civilization*. There is an "Under-Man," Stoddard tells his readers, within each individual, a compendium of instincts, drives, unconscious compulsions. And though this "Under-Man" is a constant in every individual, he is especially strong in particular strata of society, "the lower social strata, especially the pauper, criminal, and degenerate elements—civilization's 'inner barbarians.'"[148] These foment unrest and revolt within society, which is analogous to mental illness in an individual. As these lower layers are augmented by immigration, the power of reason in society steadily decreases until it begins to seem positively insane.

In this way, Stoddard advances a very common model of the psychological public sphere, stratified so that his own ethnic group and social class is identified with reason, immigrants and the lower classes with the unconscious.[149] This is a more or less direct application of conventional crowd psychology, which had been teaching since Le Bon that "masses are the unconscious."[150] Stoddard associates the "Under-Man" so thoroughly with the subconscious as to make him seem subhuman. The "primitive animality . . . of the brute and the savage"[151] is described in such bloodcurdling terms the reader almost begins to see actual Huns and Visigoths thundering through the streets. Of course, there is a good deal of competition in this respect, at a time when it was quite common to describe certain social classes as if they were peopled mainly by cavemen.[152]

On the other hand, Stoddard also associates the primitive with what he calls "destructive criticism": a "spirit of morose pessimism and incipient revolt against *things as they exist.*"[153] This revolt is visible everywhere, but most especially in the arts, which Stoddard feels are dominated by "a fierce revolt against things as they exist, and a disintegrative, degenerative reaction towards primitive chaos."[154] Here Stoddard neatly associates innovation with regression in a way rather reminiscent of the modernists themselves, if quite different in spirit. For Stoddard sees innovation as inherently mischievous, since there are, to his mind, no rational grounds of complaint against "things as they exist." Thus criticism is associated not with the intellect but rather with the body: "This new social revolt . . . is not merely a war against a social system, not merely a war against our civilization; *it is a war of the hand against the brain.*"[155] Criticism is thus the antithesis of thought, not just its opponent but in fact its very negation.

Obviously, this view must rest on a rather odd definition of thought. Intelligence for Stoddard, as for his cohorts in the nativist ranks, is innate and to a very great degree inanimate. Though there is a well-developed and highly romantic myth running through the nativist literature about the bold intrepidity of Nordic thought, Stoddard actually gives his vigorous Nordics very little to think about. The whole notion of innate intelligence begins to seem a contradiction in terms, since patterns of behavior that are innate require no thought and make no call on intelligence. Like Terman, Stoddard fetishizes intelligence, worshiping and distrusting it in equal measure. The same inconsistency complicates his picture of the Under-Man, who seems to be too conscious and too unconscious at the same time. Try as he might, it is hard to make his subhuman caveman also look like a dangerous social critic. In fact, as Alvin Johnson suggests in the *New Republic*, it is Stoddard who is the archcritic; and if unhappiness with "things as they exist" is a mark of the Under-Man, then the morose and dissatisfied Lothrop Stoddard is "under" just about everyone.[156]

It is in this inconsistency, however, that the real truth behind both Stoddard and Lippmann is to be glimpsed. The famous liberal and the archconservative both tend to see the social diversity brought about by immigration in the negative terms dictated by traditional crowd psychology, as if it lowered the general intellectual tone of society and surrendered power to the unconscious, but the works of both men imply just the opposite. Stoddard fears the self-conscious questioning of "things as they exist" that comes when a society is exposed to different points of view. Lippmann is himself both an example and an exponent of this self-conscious questioning, who by his own theory ought not to exist at all. The controversy over immigration shows how a society exposed to social diversity becomes self-conscious and self-critical, though it may very well choose to reject the results of that criticism.

Times of increased change and diversity seem to be ruled by the sort of prejudices and stereotypes Lippmann describes in *Public Opinion* not just because these become stronger in such times but also because they become more visible. As Hans-Georg Gadamer puts it, "It seems, rather, to be generally characteristic of the emergence of the 'hermeneutical' problem that something *distant* has to be brought close, a certain strangeness overcome, a bridge built between the once and the now. Thus hermeneutics, as a general attitude over against the world, came into its own in modern times, which had become aware of the temporal distance separating us from antiquity and of the relativity of the life-worlds of different cultural traditions."[157] Prejudice can only really appear as such when "things as they exist" are exposed to the "relativity . . . of different cultural traditions." The pain of this exposure is what links Stoddard and Lippmann.

The connection between psychology and immigration can thus be seen to have a different basis from the one so commonly offered at this time, for both these social developments made people aware of the many ways in which they are unaware. Society had not become, as both Lippmann and Stoddard feared, dull and stupid but rather hyperconscious and painfully self-aware, as both Lippmann and Stoddard revealed in their own work, and it seems fairly clear that the increasing diversity of American culture had a good deal to do with this.[158] As American society became more diverse, social communion became more arduous and the inevitable mediation of human society became more obvious. Ordinary citizens were able to discover at home what Wittgenstein and Malinowski had to travel to discover: the relativity and contingency of human customs. The discovery of the social unconscious, of the power of custom, prejudice, habit, is in a sense an instance of the hyperconsciousness of modern life, the reflexivity that comes when ordinary custom can no longer be taken for granted. In other words, what Terman and Stoddard were resisting was not really immigration or the rule of the unconscious but rather modernity itself, or at least that aspect of modernity that Giddens has called "the institutionalisation of doubt." Psychology is perhaps one of the best examples of the peculiarly modern institutions Giddens has in mind, intellectual institutions that depend on the skeptical questioning of appearances and on a self-consciously circular process of constant qualification.[159] But it is only half true to suggest that common awareness of the unconscious made the public more self-conscious about its social prejudices and political presuppositions. Increased immigration and the exposure it brought to different languages, customs, and opinions also made the public more aware of the power of the unconscious. This is the circularity at work in the controversies over intelligence and immigration that took place in 1922.

Salome of the Tenements

In the course of 1922, *The American Hebrew* published two articles that seem to comment in diametrically opposed ways on the controversies of that year over immigration and the public sphere. The first of these to see print was Lippmann's "Public Opinion and the American Jew." The title promises an application of the thesis of *Public Opinion* to the growing controversy around the anti-Semitic quota systems being contemplated at various American universities. The result, however, is an analysis of prejudice that places the blame quite squarely on the victims. The "fundamental fact" behind anti-Semitism in America, Lippmann says, is the fact that Jews are "inevitably conspicuous," and, rather than seeking to mitigate this, far too many Jews magnify their conspicuousness by "blatant vulgarity." In the course of his argument, Lippmann provides a picture of "upper Broadway on a Sunday afternoon" that would not have been too far out of place in the *Saturday Evening Post* dispatches of Kenneth Roberts or the anti-immigration propaganda of Lothrop Stoddard.[160]

The second article is a piece of direct testimony from upper Broadway and a virtual manifesto in favor of the conspicuous. "My Ambitions at 21 and What Became of Them" is an autobiographical account by Anzia Yezierska, who was at this moment one of the most prominent Jewish-American writers. Her first book, *Hungry Hearts*, had just appeared as a motion picture, and her first novel, *Salome of the Tenements*, was about to be published by Boni and Liveright. The story told in the article is of Yezierska's struggle to "emerge from obscurity," to make herself known and heard. This story and the one told in the novel she was about to publish give the mirror image of Lippmann's prescription for Jewish success: "It is the over-emotional Ghetto struggling for its breath in the rarefied air of Puritan restraint."[161]

Between them, Lippmann and Yezierska self-consciously exemplify the two extremes of the psychological public sphere: the Puritan head and the immigrant heart; the conscious, restrained, measured upper class against the unconscious, overemotional underclass. Their very different appearances in *The American Hebrew* thus exemplify the conflict then being waged over immigration, intelligence, and the unconscious, a conflict that Dewey was just then restating in *Human Nature and Conduct* as the conflict between habit and impulse. In fact, there is a good deal of evidence to suggest that when he wrote of impulse Dewey had Yezierska in mind, for the two were involved in an emotional relationship at the time Dewey was writing *Human Nature and Conduct*.[162] Dewey called in his book for a harmonious relation between the two human faculties, which may have been part of what he was trying to effect when he introduced Yezierska's work to the *New Republic*, originally co-founded by Lippmann, then very much under Dewey's influence.[163] The palpable difference in the 1922 contributions of Yezierska and Lippmann to *The American Hebrew* might be taken, then, as an index of how utopian Dewey's hopes were of a happily integrated personality in a fully integrated society.

It often seems, in this article and in the fictional work she published at this time, that Yezierska is going out of her way to exaggerate the opposition between habit and impulse, intelligence and the unconscious, almost as if she wants to demonstrate not just the failure of her relationship with Dewey but also her distance from the liberal elite he fostered. *Salome* in particular seems a fulfillment of the worst fears of the anti-immigrant alarmists, a crude and even strident celebration of the wild impulses brought to a sterile America by the new immigrants. It is also, in other ways, a confirmation of Lippmann's uneasy doubts about the relationship between immigration, publicity, and social simple-mindedness. In the end, however, *Salome* suggests that, in a society where publicity has already become second nature, intelligence and the unconscious will have a relationship, both negative and positive, far more complex than either Dewey or Lippmann could have imagined.

The title of *Salome of the Tenements* suggests a number of dichotomies. One of these is embodied in the two main characters, John Manning, a wealthy philanthropist introduced in the first chapter title as a "saint," and Sonya Vrunsky, the Salome of the tenements who dances for his head. Yezierska's rendering of the biblical parallel is rather inexact, since it conflates Herod and John the Baptist, who sacrifices his own head in this version by falling in love with Salome. As Manning dreams it one night, "he was John the Baptist loving with a self-destruction the white-fleshed loveliness of Salome, who lured and drew him with the dazzling color of her voluptuous dancing."[164] In this way, Yezierska neatens up the dichotomy of saint and sinner by making her Saint John the moral as well as the actual victim of her Salome.

That this basic dichotomy should be neat is important to Yezierska because it must suggest a whole series of other dichotomies. John Manning is also a representative of civilization and culture as against the crude savagery of Sonya Vrunsky. Yezierska gives to her main character a naive reverence for American culture that seems to ignore even the most basic historical evidence: "The Anglo-Saxons are a superior race to the crazy Russians. . . . They're ages ahead of us. Compared to them we're naked savages" (*ST*, p. 68). That there was no Anglo-Saxon culture in America at a time when Russia was a well-established Christian empire seems not to matter, as Yezierska neatly reverses the conventional relationship of Old and New Worlds. Leaving Russia for the United States is not, in this analysis, to leave an old culture for a much younger one but to repudiate the old culture so totally that it is no longer distinguishable from savagery. The immigrant must start over from scratch and begin the climb to civilization again as a primitive barbarian.

Sonya fully accepts, in other words, what was being said about her in the anti-immigrant press, and she follows her detractors further by expressing the cultural differences between her and Manning as an internal psychological conflict. Manning, as she puts it, has a head, while "I got only feelings" (*ST*, p. 38). Manning is "so sane, so logical" (*ST*, p. 145), while Sonya is whipped by storms of emotion so strong she often seems insane even to herself. The way in which Manning scorns "blind impulse" and calls upon "social experts" for a "scientific survey" (*ST*, p. 134) before he takes any significant step makes him seem almost a caricature of Lippmann. Though this can hardly be the case, Yezierska is in fact dramatizing the same conflict Lippmann describes in *Public Opinion*, between the rule of reason and the unconscious as a force in society. More overtly than the most confirmed nativist, Yezierska associates the unconscious with the immigrant, with a young woman who continually does things for reasons even she cannot understand.

Moreover, Sonya's "Russian madness," her "untamed wildness" (*ST*, p. 85), is associated with political anarchy and violence. The chapter in which the two opposites come together in marriage is entitled "The Crumbling Temple," and Yezierska makes it clear at the outset who has brought the sacred edifice down: "Sonya was like the dynamite bomb and Manning the walls of tradition constantly menaced by threatening explosions" (*ST*, p. 132). As in Stoddard, the revolt against the head, against reason, is also the political revolt of dissatisfied revolutionaries against things as they are. Yezierska thus resorts to one of the most popular caricatures of the time, the bomb-throwing anarchist, while confirming the assertions of conservatives like Stoddard that there is no legitimate revolt, only formless resistance to reason and order.

In fact, so closely does *Salome of the Tenements* repeat the arguments and even the metaphors of *The Revolt Against Civilization* that it often reads as if it had been written by Lothrop Stoddard as a cautionary tale. When Yezierska describes Sonya's desire for Manning, she makes her heroine sound like a combination of Theda Bara and Mata Hari: "In her intensity of emotion, she was the Russian Jewess rapacious in her famine to absorb the austere perfections of the Anglo-Saxon race" (*ST*, p. 66). Sonya is poverty-stricken Europe come to batten on American prosperity, as Kenneth Roberts was warning his readers in the *Saturday Evening Post*; Jewish sensuality come to degrade Anglo-Saxon reason, as Stoddard was warning the readers of *The Revolt Against Civilization*; instinct and appetite come to rule over democracy, as Lippmann was warning in *Public Opinion*. When Manning first succumbs to his temptress, Yezierska stages the scene as if it were the fall of an American Adam in a New World Garden of Eden. Greenwold, the family estate of the Mannings, is, the chapter title tells us, "God's Own Eden," and there Manning falls, "terrified at his own relapse to the primitive." He appeals "dumbly to all the traditions that had been bred into him to gain control of himself and save him from the fury of desire," but, just as Stoddard feared, to no avail (*ST*, p. 106). Sonya has her "victory," and her "conquering power" (*ST*, p. 107) overcomes the Anglo-Saxon race in the very heart of its homeland.

No more complete or more perfect an allegory of the terrible ascent of the "Under-Man" could possibly be imagined. Just as Stoddard predicted, the head of the Anglo-Saxon, site of both reason and authority, is lopped off and presented to the Jewish Salome. Yet even so perfect an allegory as this has certain complications in it. As Salome, Sonya is all wild impulse against the austere intellect of her saint; but Salome is also calculating and manipulative, and so is Sonya. She is frequently referred to by other characters as a witch, a siren, or a vamp, and she is often unpleasantly surprised herself by the devious means she uses to entrap her male victims: "Her heart pounded as she realized the questionable depths to which her guileful flirtation was leading her" (*ST*, p. 51). In fact, Sonya is so guileful and devious that many readers objected that she was altogether too reprehensible to gain their sympathy.[165] They share the disillusionment of John Manning, who realizes with horror toward the end of the book that "the woman of the people who was to bring him new life" is "a schemer, an adventuress!" (*ST*, p. 152). The half-wild, primitive creature who was to infuse Manning with some of her impulsive vitality now seems to be a sophisticated and even cynical manipulator, though this judgment, this swing away from his earlier sympathy, is no more astute than was its opposite.

Sonya is an actress capable of playing any number of different roles. With the right clothes, the right "costume" (*ST*, p. 56), as she calls it, she can play a "lady" and intimidate her landlord into remodeling her apartment. In different clothes, with a different "background," she can appear simple and unaffected. Simplicity, Yezierska makes abundantly clear, is an effect that sometimes takes great effort and expense to achieve. "Shopping for Simplicity," the chapter of that name shows us, is an arduous enterprise for those who aren't wealthy enough to afford simplicity. Sonya endures humiliation and hazards a good deal of deception to buy the dress and remodel the apartment that impress Manning with their "directness, their unscheming naturalness" (*ST*, p. 73). His enthusiasm is such "that for the moment Sonya actually believed she was simple" (*ST*, p. 73). But she is not really so simple-minded: "She had indeed been successful, because the effect of spontaneous beauty and simplicity was exactly the impression she desired to create. It would have ruined her chance with him if he guessed for a moment the effort, the struggle it had been to meet him on this plane of harmonious beauty" (*ST*, p. 74).

This does not mean, however, that Manning is right to replace the image of "unscheming naturalness" with that of Sonya as "a schemer." For Sonya is often most artless in her very role-playing. Very early in her relationship with Manning, almost before there *is* a relationship, in fact, Sonya imagines herself married to him and then giving away their millions to the poor: "The hungry and the homeless lift their hands in blessing everywhere she turns. The ragged children scamper from hovels and tenements and cling to her in childlike affection as she scatters handfuls of money among them" (*ST*, p. 13). This is so obviously a scene from the movies, complete with pantomimic expressions of gratitude and joy, that it is impossible to take at face value. Sonya's friend Gittel accuses her much later of an insatiable desire for the "limelight," for yet "another setting for your stage" (*ST*, p. 158), and this image of herself as the center of every gaze certainly seems to justify the accusation. It is, however, precisely because her desire for the limelight is so fierce that she can insert herself into the most contrived scenes without contamination.

On the other hand, the very fierceness that makes Sonya seem so wildly uncontrolled has itself a layer of contrivance. Sonya's honesty, her spontaneity, and her crudity are frequently described both by the narrator and by herself as "naked." When she appears to the dressmaker Jacques Hollins as a symbol of "naked, passionate youth" (*ST*, p. 23), however, an important inconsistency begins to appear. For Sonya has come to Hollins because dress is so important to her. She so consistently thinks in terms of "costume" that she finally ends by becoming a dress designer herself. In fact, Sonya puts so much emphasis on clothes that a new dress is for her virtually a whole new personality. When she meets John Manning while wearing a new dress, she is so excited that "her nakedness staggered him" (*ST*, p. 33), but what he takes for "nakedness" is in fact "the intoxication of being well dressed." Though Yezierska is having some fun with poor Manning, she is also suggesting that there are times when the difference between nakedness and being well dressed may disappear, times when clothes, no matter how artfully designed and arduously acquired, can be a real expression of the self: "Never before had her clothes been an expression of herself—she an expression of her clothes. It was like being free from the flesh of her body, released from the fetters of the earth."

Yezierska works a similar ambiguity into her use of the term "real." Sonya tells Manning, "I can't help being real" (*ST*, p. 36), and she wonders about him, though not aloud, "Were rich people ever real?" (*ST*, p. 46). Manning is attracted to Sonya in the first place because he fears he is not very "real," and he envies the way she lives "unveiled by any artifice" (*ST*, p. 74). Here, of course, Yezierska is nudging the forgetful reader with an ironic reference to the famous veils of her title character. Manning is entirely unaware of how "artfully" (*ST*, p. 50) Sonya has disposed her veils, how she has assembled what she herself calls a "costume" and a "stage setting" (*ST*, p. 57). But for Sonya such artifice is no less real for being coldly calculated. When she says to her friend Gittel, "I got to have *real art*" (*ST*, p. 57), she collapses the very dichotomy on which her relationship with Manning is based. On one level, she means nothing more than that the illusion of simplicity and ingenuousness she intends to create around herself must be complete; but on another level she is confessing a rather complex truth, that the fierceness Manning mistakes

for primitive artlessness is in fact a hunger for culture, for "real art," so that
what attracts him to her as if it were a polar opposite is actually her aching desire to be like him.

Of course, Manning might have suspected that someone who talks as
much as Sonya does about being "a wild savage in a dressed-up parlor of
make-believes" (*ST*, p. 37) can hardly be one. But then both of these characters talk about themselves in such stereotypical terms it is hard to separate
play-acting from sincere confession. *Salome* is full of operatic exchanges like
this one:

> "I am a Russian Jewess, a flame—a longing. A soul consumed with hunger for
> heights beyond reach. I am the ache of unvoiced dreams, the clamor of suppressed
> desires. I am the unlived lives of generations stifled in Siberian prisons. I am the
> urge of ages for the free, the beautiful that never yet was on land or sea."
>
> "And I," he breathed, impelled by her sublime candor to apologize for himself.
> "I am a puritan whose fathers were afraid to trust experience. We are bound by our
> possessions of property, knowledge and tradition." (*ST*, p. 37)

Even in their moments of wildest rapture, perhaps most especially then,
Sonya and Manning tend to think of themselves as social stereotypes, as the
"oriental mystery and the Anglo-Saxon clarity" (*ST*, p. 108). This is perhaps
the fulfillment of Lippmann's darkest suspicions, as people come to see not
just others but even themselves in stereotypical terms. Sonya's triumph, her
achievement in finally marrying Manning, is to become the cliché she has read
about in newspapers and seen on the movie screen: "She saw herself as one
of the million girl readers of society columns, who had suddenly been made
mistress of the shining palace of pleasure she had only dreamed about. She
felt like the poor girl who could only worship from a distance the hero on the
stage, transformed by the magic of marriage into the heroine by his side" (*ST*,
p. 120). Sonya's ambition, in a way, is to become the sort of person who appears in the newspapers, but that ambition has itself already become a cliché,
so her whole rags-to-riches story is governed from beginning to end by media-
generated stereotypes.

One simple explanation for all of this is that Yezierska is a clumsy writer
and *Salome of the Tenements* a very bad novel.[166] The characters are not just artistic failures but failures whose stereotypical exaggerations confirm the most
benighted prejudices of the time. In fact, *Salome* manages to confirm with a
single character Stoddard's prejudices and Lippmann's fear of prejudice, for
Sonya is motivated by blind, unconscious instinct and simultaneously molded
by the simplifications of the mass media. But Sonya is not, for all of this, a
simple character, nor is she simply drawn. When she says, "For Manning I
got to be a lily blooming out of an ash-can" (*ST*, p. 57), she reveals a self-
conscious submission to cliché vastly more complicated than the simple in-
doctrination that Lippmann imagines. Sonya is aware that her story is a story
and that, as such, it can never be original, and she draws from this realization

a measure of self-determination that far exceeds anything Manning can imagine. It might be said, in fact, that Sonya is a very early example of a personality commonly associated only with postmodernism, one who derives a certain measure of autonomy and even agency from her consumption of mass-market images.[167]

Actually, Sonya is aware that her story repeats a very specific prototype, the celebrated marriage of Rose Pastor, who was a friend of Yezierska's, to Graham Stokes, a wealthy philanthropist.[168] Groping for ideas in the midst of her campaign to win John Manning, she wonders, "How did Rose Pastor catch on to Graham Stokes?" (*ST*, p. 83). Here Sonya admits something about herself —the narrator says that "Sonya tore the last veil of deception from her eyes" —and about the novel, which is based on a number of extratextual narratives beside the story of Rose Pastor Stokes. For a novel that is as crudely written as it is, *Salome* calls upon an extremely complex set of extratextual associations, and it does so in a way that transfers the author's self-consciousness about such matters to her main character.

The most important of these extratextual sources is the story of Yezierska's own relationship with John Dewey, which she told and retold in a number of different forms throughout her life. The intense ethnic self-consciousness of Manning and Sonya is apparently transcribed directly from life, or at least all the available evidence suggests that Dewey and Yezierska saw their relationship as a meeting of Anglo-Saxon head with Russian Jewish heart. One of Sonya's most impassioned speeches seems to have been adapted from a poem that Dewey wrote to Yezierska:

> Generations of stifled words reaching out
> Through you,
> Aching for utt'rance.[169]

In fact, for many years, the only version of this poem in public existence was the one that Yezierska included in fictionalized accounts of their relationship. In *All I Could Never Be*, one of Yezierska's fictionalized autobiographies, the character based on Dewey sends "Fanya Ivanowna" a copy of this poem, and in *Red Ribbon on a White Horse*, "John Morrow," a stifled Anglo-Saxon philanthropist, sends Yezierska several lines from a different Dewey poem.[170] In putting Dewey's unacknowledged words into *Salome*, Yezierska is playing a rather complicated game, signaling to an audience of one that the strident effusions of this simple ghetto girl have behind them the mind of the leading American philosopher of the time.

There is a more complex and substantial relationship between *Salome* and Dewey's *Human Nature and Conduct*, published in the same year. Dewey's book, originally delivered as lectures at Stanford in 1918, in the midst of his relationship with Yezierska, is all about the difficult reconciliation of habit and impulse, of intelligence and instinct. For Dewey, these are necessary complements, impulse reviving habit and custom, intelligence choosing between useful and destructive instincts. As he says, in lines that seem to have direct reference to his relationship with Yezierska:

> The separation of warm emotion and cool intelligence is the great moral tragedy. This division is perpetuated by those who deprecate science and foresight in behalf of affection as it is by those who in the name of an idol labeled reason would quench passion. The intellect is always inspired by some impulse.[171]

In *Salome*, on the other hand, the Anglo-Saxon intellectual, who calms himself at night by reading Kant, is utterly incapable of coping with his impulsive Jewish wife. Long before the melodramatic end, by which time Manning has become quite insane, Yezierska starts subtly peppering her descriptions of this cool intellectual with doubtful epithets: the "crazy philanthropist" presses his lover's arm with "savage tightness," for example (*ST*, pp. 103, 105). The intellect turns out, in this analysis, to be a form of unconsciousness, a willful ignorance of impulses that exist whether they are acknowledged or not. When they overcome Manning, *Salome* becomes an ironic rewriting of *Human Nature and Conduct*, the very notion that habit and impulse might be intelligently balanced subjected to a withering biographical critique.

At the same time, however, Yezierska imports into her novel other experiences of her own that suggest a very close, if highly ironic, dependence of impulse on intelligence. Between 1918 and 1922 Dewey had been teaching in China, while Yezierska had been to Hollywood, an experience that adds yet another extratextual dimension to *Salome*. At least two episodes from the novel are retold elsewhere in autobiographical accounts of Yezierska's own climb to fame. The scene in which Manning's maid helps the humiliated Sonya unpack her drab belongings reappears in *Red Ribbon on a White Horse*, only in this case the maid is employed by the Miramar Hotel, in which Samuel Goldwyn had installed his newest sensation.[172] The very ironic scene in which Sonya is complimented on the wonderful simplicity of her dress actually occurred after her return to New York when the critic William Lyon Phelps tells her, "Your simplicity is the essence of taste."[173] What these two parallels suggest is that Sonya's rags-to-riches story is also Yezierska's, and that Sonya is so self-conscious about the relationship between her life and media stereotypes because Yezierska had just been cranked through the Goldwyn publicity machine. It becomes clear to Yezierska early on in her stay in California that Goldwyn is interested in her not as a writer—the noted purveyor of Jewish stereotypes Montague Glass has been brought in to handle that—but as a focus for publicity. Plucked from obscurity, Yezierska represents a "swell news angle. . . . Hollywood, the golden city of opportunity, the first to recognize genius whether it comes from Russia, Poland, or even the United States."[174] She is, in other words, merely a pretext that allows Goldwyn to praise himself and Hollywood in general. Like Sonya, who becomes a "sensational nine days' wonder" (*ST*, p. 165) in the press, Yezierska becomes a "Sweatshop Cinderella," a stereotyped news story unrecognizable to herself.[175]

Sonya's laborious campaign to reproduce herself in a form that will be convincing to Manning is a private version of the Goldwyn campaign from which Yezierska had just escaped.[176] But there was no escape, for *Salome* was the focus of a very similar publicity campaign, this one mounted not by Samuel Goldwyn but rather by Horace Liveright. With what Yezierska called "his flair for the sensational," Liveright staged a publicity banquet for *Salome* at the Waldorf Astoria because he had heard that Yezierska had once unsuccessfully applied for work there as a chambermaid. Phelps covered the banquet and wrote it into his review of the novel, thus endowing "the advertising stunt with literary significance."[177] But Yezierska had already given such stunts literary significance herself within *Salome*, which is clearly a great deal more self-conscious about the creation and manipulation of personality than Phelps could ever be.

The happy ending of *Salome* finds Sonya working as a dress designer, making stage costumes for Jeritza. Her success has been made in part by talent, in part by a clever publicity campaign promoting "the Sonya model," which was popular enough that she became known as "the Sonya of the 'Sonya Model'" (*ST*, p. 173), the original, as it were, of a manufactured line of copies. Into this happiness bursts John Manning, now utterly deranged, a "savage beast . . . starved into madness for the woman" (*ST*, p. 181). This rather improbable turn of events represents a number of reversals: Manning now lowered as Sonya has become happy and prosperous; Manning savage and primitive as Sonya has become the height of fashion. But at a more fundamental level, there has been no reversal at all, for Sonya has always been more self-conscious than Manning, who was under the illusion that there was such a thing as simplicity. That notion now seems synonymous with insanity, while Sonya's duplicity has ended in psychic health and happiness. "Everything she did pulsed with reality," thinks the Sonya of the "Sonya model," and it now seems possible to move the word beyond irony. For Sonya has a stronger grip on reality than Manning precisely because she has never imagined it as an ideal uncontaminated by art.

Toward the beginning of this quintessentially American saga of self-realization, Jacques Hollins inspires Sonya with this assurance: "You don't have to be a second-hand pattern of a person—when you can be your own free, individual self" (*ST*, p. 26). At this point, the metaphor seems suspiciously inapt, even surreptitiously ironic, evoking as it does the dressmaking patterns by which Hollins makes his living, and it seems even less appropriate at the end, when Sonya actually becomes one of those patterns, the Sonya of "the Sonya model." Sonya's progress through the book, however, has been one long demonstration of the fact that one can become a "free, individual self" by adopting and inhabiting a "second-hand pattern." Sonya's wild impulsiveness, her untrammeled instinctive desire for freedom, actually does find its most successful expression in the marketing campaigns of the fashion houses for which she works. Though the imagined reconciliation of her wild unconscious with the cool rationality of Manning does not occur, a different and perhaps more topical reconciliation is accomplished when her self-expression in dress becomes a marketing success.

In this melodramatic conclusion, then, Yezierska offers her response to the controversies surrounding the public unconscious in 1922. On the surface, Sonya is the embodiment of everything that Lippmann and the nativists feared. Wholly irrational herself, she becomes first a creature and then a creator of publicity and advertising. But Yezierska also portrays in Sonya precisely what Lippmann finds it so difficult to notice: the public self consciousness about the unconscious of which he is himself a most notable example. To proclaim one's instinctive impulsiveness as loudly as Sonya does, to theatricalize it as she does, is to make it an object of consciousness, a vector of difference that makes everyone reflect, sometimes painfully, on their own differences. When Lippmann advises American Jews to dissimulate their unfortunate presence, he is actually trying to counter this sort of self-consciousness, to make it unconscious again so that prejudice can forget about itself. He is complaining against the reflexivity of modern life, a reflexivity that Sonya not only accepts but helps to produce when she reproduces herself as the "Sonya model." And though Yezierska is not in any traditional sense a modernist, and Sonya, so desperate to succeed, is not a social critic, in producing this reflexivity both author and character provide the sort of irritation that Stoddard decried as "destructive criticism" and that he associated with innovation in the arts.

What this means in the end is that the literature of 1922 was allied with publicity on one hand and psychoanalysis on the other in a much more complicated way than Bernays could have imagined. If it glamorized the unconscious and thus helped to produce the state of bemused complicity that Bernays apparently desired, it also helped to keep the unconscious public and thus exacerbated the reflexivity that makes modern life inherently disorienting. In this way, literature helped to establish a relationship between reason and the unconscious—between the qualities that Dewey called habit and impulse—of complex interdependence. As such different writers as Yezierska and Woolf demonstrate in their works of this year, it was in very large part the new media that were making this reflexivity not just possible but also obvious, yet at the same time the new media were also promising to make it disappear.

3

Tourists in the Age of the World Picture

What every picture, of whatever form, must have in common with reality in order to be able to represent it—rightly or falsely—is the logical form, that is, the form of reality.

Ludwig Wittgenstein, *Tractatus*

SOMETIME IN THE MID-1920S, two creatures were born who have come to be
more commonly recognized than any movie star, politician, or rock musi-
cian. Unfortunately, these creatures cannot be named or described, only depicted, because they were created to circumvent language, with all its inconsistencies and disparities. They are, of course, the male and female silhouettes
visible on public facilities all over the world, symbols first formulated by Otto
Neurath as part of his attempt to create an international pictorial language to
be called Isotype. Neurath, a founding logical positivist, hoped to extend the
concept script of Frege and Wittgenstein into public life by formulating a set
of minimal, logical, and culturally unspecific symbols that would facilitate international communication. By the mid-1930s, he was collaborating with C. K.
Ogden and had translated Ogden's Basic English into Isotype, thus producing
a complete, if limited, system of international pictorial communication.[1]

It does not take a great deal of penetration to see how culturally specific
Neurath's isotypes actually are: the female figure wears a skirt and not, for example, a head scarf. In fact, as Julia Lupton and J. Abbott Miller have pointed
out, the very neutrality of the figures, their "clean, geometric character," was
"loaded with cultural associations —'public,' 'neutral,' 'modern.'"[2] And yet, this
fact in itself means that, however useless the isotypes might be as counters in
some eternal logic, they are quite economical signifiers of certain common
ambitions of the 1920s.

One of these was, of course, Wittgenstein's ambition to perfect a concept script that would contain none of the ambiguities of the natural languages. As Russell puts it in his introduction to the *Tractatus*, "The first requisite of an ideal language would be that there should be one name for every simple, and never the same name for two different simples."[3] But the projects of Neurath and Ogden, which followed and were to some extent inspired by that of Wittgenstein, were also a good deal more practical. The problem Neurath was addressing was that of international communication in a world system larger and more various than any that had ever existed. As Charles Beard put it in lectures delivered at Dartmouth in June 1922: "There is now a web of international relations—trade, finance, and intercourse—so fine in mesh and so tough in fibre that no sword can cut it. The East and the West have met and are one. The world is an economic unit."[4] The truth of Beard's statement at the highest level of generality was exemplified by the series of international conferences that took place in this year at Genoa, Washington, D.C., and Rapallo. These conferences were part of an attempt to establish order at a level of international generality hardly conceivable before the war. Isotype was an attempt to facilitate this new order by providing it with a new and unambiguous language.

That this wider and more complicated world needed a less ambiguous means of public communication was widely recognized. As Lippmann puts it rather wistfully in *Public Opinion*, "If each fact and each relation had a name that was unique, and if everyone had agreed on the names, it would be possible to communicate without misunderstanding."[5] But Lippmann also shows that the need for clear communication is only one reason to desire a neutral and unbiased language. In this newly expanded world, "our opinions cover a bigger space, a longer reach of time, a greater number of things, than we can directly observe,"[6] and therefore we are at the mercy of representations and subject to any distortions those representations might contain. Individuals need a clear and unbiased language not just so that they can communicate in this world, but also so that they can conceptualize it for themselves. As Lippmann realized, the role of that language was being filled in 1922 by pictures: "Photographs have the kind of authority over imagination to-day, which the printed word had yesterday, and the spoken word before that. They seem utterly real. They come, we imagine, directly to us without human meddling, and they are the most effortless food for the mind conceivable."[7] In other words, the photograph was already playing the role Neurath had designed for the isotype. Since it was assumed to speak directly of reality and to a diverse audience without confusion, the photograph became the popular version of Wittgenstein's concept script. Modern, realistic, and international, it seemed the one medium adequate to a various and disorderly postwar world.[8]

Like Neurath's isotypes, the photographs in popular magazines like the *Berliner Illustrirte Zeitung* and the *Illustrated London News* were supposed to help overcome the individual and cultural bias that psychology and anthropology had made so obvious. In utopian projects of this time, such as August Sander's collection of German portraits, photography was presented as if it were a universal language, with which "we can communicate our thoughts, conceptions, and realities to all the people on earth."[9] The means of this universal communication was to be the human physiognomy itself, typologized in a series of portrait photographs that was supposed to include, on its completion, an entire human alphabet. Stripped of its written languages and represented in a medium that seemed to limit cultural bias and individual intention to a minimum, humanity was to constitute its own universal language. Taken in the mass and of the mass, photographs were thus to provide what the world seemed to need most at this moment: a language that exactly and completely mirrored its subject.

In their different ways, then, Sander's photographs and Neurath's isotypes contribute to a more general modern project that Heidegger calls "the conquest of the world as picture."[10] Though Heidegger uses the term *Bild* in a way that is several times removed from the immediacy of an actual picture, it is true, nonetheless, that both isotypes and photographs help to condense, systematize, and universalize a disparate world, the ambition that characterizes modernity for Heidegger. Photography in particular serves "in the annihilation of great distances . . . the setting before us of foreign and remote worlds in their everydayness" that is for Heidegger the project of epistemological conquest at its most immediate and vulgar level.[11] In both cases, pictures allow us to reconstitute the disparate world in apparently concrete terms, to situate and "place" the foreign, to bring objectivity to what seems inherently divided by subjective differences.

Of course, if even Neurath's simplified silhouettes cannot escape the specificities of their condition, how much less so can a photograph, which needs some concrete and particular subject simply to exist? As Lippmann was well aware, it is partly because of photography that the modern world picture is so haphazard and inexact in the first place. And it is also the case that photography is not simply an art or a system of representation but also a system of distribution, of reproduction. As such, according to Walter Benjamin, whatever photography places, it also displaces, for it can bring the foreign and distant close only by separating it from its own place and time, putting a kind of intrinsic difference where it seems to show identity.[12] Thus the photograph both serves and subverts the process of systematization that Heidegger calls *Gebild*. "The fundamental event of the modern age is the conquest of the world as picture"[13] only because that conquest never takes place. Instead of producing a systematic totality, the picture reproduces all the dislocating specificity it was supposed to overcome.

In this way, the picture language promised by photography enacts on a larger and more public stage the same irony that unraveled the picture language proposed by Wittgenstein. Pictures begin to reach a wide audience at a time when psychology, philosophy, and anthropology were beginning to teach the inevitable contingency of any particular point of view. Pictures seemed to overcome that contingency, to bring the distant closer both spatially and conceptually. Every major new medium, in fact, not just photography but also movies and even the radio, came before its early audiences with the claim to be a universal language. But it was precisely the universality of these new media, their global reach, that frustrated their ambitions to uniformity. As photography made it at least theoretically possible for humanity to see itself as a totality, it also made the irreducible variety of human beings all the more difficult to ignore. In the same way, photography's promise to end mediation simply made its audience all the more aware of it. Instead of merging world and picture, the "conquest of the world as picture" made that fatal, inescapable *as* ever more obvious, until awareness of it began to seem the one true universal of the modern period.

The Grand Tour of 1922

In the course of 1922, any number of world-traveling photographers made their contributions to "the conquest of the world as picture." The most famous and successful of these was Robert Flaherty, whose groundbreaking documentary *Nanook of the North* was released in this year, as were films made by Martin Johnson in the New Hebrides. In fact, there were so many such projects that T. A. Barns, who went to the Congo primarily to bring back pictures and films to sell, complained that "the market is flooded with such pictures."[14] Many of these projects are worth investigating (and some will receive greater attention in the next chapter), but there were three world travelers, not themselves photographers, who reveal far more than the professionals could about the place of the photograph in the construction of the world picture.

The three very nearly crossed paths, all at once, on the Indian subcontinent in the early months of 1922. The Prince of Wales, who was on a diplomatic tour of the Far East from October 1921 to June 1922, passed through India just after Lord Northcliffe, the publishing magnate, who declined to extend his stay for fear of upstaging a future sovereign.[15] Northcliffe returned to England, as planned, on February 26, 1922, the same day, coincidentally, that D. H. Lawrence left Naples for Ceylon,[16] where he was to see the Prince at a vast nighttime ceremony replete with elephants, torches, and crowds of obsequious subjects. Actually, the subcontinent was crowded with famous English visitors at this time: E. M. Forster managed to see a bit of the Prince's visit before returning to England, and George Orwell arrived to start his very unsatisfactory tour of duty as a colonial policeman in Burma. But the Prince, Northcliffe, and Lawrence were all on world tours, and each tour bears particularly on the reconstruction of the world as picture. Together, the three tours suggest certain connections among politics, poetry, and the press, each of which had a role in the growing influence of images.

The most elaborate of these trips, the "Oriental Grand Tour" of the Prince of Wales, later to become Edward VIII and then the Duke of Windsor, was the longest-running British news story of 1922 despite the fact that it was also the one most peculiarly devoid of content. Between October 1921 and June 1922, the Prince visited India, Ceylon, the Philippines, Borneo, Malaysia, Japan, and Egypt, inspiring at each stop, along with the appropriate local ceremonies, the same largely unspoken question: why had he come? As E. M. Forster, himself lately returned from India and Egypt, put it in an unsigned commentary in *The Nation and Athenaeum,* "scarcely anyone in India wished the Prince of Wales to come."[17] Forster finally decided that the Prince must have come simply because he wanted to come, but the passage of time and the publication of memoirs have made it abundantly clear that the Prince was himself as bitterly opposed to his trip as everyone on whom he was visited.[18]

What Forster was perhaps simply too sensible to see was how the Prince had been caught up in a process that both exploited and effaced his individual personality. He had long since been designated the "Empire Ambassador," whose particular job it was to travel the globe demonstrating Great Britain's friendly interest in the far-flung countries over which it still ruled.[19] At no time were such demonstrations more important than in 1922, when Ireland had won partial and Egypt qualified independence and India was, after the Amritsar massacre, in its most serious political crisis since the Mutiny. One of the purposes of the Prince's tour, then, was to demonstrate—and by demonstrating reassert—the unity of the Empire. As Basil Maine put it in a book dedicated to commemorating this aspect of the Prince's life, "One immediate result of the Prince's voyages was the re-vivifying of the idea called British Empire with all its attendant ideas, not least the idea that England was a sister country."[20]

The techniques the Prince adopted toward this end seem, at this remove, positively pathetic in their irrelevance: at Benares University, where his visit was boycotted by the students, he was said to have entertained the audience assembled for him by clapping a turban on his head.[21] But this was in fact quite typical of the Prince's tactics. He wore a sombrero in South America, a feathered headdress in Canada, kilts in Scotland, an Australian coalminer's coveralls in Australia. So familiar was the Prince's talent as a quick-change artist, that his most appreciative early biographer presents him virtually as a set of paper dolls with interchangeable costumes.[22] These visually demonstrated the Prince's personal ability to mix "with his fellow men of all races, classes and creeds,"[23] which then signified the human unity of the Empire, in which different races, nationalities, and cultures could be represented mainly by details of dress. Though each individual costume was rigidly stereotyped, and stereotyping, the Prince's ability to wear them all seriatim displayed him as the human norm that made the Empire a unity. Individually, each costume change was supposed to flatter a particular audience; but taken all together, as a group of images, they were to provide visual demonstration of an imperial unity very much in peril at this time.[24]

Indian Chief, "Morning Star." The Prince of Wales, circa 1919.

That the purpose of the Prince's world tour was to justify the Empire by
producing convincing visual representations of it was recognized by the anti-
imperial opposition in India, which then set out to deny him the opportunity.
Gandhi expanded the *hartal*, or Non-Cooperation Campaign, to include the
Prince's visit because, as he said, "I consider that the visit of the Prince of
Wales is a singularly good opportunity to the people to show their disapproval
of the present Government."[25] Recognizing how intimately the struggle for
political self-representation was connected to a struggle of symbolic representation, Gandhi encouraged a boycott of the visit so that Indian crowds
could not be used to demonstrate the fitness of British rule. Thus the Prince's
attempt to display in his own person the unity of the Empire, an Empire in
which India was to be represented by himself in a turban, was frustrated by an
Indian populace that made itself far more noticeable by its absence than it
could have done by its presence.

The controversy that followed, by providing the Prince with an antagonist, made the original purpose of his tour all the more obvious. As the *Illustrated London News* put it, at the bottom of a large picture spread published in February, "The two personalities—the Prince and Gandhi—typify the situation, and it remains to be seen which of the tendencies they represent will in the end prevail."[26] But there were in fact no pictures of Gandhi, who was finally arrested, tried, and imprisoned in March. Instead, the "tendency" he represented was pictured by generic photographs of India's "teeming millions" matched with captions that read like this: "The above photographs indicate something of the endless variety of Indian life, and show some interesting types of the teeming millions among whom insidious propaganda may stir up discontent."[27] Thus dissolved into a myriad, Gandhi in his absence comes to stand for the unrepresentability of India and for the disunity and disorder that are both the cause and the effect of this unrepresentability, while the Prince becomes a focus for the attempt to represent and thus to order the "teeming millions" of the subcontinent. The illustrated press advances this analysis by means of a visual display in which the Prince becomes the center around which the multitudes of India might coalesce into a nation, while the absent and invisible Gandhi represents their dissolution into a heterogeneous mob.

The purpose of the Prince's tour, that is to say, is to establish a figurative relationship between Great Britain and an increasingly various and restive collection of colonies. The theory behind this relationship was enunciated in this same year by Lord Frederick Lugard in *The Dual Mandate in British Tropical Africa*, which was to provide the intellectual underpinnings for British colonial rule between the wars. According to Lugard, continued British rule over its colonial possessions is justified only insofar as Britain represents on one hand the interests of humankind, which he believes has a general right to all the riches of the globe not to be frustrated where the inhabitants of a particular territory are incapable of exploiting them, and on the other the unformed national interests of the colonial peoples.[28] In cases like that of India, which, it was often pointed out, had never been a nation in the European sense of the term, imperial authority represented the national interest against the sectarian claims of various ethnic or religious groups.[29] Thus the claim made implicitly in the *Illustrated London News*, that the Prince actually represents India itself while Gandhi represents something like its very antithesis, is in fact an official claim made elsewhere quite explicitly.[30]

The Prince thus acts out a colonial fantasy that had, at this moment, rather specific political significance. His costumes are up-to-date ceremonial versions of the "Oriental" disguises that British travelers had delighted in since the time of Burton, and his ability to wear them satisfies both romance and policy. The romance was available as well in certain novels of this year, particularly Harry Hervey's wonderfully lurid *Caravans by Night*, which features the improbable Euan Kerth, a British secret agent so adept at Oriental masquerade that he manages to impersonate the Grand Lama of Shingtse-

The Prince in the Uniform of the 35/36 Jacobs Horses, of Which He Is Colonel-in-Chief, Delhi (*The Prince of Wales' Eastern Book*, 1922).

lunpo.[31] Even Edmund Candler's *Abdication*, a far more substantial novel that strongly prefigures Forster's *Passage to India*, ends with its British hero becoming a "a sort of Mahatma" in Tibet after a few months of instruction enables him to become a whiz at treating cataracts.[32] The policy behind the romance is a bit more visible in Candler's novel, for here the British official, in becoming "a sort of Mahatma," is actually able to replace Gandhi, as the Prince does implicitly in the picture spreads of the *Illustrated London News*. And the argument in both cases is similar: the ease with which the British are able to disguise themselves as Orientals signifies their universality as human beings. In contrast, both *Caravans by Night* and *Abdication* feature seriocomic villains who are warped and thwarted by their inability to become convincingly European.[33] The Indian or the Tibetan remain fatally specific, unable to escape cultural conditioning and racial heritage, while the English attain a kind of pan-human divinity.

The photographs of the Prince make the same argument, to some extent simply *as* photographs. To the extent that he can be photographed in so many different contexts while remaining visibly the same, the Prince becomes a living, breathing isotype. He *is* the world as picture, simultaneously given, without apparent contradiction, a particular racial and cultural cast. In contrast, Gandhi remains unpictured because he represents the unpicturable in the Heideggerian sense: whatever cannot be reduced to system and consistency. Under his purported leadership, India is not a nation but a teeming mass of disparate individuals.

Despite the best efforts of official and unofficial propaganda, however, something unpicturable manages to invade the pictures of the Prince as well. One of the most intriguing of these, taken during a tiger hunt in Nepal, is not obviously of the Prince at all.[34] The viewer is inclined to look first at the dead tiger in the foreground and only then to notice that at least half the people in the photograph are looking elsewhere, sideways, apparently at a small, undistinguished figure slumped down on one of the elephants, which only a caption can actually reveal as the Prince. As a ceremonial expression of sovereignty, the photograph seems a dismal failure. There is none of the "English manliness" that was the stock in trade of publications like the *Illustrated London News* in the nineteenth century.[35] Instead, British power is depicted as diffident, reserved, off to one side. If it dominates at all, it does so not through sheer power, which this photograph associates with the animals in the foreground, but by persuasive authority, by commanding attention. In fact, the photograph contrives to show the difference between these two means of domination. There is an almost visible transference of power from the obvious center of the photograph, where the regal Indian beast lies dead, to the periphery, where the Prince sits. The viewer sees not just the object of his or her own gaze, but also the collective gaze itself that crowns the Prince with its attention and in so doing makes this utterly insignificant figure into a monarch.

The Prince's Tiger Shoot, Nepal (*The Prince of Wales' Eastern Book*, 1922).

What the photograph manages to portray, then, is the very authority the Prince attempted to accumulate in the course of his trip, an authority that was not just pictured in but very largely produced by photographs. Though it is clearly a candid, unplanned shot and not one of the ceremonial pictures that graced the *Illustrated London News*, it is not in fact so very different from the more calculated representations of British authority published at this time. For example, *Peoples of All Nations*, a popular ethnographic encyclopedia published by Northcliffe, among whose contributors were both Lord Lugard and Edmund Candler, began its entry on the "British Colonies in Africa" with a large photograph purporting to show colonial authorities bringing law and order to their dominions.[36] But the photograph does not contain any overt expression of dominion. Instead, the British colonial officials are pictured sitting or kneeling and off to one side, not even making eye contact with the African crowd they are apparently directing. Nor is the crowd very obviously grouped around these officials. Instead, they have formed a circle around nothing, much like the Indian assembly in the photograph of the Prince in Nepal. In this case, it seems fairly clear that the photograph is attempting to show what does not yet exist, the African nation, for which British authority is merely the stand-in. The colonial officials are merely the physical representatives of a unity that does not yet exist but which their representations will apparently help to create.

By actually picturing the process of pictorial representation, however, these photographs also manage to reveal the displacement it involves. The photograph of the Prince's tiger hunt dramatizes the distance between the man himself and the symbols of royal authority like the elephants and the tiger skin. Splayed unceremoniously and uncomfortably across his elephant, the Prince is revealed as a rather scared young man, comically small in relation to the huge weight of the ceremony surrounding him. The costume slips, as it were, and the photograph reveals what it must, the particular and the concrete, or, what Roland Barthes calls with accidentally apposite irony, "the sovereign Contingency."[37] On one hand, then, this photograph defeats the larger project of reinventing the Prince as worldwide Everyman by revealing the very particular individual behind the masks. On the other hand, it effaces the Prince altogether, so what we see when we look at the photograph is not a subject but another glance. Our gaze across the emptied-out space of the foreground is reproduced within as the gaze of the crowd across the empty space between them and the Prince, revealing something of the formal and social character of photography.

That empty space is a visual revelation of what Eduardo Cadava calls the "caesura . . . between a photograph and the photographed," the formal difference between a subject and its reproductions.[38] By staking so much on authority created through photographs, the Empire makes itself vulnerable to the inevitable gap in any process of reproduction, a gap that changes from an epistemological issue to a political one whenever people confront the actual

Administrators of Empire at Their Work of Spreading Peace, Law, and Order in Remotest Africa. British colonial officials in Africa (*Peoples of All Nations*, 1922, 1:514).

human celebrity behind the pictures they have seen. But this means that the gap is also the empty space of mechanical reproduction, of an art form that exists only in terms of wide distribution. The photographs taken of the Prince were mass-market photographs, and this photograph stands out in that it shows something of the mass and even of the way in which the Prince's authority comes to depend on that mass. If the crowd fails to look at the Prince, then he becomes essentially invisible, indistinguishable from all the other tourists in topees. The empty space within the photograph reveals the displacement of authority from celebrity to audience, which disperses again what the whole project of picturing was intended to concentrate in one place.

Thus the political version of the world picture comes apart, and the attempt to enlist the illustrated magazines in the work of empire stumbles over one of its favorite stratagems. What we see now in looking back at these photographs is not an unmediated human totality but rather the new form of mediation put in place by such pictures. Of course, our self-conscious awareness of this mediation may be specific to a much later time period. These conflicts, insofar as they are glimpsed in one or two specific photographs, remain intrinsic possibilities, of which the readers of publications like the *Illustrated London News* may never have been aware and by which they may not have been affected. But they did trouble at least one observer of the Prince's tour, and in a way that had ominous consequences for a very different kind of world picture.

The Poet and/as the Prince

When D. H. Lawrence crossed paths with the Prince, he was in the middle of a protracted circumnavigation of the globe that took him from England to Italy and then, via Ceylon and Australia, to the southwest United States and finally back to England. He was drawn to the United States by a project that was, in its way, not so very different from that of the Prince. Mabel Dodge had written to him late in 1921 proposing, in Lawrence's own paraphrase, that "one must somehow bring together the two ends of humanity, our own thin end, and the last dark strand from the previous, pre-white era," and suggesting that Lawrence was the man and Taos the place.[39] This project was but an early example of an ambition that was to become quite general among European and Euro-American intellectuals in the twenties, to such a degree that it has come to seem one of the distinguishing features of English-language modernism.[40] Lawrence himself had been seeking a certain kind of "aboriginal darkness"[41] from his first days in Italy, and for a time he apparently hoped to find it finally in New Mexico. In this case, then, the world tour is itself an attempt to effect a human unity, a project that is both reflected by and discussed in Lawrence's writings of this time.[42]

This search for some kind of link between a "thin" white civilization and its darker and more vital predecessors certainly contributes to the extraordinarily strong reaction Lawrence felt on seeing the Prince at the *pera-hera*, a ceremonial procession of elephants before the temple of the Buddha's tooth in Kandy, staged at the end of March. Lawrence's letters of this period suggest that he saw in the pera-hera ceremony a visual enactment of his own project and that what he saw both stirred and disturbed him. Over and over he sends to his correspondents the same description of the Prince, using the terminology that Mabel Dodge had applied to the whole of the white race: "Poor devil, he is so thin and nervy: all twitchy: and seems worn out and disheartened." Against this virtually invisible wisp of a man, he poses the pera-hera, which he found "wonderful: it was night, and flaming torches of coconut blazing, and the great elephants in their trappings, about a hundred, and the dancers with tom-toms and bagpipes, and half naked and jeweled, then the Kandyan chiefs in their costumes, and more dancers, and more elephants, and more chiefs, and more dancers, so wild and strange and perfectly fascinating, heaving along by the flames of torches in the hot, still, starry night."[43] The very structure of the language tells the tale: the Prince a collection of sentence fragments, the pera-hera a paratactic list in which there is always room for more.

This dichotomy in the letters is nearly the same one that characterized press coverage of the Prince's trip, with the significant difference that Lawrence sensed the Prince's own unhappiness with the ceremonial role assigned him. The poem Lawrence wrote on the occasion is so insistent about this cringing reluctance that it comes to resemble not the propaganda displays in the *Illustrated London News* but the far more unstudied photograph of the tiger hunt in Nepal. In this poem, entitled "Elephant," the Prince is not merely thin but a "pale and dejected fragment" or, even more pointedly, a "tired remnant."[44] Against this tired remnant, Lawrence poses the celebrants in the pera-hera procession, both animal and human (though it would be saying too much to suggest that he makes a very great distinction between them); both are characterized by vastness, in number and in bulk, and ultimately come to be represented by that "dark mountain of blood," the elephant.

In the poem, the Prince is not actually riding one of the elephants, but Lawrence so insistently arranges the two poles of his dichotomy in terms of space that it is easy to forget this fact: "He is royalty, pale and dejected fragment up aloft. / And down below huge homage of shadowy beasts; bare-foot and trunk-lipped in the night." The scene—white man up above, dark beast down below—clearly has an iconic power for Lawrence, who had constructed just such a scene around Gerald Crich in *Women in Love*. In this case, the furious tension between man and animal, mind and body, light and dark acquires a fairly specific political inflection. The Prince plays an important role in the development of the leadership politics that come out more and more clearly in the works between *Kangaroo* and *The Plumed Serpent*. In fact, the Prince reappears, if only in anecdote, in *Kangaroo* as a haggard, nervous man who imagines himself being slowly devoured by tiny white ants.[46] Here he is the object of Lawrence's distant, silent exhortation to rise to his true role and dominate the great panoply spread out before him. Lawrence looks to the Prince to establish a vital relationship between the individual and the crowd, between the European and the Oriental, between consciousness and the body. In his own way, and for his own reasons, Lawrence is asking the Prince to accomplish the very political task for which his trip was designed, to embody the Empire as a human totality.

That he does not, indeed cannot, do so is the tragedy of the poem. Lawrence bitterly mocks the Prince for adopting as his motto the phrase *Ich dien*, "I serve," which turns him, as Lawrence puts it, into a "Drudge to the public." What the public wants and needs, the poem insists instead, is a leader who will demand service to himself. The problem is not just that the proper relationship of leader and led has been spatially upended by the Prince's democratic affectations, but that the very character of the relationship has been fatally altered. The pledge to serve is the politician's pledge to represent his constituents, which is in fact precisely what the Prince had set out to do on his world tour. But Lawrence is looking for a relationship far closer than that of representation, a relationship made in the "hot dark blood" of the elephants, in the "kindled blood" of the "jungle torch-men" who long to pay homage to a ruler. Like his alter ego Richard Lovatt, in *Kangaroo*, Lawrence wants to feel this relationship in "his dark, blood-consciousness . . . as a passional vibration, not as mind-knowledge."[46]

The tragic difference between these two relationships is dramatized by the turn of a single word, as Lawrence describes the disappointment of the crowd:

> and tropical eyes dilated look up
> Inevitably look up
> To the Prince
> To that tired remnant of royalty up there
> Whose motto is *Ich dien*.
>
> As if the homage of the kindled blood of the east
> Went up in wavelets to him, from the breasts and eyes of jungle torch-men,
> And he couldn't take it.

When Lawrence literalizes the dead metaphor "to look up to," he suggests a political failure on the part of the Prince, who seems incapable of anything like an act of sovereignty. The literalization is also ironic, exposing as it does how the Prince's sovereignty has come to depend not on actual power and allegiance, not on "looking up to," but rather on celebrity and publicity, on mere "looking." To "look up to" is not actually to see at all, and it is no accident that servitors, once they have looked up and received the gaze of their superior, usually drop their eyes. But the jungle men of the pera-hera not only see but see through the Prince, and in the course of the poem they acquire a "strange dark laugh in their eyes," which come to seem almost a weapon, like the "lurking eyes" of the elephants.

This distinction between the homage exacted by blood and the mere attention attracted by visual display is a political version of a distinction between the physical and the visual that, as Linda Ruth Williams has shown, was crucial to Lawrence at this time.[47] *Fantasia of the Unconscious*, published in the year in which Lawrence wrote this poem, is a tirade against the visual, against the "mental, visual ideal consciousness" that disrupts the natural, visceral relationship between men and women. Later in the 1920s, Lawrence dramatized this contrast in two poems about spectatorship: "When I Went to the Circus" and "When I Went to the Film."[48] At the film, the audience pretends to feel deep emotion, even though the "black-and-white kisses" up on the screen "could not be felt." As visual images, these kisses are ideal, abstract, unapproachable,

> like being in heaven, which I am sure has a white atmosphere
> upon which shadows of people, pure personalities
> are cast in black and white.

At the circus, the dishonesty of the film relationship haunts the audience, which feels uncomfortable in the presence of "the immediate, physical understanding" that the circus performers have with their animals. Reduced by spectatorship to filmic images themselves, these people "have only their personalities, that are best seen flat, on the film." The awful irony of modern spectatorship is that people trained to consume images can no longer enjoy immediate experience except by instantly reimagining it as an image of itself.

"Elephant" is another such poem about spectatorship, one akin to "When I Went to the Circus" in that an overdeveloped "visual consciousness" disrupts what should be a natural and visceral relationship. One reason Lawrence's poem so closely resembles the photograph taken in Nepal is that Lawrence describes the Prince as if he were a photograph. The Prince's paralysis, in such sharp distinction to the fervid motion all around him, is that of a photographic image. He is pale, wispy, insubstantial because he is not a person at all but a picture of a person. Though we can be certain that Lawrence actually attended the pera-hera and saw the Prince in person, the visual experience he describes is the far more common modern experience of seeing the leader as a distant photographic image, "imponderable and touchless," to quote from "When I Went to the Circus." "Elephant" is in large part a protest against the substitution of that image for direct contact with sovereignty itself. More specifically, the poem associates the attenuated, mediated authority of the photographic image with European modernity, with a society that, like its sovereign, has become a mere remnant of itself, that remnant being the image left behind when the substance has departed.

In other words, Lawrence identifies the self-defeating irony by which the photograph disrupts the universality of the world picture. Photographs can bring together distant things only by separating them from their immediate context, abstracting them, as it were, and investing them with a new and more powerful kind of distance. As Heidegger puts it, "The rushed abolition of all remoteness brings no closeness; for closeness does not consist in the reduction of distance. What is least removed from us in terms of expanse, through the image in film or through sound in radio, can still remain remote."[49] Actually, the irony in "Elephant" is even tighter, since it shows how the habits of visual consciousness can make even the immediate remote by teaching the audience to look at physical spectacle as if it were already rendered and reproduced as an image.

Lawrence ends the poem by stepping into the gap left between image and reality, into the power vacuum left by the reduction of the sovereign to a picture of himself. He begins his progress through the poem by going down, "stepping down the bank, to make way" for a passing elephant, and he ends it, at least in imagination, up above, in the Prince's pavilion, thus righting the spatial imbalance created by the Prince's abdication:

> I wish they had given the three feathers to me;
> That I had been he in the pavilion, as in a pepper-box aloft and alone
> To stand and hold feathers, three feathers above the world,
> And say to them: *Dient Ihr! Dient!*
> *Omnes, vos omnes, servite.*
> *Serve me, I am meet to be served.*
> *Being royal of the gods.*
> And to the elephants:
> *First great beasts of the earth,*
> *A prince has come back to you,*
> *Blood-mountains.*
> *Crook the knee and be glad.*

Lawrence's desire for this position is in a sense self-validating: just as the Prince loses his place because he is so diffident, Lawrence acquires it because he wants it so much. The desire for power answers the desire for subservience in a way that not only need not but should not be argued. But Lawrence's ascent to power is not purely personal. It also depends on an implicit argument for poets over politicians and for poetry over photography.

In other words, the poem itself justifies Lawrence's transformation from pauper into prince not by describing a visceral unity but rather by enacting one. This it does by rhythmically recreating the "passional vibration" that Lawrence opposes to the "mind-knowledge" that comes by way of vision:

> More elephants, tong, tong-tong, loom up,
> Huge, more tassels swinging, more dripping fire of new cocoa-nut cressets
> High, high flambeaux, smoking of the east;
> And scarlet hot embers of torches knocked out of the sockets among bare feet of
>   elephants and men on the path in the dark.
> And devil-dancers luminous with sweat, dancing on to the shudder of drums,

> Tom-toms, weird music of the devil, voices of men from the jungle singing;
> Endless, under the Prince.

Lawrence clearly wants to create, through repetition, a rhythmic analogue of the beat of the tom-tom or the tong-tong of the elephant bells and to make that repetition dynamic by piling up participles such as "dancing" and "singing." Such poetry would have an impact as visceral as the sounds of the pera-hera and would substitute its own "passional vibration" for the unsatisfactory visual image of the Prince. This puts Lawrence in the rather strange position of trying to make language more immediate than photography, when it was the mediacy of language that pictures were supposed to repair in the first place. And it cannot be said, no matter how much the poem comes to depend on sound effects and aural repetition, that it manages to escape the trap of the pictorial.

Where the poem ultimately fails itself is in its inability to imagine a more viable form of communication between sovereign and subject, poet and audience. Though the implication of the ending is that Lawrence manages to communicate to his Ceylonese subjects by means of natural signs, the three feathers of the pera-hera ceremony, he still represents himself as speaking to them, rather comically, in German and Latin. Why this Ceylonese crowd should be stirred by the Prince's German motto or by the Latin injunction *servite* is rather hard to imagine. The Latin in particular shows Lawrence reaching for a form of linguistic authority that can have little meaning in this context. For all Lawrence's efforts to reduce language to pure sound, pure rhythm, the arbitrariness of it as a signifying system reasserts itself.

Rather more damaging, however, is the fact that the Ceylonese subjects are given no way of communicating with their sovereign at all. Their language is represented from time to time, but it is never quoted or transcribed, apparently because Lawrence did not understand it. In order to sense their frustration with the Prince, Lawrence must read their faces, turning "a glint of teeth, and glancing tropical eyes" into signs. But this means that Lawrence is doing to the Ceylonese crowd precisely what he does not want them to do to the Prince, treating them as if they were a picture. And in this case the act of pictorialization seems much more violent, since it reduces a vast crowd of individuals to a few vivid visual details.

This guilty resort to the visual is, as Williams has shown, a common one in Lawrence's novels, in which the reader is often invited to gaze raptly at men in various stages of deep self-absorption.[50] As is the case here, these men are frequently non-European, but even when they are not, their self-involvement makes them paradoxically magnetic to the Lawrentian eye. For it is fairly clear that what makes the non-European attractive to Lawrence is its disinclination to look, its relative lack of awareness of the European world of self-conscious visual display, a quality that is usually rendered in Lawrence's works as "darkness." However, "darkness" in Lawrence does not mean "that which cannot be seen" but rather "that which cannot see," and one of the great paradoxes of his work is that this disinclination to look is so attractive to the eye.[51] What brings Lawrence halfway around the world is a search for this darkness, for a passional life lived in the blood and not in the cerebral cortex or in the eye, and yet when he finds it he can do nothing more than stare.

The reasons for this are partly personal and partly cultural. Lawrence deeply despises what might be called desire at a distance, desire that cannot be passional and immediate, and yet when he feels such desire himself he is rarely able to actualize it. When its object is, as so often it is, other men, residual cultural taboos and personal reticence prevent full expression. There are exceptions, of course, especially the famous massage scene in *Aaron's Rod*, but even such scenes as this seem more about the restraint of desire than its expression. More often, and especially when the desired object is non-European, Lawrence contrives a purely visual expression of desire like the tableaux in which he places Ramon in *The Plumed Serpent*. Simultaneously drawn and repelled by cultural difference, the novelistic eye hovers over its object as if in a kind of trance. In other words, no matter how much Lawrence wishes his characters to meet as pure body, cultural inhibitions and prejudices keep them apart, and thus their relations must resort to the visual.

To link Europe with "aboriginal darkness" was the program of Lawrence's world tour, and it seems fairly clear that this means linking a sick visual consciousness back to a visceral consciousness that has no particular wish to see. This also means finding populations with no connection to the mass distribution of images, populations that have not been turned into audiences. And yet in this desire Lawrence simply reproduces one of the great clichés of twentieth-century spectatorship, which is driven forward by an unresolvable paradox. The desire that drove Flaherty to Canada, Johnson to the New Hebrides, and Lawrence to Ceylon was a desire to find something different, something that escaped the "world picture" as it had come to be constructed. Barns is probably the frankest in confessing this appetite when he compares himself to the "cannibals" he is photographing. Cannibalism, he says, can be traced to "the craving of the semi-human Congo savage (without such a thing as pity in his composition or language) for a change from his insipid vegetable diet and for excitement to break the monotony of his *forest-bound* life, in other words the longing for a 'thrill' which besets even ourselves to this day, good and bad alike, and which is in fact at the root of the general interest taken in cannibals and the wish of my friends to hear about them."[52] In fact, the photographic project seems even more truly cannibalistic than Barns' "cannibals," for it literally consumes that which it seeks: the undocumented, the unphotographed, human behavior so remote in space and in morality that it has never before been recorded by the camera. The camera-eye and the audience it serves are both attracted by what is different, what has not before been photographed, and yet the result of this curiosity is the progressive incorporation of every inch of human experience into the world picture.

Lawrence's world tour thus plays its part in the construction of the world as picture, no matter how much he may disapprove of the reduction of all experience to visual representations. The attraction he feels for the "darkness" that has not yet been photographed is not so different from that of the mass audience he despised; instead, the desire for something outside European experience that drove him around the world is actually what links him most closely to the European public that flocked to the pictures of Flaherty and Johnson. In fact, Lawrence may well have been one of the many thousands who consumed the most elaborate, the most contradictory, and the most revealing reconstruction of the world as picture that appeared in 1922: Lord Northcliffe's *Peoples of All Nations*.[53]

The World Tour and the Pictorial Press

Alfred Harmsworth, Lord Northcliffe, who took his "Oriental Grand Tour" between July 1921 and February 1922, was so utterly synonymous with a particular kind of publishing that it had come to be called the "Northcliffe Press." The part of it he actually owned was very large: through the Amalgamated Press he controlled the *Daily Mail*, the *Daily Mirror*, the *Evening News*, the *Times*, dozens of specialized magazines, and an unending procession of serialized books. But Northcliffe had a profound effect on publishing far beyond the portions of it he actually owned. When he died just a few months after returning from his world tour, he was widely credited with having altered "the mental habit of the nation," bringing to it "an added quickness, a heap of photographic impressions, a mass of unrelated knowledge of not very vital things, and a store of easy-gotten pleasure for hard-working people."[54] He was, more than anyone, responsible for making pictures the medium of national communication.

The whole Northcliffe enterprise had begun with the periodical *Answers*, whose subtitle was "on every subject under the sun."[55] This motto typifies the ambition of the Northcliffe press, which was to construct an empire of information at least as extensive as the British Empire itself.[56] Perhaps the fullest realization of this ambition came in the serialized encyclopedias that were one of Northcliffe's most popular and profitable enterprises. Issued weekly or biweekly in paperbound installments, these "part works" were so successful that, according to J. A. Hammerton, who edited many of them, they had made the word "encyclopedia" synonymous with the word "profit."[57] The *Children's Encyclopedia*, for example, had sold fifty-two million volumes by 1946.[58] The appeal of these encyclopedias was based very largely on their claims of universality: they carried out the Northcliffe program of offering "everything" to "everybody," covering the widest possible range of subject matter in a way designed to appeal to the largest mass audience.[59] *Peoples of All Nations*, which began its fortnightly appearances in the spring of 1922, was one of the most successful of these projects, appropriately enough, since it promised to deliver to its readership nothing less than the entire world.

Such encyclopedias were not just aimed at a mass audience; they were also produced by a collective author. *Peoples of All Nations* justified its claim to be "an anthropological survey of the entire world" in part by enlisting professional anthropologists such as G. Elliott Smith, who provided a rather brisk discussion of the "Distribution of Races" for the final volume. However, the encyclopedia depended more heavily for its opinions of foreign peoples on retired colonial officials like Lord Frederick Lugard and Sir H. H. Johnston, both of whom contributed articles on Africa. In this sense, it expressed a quasi-official view of the world and pursued a political project not very different from that pursued at the same time by the Prince. But the encyclopedia also sought another sort of authority for its views of far-flung places, an authority to which it appealed most openly in a large advertisement for the next Northcliffe project, *Countries of the World*, which was to have been introduced by "The Romance of Travel" by Joseph Conrad. As Richard Curle claimed within the encyclopedia itself, it was Conrad who was the "deepest spiritual interpreter [of] the romance, the heaviness, and the glitter of the East" (*PAN*, 5:3717). To register these aesthetic qualities, the encyclopedia employed a number of popular novelists, several of whom paid specific homage to Conrad either in the encyclopedia, as Curle did, or in their other work, as did Edmund Candler.[60]

As a text, then, *Peoples of All Nations* represents a collaboration of imaginative writing, social science, and politics on a kind of collective world tour, a version of the tours of Lawrence and the Prince broad and general enough to contain them both. However, it was not the text at all but rather the pictures that made *Peoples of All Nations* what it was. By the time the fifth part was issued, the editor was confident enough of success to proclaim it "The Finest Pictorial Work of This Century." It is quite obvious from this and other self-advertisements, and from the general preponderance in the encyclopedia of pictures over text, that the Northcliffe press considered photographs to be the most appropriate means of communicating to a mass audience. But there is also in evidence a faith in pictures *in* the mass, a truly encyclopedic faith that enough pictures of enough subjects must sooner or later reveal humanity in the whole. The encyclopedia is, in other words, the place where photographs come together to make literal what Heidegger calls the world picture. As Samuel Weber puts it, "When such a movement is understood as encompassing the totality of beings as such, the 'world' itself has become a 'picture' whose ultimate function is to establish and confirm the centrality of man as the being capable of depiction."[61] The goal of the pictorial encyclopedia is, in a sense, to remove the scare quotes from around the words "world" and "picture," to make a systematic world totality available in the physical form of an anthology of photographs.[62] And yet it is precisely here, where the world picture becomes concrete and actual, that the photograph lets the encyclopedia down.

Like the other world tours, *Peoples of All Nations* begins by presuming the unity of its subject matter. Virtually the first picture it published was a photographic genealogy deriving three major human races from what it called "Our Ancestral Black" (*PAN*, 1:xi). In this chart, the Negroid, Caucasoid, and Mongoloid are variations of the Australoid, who serves the encyclopedia as stand-in for Stone Age man, allowing him to be photographed. That there are such different variations of the basic racial stock of humankind is attributed by the encyclopedia to a "tribal spirit," an innate "clannishness" that divides humanity into jealous groups and ultimately into different races. In the end, it sees these two forces, which it calls "integration and disruption" (*PAN*, 1:xxiv), as waging incessant war within human society—on the one hand tending toward amalgamation, on the other toward infinite differentiation.

Though the merits of this as an analysis of human society are questionable, it does serve as a very illuminating introduction to the encyclopedia itself, where there is an incessant war between the inclusive and the exclusive, one that reflects to some extent an inconsistency in the encyclopedic form, which both amalgamates and categorizes, to some extent real political confusions within Great Britain about the nature of the Empire, and the peculiar instability of the photographic archive as a repository and communicator of knowledge. All of these inconsistencies can be glimpsed at once in the very title of the encyclopedia, which admits at the outset that "peoples" and "nations" are two very different things. "Nations" form the organizational backbone of the encyclopedia, on which depend its claims to comprehensiveness, since the world can be divided, though not without controversy, into exclusive, nonoverlapping, national units. But "peoples" cannot be so successfully divided, nor in the same ways, so that one term is always taking apart what the other builds up.

This is not to say that the contributors to the encyclopedia do not struggle to amalgamate the two terms and imagine nationality as embodying the character of a particular people. As William Harbutt Dawson puts it in his article on Germany, "Every nation has temperamental qualities peculiar to itself" (*PAN*, 4:2400). The Germans are, he tells us, "a bluff but hearty and kindly people" (*PAN*, 4:2417). The ascription of such personal qualities to the nations of the world is in fact a large part of the task to which the encyclopedia assigns itself, and the attempt to find these qualities often extends to fairly desperate measures. G. E. Mitton tells his readers that it is easy to distinguish between the two major peoples of Ceylon: the Sinhalese "make excellent table servants, and are deft, attentive, and quiet. The Colombo Tamil prefers running in a rickshaw for hire" (*PAN*, 2:1196).

Such monumental smugness might seem insurmountable, and yet the attempt to solidify the abstract notion of national citizenship with the somewhat more concrete and specific materials afforded by racial prejudice fails again and again. The very first entry in the encyclopedia, on what Europe then called Abyssinia, is subtitled "Ethiopia's Strange Mixture of Races." The text attempts to dispel the palpable discomfort of the title by making Ethiopia a special case: "Abyssinian means 'mongrel,'" according to Herbert Vivian, M.A., "and there is hardly on earth a more mixed population" (*PAN*, 1:2). But this attempt to save the category of nation by making Ethiopia the nation of mongrels does not survive even into the next entry, which begins, "Afghanistan, as the name implies, is the country of the Afghan. But who is the Afghan?" (*PAN*, 1:23). That there is no adequate answer to this question does not, however, prevent the encyclopedia from using the category of Afghanistan and, indeed, of the Afghani, who is "daring and brilliant in attack, [but] quickly discouraged in defeat," even if he is merely a political abstraction.

Painful, inept, and offensive equivocations such as these become in fact the rule as the encyclopedia works its way inexorably through the alphabet. Belgium has what Hamilton Fyfe calls "a peculiar makeup," being composed of "two distinct races, the Flemings and the Walloons" (*PAN*, 1:352), but it can hardly be more peculiar than Burma, which, Sir George Scott informs his readers, is largely made up of non-Burmese, including the Taungyos, who are called in a picture caption "Indeterminate People Who Dwell in a Debatable Land" (*PAN*, 2:1070). This at least wears its confusion openly, unlike the ubiquitous Hamilton Fyfe, who delivers a dozen different variations of the formula "In Spain there are several distinct races" (*PAN*, 7:4713). Here, and in all the other instances in which the formula is used, the supposed distinctness of race is called upon to solidify and make concrete the abstract national groupings that might otherwise seem entirely too arbitrary and equivocal, and yet distinctness itself undermines those groupings. Peoples, despite the title of the encyclopedia, are not *of* nations at all but exist in painful contradistinction to them.

What appears here is in part an organizational difficulty of the encyclopedia per se, since encyclopedias are forced by their very form to categorize and subdivide even as they assert that the body of knowledge they transmit possesses some essential unity. This difficulty is liable to strike with particular power at an encyclopedia of peoples and nations since, as Etienne Balibar has said, "the racial theories of the nineteenth and twentieth centuries . . . define communities of language, of descent, of tradition that fail to coincide, as a general rule, with actual nations."[63] But it may also be the case that this particular encyclopedia of peoples and nations, depending as it does so heavily on photographs, suffers from an especially exacerbated form of this difficulty.

Peoples of All Nations sold itself very largely on the implied claim of the photograph to deliver information. As J. A. Hammerton put it in his editorial introduction to the entire set: "Each photograph—and none but direct camera reproductions of actual life appear—has some lesson to teach, either in racial character, native craftsmanship, or custom" (*PAN*, 1:ii). Even in its most limited sense this claim to provide "direct camera reproductions of actual life" must be questioned, however. Some of the photographs accompanying the article on Algeria, for example, are actually French erotic postcards of the

Arab Witchery Unveiled (*Peoples of All Nations*, 1922, 4:2908).

kind recently analyzed in Malek Alloula's *The Colonial Harem*.[64] Beyond that limited sense, the claim to provide pictorial knowledge becomes even more equivocal. There seems to be no sense here, or elsewhere in the encyclopedia, that racial character may be more difficult to capture in a photograph than craftsmanship or custom. Indeed, the captions exude such a breathtaking confidence in the revelatory power of these pictures that the very necessity of captions is called into question. If, for example, the picture of a young Iraqi woman subtitled "Arab Witchery Unveiled" really is "eloquent of the torrid East," one wonders why the caption need be quite so insistent about it. The arbitrariness of such "information" is apparent even within the encyclopedia itself: elsewhere it tells its readers with equal confidence that the "followers of Islam for the most part wear an expression of dreary resignation" (*PAN*, 7: 5011). These examples do more than point out an inconsistency in English racial attitudes toward the Middle East, however. They reveal as well the process by which the photographic encyclopedia makes that inconsistency inconspicuous by enclosing it within another, an inconsistency between the knowledge promised by the encyclopedia and the aesthetic pleasure afforded by the photographs.

This inconsistency becomes most blatant whenever the sanctimonious tone of moral uplift and education runs up against one of the many pictures of bare-breasted maidens. But it does its most powerful work when it does not appear, when the contributors silently elide the difference between aesthetic reaction and ethnographic knowledge. The term "attractive," for example, is used over and over as if it were neutrally descriptive: "This young lady has charms exceptional among women of Kru origin, who are usually very unattractive physically and have lamentable lack of taste in dress" (*PAN*, 5:3323).[65] At times the term is allowed to stand unmodified, as if it needed extenuation no more than it needs argument: "[The Russian character] is vastly more attractive than the Polish character, which is pure Slav" (*PAN*, 6:4269). The value scheme behind this usage is revealed most clearly by the unwittingly eloquent Hamilton Fyfe when he calls the Orkneys "foreign though attractive" (*PAN*, 6:4522). In fact, the whole of the encyclopedia, its thousands of pages and its thousands of photographs, might be summed up in that short phrase, balancing as it does the whole enterprise on the knife edge between prejudicial repulsion and the seductions of the unknown.

Yet the encyclopedia does not quite balance itself, for the heavy stake it has in the attractive, as a work that sold itself primarily by means of pictures, gives that quality a value of its own, one independent of knowledge or other values. The picturable, or the picturesque, to use the term favored by the encyclopedia, becomes a value in itself. Very frequently the contributors use this term to justify putting before their readers scenes or even people who might otherwise seem to an English sensibility quite deplorable. The people of Santo Domingo, for example, seem to Percy F. Martin to have a number of regrettable traits: a "fiery temperament," an inordinate love of "political excitement," a propensity toward extravagance. But taking it all into account he is able to conclude, "At least, they succeed in being a picturesque and an interesting people" (*PAN*, 6:4437). This, in fact, becomes their predominant trait as advertised in the title of their article: "Picturesque Islanders of the Caribbean."

The air of apology with which the picturesque is frequently introduced reveals its potential dangers to the encyclopedia. There is sometimes even a sense of reproach, as the picturesque is disciplined and prevented from interfering with the more important work of prejudicial condemnation: "Content to sit and meditate in their picturesque rags, these Georgians sometimes do not stir from their home all day" (*PAN*, 4:2355). At such times the encyclopedia is perilously close to identifying and repudiating its own most powerful source of appeal. The "resident white population" of Hong Kong, we are told by another caption, is attracted to the Dragon Boat Festival by its "fantastic gaudiness, its oddity, and garish freakishness" (*PAN*, 2:844). The caption seems almost to be trying to inoculate its audience against the power of the picture, and in its uneasiness it reveals the power of the picture to present as interesting or attractive precisely the difference that the text is so insistently disparaging.

It is not so much that pictures of attractive foreigners undermine a project devoted to displaying British superiority as that the installation of the

Where Women Work and Men Are Idle. Georgians in their "picturesque rags" (*Peoples of All Nations*, 1922, 4:2355).

picturesque as a value in and of itself makes the organization of the world into abstract categories a good deal more difficult. Thus the encyclopedia is constantly pulled in two different directions: toward the abstract, rationalized categories that are its official reason for being and also toward the odd, the contingent, the peculiar, which provide its chief source of visual attraction.

The picturesque thus threatens the encyclopedic project in a very fundamental way, for it is quite obvious that the nation is not picturesque. Since it is an abstract grouping of rather different peoples, it frustrates the encyclopedic eye in its attempts to visualize its own categories. One caption calls a very distant bird's-eye view of a crowd facing well away from the camera "a unique photograph of a typically Bolivian group at La Paz, in which Spaniards, Cholos, and Indians are indiscriminately mixed" (*PAN*, 1:469). Here the encyclopedia attempts to imagine for its readers, as it so often does, the typical state of an indiscriminate mixture, and yet the logical conflict pales beside the visual difficulty of picking from the crowd distinct racial types while simultaneously mixing them together. If this is difficult where crowds are concerned, however, it proves positively painful in the case of individuals: "Racial traits in the Hollanders do not leap pure to the stranger's eye. . . . Nevertheless, some such . . . types, much mixed and with many foreign additions, do visibly enough survive" (*PAN*, 5:3613). "Visibly enough" for what? The dependence of the encyclopedia on the picturesque emerges here almost as if it were a guilty secret.[66]

This guilty secret is on one level the simple inconsistency of peoples and nations, which the encyclopedia struggles mightily to compose and which its chosen medium, the photograph, forces it unwillingly to acknowledge. But there is a more fundamental inconsistency as well between the picturesque, which favors the exceptional, and the encyclopedic project, which is busy slotting things away in its epistemological grid. The project of the world picture is, as Samuel Weber has insisted, to *place*, and yet "the more technology seeks to put things in their proper places, the less proper those places turn out to be, the more displaceable everything becomes and the more frenetic becomes the effort to reassert the propriety of place as such."[67] The photograph, which is supposed to offer concrete evidence of the truth of categories, continually disrupts those very categories with evidence of the specific, the accidental, and the exceptional.[68]

If this is true of the world picture as it is depicted by the encyclopedia, it is even more true of the world picture that the encyclopedia seeks to constitute in the form of its mass audience. Photography is the favored medium of the whole Northcliffe enterprise in part because of a naive belief that it speaks more successfully to a new mass audience because it speaks directly. The encyclopedia makes without irony the claim about photographs that Lippmann paraphrased in *Public Opinion*: "They come, we imagine, directly to us without human meddling, and they are the most effortless food for the imagination possible."[69] Implicit in this naive faith is the further belief that the photograph speaks uniformly to its audience, that since it works without mediation it works identically for every viewer. And surely this is the assumption behind all those captions that so coolly presume that every English reader of 1922, from Austen Chamberlain to Virginia Woolf, will share in their prejudices.[70] In other words, this sort of photographic enterprise presumes for its audience the same congruency of peoples and nation that it pretends to show in its subjects.

Audience and subject become one, it would seem, when the encyclopedia inevitably turns its attention to England itself. In this case, the problem of peoples and nations is handled with amazing dispatch: though the English are

Public Curiosity in the Capital of Bolivia at the Execution of a Military Officer. A "typically Bolivian group" (*Peoples of All Nations*, 1922, 1:469).

descended from "Norman and Saxon and Dane," these "had the same general characteristics, which are the characteristics of the English people" (*PAN*, 3:1763). The related problem of the dispersal of the English around the globe is similarly dismissed: the Canadians, the New Zealanders, the South Africans, the Australians all turn out to be more English than the English themselves. And it is relatively easy to specify what that Englishness consists of: "a spacious, comfortable life; it speaks in a slow, masterful way, with an accent of cultivation" (*PAN*, 7:4678). True English life, that is to say, is countrified, class based, and possessed of a traditional, if undefinable, culture. It should be no surprise, then, that of the 244 photographs accompanying the article on England, ninety-two are of field and/or cottage, a category rivaled only by organized sport, which occupies another forty-four photographs. In contrast, there are only twelve photographs including any kind of wheeled transport. At times there is a disparity between text and photograph so pronounced as to seem strategic. The section entitled "The 'Classes' & the 'Masses'" includes a good deal of commentary on social change, culminating in a rather stern discussion of "what might almost be called a Third Sex. This was made up of women who, foreseeing no probability of marriage to provide them with interest and occupation, either worked for a living or threw their energies into work of a social or charitable kind" (*PAN*, 3:1891).[71] Far from including any photographs of such women, however, the article concludes with thirteen pictures of cottage life, many of them with female subjects in poses of picturesque drudgery.

This contradiction between text and photograph is nothing, however, in comparison to the contradiction inherent in the photograph itself. In its desire for the picturesque, the photograph systematically occludes its own conditions of existence. For a work that prided itself on being up-to-date in its information and its methods, a work that also frequently criticizes the backwardness of the people it depicts, *Peoples of All Nations* is surprisingly hostile to the modern. The opinion voiced by Dawson in his article on Germany is quite general among the contributors: "There is far more real character in the rural districts of any country than in the towns, where all the influences of modern life favour conventionality and tend to reduce mankind to a dead level of uniformity" (*PAN*, 4:2423). This is why there are so few urban scenes in the encyclopedia, why one feels, on looking through it, that the camera, a machine itself, is somehow incapable of capturing other machines. Even when there are a good many urban scenes, as there are in the entries on the Soviet Union and the United States, the text steers the reader toward the rural. The large tinted section at the center of the Soviet Union entry, for example, is called "Real Russia: The Land of the Mouziks" (*PAN*, 6:4297). Beyond the nation, in other words, there lies a category even less picturesque because it is even more general, that of industrialized modernity.

Peoples of All Nations was produced, bought, and read in a urban industrialized world that its contributors deem inauthentic and that its photographers shun. Thus the most egregious gap between people and nation appears within the encyclopedia itself, for the articles and photographs claim that England is ethnically and culturally cohesive, close to the land, and steeped in tradition, while the whole project of the encyclopedia is unimaginable outside the conditions of urban mass production and distribution. The mass audience that bought *Peoples of All Nations* was, it seems, no more "picturable" than the Indian crowds that followed Gandhi. If, as Benjamin famously asserts, the photograph offers the mass a chance to see itself, it is also true, as Cadava puts it, that "the gaze the mass directs at itself can only miss its target."[72] This is true because what makes the mass a mass is not a visual quality such as similarity but rather the structural quality of occupying a particular position in the system of manufacturing and distribution. Unlike physiognomy or costume, class difference is, in the words of Sabine Hake, "inaccessible to the camera."[73]

In the case of the photographs themselves, what is fundamental to the mass market is not any aesthetic quality inherent in them but rather the facility with which they can be reproduced. By so assiduously focusing on the premodern, however, the photographers of *Peoples of All Nations* associate their medium with that which is unique, organic, and natural, almost as if such subject matter could overcome the fundamental nature of the medium. As a whole, the encyclopedia applies the same process of mystification, systematically replacing the miscellaneous urban audience that bought it with a picture of humanity unified by particular ties of blood or culture. As a mass-market encyclopedia, *Peoples of All Nations* thus becomes its own antithesis.

To some extent the conditions that the photographs try to obscure are still visible, even palpable, in particular copies of the encyclopedia. Because it was printed and sold biweekly in paper-covered installments, readers were left to compile the whole encyclopedia themselves. Obviously, only those copies that were bound have survived; most must have disintegrated to pulp in attics or dustbins. But even the bound copies differ from one another: some have the original paper covers; some do not; some are missing pages or whole sections, very often those with revealing pictures of native maidens. The encyclopedia was dependent on its readers for its final state of encyclopedic completion, and the evidence suggests that this ideal unity was often rather severely compromised. There must have been quite a few readers who missed sections altogether, whose enthusiasm waned as the encyclopedia wound its way through the alphabet and who ended up with an incomplete version of the globe on their shelves. Usually surviving copies of the encyclopedia contain a certain amount of advertising for other Northcliffe projects, and this too reveals how the encyclopedia is a creature of a market economy. In short, what the articles and photographs disdain is still evident in the encyclopedia, whose attempt to make the entirety of humankind visible as a whole is disrupted by the very conditions of mass reproduction and distribution that make it feasible in the first place.

Here, in the incompletion of the surviving versions of the encyclopedia, the reality behind the world picture finally reveals itself. For it certainly is the case that there was, as of 1922, a world unity unimaginable in earlier times: the mere presence of Lawrence, Northcliffe, and the Prince of Wales on the Indian subcontinent at the same time signifies how small the world had already become. And this world unity is certainly fostered by pictures, which were already so ubiquitous that Lawrence found their logic at work even in Ceylon. But the unity thus made is not based on what Nelson Rockefeller called, apropos of the infamous Family of Man exhibition, "the essential unity of human experience," nor is it the natural expression of an unmediated sign system. The world unity that Lawrence found so inescapable is not actually made by pictures themselves at all but rather by their distribution. As Alan Sekula has put it, "The worldliness of photography is the outcome, not of any immanent universality of meaning, but of a project of global domination. The language of the imperial centers is imposed, both forcefully and seductively, upon the peripheries."[74] The collective experience behind this world unity is, as Arjun Appadurai has said, not that of face-to-face contact nor of subjection to a particular authority nor of participation in particular religions or political systems, but rather that of sharing the same imaginative experience as spread by the reproduction of words, sounds, and pictures.[75] But this also means that this "worldliness" does not offer what Lawrence, Northcliffe, and the Prince were all looking for in their world tours: uniformity. The distribution of reproduced images makes a world unity that is ubiquitous without being uniform or self-similar, and this is at once what makes photographs such frustrating instruments of domination in the hands of Northcliffe and the Prince and what makes them much stronger works of art than Lawrence seems to have imagined.

Cutting up the World Picture

Lawrence's hatred and distrust of the mass market image was hardly unique in the 1920s. According to Siegfried Kracauer, writing in 1927, "the invention of illustrated magazines is one of the most powerful means of organizing a strike against understanding."[76] The early twenties was also, however, the heyday of photomontage, most of the materials for which came from the very magazines Kracauer despised. In 1922 photomontage was the preferred form of Berlin dada, of Alexander Rodchenko in Russia, and of Max Ernst. In each case, the raw materials came from mass-produced sources. For example, Hannah Höch, whose *Dada Dance* dates to 1922, worked for Ullstein Verlag, Germany's largest mass-market publisher, and the vast majority of the pictures in her photomontages from the twenties and thirties came from its publications.[77] In 1934 Höch commented on the coincidental appearance of photomontage in France, Germany, Russia, and Switzerland and attributed it to film and mass-market photographs, which were already being rearranged and recombined in the popular press.[78]

Cut from their original contexts, combined with other images at different angles and in different scales, juxtaposed to type in the form of billboards, slogans, and bits of ad copy, these photographs "began to *signify*," to quote Louis Aragon on the work of John Heartfield.[79] In one way, the photomontage seems at the furthest remove from the utter rationalization of the encyclopedia. What the encyclopedia tries to systematize and define, the photomontage confuses. The encyclopedia also aspires to a certain invisibility in its chosen medium: the photograph is supposed to be a language that communicates without effort. The photomontage makes the linguistic qualities of the photograph reappear, sometimes by combining it with lettering, sometimes by constructing a kind of rebus that seems to demand interpretation. In this way, it might be said that the photomontage brings back into the photograph the significance the encyclopedia tries to occlude.[80]

It would not be fair, however, to think of the photomontage as merely an extremist experiment. Höch's works frequently began in the scrapbooks she kept, like the scrapbooks kept by many other readers of mass-market publications, perhaps even those now-unknown readers who clipped pictures from *Peoples of All Nations*.[81] These scrapbooks rearrange the periodicals she bought, but they also reproduce the ordinary way in which pictures impinge on a modern consciousness. Even the experience of looking at a completed photomontage is closer to everyday experience in a media age than is flipping through the encyclopedia, for it is a simple fact that images do not come to us in logical array but rather confused and intermingled with other images. For this reason, it might be said that the mass-market photograph is not the concrete expression of what Heidegger calls the world picture but rather its virtual antithesis. As images actually come to us, they disarrange and break down the very project of unified and unmediated seeing that photography as a category sometimes promises. The promise of direct communication held out by *the* image can never be carried over to images in the mass or for the mass, for combination and reproduction reintroduce all the variability that unmediated eyesight was supposed to eliminate.

Living in this world of mass-market images was a repellent experience for Lawrence, as it apparently was for other modernists such as Pound, whose most positive comments on photography and film are filled with grudging qualifications.[82] But other modern writers seem to have followed, as far as the limitations of language would allow, the same practice as Höch, clipping images from the incessant supply and rearranging them as art. William Carlos Williams, for example, took a 1921 news photo from the *New York Tribune* and made it into a poem entitled "Picture Showing":

> Picture showing
> return of bodies
> ZR-2 victims.[83]

The clipped, compact, discontinuous nature of the language here, the very fact that the poem begins, progresses, and ends without any of the usual framing devices of literature, the whole aesthetic of the poem, in short, seems to have been taken over from the news photograph. The real subject of the poem, as the title and first line indicate, is not the subject of the photograph but rather photography's ways of showing, and particularly the oddly intrusive and disruptive way that pictures insert themselves into everyday life. Here Williams becomes conscious of the picture as a picture, of the distanciation created even as the medium brings things closer, and he seems to take it as a model for a poetry that would make its own devices disorientingly obvious.

What can such examples suggest about the other literature of 1922, especially those hugely influential works that Franco Moretti has called "world texts"? If, as Moretti suggests, a world text is inherently encyclopedic,[84] then wouldn't it be implicated in the project of objectification and systematization that Heidegger criticizes under the name of the world picture? On the other hand, *Ulysses* and *The Waste Land* both seem as devoted to montage as the dadaists. The difficulty here is obviously one of the most basic of those facing critics of modern literature, and there seem to be as many potential solutions as there are critics. Is modern literature to be seen as attempting to restore some of the immediacy that mechanical reproduction had stolen from experience and some of the organic unity that industrialism had qualified, or is it to be seen along with dada as a play on the artificial mediation so prominent in modern life? After so much essentially inconclusive dispute on these questions, it might seem worthwhile to go back to the beginning, to see what reasonable and unreasonable observers of 1922 might have thought about the relationship between the literature of the time and the new mass media, for photography was but one of the art forms offering itself as a universal language in this year.

4

Across the Great Divide

ONE OF THE MOST significant cultural events of 1922 took place some time late in the year outside the Winter Garden in New York. There, Gilbert Seldes, managing editor of *The Dial* and frequent contributor to *Vanity Fair*, among other magazines and journals, announced his new writing project to a somewhat incredulous audience of two.[1] Though his first audience was skeptical, the project, published in 1924 as *The Seven Lively Arts*, was a success, so much so that it is remembered even today as "the first sustained examination and defense of American popular culture."[2] It seems fairly safe to say, in fact, that before *The Seven Lively Arts*, American popular culture received no such examination and defense because it was not even recognized as a possible field of criticism. Writing about the movies, vaudeville, popular music, musical comedy, newspaper columns, and the comics together in one place gave these ephemeral forms of art a collective weight that helped to counterbalance critical prejudice against them. So when Seldes announced his new book project, he was announcing the birth of "American popular culture" as a critical category, as a concept independent, to some extent, of its individual constituents.

His announcement is significant for another reason as well, for at that same moment Seldes was intimately involved in another publishing project, which was to have an influence far greater and seemingly very different in character from his own. This project was *The Waste Land*, which *The Dial*, after protracted negotiations, published in November.[3] Seldes had been heavily in-

140

volved in those negotiations, in the course of which the editors of *The Dial* agreed to give Eliot their 1922 award for outstanding service to American letters, and he was certainly the very first critic to acclaim the poem as the quintessential example of literary modernism. Making use of his privileged position as editor, Seldes inserted into an unrelated article of his own in the very issue that contained *The Waste Land* the opinion that it was, along with *Ulysses*, a "complete expression of the spirit which will be 'modern' for the next generation."[4] Seldes was also one of the first to publish a formal review of the poem. His essay in the December 6 issue of *The Nation* appeared about the same time as Edmund Wilson's famous explanation in the December issue of *The Dial* and was more acceptable to Eliot himself.[5] It is safe to say, then, that Seldes' role in the nearly instantaneous canonization of *The Waste Land* is unique, since he was the only one involved in the extensive private negotiations that brought it to *The Dial* who also helped to shape public perception of it after publication.[6]

If it now seems somewhat remarkable that the same person who made American popular culture a legitimate object of criticism also played a central role in formulating the public definition of literary modernism, and that he should have done these two things at exactly the same time, it is because antipathy to popular culture has become, over the years, an indispensable part of accepted definitions of modernism. At first the line was drawn as a cordon sanitaire around the great works of aesthetic modernism by their critical advocates, disciples of Eliot like Clement Greenberg, whose famous essay "Avant-Garde and Kitsch" begins by insisting that though "the same civilization produces simultaneously two such different things as a poem by T. S. Eliot and a Tin Pan Alley song," there is in fact no essential connection between them.[7] As Greenberg became the ritualistic straw man of postmodernism, the distinction he had drawn became a "great divide," though it was now the previously canonized works of modernism that were on the far side.[8]

The one thing that Greenberg and his critics might agree on is that someone like Gilbert Seldes, who wrote appreciatively about T. S. Eliot *and* Tin Pan Alley songs, should not have existed. Of course, the important fact is not simply that Seldes, like Eliot and Joyce, for that matter, personally *liked* Tin Pan Alley songs and movies and comic strips, nor even that Seldes himself saw interesting and significant connections between these seemingly different varieties of cultural production.[9] Rather, his career demonstrates the larger social and cultural connections between popular culture and literary modernism at the moment when both emerged as distinct entities in the public consciousness.

Modernism and popular culture are natural associates in Seldes' writing at least in part because they were commonly associated in the cultural controversies of the early 1920s. Modernist experiment in the arts was seen by its critics as part of a larger cultural change in which public life and private consciousness came to be dominated by representations, by images in the wide and generally pejorative sense of the term. Criticism of this change concentrated its fire on the movies, but it spread out as well to include popular music and new literature. Some writers rejected the association, but others, including Seldes, embraced it and in so doing suggested that modern literature and popular culture shared something more fundamental than a common enemy.

Popular Culture and the Young Intellectuals

The Seven Lively Arts began as Seldes' contribution to an intergenerational controversy that had been developing since the publication of Harold Stearns' *America and the Young Intellectuals* in 1921. Stearns' book made "the young intellectuals" at once a catchword and an inviting target for older intellectuals like Brander Matthews, who held forth in the *New York Times Book Review* on the "juvenile highbrows."[10] Though Stearns had meant to focus attention on America by advertising the discontent of its young intellectuals, he succeeded instead in making youthful discontent itself the subject of scrutiny.[11] In time, this youthful failing acquired a name, and that name was "modernism." As Joel Spingarn explained it in a manifesto entitled "The Younger Generation," modernism "is a disease of our own time, confined to a somewhat narrow and unorganized but very articulate group." It is "a disease of the intellectualist who strives to make up for his artistic emptiness by the purely intellectual creation of 'new forms,'" one that subjects both ideas and art to the sole test of "modernity."[12]

Spingarn's attack recapitulates a critique at least as old as the avant-garde itself. As early as 1909, conservative commentary in France had zeroed in on what Camille Mauclair called "The Prejudice of Novelty in Modern Art." Like Spingarn, Mauclair sees novelty as an empty, self-justifying value that threatens to displace all other motives in art: "*Faire nouveau* is the entire program."[13] Worse yet, the emphasis on novelty associates art with other modern developments that have made the new the sole virtue of society at large. Art joins advertising, publicity, and fashion in ceaselessly overturning the old simply so that something new might be sold.

Spingarn's quarrel with the younger generation, with several of whom he had close intellectual ties, was actually rather a mild one; nor was he, politically a liberal, entirely averse to change.[14] But his attack on "the prejudice of novelty" was echoed by such virulently reactionary writers as Lothrop Stoddard, whose 1922 volume *The Revolt Against Civilization: The Menace of the Under Man* included a diatribe against the "spirit of feverish, and essentially planless, unrest [that] has been bursting forth for the past two decades in every field of art and letters." In Stoddard's view, the only aim of the new literature is novelty, and the result is the withering away of every other characteristic: "Structure, grammer [*sic*], metre, rhyme—all are defied. Rational meanings are carefully avoided, a senseless conglomeration of words being apparently sought after as an end in itself. Here, obviously, the revolt against form is well-nigh complete. The only step which seemingly now remains to be taken is to abolish language, and have 'poems without words.'"[15]

The real threat of this mindless emphasis on novelty comes from the way it reinforces other tendencies in society. For Stoddard the "'new' art" and the "'new' poetry" are simply "one more phase of the world-wide *revolt against civilization* by the unadaptable, inferior, and degenerate elements, seeking to smash the irksome framework of modern society, and revert to the congenial levels of chaotic barbarism or savagery."[16] By the same logic, modernism in the arts could be associated with the revolt of a racial or ethnic underclass, as Royal Cortissoz did when he called modernism "Ellis Island Art," or with the demands of newly enfranchised women, as the *New York Times* did when it mocked the young intellectuals as "intellectual and artistic flappers."[17]

This last sally was in fact aimed directly, and by name, at Gilbert Seldes and *The Dial*. The tactic behind it—to demean the modern by impugning its manhood and to trivialize modernism in the arts by associating it with jazz and gin—is brutally clear, and it was effective enough to give the phrase "artistic flappers" a certain currency in the middle of 1922. Albert Jay Nock repeated it in *The Freeman* in a defense so drenched in crocodile tears it was more offensive than an outright attack. This prompted a bitter retort in the September issue of *Vanity Fair* from Paul Rosenfeld, who set out, armored in self-righteousness, to show that T. S. Eliot, Ezra Pound, Sherwood Anderson, William Carlos Williams, and Georgia O'Keefe, among others, were *not* "intellectual and artistic flappers." The whole shallow and petulant exchange is still of interest because it shows how early modernism began, long before Clement Greenberg, to distance itself from the social changes of modernity and from the sort of popular culture implied by the term "flapper" in response to attacks on its legitimacy from established intellectual authorities. Rosenfeld in fact makes exactly the sort of case *for* modernism that critics nowadays make against it: Eliot "steeps himself of will in the Elizabethans"; Pound is "the transmitter of old English, old French, old Chinese poems"; and modernism is distinguished from flapperism by a calculated slap at "the genus of Edna Ferber."[18]

Thus Rosenfeld manages witlessly to confirm the very prejudices he set out to attack, and in so doing he helps to produce a version of modernism carefully separated from those new social forces that were so alarming to Lothrop Stoddard. But this was not the only version of modernism current in 1922, for the actual object of these attacks, the intellectual and artistic flapper himself, took a very different course. In these same months, Seldes was writing and publishing the first articles that would go into *The Seven Lively Arts*, and these carried on the war against the elders not by repudiating the imputed association with popular culture but rather by embracing it. In the same issue of *Vanity Fair* in which Rosenfeld trumpeted the debt of Eliot and Pound to Dante, Seldes wrote this on the antipathy of the genteel for slapstick: "For us to appreciate slap-stick may require a revolution in our way of looking at the arts;

having taken thought on how we now look at the arts, I suggest that the revolution is not entirely undesirable."[19] Thus Seldes accepts the challenge that Rosenfeld ducks, gladly admitting the one incontrovertible social fact revealed by this whole exchange: the revolution modernism was to make in the arts and the one being made by American popular culture were inextricably associated.

The force of this association was most obvious, perhaps, in the case of popular music, dominated at this time by an up-tempo derivation of ragtime that most everyone called jazz. During the months in which Spingarn, Nock, and *The Times* were putting Seldes on public trial for flagrant flapperism, *Vanity Fair* carried two humorous pieces on the current trials of jazz. Both of these poked fun at a play that had opened on Broadway in January and which epitomized the anti-jazz crusade of the time: J. Hartley Manners' *The National Anthem*.[20] Manners' attack on jazz as "modern civilization's saturnalia" seemed patently ridiculous to the sophisticates at *Vanity Fair*, but, according to Bruce Bliven, it was convincing enough to the audiences that came in from the suburbs to see it to help make jazz "a burning issue."[21] In October, New York City became the first of at least sixty communities to ban or regulate jazz in the course of the 1920s.[22]

In the play itself, the chief danger of jazz seems to lie in the occasions it offers for drinking and sensuality. It answers in the affirmative the question posed by *The Ladies' Home Journal* late in 1921: "Does Jazz Put the Sin in Syncopation?"[23] It is only too inevitable, however, given the nature of the time, that this surrender of the mind and will to the lower passions would also have been presented in racial terms. Manners did this in his introduction to the play, which remarks in horror how "the sexes mingle in degrading embrace to tunes the Indian and the Negro would despise," as did Laurette Taylor, his wife and the star of *The National Anthem*, in interviews she gave while the play was running.[24] The play thus echoes the argument of Stoddard's *Revolt Against Civilization*, in which the revolt of the passions against the intellect, of the dark races against the white, are mere versions of a general upending of the traditional hierarchy of values. Thus, the heavy irony of the title of Manners' play implies that jazz fanatics commit the ultimate irreverence of treason. This switch of allegiance from *The Star Spangled Banner* to a jazz tune could only take place, Manners claims in his introduction, in a time utterly severed from its own past, a time in which youth has prematurely supplanted experience and the only value is the new and up-to-date.[25]

Jazz was most threatening, in this analysis, as a species of modernism, as part of the coming reign of mere novelty, and thus the controversies about it overlap with and echo the controversies surrounding the "young intellectuals." In fact, it became relatively common in the course of the twenties to compare modern literature and jazz in terms unfavorable to both: "Jazz is to real music exactly what most of the 'new poetry,' so-called, is to real poetry. Both are without the structure and form essential to music and poetry alike, and both are the products, not of innovators, but of incompetents."[26] Readers across

America and Great Britain were made aware of something called "jazz literature," which, like "jazz music," is, according to the *Times*, "the product of an untrained mind."[27]

The most specific and the most negative such comparison was offered in 1922 by Clive Bell. In "Plus de jazz" Bell advanced two interdependent and equally questionable assertions: that jazz was dead and that its passing had spared a whole group of promising young writers and artists, including Eliot, Joyce, and Woolf, over whom its influence had been alarmingly strong. Eliot, "about the best of our living poets," according to Bell, is "as much a product of the Jazz movement as so good an artist can be of any," and yet the influence of jazz has produced in his poetry "a ragtime literature which flouts traditional rhythms and sequences and grammar and logic." In prose, James Joyce, a far less significant writer, in Bell's opinion, also "rags the literary instrument," "throwing overboard sequence, syntax, and, indeed, most of those conventions which men habitually employ for the exchange of precise ideas." Even Virginia Woolf, in her more recent work, had begun to flirt dangerously with techniques that Bell darkly and inexactly terms "syncopation."[28]

As the diatribe goes on, it becomes clear that it is not so much jazz that bothers Bell as it is jazzing. As Paul Whiteman explained in his far from definitive work on the subject, jazz has been "variously a verb and a noun."[29] As a verb, it was commonly explained at this time, jazz was nothing more than a manner or method of playing, a stylistic treatment that might be applied to any composition. In this it follows the word *rag*, which can also be either noun or verb. To jazz is the same as to rag: in Whiteman's words, "one threw the rhythm out of joint making syncopation."[30] In fact, one of the most popular forms of this practice was "jazzing the classics," a phrase that the *Oxford English Dictionary* first finds in Carl Sandburg's *Slabs of the Sunburnt West*, published in 1922.

"Jazzing the classics," as sophomoric as it may sound, is exactly the aspect of literary modernism that Bell found most objectionable. In his essay he speaks quite feelingly against the "impudence which rags." He seems almost viscerally revolted by the "jeers and grimaces" of jazz mockery, by the idea that "Lycidas" and the Sistine Chapel might come under criticism from "the coloured gentleman who leads the band at the Savoy." As a practice of impudent parody, jazz threatens to upend a whole system of value, to demolish the basic principle "that one idea or emotion can be more important or significant than another." And this is the danger he finds in the new writers as well, especially in Eliot, whom he calls "irreverent" and "impudent" and whom he accuses of "playing the devil with the instrument of Shakespeare and Milton."[31]

What is most remarkable about this indictment is that it is not aimed at *The Waste Land*, which did have in it at least one reference to ragtime, because that poem was not finished at the time Bell wrote. In his attack on Eliot's literary impudence, Bell apparently has in mind the rather severe satirical exercises of

Ara Vos Prec.[32] It is not jazz as a subject, as a noun, that concerns him, but jazz as a verb, as an insubordinate activity that might be discerned in poems with no overt musical reference at all. Yet the formal similarities between modernist literary experiments and the improvisations of jazz alarm him because of the social significance he attaches to both. Like Stoddard and Manners, Bell sees jazz as an attack from below on the hierarchy of values that sustains the current social hierarchy. It is, in a sense, the notion of popular culture in and of itself that outrages him, insofar as it lends legitimacy to social practices that had always kept a respectful distance from art. To protect art from such incursions, to keep Shakespeare and Milton segregated from "the coloured gentleman who leads the band at the Savoy," is Bell's purpose in "Plus de Jazz," as it is in all the writings contained in *Since Cézanne*, and in this effort he found modernist literature not an ally but a deadly enemy.

"Plus de Jazz" was greeted with predictable impudence by the younger American writers, not because they rejected the jazz comparison as far-fetched but rather because it seemed so natural as to be an innocuous commonplace. Harold Loeb's lofty sarcasm in the September issue of *Broom* is hardly surprising considering that the magazine would soon advertise "THE JAZZ BAND" as one of the models for the literature it hoped to print.[33] Once *The Waste Land* appeared in October, comparison of the new poem to jazz became almost ritualistic. In his influential review, Edmund Wilson noted how the language of *The Waste Land* turned "suddenly and shockingly into the jazz of the music-halls." John McClure called Eliot's poem "the agonized outcry of a sensitive romanticist drowning in a sea of jazz." And finally Burton Rascoe, writing in the *New York Herald Tribune*, called Eliot "poet laureate and elegist of the jazz age."[34]

Two longer and more thoughtful responses to Bell's attack showed, once again, how the early proponents of modernism would diverge in their defenses of the new art. John Peale Bishop, writing in the October 1924 issue of *Vanity Fair*, tended to agree with Bell about jazz, and thus he defended Eliot by raising him above it, arguing that in his work jazz had achieved "a tragic intensity."[35] But Seldes, who responded in the August 1923 issue of *The Dial*, gave his article the title "Toujours Jazz" to show how basically he disagreed with Bell, not just about Eliot and not just about jazz but also about the implications of connecting them. By this time, Bell and Seldes had become fast friends, and Bell is in fact an important silent presence in *The Seven Lively Arts* as the unnamed friend who takes Seldes to Picasso's studio in the climactic chapter.[36] And the generally dismissive ignorance with which Seldes treats the African American origins of jazz is not much better than Bell's frank racism.[37] But his disagreement with Bell about the necessity of preserving art from contamination by the popular goes to the heart of *The Seven Lively Arts*: "I have used the word art throughout this book in connexion with jazz and jazzy things; if anyone imagines that the word is belittled thereby and can no longer be adequate to the dignity of Leonardo and Shakespeare, I am sorry."[38]

Yet Seldes does have fell designs on the word "art," which he feels protects a good deal of second-rate rubbish, and he values in jazz its capacity to "rag" these pretensions. Thus he spends a good deal of time in "Toujours Jazz" discriminating between pointless and useful musical parody, and he tries to assess the irony of Joyce and Eliot in the same terms.[39] When he praises *Ulysses* as a "gigantic travesty" and a "burlesque epic," he is singling out precisely those qualities that Bell found so distressing.

As Seldes remarked when *The Seven Lively Arts* was reprinted in 1957, it seems preposterous that the music discussed in "Toujours Jazz" could have been considered a danger to public order, especially since the "jazz" at issue was the gentrified version popularized by Paul Whiteman, George Gershwin, and Irving Berlin.[40] Yet even this music could seem threatening in context, as one example of the emergence of a new social force that Bell, Manners, Stoddard, and many others feared would upend the world they knew. Terms like "travesty" and "burlesque" seem to be chosen purposely to provoke these fears, for they gladly admit the truth of the most serious charges against the new art—that it lacks seriousness and sincerity, that it is "impudent" and irresponsible. The terms also admit to a desire to affront that was commonly associated at this time with social and political disorder. At the moment Seldes wrote, however, the term *burlesque* would have carried another threatening resonance as well, for Great Britain and the United States were both in the throes of major controversies about censorship.

Movies, Modernism, and the Censorship Menace

> It seemed for a moment, in 1922, that if a convicted murderer were set free by a jury, he or she went into the movies; but if a moving-picture actor was declared innocent, he was barred from the screen.
>
> Gilbert Seldes, *The Seven Lively Arts*

Here Seldes laments the disappearance from the screen of one of his favorite slapstick artists, Fatty Arbuckle, whose sensational trial for murder, coinciding with the still-mysterious death of the director William Desmond Taylor, brought to Hollywood the sort of hostile attention that, for a time at least, kept people out of the theaters instead of bringing them in. The *Daily Mail* claimed that in the course of 1922 65 percent of the theaters in the United States had closed their doors, and though these figures seem exaggerated, every review of the film year agreed that there had been a dramatic slump in business.[41] Most reviewers explained the slump as a result of the outrage caused by the Arbuckle case and the attendant moral crusade against the movies in general.[42]

To head off this crusade, the movie industry called on Will Hays, post-master general in the Harding administration, whose irreproachable Republican dullness was to protect the studios from the menace of nationwide film censorship. As president of the Motion Picture Producers and Distributors of America, Hays was supposed to prove that the industry was perfectly capable of censoring itself, and so he traveled the country throughout 1922 attacking governmental censorship as un-American while sternly charging the movie industry to accept its educational and social responsibilities.[43]

The appointment of Hays, at the purposely spectacular salary of $150,000 a year, signified how seriously the movie industry took what critic Robert Sherwood called "the censorship menace."[44] Films had been censored in a desultory and decentralized way for some time in both England and America, but 1922 marked a definite increase in demands for nationwide, standardized, prior censorship of all films. In England, T. P. O'Connor, head of the British Board of Film Censors, reached agreement with the London County Council establishing a film rating system and wrote a set of guidelines, *The Principles of Film Censorship*, which was to make similar standards uniform all over the British Isles.[45] In the United States, O'Connor's comrade in arms, Ellis Paxson Oberholtzer, head of the most vigorous regional panel, the Pennsylvania State Board of Censors, published *The Morals of the Movie*, a rather remarkable conglomeration of moral exhortations, lurid case studies, and practical hints for turning noxious films into innocuous ones with a few deft incisions and some new title cards.[46]

Hays and his supporters in Hollywood succeeded in fighting off the censorship menace in its most rigorous form, but the crusade had a strong effect on the industry nonetheless. The *Film Year Book*, which was aimed primarily at distributors and theater owners, contained page after page of detailed censor board standards, from state boards like those in Maryland and Pennsylvania, both of which banned any discussion of birth control; to the provincial boards of Ontario and Quebec, which were quite sensitive to the display of foreign flags; to the British Board, which even sought to eliminate "salacious wit."[47] Books on the writing of successful "photoplays," of which there were quite a few in these years, began to include special chapters on anticipating the demands of the censor. William Lord Wright, for example, included in *Photoplay Writing* an extensive list of standard cinematic devices, most of them staples of the serials, that were now ruled out by "the requirements of censorship."[48]

It should go without saying that nudity and sexual relations were the most frequently and universally banned of all the standard cinematic devices, but birth control and even childbirth were also taboo, and Pennsylvania also banned discussions of eugenics or "race-suicide."[49] In England, the most extensive controversy of the year was over the film version of Marie Stopes' contraception classic *Married Love*, which was finally allowed release as *Married Life*.[50] Objection to the depiction of crime was so great that in the United

States a reenactment of the murder of Abel was removed from one film as "tending to corrupt morals," and in England the Jackie Coogan version of *Oliver Twist* was cut.[51]

Oberholtzer provides a full page of lurid titles to illustrate the kind of thing from which censors must guard the public: "The Sin Woman" (a title so provocative it is actually listed twice); "The Sex Lure"; "The Gutter Magdalene"; "Satan's Daughter"; "The Devil's Toy."[52] These make it sound as though sexual prurience and crime were the major targets of the censors, and perhaps they were; but it is also clear that anything tending to demean or even question authority came under special scrutiny. In England O'Connor's standards prohibited "scenes in which the king and officers in uniform are seen in an odious light." Attention to these standards, which extended to the wives of military and government officials, was especially vigilant in films with foreign settings.[53] The ever-popular story line that the BBFC summarized as "white men in a state of degradation amidst native surroundings" was specifically prohibited, as was anything else which, in the view of the board, would "demoralize an audience."[54] In the United States similar standards made it virtually impossible for the movies to portray the industrial unrest that was so widespread in the early twenties. According to Sherwood, William S. Hart's *The Whistle* was "cut to pieces in Pennsylvania because the hero was a laborer, and his boss a villain."[55]

The crusade against immorality, that is to say, was also a crusade against demoralization, which meant nothing more nor less than loss of faith in authority. While there is little doubt of Oberholtzer's genuine abhorrence of obscenity, it is also quite clear that, like Stoddard, he feared a more general reorientation of values. The sensationalism of the movies was threatening in part because it titillated the senses, but also because it relied on novelty and surprise in a way intrinsically threatening to the status quo. Attempts to get control of the movies, like similar attempts in the case of jazz, were attempts to subject novelty to some rule other than itself.

For a number of different reasons, literary modernism was implicated in the censorship controversy. For one thing, some of the classic works of literary modernism were subject to the same sort of censorship that Oberholtzer was bringing to the movies. Issues of the *Little Review* containing chapters from *Ulysses* were impounded in 1921, and the editors were eventually forbidden to publish further excerpts from the novel, which was itself unavailable in the United States until 1934.[56] The first commercial edition of *Women in Love* published in the United States, which appeared in 1922, was seized and unsuccessfully prosecuted by the Society for the Suppression of Vice.[57] Such actions were common enough at this time that the younger writers began, sometimes rather gleefully, to anticipate them, as when the editors of *Secession* assured their readers that Waldo Frank's mildly salacious interracial love story "Hope" would have to be privately printed to avoid prosecution.[58]

At this time, John Sumner, head of the Society for the Suppression of Vice, decided to concentrate his efforts on two New York publishers who were publicly associated with modernist literature: Toby Seltzer, who had published *Women in Love*, and Horace Liveright. Liveright fought so many court cases in this period that he kept the law firm of Arthur Garfield Hays on permanent retainer. When Sumner and his society presented a proposed Clean Books Bill to the New York State legislature in 1923, Liveright led the opposition to a measure that would have permitted the suppression of virtually any work, no matter how innocuous or reputable. In this he was virtually without support from older, more established firms, which apparently felt that all the trouble had been stirred up by a few rebels deliberately flouting the accepted standards of society.[59]

Even the most esoteric gestures of early modernism might have been implicated by contact with these controversies. When the first readers of *The Waste Land* encountered the epigraph from the *Satyricon*, they might have been abashed by its abstruse combination of Latin and Greek, or they might have imagined a more topical reference, for Liveright had just successfully defended his new edition of the *Satyricon* from prosecution for obscenity.[60] And Ezra Pound's 1922 contribution to Liveright's list, his translation of Remy de Gourmont's *Natural Philosophy of Love*, might well have been printed "privately," like a number of other Liveright publications of this time with similar titles.[61]

Another work from Liveright's list of 1922, E. E. Cummings' *The Enormous Room*, shows in more detail how sharing the threat of censorship brought literary experiment and popular culture together, at least in the minds of their early proponents. According to Charles Norman, *The Enormous Room*, a factual if fanciful account of Cummings' term in French prison during the First World War, was ready for sale by the end of April 1922, at which time Sumner threatened to confiscate it. Liveright, even at that time in negotiations over the publication of *The Waste Land*, agreed to a desperate last-minute expedient: since the Sumner group was most offended by Cummings' use of the word "shit," the publishers had all instances of it laboriously inked out of every copy by hand.[62] The whole episode, in which a respected and adventurous publisher is reduced to the level of a little boy scrubbing words off the bathroom wall, shows how trivial the struggle with censorship could become, and yet the calculated indecency of *The Enormous Room* was an important part of the intellectual controversy of this year.

Cummings had long been one of the strongest connections between the group that edited and published *The Dial* and what Seldes was to call "the seven lively arts." A Harvard classmate of Sibley Watson, who resurrected *The Dial*, Cummings began very early in the magazine's new existence to publish drawings of dancers, boxers, and comedians such as those who appeared at the Winter Garden.[63] One of these was reprinted in the vaudeville chapter of *The Seven Lively Arts*, as was a rather precious abstraction of Charlie Chaplin.

But the Winter Garden was more than just a shared interest between Cummings and Seldes, who were close friends; it was, as Seldes suggested by announcing his new book there, the center of an aesthetic, one that linked modernism and popular culture in an alliance against the censor.

The Enormous Room was itself, as Cummings' friends noted at the time, an extended vaudeville turn, a work whose very structure was taken from burlesque.[64] There are essentially three types in the book: the jailers, in which group Cummings would include the military authorities; the female prisoners, who are loud, boisterous, and sensually unashamed; and the male prisoners, who are almost to a man weak, small, and romantically ineffectual. The novel is populated, that is to say, by the female exhibitionists and baggy-pants comedians of burlesque, with whom Cummings and his compatriot make common cause against the jailers and warmongers of the outside world. Tenuously tied to reality as it is on one side, and inflated to fantasy as it is on the other, *The Enormous Room* is also an allegory of the alliance of artistic young men of the 1920s with the comic, the indecent, and the impractical against the deathly conformity of the old order. Sumner's prosecution simply makes the allegory concrete.

The Seven Lively Arts is informed from the beginning by the same dichotomous struggle. The first chapter, which was published in *Vanity Fair* in September 1922, delineates the two sides, and, incidentally, takes part in the current debate about film censorship by blaming "the genteel" for a decline in "the purity of slapstick."[65] Seldes sees the movies and, by implication, the popular arts in general, at a great turning point, about to be diverted forever by the forces of genteel disapproval from their true sources of strength. He notes the same danger in the chapter on vaudeville, also originally published in 1922, which singles out "effrontery" in its very title as the chief virtue of the art.[66] "Effrontery" and "impudence" were, at bottom, what the cultural war of 1922 was about: what disgusted Bell, what startled Manners, and what prompted Sumner to prosecution was the insubordination implicit in the "popular" itself.

And this is precisely the quality that Seldes was singling out for praise in the new works of literary modernism. *Ulysses* is, according to the review he published at the same time as his essay on slapstick, a "gigantic travesty" and a "burlesque epic."[67] Seldes links this burlesque epic back to the original satyr-play, but it is also clear that at a time when he was frequenting the Winter Garden, defending E. E. Cummings, and writing in praise of vaudeville, the term would have had direct reference to the popular art that linked sexual exhibitionism, obscenity, and comedy. Nor was he alone in making this link. Eliot's first published comment on *Ulysses*, which appeared in the September issue of *The Dial*, also called the novel a "burlesque."[68] The term is, of course, innocent and ancient enough, and yet *The Dial* had, through the writings of Seldes and the drawings of Cummings, made contemporary burlesque an integral part of its aesthetic.[69] Of course, Eliot was to publish, in his next contribution to *The*

Dial, after *The Waste Land* itself, a eulogy of Marie Lloyd and a lament for the music hall tradition that seemed to die with her.

"Burlesque" is such a key term at this distinct moment in the history of literary modernism because it links the obscene and the critical and thus identifies what is most provoking to censorship in both the movies of the time and the literary works. In a sense, the term suggests a tradition, beginning with the satyr-play, in which the obscene *is* critical in and of itself, the exposure for examination of what is supposed to remain tacit being one of the most dangerous things an artist can do.[70] Seldes identified this exposure as a defining characteristic of popular culture as such, since what made popular culture distinct as a category from the carnivals of the past was its unignorable presence on a national stage. As Bell so acutely sensed, it was not so much that jazz existed—such things had always existed—but that people who had traditionally cared only for Art were somehow expected to pay attention to this jungle noise. The importunity of it was the key, the very worst of it if, like Bell, one hated "impudence," the very best if, like Seldes, one admired "effrontery." In either case, literary modernism was linked to the popular in its affront to the cultural hierarchy of the past.[71]

Seldes was perhaps emboldened by the fact that burlesque, both as a term and as a practice, had already been legitimated for art by the French avant-garde. As a term, "burlesque" had been used both in attacks on and defenses of new art movements in France. As Jeffrey Weiss has shown, cubism had in particular been attacked as a confidence-trick, a sham, an act of bare-faced effrontery. And it had also been celebrated in those terms, so that Picasso's costumes for *Parade* could be described as "burlesque . . . without [its] being taken to mean anything less than that they were a complete success."[72] Of course, *Parade* could be described as "burlesque" in another sense, for it frankly modeled itself on the music hall. In fact, the association between the art movements of the French avant-garde and popular entertainment of this kind is so close that Weiss has termed it "music-hall modernism."[73]

In part, the association depends on simple enthusiasm for popular forms that seem fresh and unacademic. But the music hall also provides a formal model for the avant-garde, a model of ironic juxtaposition in which quick transitions between the high and the low, the comic and the bathetic, the artistic and the commercial deflate pretensions and level out specious distinctions. This model is most obvious in actual stage productions like *Parade*, but it is also at work, Weiss suggests, in the visual art of Picasso and Duchamp, and it can be found as well in the literary masterworks of 1922. *The Waste Land* was originally to have begun with snatches of popular song and with a drunken visit to Boston's Grand Opera House,[74] and though this material was excised in revision, there are still a few bits of popular music in the final text. More importantly, the whole structure of the poem, its rapid cuts from subject to subject and its juxtapositions of high art and low life, may have been suggested by the minstrel shows that had such a powerful influence over Eliot's imagination at this time.[75] As Cheryl Herr has documented in such detail, the music hall had a similar hold on the imagination of Joyce, who once wrote, "The music hall, not Poetry, [is] a criticism of life."[76] The results are clearly visible in the dramatic structure of the "Circe" chapter of *Ulysses*, though it has been suggested that the "turns" of music hall provided a formal model for the entire novel.[77]

With this structural model comes a peculiarly modern attitude, a fusion of two seemingly incompatible qualities. The first of these is a flair for publicity, "the relentless refusal, by definition, to self-efface."[78] This is the quality Seldes celebrates as effrontery, and it links modernism to the popular as such. At the same time, the music hall depends on a strategy of innuendo, of shared but hidden meanings, that were developed in part to frustrate censorship rather than to defy it. As Weiss shows, a good deal of the allusiveness of the early French avant-garde is taken over from this strategy in the popular arts. Both art forms, he argues, foment "a breach of decorum which substitutes quick wits for slow study."[79] What proved most attractive to the avant-garde was this new combination of the public and the private, the banal and the obscure, the obvious and the devious. It allowed the artist to assume a public role, to take a public pose, without necessarily pretending to believe in it, and this was, of course, one of the infuriating things about modernist burlesque for its critics. For it meant that art merged itself with a new public world in which sincerity and honest intentions counted for very little, in which appearances might be enjoyed even as they were exposed merely as appearances.

This merger took place within works like *The Enormous Room*, *The Waste Land*, *Ulysses*, and *Parade*, but it also took place as those works were received into the larger and more extended version of the music hall represented by magazines like *Vanity Fair*. Under the guidance of editors and contributors like Seldes, *Vanity Fair* made popular forms like burlesque intellectually fashionable while also introducing to a larger public difficult works from the avant-garde. It was not unusual in the course of 1922 to find articles by Cocteau or Tzara next to advertisements for the new line in automobiles, or political analyses by Walter Lippmann next to the purposely playful pieces of Gilbert Seldes. With this heterogeneous mixture, so strongly reminiscent of the mixtures effected by the music hall, comes the attitude that Weiss identifies with music hall modernism. In fact, Michael Murphy has recently argued that it is precisely this attitude that *Vanity Fair* sold to its subscribers. According to Murphy, *Vanity Fair* offered the sensation of being up-to-date and in-the-know, a sensation that peculiarly combines elitism and commonality. For the glossy magazines, "bohemia was itself a marketplace, and marketplaces turned out to be the ultimate bohemias."[80] What linked the two apparent opposites was a knowing awareness of the commodification behind fame and fashion and of the way that commodification broke down the notion of intrinsic value. This awareness freed both the artist and the audience to play with representations, to produce and consume the ironic knowledge that behind appearances there was nothing but last year's appearances. In magazines like *The Dial* and *Vanity Fair*, aesthetic modernism met and merged with a cultural marketplace that was essentially modernist itself, in that the only value respected there was change. Art, in short, was entering the new public sphere created by the twentieth-century media, where it might leave the relatively innocent ambiguities of the music hall very far behind.

Movies and the Public Sphere

In most accounts of censorship, the antagonists are a community and an individual. In fact, the legal exercise of censorship, in the United States at least, usually involves the application of something called "community standards." The implication, of course, is that the censorable is by definition something individual, capricious, exceptional. Not only does this exaggerate the distinction between the censoring community and the offending individual, who often have a good deal more in common than either would like to admit, but it ignores the possibility of censorship episodes involving two different communities. The controversies in 1922 over film censorship in particular seem less a conflict between one community and one or more renegade individuals than a conflict between two completely different kinds of communities, one clinging to a model of face-to-face contact that was already seriously outmoded, the other constituting itself in the insubstantial public fora created by the new media of the twentieth century. Beyond relatively simple conflicts like that between the individual and the community, or even between an insurgent avant-garde and the affronted bourgeoisie, there lies this larger conflict, in which censorship attempted to preserve a community that new means of communication were redefining out of existence.

The cultural controversies of 1922, in other words, were really about the entirely new public sphere that movies, recordings, and the infant industry of broadcasting were in the process of creating. What Hartley Manners most disliked about jazz was its ubiquity; it was the new "national anthem" because everyone listened to it everywhere. There was something disquieting to him about the sheer fact of its popularity, the way it tended to efface boundaries of class and geography. Even Nanook of the North, in Robert Flaherty's famous 1922 documentary, could listen to jazz, courtesy of Flaherty's portable victrola. Of course, *Nanook* also demonstrated the ubiquity of the movies, both their insatiable desire to document every corner of the world and their inevitable expansion as universal entertainment. Flaherty made the Arctic into both a sound stage and a movie theater, showing his rushes to an appreciative Eskimo audience, as Martin Johnson did at about the same time in New Guinea.[81] And though neither filmmaker quite had the opportunity to take the next step and show *Nanook* in New Guinea, the mere possibility of such a thing gave the movies an unprecedented power: "They bring Alaskan glaciers to the Desert of Sahara, and South Sea lagoons to Siberia. They bring the canals of Bruges to Quito, Peru, and the glamour of Mediaeval England to Butte, Montana." As Robert Sherwood, author of this testimonial, goes on to say: "The press, which has always been considered the most powerful medium of expression, knows the limitations of time, location, and language; the movies know no limitations whatsoever."[82]

Movies were, in this analysis, both the creators and the beneficiaries of a new global public sphere.[83] According to the *Film Year Book*, there were 600 movie theaters in Japan, 168 in Burma, India, and Ceylon, and 250 in Java, one of them large enough to hold 4,500 spectators.[84] The vast distance between these theaters and the major movie studios in the United States and Great Britain created entirely new problems in censorship. Indian audiences were apparently frequently affronted by the frankness of American films and disappointed by the stereotyped images of India promoted by the studios.[85] On the other hand, the *Daily Mail* complained that in India, Burma, and what it called Mesopotamia, "the natives have been shown pictures in which the white woman has figured in an unfavourable light."[86] The problem of reaching vastly different audiences was illustrated vividly in Java, where, according to the *Film Year Book*, "theaters are so constructed that the screen divides it into two parts—the Europeans and foreign orientals sitting on one side of the curtain and the natives on the other." The account concludes with one of those brief statements that can inadvertently sum up global complexities: "The picture is projected from the side of the Europeans."[87]

Despite such evidence, the ubiquity of the movies was regularly used as an argument against film censorship. One of the strongest arguments that Will Hays could mount against the forces of censorship was that restrictions on the universal language of the screen would destroy the world's most powerful instrument for international understanding. Hollywood self-promotions like Samuel Goldwyn's *Behind the Screen* and Edward S. Van Zile's *That Marvel— The Movie* were particularly fond of the notion that movies were a universal language, an Esperanto, as both writers put it, of the eye.[88] This represents an extension to film of the claim made for photography as early as 1841.[89] Miriam Hansen has traced the film version of this trope back to Griffith, who may have derived the idea in his turn from a reading of Vachel Lindsay's *The Art of the Moving Picture*, the reissue of which by Boni and Liveright in 1922 may explain the currency of the comparison at this time.[90] For Lindsay, movies represent the modern version of the union of painting and writing that existed at the beginning of civilization in the hieroglyph or ideogram. Movies thus realize the desire of the American imagist poets for an immediate and concretely sensuous language, and Lindsay revels in the possibilities that film offers to the imagist movement: "Imagist photoplays would be Japanese prints taking on life, animated Japanese paintings, Pompeian mosaics in kaleidoscopic but logical succession, Beardsley drawings made into actors and scenery, Greek vase-paintings in motion."[91]

The trope links together film and literature, the eye and the mind, in a union in which the sense of difference overcome is itself functional. Because the movies have effaced the difference between the visual and the written, the argument runs, they can also efface the differences between classes and nations that are caused by the arbitrary specificities of the written languages. There is, as Hansen says, a utopian democratic universalism at the heart of this belief, one that can be traced back to American transcendentalism.[92] In the early 1920s, this universalism had a specific polemical thrust, aimed at the genteel notion that art had to be a specialized activity and the province of a particular class. As Sherwood insists, it is through their universality, their appeal "for the high and mighty, and for the meek and lowly, without distinction," and their ability to travel the globe, that the movies "perpetrate their greatest offense against those who like to believe that art is their own exclusive esoteric property."[93]

The most convinced, if not the most convincing, proponent of this argument was Van Zile, whose entire book is an argument against tampering with "the first antidote the race has discovered against polyglot poison."[94] But it was a consistent theme in the movie industry's various defenses of itself at this time, from Rupert Hughes' novel *Souls for Sale* to John Amid's boy's book *With the Movie Makers*, which recapitulates the entire argument.[95] In fact, perhaps because of its utter artlessness, Amid's book exposes more blatantly than any other source the contradictory self-interest lurking within the universalist argument. For Amid, as for the others, movies are a universal language, "the oldest language of all," with a pre-Babelian purity and international reach, but "the really big thing about American films abroad—in Europe, in Asia, in Africa and South America—is that they carry American ideas, and American ideals and American influence, around the world." To the censors, the warning is clear. Tampering with the movies is un-American not because it violates American ideals of free speech but because it hobbles America's most potent international weapon: "It is probably not too much to say, although the bare thought itself is a staggering one, that to-morrow the country that excels in the production of popular motion pictures will dominate the world."[96]

As Amid's rather brazen promise of world domination reveals, the movies did not so much oppose censorship as offer to accomplish it by other means. In Griffith's formulation the universal language of film accomplishes *formally* what Oberholtzer and his fellow censors wanted to accomplish in substance. The notion that every audience receives visual stimuli in the same way brutally elides every category of difference. It was the work of Griffith and the emerging photoplay not merely to postulate this "ideal," standardized observer but also to produce it, to create in film a model of standardized reception apparently emptied of every specific characteristic but actually modeled on the point of view that brought forth *Birth of a Nation*. To standardize reception in this way is to accomplish the most thorough prior and universal censorship possible; it is to make the censor—whom Oberholtzer calls "someone, seeing all from a height and representing the common interest"—and the viewer one.[97]

Film industry apologists like Van Zile promised a world of infinite transparency, a world in which everything would be equally and identically visible to everyone: "The Esperanto of the Eye, which found its alphabet when Edison invented the kinetoscope, has now become a universal method of expression fitted to reveal eventually all human knowledge to the race in such a manner that it can be sensed, if not comprehended, by even illiterates and morons."[98] It is a world in which censorship is simply unnecessary because the possibility of deviance has ceased to exist. On this, the dark side of the universalist utopia, the film industry promises a uniformity greater than anything the censors could even have dreamed of, a world picture that not only contains everything that can be seen but every person capable of eyesight. And yet the censors were not mollified by the promise of infinite visibility, which seemed to them to call if anything for even greater vigilance.[99] The danger was not just that films were so much more widespread than previous forms of art. There was something particularly pernicious in the very universality of film, in the new public sphere it creates out of a heterogeneous and disparate world.

For Oberholtzer censorship is so necessary and natural it is essentially synonymous with community itself: "We censor our thoughts before we utter them, if we are esteemed as neighbors and citizens."[100] The threat posed by film to this sort of community decency is obvious: the vast audiences it assembles are no longer neighbors or fellow citizens, and thus they no longer share those tacit assumptions that keep the unspeakable unspoken. But sheer size and extent is only part of the threat of film to Oberholtzer's notion of community decency; far more serious is the way it substitutes illusory and immaterial contact for the immediate personal proximity of "neighbors and citizens." There is far greater danger of what he calls "daring and repugnant situations" in film than there is in the theater, because in the former "there is no personal relationship between the actor and his audience."[101] Since actor and audience are not actually in the same neighborhood at all, the natural censorship of a real community cannot operate. Since the relationship between actor and audience is neither immediate nor reciprocal, since the actor cannot see himself being seen, the sense of shame is severed from that of sight. What Oberholtzer seeks in a national film censorship board is a way of making this new scattered and impersonal public space operate as if it were a community founded on face-to-face contact. It is, in other words, the very universality of film, its independence of any particular community, that makes it dangerous and inherently in need of censorship.

Oberholtzer's uneasy realization that an entirely new kind of public space had been created was shared by other, rather more liberal, observers of the time, including Walter Lippmann, who also worried that the old model of individual democratic participation had simply been made irrelevant by a situation in which most issues would come to the individual citizen in the form of distant representations. Lippmann's solution is also a kind of censorship, though he would never have used the term and would probably have quailed at the very idea. But he believes that, given "the failure of self-governing people to transcend their casual experience and their prejudice, by inventing, creating, and organizing a machinery of knowledge," such a machinery must be created for them.[102] To create such a machinery was also the project of Ogden and Richards, who proposed their new science of symbolism primarily as a way of helping the "new mass of voting citizens" to "test the truth of language—language as publicity, advertising, political propaganda, yellow journalism, language coming over the airwaves, the loudspeaker, the cinema."[103]

As different as these writers were in their political opinions, they all shared an essential conservatism where the new public sphere was concerned, for all their efforts were bent on arming citizens to resist the changes they saw coming. Their efforts on behalf of truth and morality depended on a faith that these remained unchanged and that the difficulty presented by new and more powerful means of generating representations was primarily that these made truth and morality harder to discern. What Lippmann found as hard to accept as Oberholtzer was the possibility that the more powerful and far-reaching proliferation of representations had changed what counted for truth and had therefore made the regulation of morality a far more difficult and doubtful thing. Yet this is precisely what the more brazen defenders of the popular arts were suggesting.

One of Oberholtzer's peskiest antagonists was a novelist, screenwriter, and director named Rupert Hughes, who had originally been recruited to Hollywood as part of a highly publicized campaign to bring good literature to the screen. Exemplifying as he did what passed for artistic prestige in the Hollywood of the time, Hughes was a valuable ally in Hays' campaign against governmental censorship.[104] He was also, not incidentally, one of the most frequently censored of the prominent writers, having made a specialty of racy titles like *Gimme*.[105] One of his most provocative titles, one that was in fact singled out as especially objectionable by Oberholtzer, was *Souls for Sale*, which was first a book, published at the height of the censorship controversy in 1922, and then a highly publicized and commercially successful film.[106] On one level, *Souls for Sale* is nothing more than a bold-faced denial of every criticism ever leveled at Hollywood, which appears in the novel as a close-knit small town of hard-working folks who just haven't got the time to sin. On another level, however, the novel is an attack on suppositions about truth and morality that are so deep Oberholtzer cannot even articulate them.

Early on, when things look very dark for the heroine of *Souls for Sale*, the narrator, speaking with an oracular privilege the narrators in more serious novels had long since disavowed, promises her success. He sees a future in which "she appeared in a hundred places at once by a diabolic telepathy in a multiplication that made of one shy, frightened girl a shining multitude. And at times each of her was of an elfin tininess, at times of titanic size. But all of her was always of more than human sympathy, and spoke a language that men of every nation understood."[107] What the narrator promises this heroine is the universality and infinite intelligibility that were, according to Griffith, Hays, Van Zile, and its other defenders, the chief social virtues of film. But this universality is accomplished not by any peculiar formal virtue intrinsic to film, not by pantomime on the part of the actor nor by particular strategies of framing or pacing on the part of the director, but rather by the method of reproduction by which films are distributed. The heroine acquires her universality by herself becoming a multitude, and as a series of copies of herself she triumphs over the constraints of time and space.

Already Hughes has singled out for praise one of the most troubling aspects of the new arts, which differed from previous forms of reproducible representation like print in that they did not seem like representations at all but resembled with disturbing fidelity the thing itself. But there is another and more threatening sidelight to this crude Hollywood boosterism, because the heroine is already infinitely reproduced and scattered across the globe even before she becomes a star, even before she leaves home to enter the movies. At the very beginning of her melodrama, she is advised by a kindly hometown doctor who has "tried his hand at the newest indoor sport, the writing of stories for moving pictures," and who "improvised for Mem's future what a moving-picture man would call a 'continuity.'" She agrees to "play the part as best she could. . . . She was in haste to begin her career."[108] At this point there is no hint that this "career" will be in the movie industry itself, but the movies provide her with a "career" nonetheless by suggesting to her continuity-writer a pattern of behavior, a role and a drama in which to play it. Hughes suggests, in other words, that his heroine is already part of a multitude, one of an infinite series of reproductions. The only difference is that in her triumph as a star she becomes the source for others to copy, but, of course, the most ironic possibility suggested by the novel is that this isn't a difference at all.

In one way, then, the relationship between the audience and the star is much closer than the old face-to-face relationship that Oberholtzer laments. As Lary May has shown, the two biggest stars of the time, Douglas Fairbanks and Mary Pickford, were carefully marketed as model consumers, so the audience was led to identify with the stars because the stars were themselves a kind of idealized audience.[109] The longing to be in the movies, which was also fed by dozens of books like John Emerson and Anita Loos' *How to Make It in the Movies*, is a longing to realize this promise, in which performing in the movies is simply a more perfect version of watching them. The fact that the audience and the performer can no longer see one another at the moment of performance hardly seems to matter, then, considering that if it achieves its goal at all the performance makes the difference between acting and watching disappear.

This is perhaps part of what Benjamin meant when he ascribed the "contemporary decay of the aura" to the "desire of contemporary masses to bring things 'closer' spatially and humanly, which is just as ardent as their bent toward overcoming the uniqueness of every reality by accepting its reproduction."[110] The public space in which Hughes' heroine has her existence is in one sense suffocatingly close because the relationship of the individuals in it is one of mimicry. Such mimicry represents for her not a loss of individuality but rather a gain in mobility, as she moves up the great chain of mimicry to the top. It is a public space in which people also lose their aura, their halo of sacred individuality, and become reproducible commodities, which is certainly one of the things about it that disturbs Oberholtzer without his being quite able to articulate it. Yet this is precisely what Hughes holds out as the greatest promise of the movies, that they make people reproducible commodities, as his heroine realizes in the crassly uplifting conclusion of his novel: "She had a soul to sell and it was all her own, and she was going to market."[111] Here there is not just an acceptance but an ardent embrace of commodification and the loss of aura it entails, which in this case is also the loss of the very thing that Oberholtzer's morality intends to preserve: the soul.

The ultimate fulfillment of the promise of the movies to link the whole world together in a huge, universal audience is thus the marketplace itself, a place where souls are sold only in the sense that the reduction of everything to the mechanics of selling has already ruled the soul out of existence. This is the more daring part of *Souls for Sale*, which defends the movies from Oberholtzer's charges of immorality by asserting both that the movies are highly moral and that they are profoundly amoral. And this second and more daring assertion touches the core of the conflict between the popular arts and the censor, which is not really over the relative niceness or naughtiness of the content of the arts, nor even about the moral implications of their formal innovations, but over the more fundamental question as to whether the methods of mechanical reproduction make the whole issue of morality obsolete.

Lippmann, of course, was concerned not about morality but about truth and about the survival of an enlightened and engaged citizenry in a world of reproductions. But Benjamin, for one, felt that a people exposed to the constant circulation of reproductions might become more critical and canny rather than less so, and another popular Hollywood treatment of 1922 seems to bear him out. Harry Leon Wilson, unlike Hughes, was a temporary and somewhat critical visitor in Hollywood, but his novel *Merton of the Movies* did far more than *Souls for Sale* to establish the early mythos of film. In the course of 1922, *Merton* was serialized in the *Saturday Evening Post*, published as a novel, and produced on Broadway in a treatment by George S. Kaufmann and Marc Connelly. In 1924, having already inspired a whole series of films with titles like *Mary of the Movies* and *Hazel from Hollywood*, it was itself made into a movie, for the first of at least four times.[112] While Seldes noticed it somewhat grudgingly in *The Seven Lively Arts*, Sherwood called it "the sagest book that has ever been written about the silent drama."[113]

Sage or not, *Merton* does capture much of the uncanniness of the relationship between the film audience and its art. Merton Gill, come from Illinois to Hollywood to be a star, is at first an utter failure, so much so that, after a single walk-on role, he is reduced to living on the lot. The young man who was such a quintessential spectator that he could be referred to simply as "the watcher" crosses over and becomes as immaterial as the "phantom crowds" who disappear once the shooting stops.[114] From behind the screen, as it were, his old life appears as if it were itself a film, one he writes, directs, and watches again and again as hunger and fatigue make him almost continuously delirious. One irony of the reversal is that, as in the case of Hughes' heroine, Merton's life was already a film, Merton having long since turned himself into what Hollywood called "a type," or rather a series of types, represented by the set of studio photographs for which Merton has religiously posed in a series of stereotypical costumes. Long before he actually goes to Hollywood, Merton comes to see his actual life in a smalltown drugstore as a false imposition on the true life he leads as the subject of those photographs. His disappearance is, therefore, simply the realization of a cherished dream to become a visual image.

True to the promise of Hollywood, this dream, the dream of the quintessential spectator who cannot imagine that anything is real unless it is registered in a photograph, makes Merton a star. Filmed gazing at his own publicity stills, he is so hilariously sincere he becomes a comedy sensation. Since it is finally nothing more than his intense desire to become a star that makes him a star, albeit a different kind of star than he imagined himself, Merton is a very pure example of the empty mimicry that links audience and performer. What Merton admires in the stars he reveres is simply that they are famous, so in a very real sense he is simply admiring his own admiration; he becomes a star himself when the intensity of this self-regard becomes so great that others are willing to admire it in him.

Of course, there is one final turn in this hall of mirrors, in which the audience watches the star fondly watching himself: since Merton's movies are comedies in which Merton's pretensions are held up to ridicule, the audience is in fact invited to watch itself, in the role of Merton, watching the star watch himself. The empty mimicry of the whole process is ruthlessly exposed, and everyone involved trembles with fear when Merton finally realizes that he is not a romantic hero but the unwitting butt of a series of low comedies. But it is just here that Merton shows himself to be a true representative of the audience, for his very real gullibility seems somehow to coexist with a cynicism so deep it confounds the most hardened studio executives. Without ever revealing his own feelings, Merton accepts stardom on the terms offered. He ends the novel acclaimed as a comic genius, a performer whose art is so carefully controlled it appears effortless, whose offstage demeanor is so natural one would never suspect he is a great actor. The novel concludes with Merton telling a gossip columnist the utter truth about himself, that he is a simple person simply playing himself on screen, but since he does this by quoting word for word an interview he had read years earlier in a screen magazine, the reader can only conclude that for Merton success means that the difference between sincerity and mimicry has finally disappeared.

Like *Souls for Sale*, *Merton* describes a public space in which the relationship between audience and performer is both close and distant at the same time, since mimicry, like reproduction, implies both similarity and difference. In this public space, truth and falsehood are not so much at war with one another as in constant resonance, and *Merton* is more radical than many works of its time in suggesting that it is precisely this resonance that the audience enjoys. Where Lippmann fears an audience at the mercy of manufactured representations, Wilson describes a situation closer to the one Max Ernst was imagining at exactly the same time, "this being caught inside the illusion and this looking on nonetheless from without," as Rosalind Krauss puts it.[115] An observer of 1922 might find this dialectic dream state in Ernst's surrealist collages or in the most ordinary boy's book introduction to the movies, one like John Amid's *With the Movie Makers*, which originally ran as articles in *The American Boy*. Half a century before Roland Barthes, Amid told his young readers of the importance to the movies of "a good 'reality' element," the quotes making it clear that "reality" was an ingredient to be added to a movie rather like suspense or atmosphere.[116] Amid showed his readers in some detail exactly how the reality effect was achieved, not to ruin their enjoyment or to armor them against deception but rather to produce that surrealistic state of being caught inside the illusion while looking on from without which was already an essential part of enjoying the movies. As Jean-Louis Comolli has said, movies "lay out a contradictory, representative space, a space in which there are both effects of the real and effects of fiction, of repetition and difference, automatic devices of identification and significant resistances, recognition and seizure." The real power of the movies lies not in their ability to deceive but rather in their invitation to enjoy the tension between awareness and self-deception. "The more one knows," Comolli says, "the more difficult it is to believe, and the more it is worth it to manage to."[117] The contradictory tension thus created was, as Krauss shows, an essential device of the European avant-garde of this time, but it was also an ordinary part of everyday moviegoing, and it was in this tension, perhaps, that modernism and the popular arts found their most significant common cause.

Beyond music hall modernism, then, there may lie a kind of movie screen modernism, which would push the seemingly impossible conjuncture of publicity and private meaning to new extremes. Surely the worldwide proliferation of reproduced images creates powerful new possibilities for "burlesque," for public irony of the kind that both Weiss and Krauss associate primarily with the avant-garde. Wilson himself may have had some small influence in this regard, for Gertrude Stein thought *Merton* "the best book about twentieth century American youth that has yet been done," and she arranged to meet Wilson when she returned to California in the 1930s.[118] But the most appropriate representative of movie screen modernism, and the most thorough illustration of the cultural and aesthetic possibilities of an association between movies and the avant-garde, is another personality Stein met on her tour, one who had long enjoyed a significant relationship with modernist literature: Charlie Chaplin.

The Modernist Charlie Chaplin

If there is any cultural icon of this time that represents how thoroughly mechanical reproduction had made for itself a new global public sphere, it is the derby hat and rattan walking stick of Charlie Chaplin. The slogan used to advertise the early Chaplin films was, according to Seldes, "I Am Here To-Day," and the faintly ridiculous iterability of all the terms suggests how identifiable and ubiquitous Chaplin was.[119] If one had to choose one thing that every human being living in 1922—from Evelyn Waugh to Walter Benjamin—could have agreed upon, it would probably be Charlie Chaplin. In Russia he was the darling of the futurists; in Germany he was a model for the dadaists; in England he was praised by Eliot; in France he was the subject of the first full-length book devoted to any movie star.[120] The election day crowds gathered in Trafalgar Square late in November were entertained by a Chaplin film projected on a vast screen, and fighting broke out not over political differences but because not everyone could see.[121]

Chaplin's trip to Europe in 1921, his first since the beginning of his American movie career, marked, according to one biographer, "the very peak of [his] phenomenal popularity."[122] In *My Trip Abroad*, the account he published in 1922, Chaplin appears genuinely unprepared for the sheer mass of adulation that awaited him: in his first three days in London he received 73,000 cards and letters.[123] This trip also marks the beginning of the sort of suspicious distrust that would eventually drive Chaplin into exile: in America he was rather frequently asked if he was a Bolshevist, and the FBI opened its first file on Chaplin in this year; in England a number of those 73,000 cards and letters contained a white feather, critically symbolizing Chaplin's absence during the war.[124] Though his sexual morals had not yet put him in legal jeopardy, his first divorce in 1920, coinciding as it did with the highly publicized divorces of his friends Mary Pickford and Douglas Fairbanks, did add to the outrage gathering around Hollywood.

A number of articles written by, about, or to Chaplin in the course of 1922 suggest that he had reached a critical point in his career, one that coincided in suggestive ways with the crisis of the movies in general. As far back as 1918, *Photoplay* had popularized the notion that Chaplin was a dual per-

Charles Chaplin as You Have Probably Never Seen Him, and, below, the Charlie Chaplin Everybody Knows. The two Chaplins. (*Ladies' Home Journal*, October 1922).

sonality, Charles vs. Charlie, as an article in *Current Opinion* put it in February 1922.[125] "Charles" read Kant and Schopenhauer and longed to retire from pie-throwing to a life of serious study among his books, but the public demand for "Charlie" was insatiable. In October *The Ladies' Home Journal* published contrasting pictures of the two Chaplins, in and out of costume.[126] The private conflict between the two Chaplins became a public war when Stark Young published an open letter in the *New Republic* in August demanding greater artistic seriousness from Chaplin in the future, to which Seldes responded by calling it "intellectual nonsense."[127] When Chaplin published "In Defense of Myself" in November, his readers might legitimately have wondered which self he was defending, and from whom.[128]

Since Chaplin had come to symbolize the movies, it is appropriate that he should also symbolize the conflict that gripped the movies. Public calls for greater seriousness from him were roughly parallel—in character if not in motive—to Hays' campaign for movies responsible enough to avoid censorship. But Chaplin's dual personality symbolized something else as well: the conflict between Charles and Charlie incarnated the relationship between popular culture and the young intellectuals. Whether Charles might ever express his deeper intellectual yearnings *as* Charlie, without losing any of his popular appeal, is a question that seemed very much in the balance in 1922, and it was a question full of implications for American popular culture, the young intellectuals, and the relationship between them.

That Chaplin was, as Seldes put it, "a universal genius capable of holding the multitude and exciting the speculations of the intellectuals" had long been an accepted part of his public image, even in 1922.[129] As early as 1916, Chaplin published an article in Robert Coady's legendary little magazine *Soil* on "the irreverence of comedy toward authority."[130] Seldes claimed to have written on Chaplin in the same year, having been preceded only by Vachel Lindsay and Waldo Frank.[131] By the next year, however, Chaplin had received a seal of approval from the *New Republic*, and in 1919 he met Max Eastman, through whom he was to meet a number of other writers and intellectuals, including Claude McKay.[132] Through Frank he met Hart Crane, who was one of a number of well-known American poets to write poems about Chaplin at this time.[133] Another was Carl Sandburg, whose meeting with Chaplin just before the European trip is commemorated in "Without the Cane and the Derby."[134] Chaplin also became acquainted with the editorial staffs of some of the livelier magazines, including *Vanity Fair*, where he came to know Seldes, Bishop, and Wilson.[135] In 1919, in fact, Chaplin had contributed money toward the creation of a new magazine to be edited by Gorham Munson and entitled *The Modernist*.[136]

The Modernist never materialized, but the little magazines that did publish modernist work were full of references to Chaplin in 1922. In *Broom*, to take just one example, he was hailed by Matthew Josephson in June as the only faithful representative of the "astounding American panorama," by Harold

Loeb in September as one true instance of American art that appeals to the
masses, and by Malcolm Cowley in a poem in November that makes him,
along with Theodore Roosevelt, Jack Johnson, and an anonymous country
fiddler, one of "four angels bathed in glory round my land."[137]

Chaplin was so much in the public eye at this time that it may not seem at
all odd that even the littlest of the magazines should have noticed him, especially considering his popular reputation as a closet intellectual, but the intellectuals did not celebrate him because he was supposed to have read Kant and
Schopenhauer. Quite the opposite in fact. What seemed most to fascinate the
writers was Chaplin's perfect silence. As Elie Faure put it in one of the most
fervent of these early tributes, "The master of this new art never speaks,
never writes, never explains."[138] Seldes repeated this point many years later, insisting quite erroneously that Chaplin never even mimicked the actions of
speech.[139] Accurate or not, such praise exposes a general intellectual desire to
see Chaplin as having succeeded more completely than any other screen actor
in turning himself into a purely visual object. By not writing (surely not a particularly distinctive trait in the movies), Chaplin heals the split that writing creates between the sign and the thing it represents. In so doing, he also closes
the related gap between the senses and the abstract intellect. Ironically, it is not
by reading Kant and Schopenhauer that Chaplin brings the intellect together
with the visceral appeal of the comic—not in fact by reading at all but precisely by not reading or writing or even speaking, because it is language that
created this dichotomy in the first place.

Chaplin is sometimes held to have created, out of himself, an entirely new
form of language. When Seldes calls the tramp costume "the universal symbol of laughter," he suggests, as many others did at the same time, that film
comedy triumphs over the limitations created by the arbitrariness of the natural languages.[140] Since "the slapstick is universal," as St. John Ervine insisted
at this time in *Vanity Fair*, Chaplin "has taken Englishmen and Irishmen,
Spaniards and Russians, Frenchmen and Germans, Americans and Japanese,
and reduced them all to their elements; and in so doing has achieved very
largely what the more sober Dr. Wilson failed to do at Paris."[141] The fond
hope behind Ervine's pronouncement is clear: in a world bewildered by its
own variety, Chaplin appealed as the symbol of a symbol, one so purified of
the abstract and arbitrary that it could be read and understood universally.
This hope veils a corresponding anxiety, more particular than the age-old anxiety about the mediacy of any symbolism, that the written languages would
not be adequate to the much larger and more various audiences, both international and domestic, of the postwar era.

In portraying Chaplin as the symbol of a universal system of symbolism,
writers like Seldes and Ervine are simply following the comedian's own lead.
He liked to claim, as he did at this time in "In Defense of Myself," that he had
come to throw away "the crutch of words" and refine the art of pantomime
by playing with Fred Karno's troupe before audiences that could speak no

English: "But although I used this device first as a substitute for words, born of necessity, I discovered that in many cases the pantomime carried over the idea more vividly and with more telling effect than words, and I began later to rely upon pantomime before English-speaking audiences." At times, in fact, Chaplin liked to hint that he had gypsy blood and had inherited with it his ability to communicate through sign language.[142]

As a soundless comic, Chaplin embodies more perfectly than any other star of the time the promise of the movies as a universal medium, and the intellectual clamor over him at this time shows how great a stake the younger writers had in this same project. By lionizing Chaplin, writers like Seldes were throwing support to someone who seemed to symbolize the common aim of popular culture and the modernist avant-garde. What fascinated them in him was the same sense of the universal, of social and geographical ubiquity, that dismayed Oberholtzer and Manners. For them Chaplin was a representative of the democratic universalist hopes that Lindsay had long since invested in film. But Chaplin also represented, more so than any other star of the time, the sort of universality film achieved by means of mechanical reproduction, a universality neither uniform nor self-similar and one that touched the avant-garde in a much more fundamental way.[143]

At a time when Fairbanks and Pickford were doing everything they could to erase the differences between their images onscreen and their offscreen lives, Chaplin was conspicuous as a double personality.[144] The difficulties thus caused were an inescapable irritant during his 1921 trip. The massive crowds that turned out wherever he went were obviously motivated by the chance to see the "real" Chaplin, that is to say, the man Charlie Chaplin as distinct from the screen role he played as the tramp. As one fan put it, in a witticism already ancient, "I have seen you so much in 'reel' life that I wanted to talk to you in 'real' life."[145] Yet there was a constant sense of disappointment that he was not in costume, and Chaplin's strategic decision to leave behind the mustache and large shoes, the derby and the cane, caused more and more disgruntlement: "There are grave doubts as to whether I am Charlie Chaplin or not."[146] In fact, there was so much disappointment on board the ship he took across the Atlantic that there was a kind of rebellion against him: a crew member paraded the decks dressed as the tramp; there was a nasty confrontation with a photographer demanding his picture; and finally the entertainment chairman announced that it hardly matters whether Chaplin performs or not "as they could see Charlie Chaplin at any time for a nickel."[147]

This last comment focuses the whole controversy on a single point. The crowd seems spellbound by the aura of the famous individual, and yet it also seems intent on destroying that aura, so much so that it resorts to duplicating him against his will and then taunting him with its power to possess his duplicates. Chaplin suffers the feeling of strangeness that Benjamin says is peculiar to the film actor before the audience, which is "basically the same kind as the estrangement before one's own image in the mirror."[148] But the audience is also confronted with the mirror image, and it may be that Chaplin was such a compelling figure at this time because he allowed the audience to contemplate its own fate in the mirror.

The notorious difference between Chaplin in film and Chaplin out of it was also a structural principle within the films of this period.[149] Chaplin himself played dual roles in *The Idle Class*, made just before his trip to Europe, and *The Pilgrim*, made just after. *A Woman of Paris*, started in 1922 and released the next year, had no role for Chaplin in it, perhaps to confound an audience that thought it could have him at any time for a nickel, but it was based on a contrast between rich sophisticate and poor artist that most critics have traced back to Chaplin himself. The ancient devices of mistaken identity that motivate *The Idle Class* and *The Pilgrim* almost seem, in the context of the time, allegories of unwilling reproduction, Chance dropping the tramp into situations in which he must face and in some cases fight his mirror image.

As Charles Musser points out, the tramp had always been quite willing to double up, to accept masks or new identities whenever they might come along.[150] The tramp costume itself is so stylized and so faithfully reproduced in film after film once it achieves trademark status that it seems both a mask and a character in its own right at the same time. In fact, everything the tramp does, from his finicky hand gestures to the stuttering walk, is so perfectly stylized and stereotyped as to suggest a character operating on its own, utterly separable from and independent of the actor playing the role. The tiny automatisms of the tramp's movements, the mechanically geometric squareness of his steps and gestures, suggest a figure not just in but created by the movies. It is as if a human being had internalized the metronomic stop action that paradoxically makes the movies move, "as hitching up his pants and bouncing his cane he imitated the tremor that constantly palsied the visual space of primitive cinema, everyone seeming to march to the sound of an invisible drummer."[151]

While Fairbanks and Pickford were doing their best to create a free and natural persona that could travel easily from Pickfair to the screen and back again, Chaplin was taking the machinelike regularity of the film camera deeply into his character and producing a screen persona that advertised itself as produced and reproduced. As Benjamin put it, he "raises the law of the filmic sequence of images to that of human motor actions."[152] Thus the most basic kind of slapstick can sometimes reflect more deeply than complicated plot doubling the effects of mechanical reproduction. This is certainly the case in *Pay Day*, Chaplin's one 1922 release. What would otherwise be a relatively ordinary and old-fashioned film contains two inspired sequences set on a building site. In the first, two men toss bricks up to Chaplin, who is standing on a thin scaffolding. Two men throwing and one man catching is a recipe for disaster, but Chaplin turns it into ballet, catching bricks under his chin, behind one knee, in the crook of an elbow, on a heel, even perching one delicately and impossibly at the base of his spine. The miracle is made possible, of course,

Chaplin on the lift (*Pay Day*, 1922).

by cranking the camera backward as Chaplin balletically drops the bricks to his coworkers below. In fact, the scene works rather better if this fact is obvious, as it would have been to any audience within easy reading distance of the many books and articles that explained such effects. The comic beauty of the scene is all in the death-defying unreality of it, in the freedom from gravity that the trick photography affords. What better and more concise recipe for comedy than a machine that turns work into play simply by cranking back-ward?[153]

Of course, a machine that cranks backward can also crank forward, and part of the giddiness of the brick throwing scene comes from the sense of in-finite reversibility that it imports into the linear and instrumental world of work. Chaplin takes this one step further in another scene, or set of scenes, centered on a primitive lift. As the workers settle down for lunch, they set var-ious food items down on what seems an ordinary section of wooden floor, which turns out to be a lift with a mind of its own. It proceeds to rearrange lunch, lifting a banana up one floor, dropping a loaf of bread down, until everyone is thoroughly confused and angry. The lift itself, rising and falling, taking and leaving, seems a representation within the film of the shutter that, opening and closing, hiding and revealing, makes the film possible in the first place. The blink of sightlessness within the seeming fluidity of filmic sight is dramatically echoed by the inattention of the lunchers to the lift; they turn away just for a second and turn again to find a whole new reality in place. The elemental back and forth of infantile comedy, now-you-see-it-now-you-don't, is produced in this case by a witless machine whose utterly random automatism invades the workplace and turns its routines into chaos.

Now-you-see-it-now-you-don't also appears in a slightly more pointed and specific form: here-today-gone-tomorrow. Chaplin himself has no lunch, but he is served nonetheless by the obliging lift, which brings him bits of food from the boss's lunch like some gigantic dumbwaiter. Here in its most basic form is the dramatic doubling of *The Idle Class*, *The Pilgrim*, and even perhaps *A Woman of Paris*, in all of which the difference between rich and poor, respectable and contemptible, is the product of pure accident and, as such, is easily reversible. What makes Charles rich and Charlie poor? And how fundamental can this difference be if Charlie can walk into Charles' world without anyone being the wiser? What one witless machine can do, another can undo, and so the lift is both the industrial machine that manufactures distinction and the cinematic machine that discombobulates it.

Or perhaps it would be more accurate to say that the lift represents the cinematic apparatus in both its phases, as commerce and as art. The literal machine that can run both forward and backward, bringing food and freedom and then taking them away, is just the tool, of course, of an industrial machine that could make someone like Chaplin unimaginably wealthy almost, it seemed, by accident. In either case, the difference between having and not having, seeing and not seeing, doing and not doing is simply effaced by the automatism of the machine. *Pay Day* teaches, in other words, the lesson that Benjamin said film had taught dadaism: "the pervasion of reality by the apparatus."[154] Pervaded as it is by the machine, reality simply ceases to be unitary and consistent, and if there is bewilderment in the arbitrariness of it there is also a certain measure of freedom.

Chaplin is Benjamin's symbol of popular enjoyment of this condition, an enjoyment of deflation and disorientation that dada had tried to bring about with much more limited success. The emulative envy of dada is suggested by a collage that Erwin Blumenfeld produced in 1921, in which he appears half-transformed into an exotic dancer, under the scrawled label "President-Dada-Chaplinist." The label is also given in French, so that "Chaplinist" becomes "Charlotin" or "charlatan."[155] Thus Chaplin is the symbol of double identity, of irony and put-on, of word-and-picture-play, of the sort of public duplicity that Weiss associates primarily with music hall modernism. The collage suggests that there was in the widespread intellectual enthusiasm for Chaplin in the early twenties something different in character from the dreams of universal communication that figure so prominently on the surface, an appreciation for an unfixed and disorienting universality peculiar to modern media like film.

The aesthetic figure for this disorientation was the mechanical jerkiness of Chaplin's movements, the jerkiness that made him visibly a representation of himself. Cocteau imported this "vibration" into *Parade*, in which the character of the "American girl" is supposed to "'vibrate' like a silent film, imitate Charlie Chaplin, chase a pick-pocket with a revolver, and dance a 'Ragtime.'"[156] Here, music hall modernism is visibly turning itself into movie screen modernism, imitating the stuttering movements of film because these make the constructed quality of representations all the more obvious. There was a similar Chaplinesque figure in *Le ballet mécanique*, which P. Adams Sitney suggests was an influence on the portraits of Gertrude Stein. Whether this is true or not, it is clear that Stein also admired the stylized rhythm Chaplin achieved through repetition. When she met him in 1934, they agreed that to "change the rhythm" was the most difficult task of both filmmaking and writing.[157]

A very similar comment finds its way into *The Seven Lively Arts* and thus into the American intellectual controversy about Chaplin. In a 1923 issue of *The Criterion*, Eliot remarked, "The egregious merit of Chaplin is that he has escaped in his own way from the realism of the cinema and invented a *rhythm*. Of course the unexplored opportunities of the cinema for eluding realism must be very great."[158] Seldes was not the only American writer to seize on this comment; it appears also in a mock dialogue on the movies that John Peale Bishop published in *Vanity Fair* in 1925.[159] What is interesting about the comment is that rhythm is not, except by metaphorical extension, a visual quality at all; the opposition suggested by both Eliot and Stein between rhythm and realism is, in this sense, an opposition between a quality associated with language, music, or song and the visual representationalism of photography. Chaplin is praised, that is to say, not for purging the linguistic from movies, but rather for bringing it back in, the stylized and mechanically repetitious movements so characteristic of his comedy bringing the arbitrary back into a medium that seems more able than any other to ignore it.

What these writers find most compelling in Chaplin, then, is the way he defeats what would seem the primary power of film, the illusion of presence, of immediacy, that it is able to give. In bringing a rhythm back into realism, he stalls or syncopates or reverses the seemingly natural order of things, disrupting that powerful sense of the given that always attaches to the purely visual. In particular, the repetitiousness of his movements, or of certain props like the wayward lift, makes the whole process of copying, without which movies are unimaginable, visible, and in so doing it highlights the inherent instability of every object and person in a film. These are all activities that Benjamin, and after him such theorists as Rosalind Krauss, associates with surrealism and dada, both of which adopted devices associated with film because of the way they duplicated and divided the unitary objects of a conventional visual consciousness. But an appreciation of these possibilities may have been a good deal more widespread than this in the early 1920s. It may be, in fact, in this fundamental disruption of the universal that the year 1922 found its most universal theme.

This is certainly a significant part of what critics like Oberholtzer and Stoddard found so threatening in both the popular arts and aesthetic modernism. When Bell accuses Joyce, Eliot, and Woolf of "syncopation," he is accusing them of disrupting a natural rhythm with mechanical embellishments. He is defending a natural order against irony and disruption, an irony and disruption he senses has come to art through the widespread reproduction and dissemination of popular materials. "Syncopation" is his negative figure for the fact of mechanical reproduction itself, a negative version of the vibration that Cocteau wanted to bring into *Parade*. The sense of this new rhythm was fairly widespread at the time; even the *Evening News* observed of *Ulysses* that its "style is in the new fashionable kinematographic vein, very jerky and elliptical."[160] A syncopation of sight, this jerkiness suggested the uncanny way in which the new media created copies at such a slight and enigmatic remove from originals as to make the difference disorienting. Once sound and sight had been broken open in this way, as Bell, Stoddard, Oberholtzer, and Manners all dimly sensed, it would be hard to make anything whole in the same way again.

For other eyewitnesses of the time, however, such breaks in the apparent wholeness of the senses were what made the modern scene so appealing. When Nick Carraway walks the streets of New York in the summer of 1922, he is enticed by what seems an entirely new kind of visual phenomenon: "I began to like New York, the racy, adventurous feel of it at night and the satisfaction that the constant flicker of men and women and machines gives to the restless eye."[161] Here, Fitzgerald finds the most appropriate term for the change of rhythm that Eliot and Stein commend, the "syncopation" that Bell decries, for "flicker" is, of course, an early disparaging term for the movies, and Nick's use of it suggests that his visual pleasure comes from seeing reality as if it were a film. The "flicker" of the New York streets is the quick coming and going of the urban crowd, the way that constant motion resembles the motion that film brought to pictures, and the odd oscillation between actuality and its filmic counterpart, an oscillation so destabilizing that it actually makes reality shimmer and seem to disappear. Writers like Fitzgerald, Seldes, Cummings, Stein, and even Eliot were intrigued, if not always attracted, by the ways in which the popular arts were rearranging experience, given the powerful new means of reproduction at their disposal. Cheerleaders for the popular arts like Seldes and conservative opponents like Stoddard and Oberholtzer sensed that something fundamental was changing in the way that art and society informed one another, and both sides felt that modernist literature was part of that change. For someone like Seldes, in fact, it was the very convergence of modernist literature and popular culture that made 1922 so significant a year in the history of the modern.

5

All Nice Wives Are Like That

ANY NUMBER OF writers might have looked back at 1922 as a year of important beginnings, but perhaps only Willa Cather looked at it as a definitive end. In a book of essays published in 1936 under the defensive title of *Not Under Forty*, Cather announced, "The world broke in two in 1922 or thereabouts, and the persons and prejudices recalled in these sketches slid back into yesterday's seven thousand years."[1] Though it has always been hard for Cather scholars to explain why she placed this watershed so precisely in 1922, it is not hard to see what it divided. The preface starkly distinguishes the "forward-goers" from "the backward" and ironically addresses itself only to the latter. In this rather chilly way, Cather invites into her book only those readers pleased to have passed forty and proud to be numbered among the "backward."[2]

Letters Cather wrote to Dorothy Canfield Fisher in 1922 suggest that this stern antimodernism began with disapproval of avant-garde experiments in the arts, and it is certainly the case that 1922 marked the triumphant arrival of a kind of literature for which she had little obvious affinity.[3] In fact, Cather may seem to epitomize the kind of writing that literary modernism notoriously sought to displace. Her works were stylistically conventional, popular, nostalgic, and regional at a time when writers like Eliot and Pound were demanding that literature be difficult, up-to-date, and international.[4] These differences were rather harshly focused by the award of the 1922 Pulitzer Prize to Cather's *One of Ours*, just the sort of conventional success that made it an inviting target for younger critics such as Gilbert Seldes and Edmund Wilson. For writers like Seldes and Wilson, 1922 was not a low point but rather "the peak of the younger generation," as their friend F. Scott Fitzgerald put it, and their evident distaste for *One of Ours* seemed destined to make Cather feel the generational difference.[5] Though her distrust of aesthetic modernism predated this controversy, it must certainly have sharpened her sense of living in a world whose traditions had suddenly been rendered obsolete.[6]

The fact that Cather was not just old and conventional but also female was not at all irrelevant to the controversy. The literary qualities she seemed to epitomize—the simple, the popular, the nostalgic—together made up one of early modernism's announced targets: the ladylike. Joyce is usually held to have provided the best summation of this animosity when he announced that *The Waste Land* "ends [the] idea of poetry for ladies."[7] Some of the early criticism of *One of Ours* seemed to be determined by a parallel desire to end the idea of novels for ladies. Seldes cast some complex and intriguing aspersions by titling his review "Claude Bovary," renaming and regendering Cather's main character.[8] Wilson participated by publishing a similarly hostile review, which elicited a now-notorious letter from Ernest Hemingway in which Cather is attacked and patronized at once as a "poor woman."[9] Thus Cather's feeling that this year broke the world in two might have a sexual as well as a temporal sense, though the two categories tend to merge when the future is figured as male and the hopelessly passé as female.

Younger male modernists like Seldes, Wilson, and Hemingway might have found some evidence for this equation in the work of the linguist Otto Jespersen. *Language: Its Nature, Development, and Origin*, which Jespersen published in January 1922, contained an entire chapter on "The Woman," primarily on her role as an agent of linguistic change. In Jespersen's opinion, the influence of women on language is rather slight, since they tend to be correct, conservative speakers rather than innovators:

> the highest linguistic genius and the lowest degree of linguistic imbecility are very rarely found among women. The greatest orators, the most famous literary artists, have been men; but it may serve as a sort of consolation to the other sex that there are a much greater number of men than of women who cannot put two words together intelligibly, who stutter and stammer and hesitate, and are unable to find suitable expressions for the simplest thought. Between these two extremes the woman moves with a sure and supple tongue which is ever ready to find words and to pronounce them in a clear and intelligible manner.[10]

In other words, women embody linguistic convention, while men are the innovators. Men, in Jespersen's view, are simply more various, for good and for ill, than women. This explains, perhaps, why there is no chapter in *Language* on men, who are simply too vast for a single category.

With such pseudo-scientific conclusions,[11] Jespersen reinforces the general prejudice about women and language visible in the condescension of Seldes and Wilson toward Cather. Her work is seen as conservative, conventional, and dull next to the exciting literary experiments of the male avant-garde. The feminine, in this analysis, is both homely and artificial, the male somehow simultaneously more realistic and more imaginative. In this very inconsistency, however, it begins to be apparent how this notion of the feminine allows its believers to resolve certain difficult ambivalences, particularly the rather obvious one between aesthetic creativity and a masculinity defined by its crude practical power. Part of the male hostility toward Cather's work may in fact come from the way it pries this contradiction open. Some of the sense of hostile conflict surrounding her in 1922 may in fact be related to larger changes in British and American society, which were making this contradiction painfully obvious. And some of the emotional charge built up at this time may come from the guilty secret harbored especially by Hemingway, that male modernism itself was not so much a defiance of convention as an exacerbation of the contradictions within it, a fact exemplified by the very close relationship this master misogynist was just beginning with a writer intriguingly similar to Cather, Gertrude Stein.

The Old Beauty

Cather herself reflected on the relation between gender and aesthetic convention in a little-known story written at the same time as the preface to *Not Under Forty* and set in the year that preface names as a breaking point in history.[12] The title of the story, "The Old Beauty," refers specifically to the heroine, Gabrielle de Couçy, formerly Lady Longstreet, who dies in a kind of temporal exile at Aix-les-Bains in September 1922, but it also refers to a kind of aesthetic distinction, a beautiful kind of art, that Cather apparently felt had died its own death in that year. Cather covertly associates this beauty with her own work, since Gabrielle de Couçy, who has virtually the same name as one of the characters in *One of Ours*, dies in the very month in which that novel was published.[13]

It seems, in fact, on a first reading, that the story is constructed defiantly to confirm the assumptions behind the most gender-based of the attacks on *One of Ours*. Art is represented by a lady who is a lady in the old sense: genteel, conservative, reserved to the point of frigidity. Moreover, the death of this lady is caused by the passage of time in a more general and abstract sense than usual. Though there is a slight accident, there is no acute injury or illness: she dies apparently because she has become terminally outmoded. She passes, in a sense, because ladies no longer exist in a world in which young people bathe "naked."[14] Though the story sometimes takes a humorous distance from this exaggerated prudery, it is not in fact very different from Cather's own feelings in 1922. One of the things that depressed her, as she told Dorothy Canfield Fisher at the time, was a decline in the sense of sin, an immorality that she associated equally with sexual behavior and modern art.[15] In fact, the feeling she reports to Fisher—"We knew one world and knew what we felt about it. Now we find ourselves in quite another"—is the same one that bewilders Mme. de Couçy: "You see she thought, once the war was over, the world would be just as it used to be. Of course it isn't."[16] The world, that is to say, had broken in two.

The incident that precipitates the break seems to make even more explicit the notion that this lady dies because ladies can no longer exist. While on a drive in the country, Mme. de Couçy and her party nearly collide with another car belonging to two American women, who are "bobbed, hatless, clad in dirty white knickers and sweaters."[17] Both the characters and the narrative seem to feel an inordinate hostility toward this pair. Mme. de Couçy is appalled by their "white breeches," which to her are a greater injury than a few bruises from the crash, and she dies mysteriously the next day. This is both the dénouement and the main dramatic weakness of the story, forcibly imposed as it seems to be by Cather's desire to draw an abstract distinction between the degraded, even "dirty," mannishness of the two women in breeches and the traditionally feminine beauty of the old woman. To make the point even more obviously clear, the two women address each other "as 'Marge' and 'Jim.'"

This, it seems, makes the allegory complete. Aesthetic beauty is so thoroughly associated with the rigid gender divisions of the past that it cannot survive in a world where a woman might be known as Jim. But it is also this detail that throws the whole rather cumbrous allegory off its foundations. For any reader of Cather, the name "Jim" is sure to recall Jim Burden of *My Antonia*, whose experiences so closely resemble Cather's own that he is generally considered to be a reimagination of herself as a boy.[18] More knowledgeable readers will recall that there is another woman named Jim in Cather's work, one Jimmy Broadwood, the actress specializing in trouser roles, who represents a node of sanity in the short story "Flavia and Her Artists." And finally, there is in "The Old Beauty" itself a new version of Jimmy Broadwood in the person of Cherry Beamish, the retired male impersonator who is now Mme. de Couçy's cherished companion.[19] How can Mme. de Couçy be horrified actually unto death by the specter of a woman in breeches when her dearest friend and companion has made a life of wearing breeches on the stage? For that matter, how can the narrative exude such an obvious dislike of these mannish women when the author herself had worn breeches, played trouser roles, and, for a time, asked to be known as William?[20]

There is, of course, a significant difference between Cherry, who is "such a womanly woman in private life,"[21] and the bobbed and knickered Jim. For Cherry, the male persona is a work of art, and it is perhaps because she is an artist that she is able to appreciate Mme. de Couçy so deeply as to devote her life to her. But this also means that art can be just as much a matter of defying or playfully subverting gender conventions as it seems for most of the story to be a matter of defending them. In fact, when Mme. de Couçy is finally laid to rest in Père Lachaise alongside Adelina Patti and Sarah Bernhardt, it seems that her life was no less theatrical than theirs, her great beauty no less a role than the boyishness of Cherry Beamish. Together they are, as Cherry says, "the queerest partnership that war and desolation have made,"[22] queerer even than Marge and Jim, because their particular travesty of the conventional male-female couple contains in it more of the uncertainty of art.

Cather may have had private reasons for drawing a sharp distinction between Cherry's male impersonation and the open and aggressive mannishness of Marge and Jim. If she was, as Sharon O'Brien has argued, a secretive and somewhat guilty lesbian, then she may well have feared the openness very common among American expatriates in France at the time in which her story is set. The dress in Natalie Barney's circle, for example, did not generally run to dirty white knickers, but it was decidedly masculine.[23] "The Old Beauty" may thus record a generational clash among lesbians, and Cather may be associating the aesthetic not with the female as against the male but with an involuted and cryptic lesbianism as opposed to a more overt modern version. Thus "The Old Beauty" might be considered a story of lesbian panic, in which Mme. de Couçy dies because she has suddenly been confronted with a truth about her relationship to Cherry that conventional life cannot allow.[24]

Such a narrow biographical reduction does not explain, however, the close relationship Cather suggests between this story and *One of Ours*, a novel about the painful maturation of a young man. There is a good deal of difference between the squeamishness of the character and the boldness of the author, who, very much like Cherry Beamish, imagines her way into the psyche of a young man in order to write her novel. What allows both Cather and Beamish their leeway to experiment is simply aesthetic convention itself, the acknowledged artificiality of a role, within which human ingenuity can contain all sorts of behavior not possible off-stage and beyond the pages of books. This means, however, that in "The Old Beauty" aesthetic convention is not to be unambiguously associated with conventional femininity but also with a rather drastic freedom from conventional gender constraints.

The very title of Cather's story thus seems to contain a rather complex argument about art and gender. One kind of "old beauty," the quintessentially feminine aesthetic of Mme. de Couçy, is accompanied by—complemented but not cancelled by—another "old beauty," the well-worn stage routines that allow Cherry Beamish to stretch the bounds of gender. By placing the story so pointedly in 1922, Cather seems to suggest that those two kinds of beauty came to some sort of crisis in that year and that *One of Ours* is also in some way about that crisis. She also suggests that modernism, a "new beauty," might make its way in the world not by repudiating convention in favor of some putative reality, but rather by putting convention, in language and behavior, in some sort of critical resonance until it yields up the freedom inherent within it. In this, she turns out to be closer to the sort of modernism Gertrude Stein was offering in 1922 than at least some of her male antagonists.

Claude Bovary

By most practical measures, *One of Ours* was Cather's most successful novel to date. Her first with Knopf, it sold well—well enough, in fact, to be considered a best-seller—and it achieved enough critical esteem to be awarded the Pulitzer Prize.[25] At the same time, a number of the critics Cather most hoped to please were disappointed by the book. H. L. Mencken and Sinclair Lewis, for example, wrote generally critical notices, and many of the younger critics were harsh and even dismissive.[26]

In some of these there was an undertone of generational polemic, a negative version of the propaganda on behalf of modernism being carried out in the same journals by the same critics. In *The Dial*, for example, Gilbert Seldes based his review on a truism drawn from "modern aesthetics" to the effect that "expression" and "impression" should coincide. Where they do not, where the language of the novelist is inadequate to the impressions to be conveyed, then the result is mere reportage, as distinguished from art. Seldes rather cruelly titled his review "Claude Bovary," playing on the midwestern cloddishness of the main character's name, to dramatize the differences between Cather's reporting and Flaubert's art.[27] Edmund Wilson, who found the novel "a pretty flat failure," made the same unfriendly comparison, citing Joyce's *Ulysses* as a better example of Flaubertian "economy of detail."[28] The sheer audacity of praising *Ulysses* for "economy of detail," even at a time when very few could have read it, betrays the ulterior motive of these reviews, which is to condemn as vulgar and inartistic certain novelistic conventions to which modernism was opposed.

What must have made this particularly irksome for Cather is the fact that she had just made many of the same points herself, though less tendentiously, in "The Novel Demeublé," published in the *New Republic* in April. In this, her credo as a novelist, she came out against description for its own sake and for the same fusion of impression and expression that Seldes and Wilson were demanding. In fact, she even found hopeful signs in the influence of "modern painting" on "the younger writers," which seemed to be moving them in this direction.[29] Though there is no explicit mention of Flaubert in the essay, he had been Cather's model when Seldes and Wilson were still in short pants.[30] In other words, Cather was not at all unfriendly, in general terms, to the aesthetic regime represented by the younger critics.

Of course, it is possible that *One of Ours* simply failed to live up to aesthetic standards held in common by the novelist and her critics. But the tone of some of the attacks on the novel suggests that something else was involved. Most of the hostile reviews concentrated their criticism on the second half of the book, in which Claude Wheeler leaves Nebraska for the battlefields of France. The explanation for the relative failure of this part of the novel was, for most reviewers, not far to seek. According to Sidney Howard, writing in *The Bookman*, *One of Ours* shows "what a woman can write supremely and what she cannot write at all."[31] Ernest Hemingway made the same analysis more explicit when he claimed to Edmund Wilson that Cather had taken all her battle knowledge from the movies: "You were in the war weren't you? Wasn't that last scene in the lines wonderful? Do you know where it came from? The battle scene in *Birth of a Nation*. I identified episode after episode, Catherized. Poor woman she had to get her war experience somewhere."[32] In one way, the crude realism of such criticism is wholly at odds with the complaints of Seldes and Wilson that *One of Ours* is full of unnecessary reportage. In another way, however, this very inconsistency reveals something unstable in the modernist objection to the conventional, which is seen as effete and excessively refined, distant from experience, but also as lumpishly realistic and unimaginative. As Rita Felski puts it, "Although the male intelligentsia disputed whether naturalist or modernist techniques were more suited to representing the complexities of the modern age, they were largely united in their disdain for an idealist aesthetic associated with an outmoded and cloying feminine sentimentality."[33]

The reception of *One of Ours* thus seems a classic instance of the way in which literary modernism was defined negatively by distinguishing it from a popular literature associated primarily with women. Whether this modern literature was to be toughly realistic or aesthetically experimental, it could define itself in contradistinction to a passive, sentimental, and essentially conformist female art. And yet, drawing the lines in this way is to accept without much probing both *One of Ours* and the male response to it, which need not have been quite so fierce if Cather really were, as Hemingway pretends, merely an object to be pitied. It may be that the massive condescension of the younger male writers to their older female colleague masks another reaction, that distinction is insisted on, as it so often is, precisely because the resemblance is too close. If this is the case, it may require some rethinking of the crisis of art and gender that Cather herself located in 1922.

Though *One of Ours* is never discussed in histories of modern literature, a few of Cather's contemporary critics have noticed how closely it resembles other works published in the same year. Especially clear is the general pattern of disillusionment and expatriation that would come virtually to define the "lost generation."[34] Claude Wheeler, the Nebraska farmboy who is Cather's protagonist, is restless and discontented, "one of those visionary fellows," his father speculates, "who make unnecessary difficulties for themselves and other people."[35] Like any number of other modern protagonists, remarkably like Hemingway's Harold Krebs, for example, Claude is paralyzed by the pointlessness of an exchange economy stripped of its religious justifications: "He could not see the use of working for money, when money brought nothing one wanted. Mrs. Erlich said it brought security. Sometimes he thought this security was what was the matter with everybody; that only perfect safety was required to kill all the best qualities in people and develop the mean ones" (*OO*, p. 102). Lost in a purely instrumental world, a world in which people

have become mechanical and dead and objects have acquired a perverse
power, Claude has a vision that essentially paraphrases the opening of *The
Waste Land*:

> Rubbish . . . junk . . . his mind could not picture anything that so exposed and con-
> demned all the dreary, weary, ever-repeated actions by which life is continued from
> day to day. Actions without meaning. . . . As he looked out and saw the grey land-
> scape through the gently falling snow, he could not help thinking how much better
> it would be if people could go to sleep like the fields; could be blanketed down
> under the snow, to wake with their hurts healed and their defeats forgotten. (*OO*,
> p. 223)

Like the voice that speaks at the beginning of *The Waste Land*, Claude wants
simply to be buried now that he is, to all intents and purposes, dead, but the
peculiar horror of modern life is, as in so many other works of the time, to be
dead and not to be buried or even, for that matter, to be unconscious.

In many readings of the novel, what saves Claude from this death-in-life is
the life-in-death of a military hero. Fallen in battle, Claude has finally "found
his place" (*OO*, p. 457), or so, at least, his mother thinks. The last section of
the novel suggests, however, that in France Claude had "found his place" in
a different and more complicated sense. In a way, Claude had been destined
for France from birth, or at least from the moment he was christened with the
unfortunate name that Nebraskans always pronounced "clod" (*OO*, pp. 130,
208). Early on, in the home of the Erlichs, Claude discovers within himself
another Claude, Claude Melnotte, a romantic hero from the pages of Bulwer-
Lytton, but it is not until he actually goes to France that he finally escapes
cloddishness by acquiring his right and proper name in a land that can prop-
erly pronounce it. This suggests that it is not so much war as it is France that
saves Claude from the sense of spiritless materiality that makes him feel as if
he actually were a clod.

Yet, it may not be France itself that saves him as much as the sheer experience of expatriation. For France turns out remarkably to resemble Nebraska,
so much so that the troops roar with laughter when their train passes a field of
alfalfa: "alfalfa was one thing, they believed, that had never been heard of outside their own prairie states" (*OO*, p. 339). Claude himself is constantly redis-
covering bits and pieces of the prairie home, like the evening primrose: "He
had never thought it very pretty, but he was pleased to find it here. He had supposed it was one of those nameless prairie flowers that grew on the prairie and
nowhere else" (*OO*, p. 388). Like himself, the evening primrose acquires a name
and a distinction through imaginative transplantation. What makes the dull, ordinary flower suddenly pleasing is simply the change of context, which makes
it seem new by contrast. In France, then, Claude finds "his place" in a double
sense, for France gives him back Nebraska, only filled now with "the feeling"
(*OO*, p. 386) that had been bled from it by relentless exploitation. That "feeling" cannot survive when things are constantly degraded by instrumental use;

it comes back when they are rediscovered torn from context and removed from familiarity. In other words, expatriation to France restores to Claude the aesthetic dimension without which his life had seemed numbingly material, and it does so because distance from the ordinary, especially from ordinary use, is one indispensable characteristic of the aesthetic.

Claude's particular experiences are to some extent Cather's own and to some extent those of her cousin, G. P. Cather, who actually died in the war, but *One of Ours* also makes them paradigmatic of a whole generation that fled from America to France in order to rediscover art. Perhaps the most celebrated such departure at the time was Harold Stearns' in 1921. In his preface to *Civilization in the United States*, published the year after his departure, Stearns complained that "the most moving and pathetic fact in the social life of America to-day is emotional and aesthetic starvation, of which the mania for petty regulation, the driving, regimentating, and drilling, the secret society and its grotesque regalia, the firm grasp on the unessentials of material organization of our pleasures and gaieties are all eloquent stigmata."[36] Stearns loudly departed the United States for France, where he was to end his aesthetic starvation as a racetrack columnist. The same country was put to somewhat better use in the book that Hemingway complained really deserved the Pulitzer of 1922: Cummings' *The Enormous Room*. Like Stearns, Cummings believed that the United States was "the most aesthetically incapable organization ever created for the purpose of perpetuating defunct ideals and ideas." Like Claude, though far more flamboyantly and with a great deal more self-congratulation, Cummings rediscovered "feeling" during the war in France, though it was, to be sure, in prison and not in battle: "and then at last it was lumières éteintes; and les deux américains lay in their beds in the cold rotten darkness, talking in low voices of the past,ofPétrouchka,ofParis,of that brilliant and extraordinary and impossible something: Life."[37]

It was Hemingway himself, of course, who did the most to make France seem the inevitable alternative to the aesthetic starvation of conventional American life, which appears in early stories like "Soldiers Home" in a form so close to *One of Ours* that his criticism of that novel begins to seem almost self-protective. In fact, there is very little difference between Claude and Harold Krebs except that Harold has survived the war, so the "cool, valuable quality" that had distinguished his success as a soldier was sullied by renewed contact with mercantile America.[38] Viewed in this light, the generally critical response of Hemingway's generation as a whole to Cather's novel may be seen to derive from an uncomfortable sense of recognition: the unhappy, maladjusted, aesthetically starved midwestern boy who finds himself in France is the paradigmatic figure of this generation. When Seldes sarcastically dubs this figure "Claude Bovary," he has cruelly, if unwittingly, typed his own generation.

Of course, Cather did not mean to lampoon these writers, whose works were generally contemporaneous with hers and whose animosity she could

hardly have intuited before the fact; but she does seem to have set out to de-
lineate a general crisis in masculinity, one that might have motivated some of
the opposition to her novel. Claude's aesthetic dissatisfaction, his unslaked appetite for "feeling," is in one sense neither abstract nor disinterested but
frankly carnal. For Claude is trapped in marriage with a woman who has "no
shades of feeling to correspond to her natural grace," a woman who "disliked
ardour of any kind," who had replaced physical and emotional commitment
to her husband with commitment to a series of progressive causes including
vegetarianism (*OO*, pp. 211–212). His frustration, in other words, is in part
the sexual frustration of a relatively conventional young man married to a progressively modern young woman.

The fact that Enid refuses to consummate their marriage and that Claude
dully but uncomplainingly acquiesces has always been for critics one of the
least convincing aspects of this novel, and yet, however implausible it may
seem, it is one of the timeliest elements of Cather's plot. In fact, the cold
modern wife who redirects her passions into business is one of the fixtures of
the popular literature of this year. She is the centerpiece of a far larger best-
seller than *One of Ours*, A. S. M. Hutchinson's *This Freedom*, which caused controversy on both sides of the Atlantic. Hutchinson's previous novel, *If Winter
Comes*, was still at the top of the best-seller list in 1922 and was the subject of
such widespread popularity that the *Times* sponsored a public debate on it that
ran throughout April, May, and June.[39] *This Freedom* sparked even more discussion, most of it debate about the relative plausibility of the plot, in which
a direct cause-and-effect relation is drawn between Rosalie Occleve's taking a
job and the deaths of two of her children and the disgrace of the third. Actually, the real implausibility in the novel, given the nature of the main character, is that she should have gotten married at all, since the "special function
of men in regard to women" repulses her.[40] Though she is swept off her feet
and has three children, it is the romance of business that really entrances Rosalie, and the resulting emotional impoverishment of a home deprived of a
true woman's influence leads to disaster.

Though Hutchinson was widely criticized for unacceptably stacking the
deck against his poor heroine, his book did ignite a transatlantic discussion as
to whether a woman could keep a job and manage her home and family as
well. Though G. K. Chesterton was skeptical, the prominent women polled by
the *Literary Digest* in November thought, on the whole, that it could be managed.[41] The same question was raised and rather starkly settled in Hamilton
Fyfe's *The Fruit of the Tree*. The heroine of this novel, Muriel Tanstead, agrees
to marry on the condition that she not be required either to give up her job
or to have children, and though her husband agrees, the continuing lack of
what he pathetically calls "what a man marries for" and she disdainfully calls
"the other thing" causes such distress that he takes a mistress, establishes a
parallel home, and has several children. When it all comes out, as it inevitably
must, the three principals and their spiritual adviser decide to continue the

arrangement, since Muriel wants Tanstead's intellectual companionship but not his children; Margaret, the mistress, wants the children but not especially Tanstead's companionship; and Tanstead wants both companionship and children, but finds, as Muriel wisely puts it, that "a man wants a woman to be so many different things. And generally she can't be more than one. That's the difficulty."[42]

Both novels are explicitly set in 1922 so as to make as strong as possible their connection with contemporary events. Muriel becomes England's "First Woman Barrister's Clerk" in the year that saw the first woman admitted to the bar in England.[43] Rosalie insists that her job be treated with precisely the same seriousness as her husband's in the year in which Alice Paul and the National Woman's Party was hoping to pass an Equal Rights Amendment.[44] What the *Illustrated London News* called "Women's Invasion of Parliament" was also a matter of much debate, though by the end of the national elections held this year in England and the United States there were still no women legislators who were not serving out the unexpired terms of their husbands or fathers.[45] In fact, it was still to be determined in the United States whether a woman could legally hold office or not, it having been argued in state court in Michigan that a married woman could not serve because she was "a chattel and not a person." The passage of the Cable Act in 1922 established for the first time in the United States that a woman's citizenship was not contingent on that of her husband, and this, along with various state court decisions allowing women officially to hold office, established what suffrage seemed to imply: that a woman was an independent being with rights and duties of her own.[46]

Entry into the work force, however, seemed a different matter, and it was still widely believed at this time that women worked only to supplement the income provided by husbands.[47] The vanguard of change in this respect seems to have been made up of typists, who appear in a number of works besides *The Waste Land*. In *The Fruit of the Tree*, Tanstead's godfather, a bishop, is first scandalized merely that Margaret comes to his office to type, not inappropriately considering what this arrangement ultimately leads to. In Arnold Bennett's *Lilian*, a typist also becomes her employer's mistress, though with happier results in this case, since he marries her and then obligingly dies.[48] Elinor Glyn's *Man and Maid* is also about an affair between a man and his typist, though in this case the fairy-tale ending is supposed to resolve rather more than the plot. The employer in this novel suffers both physically and mentally from wounds received during the war. Confined to a wheelchair, he spars mentally with the typist, who is resolute and strong where he is weak. Finally, he stands up out of his wheelchair and overcomes her resistance, while she happily acknowledges the "powerful brute" he has become.[49] As a number of scholars, including Billie Melman, Susan Gubar, and Sandra Gilbert have shown, there was a good deal of anxiety about women remaining in the work force after the war to vie with men, and Glyn's novel seems an explicit attempt to resolve these feelings at the level of romance.[50]

SENIOR WOMAN OF THE MIDDLE TEMPLE : MISS HELENA NORMANTON, WHO PASSED HER FINALS IN OCT., 1921.

PLACED IN CLASS THREE AT THE RECENT EASTER TERM BAR FINAL EXAMINATIONS : MISS MERCY L. ASHWORTH.

THE FIRST ENGLISHWOMAN TO BE CALLED TO THE BAR (ON MAY 10) : MISS IVY WILLIAMS, A B.C.L., M.A., AND LECTURER AT OXFORD.

THE FIRST WOMAN TO PASS THE ENGLISH BAR EXAMINATIONS : MISS OLIVE KATHERINE CLAPHAM.

IN a letter to the " Times " criticising the suggestions (mentioned below) for the costume of women barristers, Lieutenant-Colonel C. P. Hawkes writes : " It is pointed out to me that, in order strictly to conform with the regulations, it will be necessary for a lady barrister to crop her head with masculine abbreviation and incur no inconsiderable expense in obtaining mannish shirts and 'stiff high collars' of a kind which, owing to the softer trend of feminine fashions for the last ten years, are unobtainable in ordinary shops, thus putting her to an economic disadvantage as compared with a male advocate, whose expenses are limited to the purchase of wig, gown and bands, and whose 'quick-change' in the robing-room chiefly consists in the removal of his tie. Sir Herbert Stephen points out that modern forensic dress is but a survival of eighteenth-century male fashions. May I suggest that the soft lawn 'jabot' of that period (of which the bands are a vestige) should be allowed, as giving the same effect as, though more conveniently adjustable than, the stiff white collar ; and that the masculine wig, grotesque and undignified as it will appear upon a female head, should be replaced by the graceful 'coif.' "

The First Woman Called to the English Bar—and Others. Ivy Williams, the first English woman barrister (*Illustrated London News*, May 13, 1922)

What happens in such novels is that the contradiction between women and work is resolved when the woman gives up work to become a willing sexual partner. But Fyfe, among others, worried that such a resolution was not realistic, that the contradiction between women and work was so strong as to require "what might almost be called a Third Sex. This was made up of women who, foreseeing no probability of marriage to provide them with interest and occupation, either worked for a living or threw their energies into work of a social or charitable kind."[51] *The Fruit of the Tree, This Freedom,* and *One of Ours* are, to varying degrees, about what happens when a member of this Third Sex goes against her better judgment and marries. Only Fyfe can imagine a happy ending and then only by inventing a new kind of marriage joining a threesome: a man, a woman, and a member of the Third Sex.

The frustration caused by these cold and unfeeling new women is not, however, merely carnal. Claude is, in fact, not especially sensual himself, and he accepts his banishment from Enid's bed with a meekness that has astonished and disconcerted any number of critics. Even his erotic daydreams about her are curiously cool and abstract: "In his dreams he never wakened her, but loved her while she was still and unconscious like a statue" (*OO*, p. 145). And he actually seems to prefer daydreams to reality: "Often he was glad when she went away and left him alone to think about her" (*OO*, p. 145). What really seems to stir Claude about his impending marriage is the opportunity it offers him to build and decorate a house and plant its grounds. At times, these activities seem a compensation for the emotional poverty of the engagement: "He lavished upon the little house the solicitude and cherishing care that Enid seemed not to need" (*OO*, p. 177). But Claude's joy in the house is so detailed and so extreme that it seems to displace Enid almost too successfully. In fact, Claude takes to himself the domestic attitudes conventionally acted out by the prospective bride: "He hated to have anybody step on his floors. He planted gourd vines about the back porch, set out clematis and lilac bushes, and put in a kitchen garden" (*OO*, p. 183). These passages suggest what it is that Claude has actually married for, certainly not for sex nor perhaps even for companionship but rather for the opportunity to inject into the drab Nebraska world the "feeling" and beauty whose lack he feels so painfully. Marriage to Enid is to be an outlet for the aesthetic feelings that the conventional life of a Nebraska farmboy have left bottled up inside him.

Claude wants in Enid what Cather calls elsewhere in the novel an "aesthetic proxy":

> When they were classmates at the Frankfort High School, Gladys was Claude's aesthetic proxy. It wasn't the proper thing for a boy to be too clean, or too careful about his dress and manners. But if he selected a girl who was irreproachable in these respects, got his Latin and did his laboratory work with her, then all her personal attractions redounded to his credit. Gladys had seemed to appreciate the honour Claude did her, and it was not all on her own account that she wore such beautifully ironed muslin dresses when they went out on botanical expeditions. (*OO*, p. 112)[52]

Cather is not, perhaps, suggesting that Claude would like to wear those beautifully ironed muslin dresses himself, but she is saying that Claude needs someone through whom he can exercise an aesthetic sense generally forbidden to men in the Nebraska countryside. A wife is, in this sense, a sort of camouflage behind which a man can clean and plant and decorate. Because he exercises his aesthetic proclivities through her, in her name, he can enjoy the expansion of ordinary life that the aesthetic affords and still reinforce the strict gender divisions that the aesthetic underwrites. And this, unfortunately, is precisely where Enid lets him down. All her causes, from Prohibition to vegetarianism, seem to require, as Frances Kaye says, "a reduction of the beauty in the world," or at least a reduction in sensory gratification available in it.[53] Enid's very name suggests her purity, while Gladys' name, which is the female version of Claude, suggests that she is not just suited to him but perhaps *is* him, expressed in female form.[54]

In short, *One of Ours* is not at all what Hemingway said it was, the story of a woman's battle envy; rather, it is the story of a man's envy of muslin dresses and pretty flowers, and this is what made it so disconcerting for Hemingway's generation. Cather is describing in novelistic terms the intellectual and emotional self-impoverishment of men that Harold Stearns was denouncing at the same time in *Civilization in the United States*: "To an extent almost incomprehensible to the peoples of older cultures, the things of the mind and the spirit have been given over, in America, into the almost exclusive custody of women. This has been true certainly of art, certainly of music, certainly of education."[55] The general separation of the aesthetic from the practical and scientific, and the arrogation of the latter by spheres of life generally closed to women, led to an identification of the aesthetic with the feminine so utter that it seemed virtually incompatible with masculinity.[56] The male life that results is the life Cather described in *One of Ours*: sterile, frustrated, and bleak. It is the life apparently led by her cousin, G. P. Cather, who was the model for Claude and for whom Cather herself apparently functioned as a kind of aesthetic proxy.[57] And it was the life generally described and denounced in *Civilization in the United States*, a life that Stearns' generation fled to France to avoid.

The best-sellers of the year suggest, however, that this crisis in masculinity was felt well beyond the lost generation, that it extended to men who had no precise aesthetic ambitions themselves, for the feminine had gradually come to be the repository of emotional and aesthetic qualities that were all the more necessary the more they were wrung out of industrial society. Their status is symbolized best perhaps by the fairy child who appears in the dreams of George F. Babbitt at the beginning of Sinclair Lewis' best-seller of 1922: "She was so slim, so white, so eager! She cried that he was gay and valiant, that she would wait for him, that they would sail."[58] No one could be more aggressively masculine, more pedantically practical, more dedicated to business values than George Babbitt, whom the entire nation instantly recognized as a type of American masculinity, and yet his life depends on the fairy child, his aesthetic proxy, who keeps alive in dreams the very qualities Babbitt most despises when awake.

The "cold" working wives of the best-sellers of this year are rebelling against this psychic division of labor. As Havelock Ellis put it, "In old days it was conventionally supposed that women's sphere was that of the feelings; the result has been that women now often take ostentatious pleasure in washing their hands of feelings and accusing men of 'sentiment.'"[59] Rosalie Occleve, for example, in Hutchinson's *This Freedom*, snorts, "Sensitive! No, a better word than that. She was in such matters *sensible*."[60] Though Rosalie is in many ways quite romantic about being sensible, it is clear nonetheless that her unwillingness to sustain the emotional in a traditionally feminine sense dooms her family to a life of soulless routine. Choosing the sensible over the sentimental hardens her own heart and then those of her children, who are emotionally dead to their parents long before the implausible plot actually takes them to their graves. The ludicrous twists of fate that take the children one by one are not meant, however, simply to represent divine retribution. The protracted agony of losing her children reeducates Rosalie in the routines of feeling. Women had always demonstrated their greater emotional sensitivity, Ann Douglas points out, by suffering.[61] Through enforced suffering, Rosalie comes to accept the sentimental role she had once scorned.

The family in Fyfe's novel avoids the fate of the Occleves by splitting itself in two: Muriel lives her childless life in town, while Margaret raises the children in a cottage in the country. This reestablishment of the traditional psychic division of labor reveals what else is at stake in these novels. As Rita Felski puts it, "The maternal home offers a redemptive haven for those fleeing the chaos and instability of the modern world."[62] "Sensible" women threaten the implicit arrangement whereby men are able to have both the modern world of the city and the old life of the cottage. Emotionless marriage is, therefore, one of the hallmarks of modernity in works from *This Freedom* to *The Waste Land*, not necessarily because marriages were any less successful in 1922, but because the aesthetic and emotional qualities sequestered in the feminine sphere had represented the last, most necessary, bulwark against the utter regimentation of modern life. Without a convenient repository for those feelings, men must either assume them themselves and thus suffer a significant change in the conventional notion of masculinity or let modernity work its logic utterly and without qualification.

By itself, this strong resemblance between Cather's novel and male-authored works, both popular and experimental, might seem to call for a reaction very different from the one the novel received. After all, it is quite easy to read the first part of *One of Ours* as an indictment of women like Enid, as if Cather, like Hutchinson, were claiming that keeping the aesthetic fires burning is one of the immemorial duties of women. Indeed, it seems that Enid is a more conventional domestic version of the mannish women in "The Old Beauty," and she receives from her creator as little overt sympathy as they do.[63] It was not, however, this part of the novel that elicited the most criticism, but rather the later sections set in France. These, it seemed to certain male critics, violated the generic boundaries that historical experience has set around female experience. In the literary marketplace, that is to say, the novel assumed a position analogous to Enid's within the novel, quite regardless of Cather's own sympathies in the matter. The widely perceived split between the two main parts of the novel may evince a deeper discontinuity, not so much in the novel itself as in readers' attitudes toward it. While the first part might be read as a fairly conventional denunciation of the modern woman, the second proposed a very unconventional resolution for the modern man.

In part, of course, mere removal to France resolves Claude's dilemma. The emotional relation to his own countryside, which he could not express directly nor by mediation through Enid, is mediated through France instead. But Claude is not alone in France, and part of his cure is the emotional outlet afforded by his men. The role he plays toward them is, as a number of critics have noticed, generally a maternal one: feeding, comforting, tending the sick. The real fulfillment of his life is represented, however, by a particular soldier, David Gerhardt, who is the aesthetic proxy Claude had failed to find in Enid: "In the years when he went to school in Lincoln, he was always hunting for some one whom he could admire without reservations; some one he could envy, emulate, wish to be. Now he believed that even then he must have had some faint image of a man like Gerhardt in his mind" (*OO*, p. 411). A man like Gerhardt is a man who is well read, widely traveled, aesthetically accomplished, a man, in this case, who plays the violin well enough to have had a successful concert career.

Cather takes pains to tell her readers, as explicitly as she dares, that the relationship between Claude and David is not a physical one. When they shoot a German officer who turns out to be wearing a locket containing the picture of "a young man, pale as snow, with blurred forget-me-not eyes," Claude assumes the keepsake must commemorate a younger brother, and David, by far the more worldly of the two, merely smiles indulgently (*OO*, pp. 431–432). Of course, if Claude is so utterly unaware of the possibility of male sexual attraction, he may easily feel it without knowing it, but it seems safer to assume that Claude's feelings for David are much like his feelings for Enid, that what he wants is not a sexual partner but an aesthetic proxy, someone he can "envy, emulate, wish to be." For these purposes, of course, David is all the more useful for being a man, representing as he does the possibility that masculinity and the aesthetic might not be utterly at odds. In himself, David represents an eminently sensible solution to the breakdown of the old psychic division of labor, that the aesthetic and emotional qualities once lodged exclusively in women should, insofar as they remain humanly valuable, be distributed across gender. Together, David and Claude represent a solution to the demise of marriage so prominent in the works of this year: that the important consolations once provided by it be found instead, or just as easily, in same-sex friendships.

Some inkling of this redistribution of gender roles, and some instinctive revulsion against it, is apparent when Seldes renames Cather's hero "Claude Bovary." But the sarcasm is at least partly defensive, for the resolution that Cather offers is to be found just as easily in the male-authored works of the year. The most important relationship in George Babbitt's waking world is with Paul Riesling, who also plays the violin. Their friendship is so strong that when Paul goes off the rails Babbitt's life explodes as well, for without Paul life is "meaningless."[64] In fact, Paul is mixed up in Babbitt's mind with the fairy child, not necessarily because he feels sexual desire for either but because Paul, who "might have been a great violinist or painter or writer," represents the necessary repository of aesthetic and emotional values without which Babbitt cannot continue in business.[65] To take a case much closer to Seldes himself, Cummings' *The Enormous Room* also juxtaposes a male friendship against the soul-destroying forces of conformity. When the authorities threaten the quasi-autobiographical protagonist with prison if he does not abandon his friend, he replies, "With my friend, I should be well content in prison."[66] Outside America, D. H. Lawrence was obsessively worrying the same issue in *Aaron's Rod*, published in 1922, and *Kangaroo*, written in that year, both of which are about the seductive problematics of male friendship. In all these cases, the male friend threatens to make the protagonist an outcast from society, a fact that may confess a secret fear of the consequences of homosexual love. But even in Lawrence, where the male relationship is the most explicitly physical, the male friend also serves as an alter ego, a representative of the protagonist's rebellious side. He is, in other words an aesthetic proxy, a representation of those qualities that, if realized, would make life in conventional male society impossible. *One of Ours* thus reflects in a rather complex way what seems to have been a general crisis in the relation of gender to art brought about by changes in the status of women. The conventional female role, what Cather calls the aesthetic proxy, long allowed men to keep a careful distance between their aesthetic needs and male practicality. Simply by writing out this situation, Cather had exposed something that many male readers were apparently unprepared to face. Beyond that, her portrait of a male aesthetic proxy reflects what was in fact one of the most common situations of the time in male works, as male writers began to examine the consequences of female refusal to play the conventional role.

These consequences might lead in one of two very different directions. One of the most crudely written of this year's best-sellers, Zane Grey's *The Day of the Beast*, shows how tortured and complex even the most conventional solution might be.[67] Grey's story is about a crippled and apparently dying veteran named Daren Lane, who returns home, along with two similarly crippled friends, to find the world broken in two. His job has been taken by a young woman who works for lower wages, and his fiancée has embarked on a life of jazz dancing and heavy petting with the "slackers" who remained physically whole and financially secure because they stayed at home. Because it is so exaggerated, Grey's novel makes especially clear one of the major changes wrought by the war: by imposing unexampled suffering on the men who served in it, the war imposed on men a variety of experience that had been associated with the feelings and sentiments of women.[68] Conversely, at least in Daren's eyes, the women have acquired a set of characteristics conventionally secured for men. Though the young women in *The Day of the Beast*, conventional flappers every one, seem very different from the cold wives of Hutchinson and Fyfe, they are in their own way every bit as cold and calculating. This is especially galling to Daren, who declares that he fought for one reason only, to protect his women from "the apish Huns."[69] As seriously crippled as he is, Daren can take no direct action to redress this situation, so he does what he can, which is to suffer.[70] He and his two friends, all of whom eventually die, become a center of pathos, suffering so extensively and so egregiously— Daren leaves home for the slums, where he virtually starves to death—that they reimpress on one or two worthwhile girls the virtues of feeling. Thus the aesthetic burden imposed on men by the war is painfully transferred back to its rightful bearers: the women.

What happens when the balance tips in the other direction is revealed by the very title of a story written at about this time by Sherwood Anderson, "The Man Who Became a Woman." Some time in the fall of 1922, Anderson wrote this racetrack story about a friendship between one Herman Dudley of Nebraska and a young man named Tom Means. Means is in many ways the quintessential aesthetic proxy. An aspiring writer with an appropriate surname, he has a way of talking about racetrack life that invests it with unexpected meaning: "It's pretty fine but I didn't know how fine it was until I got to know Tom Means and heard him talk about it all."[71] By talking, Means also develops in the narrator an aesthetic sense he hardly knew he had: "I would never have felt the way I finally got to feel about horses or enjoyed my stay among them half so much if it hadn't been for him" (*HM*, p. 189). Like David Gerhardt in the military or Paul Riesling in the world of business, Tom Means brings into an utterly male world, in this case the world of the racetrack, a kind of feeling usually banished from it.

At first, it seems that Anderson, like Cather, seeks protection from the more unconventional implications of this "feeling": "To tell the truth, I suppose I got to love Tom Means, who was five years older than me, although I wouldn't have dared say so, then. Americans are shy and timid about saying things like that and a man here don't dare own up he loves another man, I've found out, and they are afraid to admit such feelings to themselves even. I guess they're afraid it may be taken to mean something it don't need to at all" (*HM*, p. 188). However, the defensive assertion that "I'm not any fairy" (*HM*, p. 209) turns out to be rather spectacularly beside the point, for in the course of the story Herman Dudley actually turns into a woman. At first this seems a hallucination, perhaps the effect of drink, as the narrator looks into the mirror above a bar and sees a reflection that "wasn't my own face at all but the face of a woman" (*HM*, p. 207). But gradually he is forced into a series of female roles, asked to take care of a child first and then nearly raped in a hayloft.

What seems to have happened is that Dudley has been overtaken by his own feelings. All of these feelings have been wrapped up in the image of a woman, "a pure innocent one, for myself, made for me by God, maybe" (*HM*, p. 220). Instead of finding that woman, however, he has become her: "And now I was that woman, or something like her, myself" (*HM*, p. 221). In other words, the distance maintained by the aesthetic proxy between the subject and his own feelings has collapsed, the protection afforded by the proxy has disappeared, and the male is suddenly forced to assume the weight of his own emotions. None of this need have happened, perhaps, if Dudley had been content merely to love and admire Tom Means; it is not, in other words, male-centered desire in itself that renders him a woman. What does accomplish this transformation is the desire to write, which continues to come over Dudley like a hallucinatory spell long after he returns to his own male identity: "There was one experience of that time on the tracks that I am forced, by some feeling inside myself, to tell. Well, I don't know why but I've just got to" (*HM*, p. 189). This excess of feeling is what made Dudley into a woman in the first place, and it turns him back into one when he writes the experience down, a process that he calls, without explanation, "my knitting" (*HM*, p. 193).

This association of the female with writing is revealing on another level as well, for the story of Herman Dudley's near-rape and subsequent flight seems an elaborate exaggeration of a very similar scene in Cather's *My Antonia*, published four years earlier.[72] In this scene, Jim Burden, sleeping in Antonia's bed while she is away, is attacked by the repulsive Wick Cutter, who quite naturally expects to find Antonia herself. Like Herman Dudley, Jim ends up running out into the night, though Herman is the more seriously undressed. The relationships suggested by this similarity are dizzying in their complexity. Anderson has apparently taken over and rewritten from a male point of view a woman's version of what it would be like for a man to be taken for a woman and nearly raped. Or, to put it somewhat differently, writing makes Herman Dudley feel like a woman because his creator has appropriated a woman's story about a man who is made to feel what women feel in the grip of men. Writing, then, is not to be associated simply with the feminine but rather with a more general transsexuality, an aesthetic elision of the conventional boundaries that delimit gender. In this case, such transsexuality occurs on two levels at once, within the story itself, when the desire to write pulls Herman Dudley across the boundary of the masculine, and outside the story, in its relationship to *My Antonia*, in which Anderson seems to have found a model of transsexual experience too powerful to ignore.

This relationship also casts a new light on the controversy surrounding *One of Ours* and possibly on gender relations within modernism as a whole. Seldes' flippant title for that novel, "Claude Bovary," confesses, in the very gesture that is meant to feminize Cather's writing, the fundamentally transsexual nature of her work. Complaints that the novel inappropriately invades the battlefield are at bottom complaints that Cather has violated the conventional boundaries around male experience, and in this sense they are perfectly well founded. For Cather is writing about a redefinition of gender, a redistribution of human qualities in which even a battlefield might witness behavior that is conventionally feminine.[73] This elicits resistance from younger critics like Seldes and Wilson not because it is too different from the modernist work they favor but because it is altogether too similar. Any attempt to rescue the aesthetic from its American embargo would entail as a necessary corollary the sort of destabilization of gender that occurs in the works of Anderson, Cummings, and Lewis just as it occurs in Cather. But it occurs elsewhere as well. In fact, the very writers who were to end the idea of poetry for ladies wrote their own versions of "The Man Who Became a Woman": the "Circe" chapter of *Ulysses*, in which Leopold Bloom becomes a woman, and the third section of *The Waste Land*, in which Tiresias, having been a woman in the past, shares in the meager sensations of a female typist. In Eliot there is a good deal of resistance to the transsexual implications of his own work, a harsh misogyny mixed, as Wayne Koestenbaum has shown, with feminine self-identification.[74] But in Joyce's case, the parallels with Anderson are fairly exact, for it is because there is "a bit of the artist" about Bloom that he is considered "a mixed middling," an anomalous man at least part woman even before his fantastic transformation.[75] Include Lawrence in this group as well and it becomes clear that a great deal of the modernist work of 1922, major and minor, is concerned in some way with the reorientation of gender that Cather describes in *One of Ours*.[76]

The attempt of the male critics of *One of Ours* to distance themselves from Cather's supposed conventionality may therefore represent anxiety about what was happening within male modernism itself. The idea that women are more conventional than men had long been part of an aesthetic and psychological division of labor that allowed men access to certain activities and emotions without compromising the practical power associated with the masculine. As that division of labor became unstable, the contradictions in masculinity could no longer be composed by reference to some female aesthetic proxy; they began to appear in the form of a male aesthetic proxy, a doubling or changing of the self required by the conflicting demands of male creativity. This is one of the chief features of the very work that Seldes and Wilson were preferring to *One of Ours*. The same inconsistency is visible on the stylistic level as well, for the notion that women were more conventional users of language was at this very moment being called into question by the relationship between Hemingway and Gertrude Stein.

Hemingstein

In a 1924 review that appeared in *The Dial*, Edmund Wilson introduced the first published work of Ernest Hemingway as representative of a "school" including Hemingway, Sherwood Anderson, and Gertrude Stein.[77] As Marjorie Perloff has shown, this grouping was not uncommon in the earliest years of Hemingway's career, though the mutual regard on which it was founded was to be short lived.[78] Indeed, the association of the three was at its most intense at its very beginning in 1922. In February of that year, Anderson sent Stein the text of his introduction to *Geography and Plays*, which was to be published in December.[79] Even before this introduction appeared in print, Anderson had become one of the few prominent American writers to take Stein seriously in public, and his support was supposed to be helpful in marketing Stein's new book.[80] Stein responded, apparently with genuine warmth, in "Idem the Same: A Valentine for Sherwood Anderson," which appeared in the *Little Review* in the spring of 1923 but which had been finished almost immediately after Stein received Anderson's introduction.[81] At almost the same time, Hemingway arrived on Stein's doorstep with another introduction from Anderson, this one introducing himself. Their association was, of course, to constitute the very heart of the "lost generation," Stein providing the name, Hemingway the mythology, and the two of them together its characteristic literary style.[82]

By the time he denigrated Cather's writing as that of a "poor woman," then, Hemingway was heavily under the influence of this woman who was, in some personal respects at least, very like Cather. In fact, his dispraise of Cather in the letter to Wilson is immediately followed by two paragraphs of praise for Stein: "Her method is invaluable for analysing anything or making notes on a person or a place. She has a wonderful head."[83] The virtues Hemingway praises are those of the reporter he himself had been, the one who observes directly, as opposed to the sort of person who gets experience indirectly through the movies. To have a "wonderful head" is to be both intelligent and brave, to use one's head and to keep one's head, and not to be carried away by the heart. Hemingway seems concerned to establish here, in other words, that the influence of Stein on him has been a masculine influence. Her writing might be distinguished from that of Cather because it has not been weakened by indulgence in sentiment.

This might seem to explain how Stein came to assert such influence over a writer who was already denouncing the literary capabilities of women. As a stylist noted for her avant-garde experiments, Stein was easy to distinguish from lady novelists of the past. The association of ladies and outdated writing might have worked, that is to say, in her favor: writing in an up-to-date mode made her something of an honorary man. Both personally and stylistically, however, Stein's influence over Anderson and Hemingway seems to have been far more complex. It may well be that "The Man Who Became a Woman," which Anderson was writing at this time, betrays the influence of

Stein as well as Cather, and the story that Hemingway had just finished before he met Stein, the one that betrays most obviously her early influence, is almost unique in his work as being told from the point of view of a woman. If there was, as Wilson was to assert, a "school" including Stein, Anderson, and Hemingway, the predominance of masculine characteristics within it seems problematic at best.

In this respect, Anderson's attempts to characterize Stein's style for early readers betray a curious and significant indecision. In his introduction to *Geography and Plays*, he takes pains to assure Stein's readers that she is not "a languid woman lying on a couch, smoking cigarettes, sipping absinthes," but "a woman of striking vigor."[84] Like Hemingway, he wants to emphasize for early readers Stein's manly qualities, her strength and power. Yet, at the same time, though in a different place, Anderson calls her "an American woman of the old sort, one who cares for the handmade goodies and who scorns the factory-made foods."[85] Whether he sees her as conventionally male or conventionally female, Anderson is clearly anxious to make Stein familiar, to avoid at all costs the image of the drinking, smoking woman lying on a couch, a woman, that is to say, who is neither manly nor womanly.

Anderson attempts this refamiliarization of Stein's person so that he can work a similar transformation on her words: "And what I think is that these books of Gertrude Stein's do in a very real sense recreate life in words."[86] Stein's style, that is to say, returns words that have been perverted to their true and familiar uses: "Strong broad shouldered words, that should be marching across open fields under the blue sky, are clerking in little dusty dry goods stores, young virgin words are being allowed to consort with whores, learned words have been put to the ditch digger's trade."[87] From her own proper place in the kitchen of words, that good, wholesome cook, Gertrude Stein, dispatches words to their proper places, male words to the army and female words that have strayed back to the bosom of the family. There is a clear equation in the metaphorical terminology of this praise between returning words to their proper uses and reestablishing the traditional distinctions between the genders. In fact, with its strongly antimercantile thrust, Anderson's language makes Stein the traditionally female repository of the aesthetic, the one who gives "handmade goodies" and not "factory-made foods."

By his own account, however, Anderson had originally been drawn to Stein's work by a very different quality. In the same introduction, he recounts his first reading of Stein, and he reports with approval his brother's conclusions about her style: "'It gives words an oddly new intimate flavor and at the same time makes familiar words seem almost like strangers, doesn't it,' he said."[88] To *de*familiarize words and make them seem like strangers is quite the opposite of returning them to their proper places. The terminology neatly reverses everything else Anderson says about Stein, for it suggests that her work is not to be situated in the kitchen, nor, for that matter, in the family at all, but rather with those strangers who do not and cannot belong to families, perhaps because they spend all their time drinking and smoking on couches.

Anderson is obviously uncertain about how to place Stein in a traditional arrangement of gender, and this necessarily affects his ability to place her style. His uncertainty exposes an inconsistency in the traditional claims of the avant-garde, which sometimes justifies itself as a refamiliarization, a return of the means of art to their original purity, and sometimes as a defamiliarization, changing art in order to make it new. Conventional femininity, by occupying the position of that which is simultaneously conservative and effete, helps to compose this inconsistency by offering the avant-garde a very flexible point of opposition. But Stein's very unconventional femininity opens it up again, so Anderson can never quite decide if she is to be praised as earthy and ordinary or trumpeted as something completely unfamiliar. What Anderson is trying to account for is the fact that in Stein's work the apparent contradiction between refamiliarizing and defamiliarizing, in art and in life, is no contradiction at all. For Stein, the simplest and most common uses of words are already strange, so that to return words to their most basic meanings is also to defamiliarize them. In life as well, the apparently familiar familial relationships turn out to be full of divergent possibilities, about which Stein wrote some of her most significant work.

Hemingway suffered even more obviously from these ambivalences. For him Stein was, as Mark Spilka among many others has suggested, a literary mother with whom Hemingway reenacted the double drama of submission and rebellion he had already played out with his biological mother.[89] At the same time, Hemingway confessed in very forthright language that he had considered Stein's possibilities as a lover.[90] He also considered her a colleague, and as such a sort of honorary man: "Gertrude Stein and me are just like brothers."[91] She was apparently the sort of woman he feared, the sort of woman he admired, and the sort of man he wanted to become, all at once. That she may also have been the sort of woman he wanted to become is suggested by the posthumously published novels, which show a decided fascination for sexual role-switching.[92] Stein helped to encourage this interest in a small but significant way by showing Hemingway how to cut his wife's hair. She may also have encouraged it in a larger sense by offering Hemingway a relationship in which he might act simultaneously as figurative sibling, lover, and son. Stein was, then, in the most complicated way possible, Hemingway's aesthetic proxy, a cross-gendered role model who allowed him to imagine himself as an artist and to use his artistry to imagine himself as differently gendered. Hemingway found this relationship already encoded in the weirdly proleptic nickname he had been using for some time: Hemingstein. Stein's own description of Hemingway's impressionable relationship to others is contained in the title of the portrait she produced in 1923: "He and They, Hemingway."[93]

Of the three stories that appeared in Hemingway's first book, one, "My Old Man," has long been recognized as a deliberate exercise in the style of Sherwood Anderson. One of the two others, "Up in Michigan," is perhaps the only early piece in which the influence of Gertrude Stein is distinctly visible. "Up in Michigan" was originally written in 1921 and then rewritten in the first few months of 1922, just before Hemingway introduced himself to Stein.[94] At their second meeting, he showed her the story, along with the other work he had on hand. She was not particularly impressed, but she diplomatically expressed her dissatisfaction in practical terms, remarking that a story as graphic as "Up in Michigan" could hardly be published.[95] Ironically, it was to be the first story in the first book published by Robert McAlmon's Contact Editions, which also published Stein's own unpublishable masterpiece, *The Making of Americans*.

Stein was right, however, in saying that, in any conventional sense, "Up in Michigan" was unprintable. At a time when Joyce, Lawrence, and Cummings were all subjected to official censorship, Hemingway could hardly have succeeded in publishing a story with such an explicit description of sex. But if the story is obscene, it is obscene in a complex and somewhat unconventional sense. In fact, if the pornographic is to be associated, as it so often is, with male objectification of the female body, then "Up in Michigan" is not pornographic at all, for the point of view it invites its readers to take is female, and the body at which its gaze is directed is male.

Hemingway slowly slides the narrative into this position over the first three paragraphs of the story. The first two paragraphs begin flatly with the names of the two protagonists: "Jim Gilmore came to Hortons Bay from Canada. . . . Liz Coates worked for Smith's."[96] The third paragraph, though remaining in the third person, slowly identifies the narrative point of view with Liz by acquainting the reader with her reactions: "Liz liked Jim very much. She liked it the way he walked over from the shop and often went to the kitchen door to watch for him to start down the road." As the noun gives way to the pronoun, making Liz herself just a bit less visible, the prose acquires a colloquial imprecision, as if it were taking on her speech patterns as it takes on her point of view: "She liked it about how white his teeth were when he smiled." But her "point of view" in this case is much more than a particular vantage point; it is also a physical lookout, a position from which Liz avidly watches Jim walk, smile, and finally undress: "One day she found that she liked it the way the hair was black on his arms and how white they were above the tanned line when he washed up in the washbasin outside the house" (*TS*, p. 4).

It is interesting to speculate that Hemingway might have been reading Lawrence, as well as Anderson and Stein, for this scene of the male washing-up is strongly reminiscent of similar scenes in *Sons and Lovers* and *Women in Love*. Or it may simply be that washing up is one of those times when men tend to see one another in what is usually called in other contexts "various stages of undress" and that Hemingway, like Lawrence, has chosen the obvious screen of a fictional female as a way of expressing in mediated form his own homoerotic feelings. Even if this were the case, however, the mere fact that male desire can be expressed in female terms unsettles conventional gender divisions.[97] Even if the female gaze in this passage is merely ostensible, its erotic enjoyment of male flesh still disorders the conventions by which desire is usually directed in a text.

A similar and related shift is accomplished at the same time in the smallest grammatical elements of the prose. The reiterated "she liked it the way" is clearly meant to be subliterary sentimental rot, "puppy love" talk, as Alice Hall Petry calls it.[98] Hemingway is no doubt attempting to render the feminine reliance on euphemism that Jespersen derived from "their instinctive shrinking from coarse and gross expressions."[99] The redundancy of the pronoun followed immediately by its own referent is also meant to be an index of the unsophistication of this consciousness. But as the redundant "it" is reiterated in sentence after sentence, it begins to conjure up an absent referent, not just "how white his teeth were" or "the way the hair was black on his arms" but erotic desire itself. When the paragraph ends "Liking that made her feel funny," the pronoun refers with purposeful vagueness backward to everything that Liz has gazed on and forward to the "funny" feeling that is curiously indistinguishable from "liking that." The redundant pronoun, at first mere sentimental nonsense, gradually comes to refer to the sexual feelings that Liz herself cannot acknowledge, which the reader, at this point, must experience for her.

Of course, by 1922 Elinor Glyn had already made "it" something more than a household word, so much so, in fact, that even her own characters identified her with the term: "you have what Elinor Glyn writes of in her books—that 'it.'"[100] But if Glyn's "it" is vague, it is not ambiguous, and though it was common it was not to be confused with the ubiquitous, colloquial "it." For that ambiguity, Hemingway had to look to Stein: "Melanctha loved it the way Jem knew how to do it."[101] The colloquial redundancy, one of the few in "Melanctha" that sounds at all like actual speech, is exactly the one Hemingway repeats in "Up in Michigan." More significantly, he mimics the technique by which the grammatically empty "it" comes to be a counter for the act of sex. What keeps even so explicit a phrase as "how to do it" from becoming overtly obscene, however, is the incessant repetition of it: "She loved it too, that he wanted to be married to her." Precisely because "it" is so common, so iterable, it is one of the most indeterminate words in the language, a lesson that Hemingway had clearly learned from his reading of Stein.

"Up in Michigan" may be the one exception to the general rule that, as Marjorie Perloff has shown, Hemingway's mimicry of Stein's mannerisms tends to stop before it does much damage to conventional opinion or conventional prose.[102] Hemingway might well have been baffled by Stein's objections to the story, for it seems that he adopted some of her own strategies for skirting the obscene. For example, he describes a restless night that Liz has as "all mixed up in a dream about not sleeping and really not sleeping" (*TS*, p. 5). Hemingway makes it quite clear that this dream about "not sleeping" is an erotic dream, one that comes from thinking about Jim. It is, in other words, about an act often called "sleeping" but which isn't really sleeping at all. This is a kind of negative indirection that Stein had used for similar purposes in "Melanctha": "And yet Melanctha Herbert never wanted not to do right."[103] This semantic giving by taking away keeps the exact nature and extent of Melanctha's transgressions vague. But Stein's use of the negative, as in this passage, is so complex that it begins to break down the difference between positive and negative, between doing and not doing, transgressing and behaving, as Hemingway breaks down the difference between sleeping and not sleeping. In such a situation, the use of intensifiers like "really" simply deepens the paradoxical effect, as when Stein maintains that Melanctha has not been "really married," as if there were such a thing as being falsely married, or when Hemingway describes Liz as "really not sleeping" when it is clear that "not sleeping" means something a good deal more than simple wakefulness.

All of these techniques converge in the scene that made "Up in Michigan" unprintable, the scene in which Jim and Liz finally give "it" a referent. In fact, the referent becomes more and more explicit as the scene advances from Liz's frantic "You mustn't do it Jim" through "Oh it isn't right" to "Oh it's so big and it hurts so" (*TS*, p. 9). From its general vague daydreamy reference to the "funny" feelings that Liz gets when looking at Jim, "it" advances in both specificity and crudity to designate the act of sex and then the penis itself. Here, it would seem, the pronoun becomes concrete at last, and language becomes specific and hard just as it violates the female and gives her pain. And yet, despite the unmistakable male self-congratulation behind "Oh it's so big," the predominant feeling, both emotionally and stylistically, is one of absence. The sex act itself takes place in the conventional hiatus, between paragraphs, and this indicates on the one hand a residual reticence on the part of the author, but it indicates on the other hand as well the terrible disappointment and vacancy that sex visits on the female observer. The wakefulness that sexual longing had caused in her is cruelly mocked by the dull sleep into which Jim instantaneously lapses, so that the difference between sleeping, not sleeping, and really not sleeping appears in all its irony. In the end, the story massively reverses the force of its positive-negative terminology: "everything felt gone" (*TS*, p. 10). In other words, the "it" that seemed so hard and positive it hurt is in fact sheer emptiness.

The emptiness that the story names is matched by an emptiness that it creates stylistically, and the dramatic irony of Liz's sexual disappointment runs parallel to a linguistic irony. The whole story tends toward the dramatic appearance of the absent referent of the pronoun "it," but when that referent arrives it brings with it only more absence. There is obvious sexual irony here, since the absent referent is also the ultimate referent, the phallus. But that irony is also linguistic, since it suggests that there is no referent at all, just more reference. Hemingway's version of this by-now-familiar conundrum has a particular character, however. The chief characteristic of the Anderson-Stein-

Hemingway brand of modernism was to be its restoration of direct, colloquial language. For Hemingway more purely than for any other male modernist this was a masculinist project, and clarity of reference was to be a masculine virtue. Here, however, directness of reference leads straight to a gap, a
fissure in the text of the kind that Kristeva has taught contemporary critics
to think of as essentially feminine. And in this case at least it is feminine, and
it occupies and keeps open the space that was supposed to be filled, in every
possible way, by the male.

"Up in Michigan" is both a crude and a very complicated story, and showing it to Stein was for Hemingway both an aggressive and a submissive act,
one quite eloquent of the ambivalent feelings she awakened in him. Offering to a female colleague such a story as an instance of his prowess as a writer
is the sort of gesture we might expect from so stereotypically masculine a
writer as Hemingway. On the other hand, writing the story from a woman's
point of view suggested affinity instead of domination. If Hemingway turned
himself into a woman in one sense by adopting a female point of view, and
if this expressed, as Kenneth Lynn has suggested, his fascination with the
female role in sex,[104] he also turned himself into a woman in a more fundamental sense by submitting himself to discipleship under Gertrude Stein.
This meant a good deal more than simply taking technical advice from an
older female artist. It meant exploring common sentiments and everyday
talk, even the "puppy-love" talk of such as Liz Coates, and making of them
the innovations of an avant-garde style. It meant exploring certain linguistic habits, such as the use of euphemism and the redundancy of pronouns,
that Jespersen had identified as essentially feminine. Female reliance on what
Jespersen calls "the indispensable small-change of a language" is what makes
women, to his mind, such perfectly conventional speakers, what guarantees
that men will always be "the chief renovators of language."[105] But Hemingway was showing that the "small change," the flimsy linguistic conventions
of everyday speech, had more renovative possibilities in them than anyone
suspected.

How much of this Hemingway had learned from Stein is clarified by the
work she herself was writing at this time, a work that was to be her contribution to the mutual admiration society composed of herself, Hemingway, and
Sherwood Anderson. About the time she received Anderson's preface to *Geography and Plays*, that is to say in February or March 1922, Stein wrote a response, entitled "Idem the Same: A Valentine for Sherwood Anderson."[106]
The title suggests, rather slyly, that she is returning one valentine for another,
which makes Anderson's preface seem even more ardent than it was. But, of
course, "idem" is not really the same as "the same," even though it may mean
the same thing, and so Stein is not precisely returning tit for tat.[107] In fact, in
manuscript the piece was not a valentine for Sherwood Anderson at all but
rather a valentine for Alice Toklas.[108] In reworking her original text, Stein may
be using Anderson to provide a public cover for expressions of an uncon-

ventional love, or she may be having an elaborate joke at his expense. In either case, the ambiguities that make this duplicity possible are inherent in the ordinary sentimental materials themselves.

On the surface, a valentine seems the most banal kind of writing possible, one synonymous with commercialized sentiment. With her characteristic repetitions, Stein seems rather to exaggerate this aspect of her subject:

> Very fine is my valentine.
> Very fine and very mine.
> Very mine is my valentine very mine and very fine.
> Very fine is my valentine and mine, very fine very mine and mine is my
>   valentine.[109]

This is precisely what Stein's subtitle calls it, "A Very Valentine," distilling the language of valentines to a quintessence so cloying it seems to be incapable of meaning anything. Valentines, it would seem, are always "very," always exaggerated and breathless and yet quite vague about the objects of their enthusiasm. At the same time, however, something odd and ambiguous emerges from the hackneyed language itself. For "very" still retains within it vestiges of its original meaning, "truly," apparent in cases when the adjective is used before a noun to make it exemplary, "the very thing." Stein certainly uses "very" in this sense to celebrate how truly fine and how truly "mine" her valentine is, and yet she is also pulling apart the very conventions of praise by posing the truth asserted by "very" against the exaggeration inherent in it. A "very valentine," that is to say, is both true and false at the same time, heartfelt and faithful but also insincerely affected.

Some of this ambiguity is made possible by the fact that in common parlance a valentine is both the message and the person to whom it is addressed, a duality often collapsed in the conventional query "Will you be my valentine?" Thus it is possible to read the passage as self-reflexive self-praise, not returning but rather echoing Anderson's compliments about Stein's writing. This possible reading is made the more probable by the fact that in the manuscript every instance of "mine" but one originally read "Stein." "Very fine and very Stein" may represent a drastic summary of Anderson's preface, reduced to five words, and "Idem the Same" may mean that Stein is not returning Anderson's compliment to herself but rather that she is repeating it.

There are other possibilities here as well. Both visually and verbally valentines seem conspicuously feminine: frilly and highly decorated. Yet the role of "valentine" can be played equally and interchangeably by male or female. Thus it is quite possible for Stein to deliver her valentine publicly to Sherwood Anderson and privately to Alice Toklas and to put expressions of an unconventional love in the most conventional of terms. The word "fine" is similarly ambiguous, unlike many terms of approbation that are inclined by usage to one sex or the other. At the same time, the exact nature of the relationship implied by being "my valentine" is left politely indefinite. "Will you be mine?" is a conventional version of the more common "Will you be my valentine" that is considered quite appropriate even for young children. Yet Stein's slightly intensified version, "very mine," seems to suggest a level of ardor somewhat beyond ordinary friendship. Precisely because it is not grammatically appropriate, the phrase "very mine" awakens questions in the reader's mind. In short, simply by teasing with rhyme and repetition, Stein manages to make the most innocent of all expressions of heterosexual love carry the implication of homosexual license. At the same time, the genre most utterly associated with the feminine and the popular becomes the vehicle for linguistic experimentation.

The basic technique of the piece is, as the title forecasts, to find the different in the same. The issue of feeling "differently" arises just after "A Very Valentine," apparently to be dismissed:

> Why do you feel differently about a very little snail and a big one.
> Why do you feel differently about a medium sized turkey and a very large one.
> Why do you feel differently about a small band of sheep and several sheep that
>   are riding.
> Why do you feel differently about a fair orange tree and one that has blossoms as
>   well.
> Oh very well.
> All nice wives are like that.[110]

As a whole, the passage suggests that there is no accounting for taste, and it ends by throwing up its hands in mock exasperation. The line "All nice wives are like that" may be taken to mean something like "all women have their little quibbles." But there are some obvious obstacles to such a neat reduction. The title of the section, "Why Do You Feel Differently," poses a distinctly different question than appears in the body of the section. To "feel differently" is very different from feeling "differently about." To "feel differently" is to feel different, to have different emotions and tastes than other people. It is logically impossible for "all nice wives" to "feel differently" in this respect. And yet the referent of the phrase "like that" is so vague as to leave open almost any possibility. In fact, used in this way, the phrase "like that" is one of those bits of language that presumes understanding instead of creating it. But this means that it can be used only in cases when people do not "feel differently." The same piece of language is simultaneously open to any possible difference and closed to any variation from the utter uniformity implied by the word "all."

Of course, the adjective "nice" does provide the phrase "like that" with a vague sort of target. On one level, Stein simply returns the word to its original meaning: "nice" wives are those that make fine or careful discriminations such as that between a medium-sized turkey and a very large one. "Nice" does in fact mean "fine," so that the "nice" wife of this section is related back to the "fine" valentine of the previous one. They may in fact be the same person, a person who is "fine" not necessarily because she is admirable in some way but because she is closely discriminating in her feelings. "Nice" wives are those, in other words, who make a practice of feeling "differently about."

But "nice" also carries a conventionally moral meaning quite separate from its original one. In this sense, "nice" wives are those who most definitely do not "feel differently," who are not different in their feelings. "Nice" wives are those who fit comfortably within the category of "wife," so that "nice wives" is almost, as the assonance and near-rhyme suggest, a tautological phrase. Words like "nice" and "fine" in fact exemplify a class of words that Jespersen feels are particularly appropriate to wives: "There are a few adjectives, such as *pretty* and *nice*, that might be mentioned as used more extensively by women than by men."[111] This is in part because women prefer euphemism and in part because they tend to make finer distinctions of a more trivial sort than men. There aren't "wives" and "nice wives," but rather "wives" and women who "feel differently." Once again, then, the same word seems to insist on distinction and to efface it simultaneously.

But it may be that in this situation, in the context of a valentine at least partially dedicated to Alice Toklas, there isn't any difference between wives and women who feel differently. Toklas, somewhat notoriously, "sat with the wives." In fact, it was apparently Stein's practice to refer to her companion, from the beginning of their relationship to the end, as a wife.[112] It would be quite logical in this case to call Toklas a wife after having called her a valentine. But if Alice Toklas is an appropriate member of the class "all nice wives," then perhaps the phrase "like that" means something very different indeed. This alternative meaning would still be perfectly colloquial, but the inflection would simply be changed from "*like* that" to "like *that*." With this slight change of emphasis, the line "All nice wives are like that" is changed from a smug assertion of uniform heterosexual conformity to a suggestion of ubiquitous secret homosexuality—"All nice wives are like *that*."

Stein has not cleverly inflected these words to warp them from their conventional meanings. On the contrary, she restricts herself entirely to conventional meanings, which turn out to have yet other meanings, the way a piece of paper has another side. It was this technique that Hemingway was in the course of adopting when he wrote "Up in Michigan." In a line such as "Liking that made her feel funny," Hemingway is exploiting the conventional elasticity of the pronoun in much the same way that Stein does in "All nice wives are like that." In fact, the terms on which Stein hangs all the duplicity of "A Valentine for Sherwood Anderson," "fine" and "nice," become key terms in Hemingway's later work. As Walter Michaels points out, "fine" and "nice" come to play a crucial role in the aesthetic morality of *The Sun Also Rises*.[113] "Nice" is the precisely measured term of approval that Jake applies to Lady Brett and Hemingway applies to Stein herself.[114] But by this time the piece of paper has come to have only one side, for, as Michaels says, in *The Sun Also Rises* these terms are simply incomprehensible outside the small group of aficionados that defines them. To know without having even to think what "nice" means is to be one of the aesthetic elect; to use the word improperly, as Robert Cohn misuses "fine," is to betray oneself as a boor. The ambiguity, in other words, is coercive and bourgeois in precisely the sense that Stein herself seeks to mock in the line "All nice wives are like that." In fact, the ultimate separation of Hemingway's style from Stein's influence is marked by this very phrase, used by Jake Barnes to dismiss the male homosexuals who dance so annoyingly in the *bal musette*: "They are like that." Here, Hemingway seems to count on a male readership not only knowing what "like that" means but agreeing with his narrator in finding it disturbing.[115]

In 1922, however, all the ambiguities of the line were still hanging in the air. There was the widespread male fear that "nice wives" were no longer "like that," or worse, that they were "like that" in something like the sense that Stein intended. Hutchinson and Fyfe were writing out of the simple fear that women were changing and out of the more complex fear that something long taken for granted, something soft and comforting in a harshly instrumental world, something "nice," in a word, was being lost. In Cather's work, this shift in the psychic division of labor, actual or conjectural, appears as an opportunity as well, an opportunity to redistribute human traits across gender, so that someone like Claude might satisfy his aesthetic longings and someone like Enid lead the church militant in China. On this level, there seems to be a commonality between Cather and Stein despite their significant stylistic differences. The whole notion of the aesthetic proxy depends on a duplicity within the commonplace very much like the one Stein was to make her stylistic hallmark. The linguistic relationships between the 1922 works of Hemingway, Anderson, and Stein suggest that this duplicity was on its way to becoming part of the modernist style. The apparent division between the male world of tough talk and linguistic experiment and the conventionally female world of everyday sentimental language was, that is to say, every bit as complex as the relationship between Claude Wheeler and his aesthetic proxy.

If Hemingway managed to make his use of ordinary language widely popular, while Stein's was merely notorious, it was perhaps because he had removed from it the strangeness that Stein had found for him. This means that he missed, or enjoyed only briefly, what seems the quintessential experience of 1922 and perhaps of modernity in general, the discovery of what Marjorie Perloff has called "the strangeness of the ordinary." As Wittgenstein discovered in language experiments very like Stein's, there is nothing stranger and more disorienting than a convention, once you bring yourself to see it. The conditions of 1922 made it easier than ever to see convention at work, to feel its power and its artificiality at the same time. Global travel, the self-consciousness taught by anthropology and psychology, the distanciating reduplications of the media all brought awareness to bear on the unaware, the unconscious, the automatically accepted. The writings of authors as generally unreflective as Harry Leon Wilson and Rupert Hughes suggest that these conditions had made their mark on artists a good deal less extreme than Gertrude Stein. Even the most ordinary writing, that is to say, was aware that something uncanny and strange had been exposed within the everyday, and even the strangest writing felt the attraction of ordinary language and experience, once it had been destabilized in this way. This is the context in which Wittgenstein meets Chaplin and Stein meets Rupert Hughes, where the modernist avant-garde, the human sciences, and the popular culture of 1922 find their common cause.

Conclusion

IN SOME NOTES ON THE modern inserted near the end of his monumental study of postmodernism, Fredric Jameson stipulates that the only adequate theory of modernism and its culture would be one that "worked both sides of the street and dug its tunnel from both directions." Thus in one flourish Jameson requires that modernization and aesthetic modernism be understood in relation to one another while insisting by his very metaphors that they are fundamentally divided. The tunnel he prescribes is necessary because of the great continental divide between modernism and the rest of modern culture; the street has two such distant sides because it runs through what Jameson himself calls the "frontier between high culture and so-called mass or commercial culture." Any attempt to satisfy Jameson's demand for "a comparative sociology of modernism and its cultures" is thus confronted by the common assumption of stark antipathy that postmodern theorists have made a virtual article of belief.[1]

It should have been clear for some time that this belief rests on rather uncertain foundations. For one thing, it tends to generalize across an extensive period of time. Peter Nicholls, for example, follows currently accepted practice by beginning his excellent survey of modernist movements with Baudelaire, whose self-conscious theorizing of the conditions of the modern make him an almost unavoidable starting point. And yet, making Baudelaire's fastidious irony, as Nicholls does, the very type of the modernist attitude toward modern life is to deny many decades of historical change.[2] Even by the turn of the century, irony had become less a defense against commercialized modernity and more a way of participating in it. Starting with café culture in the 1880s, the French avant-garde gradually mined music halls, newspaper advertising, billboards, and the movies for aesthetic forms and rhetorical strategies,[3] and the ratio in this emulation between mimicry and mockery was so complex that even so canny an observer as Gertrude Stein was supposed not to understand it.[4]

The same trend is apparent in other countries. By the 1920s the German avant-garde had extraordinarily close ties with the "culture industry." Kurt Schwitters, for example, had established an advertising agency, and Hannah Höch was working for Ullstein Verlag, publisher of Germany's largest mass-market magazines. The way that Berlin dada posed as a business with investment strategies and advertising campaigns was meant, of course, to be a mockery of both the disengagement of traditional art and the practicality of business, and yet there was also a good deal of genuine admiration for the forms of mass marketing, which seemed both untraditional and nonsectarian. The activities of Schwitters and Höch, according to Maud Lavin, "while sometimes critical, were more often additive and reformist—specifically, based on a belief in avant garde designs as carriers of utopian messages."[5] For a large segment of the German, French, and Russian avant-garde of this period, the art of the future was to be found in the mass marketing and popular arts of the United States, and certain artists, such as Picabia, brought this attitude back to the United States itself. As early as 1915, according to Stephen Lewis, "American commodity culture became the standard of modernity against which the post-Armory show New York avant-garde measured its work."[6] By the 1920s, this attitude had become so influential that it became itself a part of commodity culture, which promoted its own modernity in magazines like *Vanity Fair*.

According to Andreas Huyssen, the enthusiasm of the European avant-garde for American "jazz, sports, cars, technology, movies, and photography" somehow skipped over American modernism itself, returning "to America in the 1960s, fueling the fight of the early post-modernists against the high-culture doctrines of Anglo-American modernism."[7] But this remarkably discontinuous history is simply impossible to sustain in face of what would otherwise be rather unremarkable evidence that Anglo-American modernism was produced, received, and understood in association with those other aspects of Anglo-American modernity. In fact, the evidence of 1922 suggests that "jazz, sports, cars, technology, movies and photography" provided the basis for a strong association between the European avant-garde and Anglo-American literary modernism. Duchamp and Milhaud spent the year in the United States, the former soaking up American movies and the latter American jazz.[8] Gilbert Seldes, who had written widely read articles on both movies and jazz, collected those articles into a book while staying in Paris, where he hobnobbed with Picasso, Stravinsky, and Joyce.[9] Under Seldes' editorship, *The Dial* had been publishing Pound's Parisian letters, which regularly included information about dada, especially where it concerned Picabia, with whom Pound was particularly closely associated in this year.[10] Both Pound and Edmund Wilson noticed with some amusement in *Vanity Fair* how strongly influenced the French avant-garde of 1922 was by American popular culture.[11] Even a little acquaintance with this Anglo-American cultural scene, the world in which Gilbert Seldes thrived and Walter Lippmann agonized, makes it impossible to dissociate the "high modernism" that Pound, Wilson, and Seldes were promoting from the general avant-garde enthusiasm for modern culture.

This is not to deny, of course, that certain writers usually identified with "high modernism" were exceedingly critical of mass society. Even here, however, the argument often rests more on a priori reasoning than on actual evidence. To bolster his very influential opposition of modernism to mass culture, Huyssen instances exactly one brief statement from T. S. Eliot, and that one parenthetically.[12] Against this, David Chinitz has mustered a fair amount of evidence to suggest that Eliot was not deeply prejudiced against mass culture,[13] but surely the real points of contention here cannot be decided by individual statements or individual predilections. The sociology of modernism that Jameson has demanded would consider institutions, modes of dissemination and production, such as publishers, galleries, and magazines. That there has been relatively little work in this area means that disagreements about modernism have been settled by reference to the intentions of its most visible perpetrators, with all the weaknesses and limitations that such analysis entails.

It is also possible that the notion of a fundamental split between modernism and modern culture has been sustained by a rather limited understanding of the latter. For Jameson, the real difference of the postmodern comes from the fact "that aesthetic production today has become integrated into commodity production generally."[14] It seems rather easy to dispute the false punctuality of "today," to wonder whether aesthetic production and commodity production hadn't already embraced when advertising and cubism discovered one another in the first decades of this century. What happened in those decades, however, was not simply the commodification of aesthetic objects, as if art had been integrated into an essentially unchanged and unchangeable industrial machine. The machine itself began to change as its products ceased to be exclusively material and began to be notional and imaginative. It might not be possible to swing all the way around from Jameson's point of view and contend that it is commodity production that has been integrated into aesthetic production generally; but it is certainly the case that when even the most mundane product is marketed as an experience, aesthetic considerations have penetrated the market to an extraordinary degree. Though Jameson himself has written a good deal about this interpenetration, it is still rather common to suggest that modernism sets itself off from commodity culture by a process of "aestheticization," as if the hallmark of modern commodity culture were not the fact that it has itself become progressively aestheticized.

This is one of the main reasons why a reconsideration of modernism and modern culture must work from both sides, because the latter is often considered as cursorily as the former. It is not simply a matter of arguing that modernists were more positive in their attitudes toward mass culture than is usually assumed, but rather of suggesting that this relationship is more complex because mass culture is more complex. Wittgenstein's discovery of the strangeness of the ordinary is in our century a rather ordinary discovery, and it helps to bring even the strangest works back within the orbit of everyday life.

In contrast, Nicholls' assertion that irony is a minority strategy deployed against modern society depends on the assumption that irony is not already a common feature of that society.[15] As society becomes progressively aestheticized, however, as audiences begin to consume imaginative and symbolic materials as they had previously consumed material goods, then everyday life acquires an inherently ironic distance from itself. As John Thompson puts it, "The appropriation of symbolic materials enables individuals to take some distance from the conditions of their day-to-day lives — not literally but symbolically, imaginatively, vicariously."[16] The fact that more and more information comes from a greater and greater distance means that individuals are commonly acquainted with lives quite different from their own, and this makes it possible to consider their own lives as if they were at a distance. In literature, Jameson reminds us, this distance is called irony, and its prevalence in the works of early modernists such as Conrad stands as a symptom of "the penetration even of middle-class lived experience by this strange new global relativity."[17]

In fact, as experience comes less and less from face-to-face encounters and more and more from representations at a distance, the very basis of the monadic bourgeois individual begins to slip. A self perceived from a distance can be manipulated, constructed. As Thompson puts it, "the appropriation of media messages has become a means of active self-fashioning in the modern world."[18] This is widely and commonly the case, even in places seemingly far distant in space and time from Western media capitals. Appadurai finds the same process in cabaret dancers in Bombay: "What we have is a sense that they are putting lives together, fabricating their own characters, using the cinematic and social materials at their disposal."[19] This sort of self-fashioning is widely visible in the literature of 1922, perhaps most especially in the more popular examples, works like *Salome of the Tenements*, *Souls for Sale*, or *Merton of the Movies*, which are already about a kind of self permeated by the media.

The common opposition of an ironic, aestheticized modernism to mass culture thus depends on a prior generalization about mass culture that seriously oversimplifies it. As Appadurai insists, "many lives are now inextricably linked with representations,"[20] and there is no reason to limit this statement to an indeterminate "now." As of 1922, photography and film had made the linkage of everyday life with representations so obvious a fact that it appeared in the most mundane popular novels, in travelogues like Chaplin's, and in multifarious media events like the vogue for Egyptiana. Though modern professional anthropology was still in its infancy, a certain kind of anthropological relativism had already permeated society, and the "bourgeois rationality" that is supposed to be one of literary modernism's favorite targets was already shrouded in general disbelief.[21] If, as François Bourricaud has suggested, modernity can "be characterized by the impossibility of regarding mankind other than as an irreducible diversity of culture and societies,"[22] then modernity was equally entrenched in the society and the literature of 1922.

Recognizing this fact should make it possible to contain within the purview of modernist studies a good deal of material conventionally separated from the extreme literary experimentalism of Eliot, Joyce, or Stein. If Charles Beadle, Rupert Hughes, and Harry Leon Wilson show some sense of the ironic insubstantiality of ordinary life under modern conditions, then perhaps popular literature might profitably be studied along with the accepted modernist classics. As a number of studies from critics such as David Trotter and Billie Melman have shown, the popular literature of the early modernist period is often capable of an ironic self-reflexiveness every bit the equal of that found in the established writers.[23] At the very least, it should be possible to expand the canon to include writers like McKay, Cather, and Yezierska, who have never been considered modernists though they exhibit an acute awareness of modern conditions.

Of course, the problem here is that modernism has always been defined by reference to its formal properties, and there is little formal similarity between Cather and Joyce or McKay and Eliot. This objection is neutralized to some extent by the fact that the usual lists of formal characteristics do not describe even the most commonly canonized modernists very well. If the first rule defining the modernist aesthetic is, as Huyssen maintains, that the "work is autonomous and totally separate from the realms of mass culture and everyday life,"[24] then it is hard to think of any appropriate candidates— certainly not Eliot, who puts several scenes of London lowlife and excerpts from American and British popular culture into *The Waste Land*; not Joyce or Woolf, who sends Mrs. Dalloway out into London on the top of a bus; not Yeats or Pound, who were both committed polemicists, just to consider a few of the more obvious suspects. For any more specific rule, it is always possible to find one or more major modernists who do not fit, as Lawrence and Yeats defy the common requirement that modernist works are organized paratactically rather than hypotactically. Attempts to formulate a unified formalist definition of modernism have always run afoul of the fact that modernism ceaselessly creates forms and in so doing confounds critical desires for formal consistency.

Most such lists of formal characteristics are, however, simply elaborations

of a more general underlying rule enunciated a priori by Art Berman that to
be considered modernist a writer must put form before content or at least
seek to merge form with content.[25] It is not necessary that any particular formal characteristic be present as long as the writer experiments with form or at
the very least worships formal precision, as Yeats does and someone like Theodore Dreiser clearly does not. And yet, though formalism is for Berman as
for most writers on modernism a characteristic that utterly sets off modernist
works from the society around them, it may be through formalism itself that
modern works approach most critically the ordinary experience of the twentieth century.

The fact that most of the accepted modernist classics are self-consciously
formalist means that they are also highly conscious of the formalism of society, which their own works often seek to mimic. In one of the *Waste Land*
drafts, for example, Eliot complains about the "formal destiny" that holds humankind hostage, an imprisonment that the final version of the poem illustrates with its crowds of Londoners trudging around in a ring.[26] But *The Waste
Land* also illustrates this formal imprisonment through its use of rhyme,
which tends to come into the poem when its characters are acting most automatically. The young man carbuncular and the typist in "The Fire Sermon,"
for example, enact their loveless relationship in quatrains. When the typist
"smoothes her hair with automatic hand, / And puts a record on the gramophone,"[27] her routine movements rhyme with the mechanized movements of
the gramophone "arm" and with the repetitive action of rhyme itself, which
should seem just as prerecorded as the music coming from the gramophone.
If formalism is a submission to form quite regardless of content, then Eliot
is clearly using literary formalism to mime and critique a larger formalism in
society itself. In at least some long-canonized modernists, then, literary formalism is not so much a hedge against commodification as it is a parodic reflection of it. If Eliot resists commodification, it is in terms almost identical to those laid out in the founding document of Western Marxism, Georg
Lukács' *History and Class Consciousness*, dated December 1922, which also de-
nounces the way that "human relations" increasingly assume the appearance
of "objective forms."[28] For Eliot at the same time, literary forms are not exceptions to this rule but rather the most painful examples of it.

It may be a certain self-conscious formalism, then, that most closely links
modernist literary works with modern society. Certainly, the archformalist of
this time was Edward Bernays, who represented the eugenics movement one
day and the NAACP the next.[29] When Bernays describes the campaign he invented to rehabilitate the Hearst magazines after World War I, which they had
not been at all eager to enter, he maintains, "My job had no ideological connotations."[30] This disclaimer of political intent is in effect a rejection not just
of political content but of content per se. Public relations negates the notion
of intrinsic truth just as mechanical reproduction negates the notion of intrinsic value. For Bernays, "The only difference between 'propaganda' and

'education,' really, is in the point of view."[31] This was still perhaps a somewhat scandalous opinion in 1922, but it was also fashionable enough to become a commodity in its own right. Michael Murphy maintains that the readers of *Vanity Fair* "weren't interested in securing from the magazines any knowledge that they could value as information, as irreducible *truth*, but only relative and arbitrary knowledge produced in a specific historical context as an exchange object, knowledge that they could in turn continue to trade on for its exchange value—*slick* knowledge. With the rise of the slicks, that is, it no longer mattered what was *in* a magazine, only what *brand* it was."[32] In a context like this, aesthetic formalism meets a larger commodification and merges with it, since commodification was itself a kind of formalism in the first place.

That the great works of literary modernism were first received in a context determined to a large extent by men like Bernays and publications like *Vanity Fair* might mean that they were both influential and offensive for reasons rather different than is now usually assumed. According to Jameson, early modernism struck the average bourgeois reader as "variously ugly, dissonant, obscure, scandalous, immoral, subversive, and generally 'antisocial,'" but since these works have become so thoroughly familiar they now seem merely elitist.[33] Whether works like *Ulysses* have in fact become so thoroughly domesticated that they seem "realistic," as Jameson suggests, is open to question; it is certainly the case that in some very basic ways works like *Ulysses* and *The Waste Land* have become more obscure over time, particularly for American undergraduates, to whom World War I may seem nearly as distant as the Peloponnesian War. In their own context, when the contemporary materials, at least, did not require so much explanation, the works of Eliot and Joyce were likely to strike conservative readers as ugly and scandalous in much the same way that contemporary music or the movies did. The resistance of a sophisticated aesthete like Bell to Eliot and Joyce was hardly based on their obscurity. For Bell, in fact, the great sin of these works was their blatancy, a judgment shared to some extent by Virginia Woolf where Joyce was concerned. The quality that made Joyce and Eliot "scandalous, immoral, subversive, and generally 'antisocial'" in Bell's mind was not obscurity but "impudence," a quality they shared with the popular art forms that appealed primarily to the vast new audiences who had little knowledge of or reverence for Leonardo or the Sistine ceiling.

In other words, the works of Joyce and Eliot, and perhaps Woolf as well, where Bell was concerned, were perceived as part of the general commodification of art in the course of which old notions of intrinsic value would evaporate, to be replaced by the pure exchange value that accrues to the new and up-to-date. This had been the charge leveled against modernism in the arts since it had first been associated at the turn of the century with fashion.[34] It is a charge that survives in the work of Lothrop Stoddard, for whom modernism is part of a general collapse of values. The charge parallels that made by conservatives such as Oberholtzer against the movies, which they feared primarily because they represented a future in which face-to-face contact would be replaced by contact at a distance and intrinsic values would give way to the play of representations.

This is to say, of course, that Joyce and Eliot were perceived as part of what has lately been called postmodernism. The difficulty of distinguishing modernism from its supposed successor on intrinsic grounds has long been recognized, and Jameson quite sensibly stakes his final claim on context instead: "Even if all the constitutive features of postmodernism were identical with and continuous to those of an older modernism—a position I feel to be demonstrably erroneous . . . the two phenomena would still remain utterly distinct in their meaning and social function, owing to the very different positioning of postmodernism in the economic system of late capital and, beyond that, to the transformation of the very sphere of culture in contemporary society."[35] But it is precisely this last claim that is most demonstrably erroneous, since the changes Jameson points to took place much earlier in the century and were seen then to have taken place. *Post-Industrialism* is, after all, a title from 1922, and Walter Lippmann was already decrying in that same year the very transformations in the sphere of culture that seem to Jameson constitutive of the postmodern.

The purpose of making such a claim is certainly not to siphon off into the modern some of the intellectual glamor attached to the postmodern, because in the very few years since Jameson's book was published most of that glamor has evaporated. The inversely seductive notion that we happen to live in a time of unique historical crisis has lost much of its hold as the years roll on and the postmodern itself seems in need of a successor movement. This relative lull in the excitement of our own moment offers several opportunities, not the least of which is the opportunity to disabuse the present of its notion of historical uniqueness, which is often nothing more than the desire to sneak away from history altogether. A more positive opportunity is the chance to see this fading century as a whole, to see where humankind has been since Queen Victoria died, before the century she died in dies in its turn.

The most crucially unsolved problem of that century may be one that modernism and postmodernism share. If Bourricaud is correct in saying that the essence of modernity is the recognition of irreducible diversity, then what do we call the vantage point from which we recognize that diversity, how do we perceive it, and how do we include it within modernity's irreducible diversity? For this vantage point must be utterly distinct from any particular point of view, which would regard other points of view not as being relative but rather as being wrong, and it is certainly not to be identified with either a divine point of view or a neutrally rational one, both of which the very notion of mutual relativity rules out, even if the century had not already rejected them on other grounds. The forefathers of modern hermeneutics attempted to solve this problem by postulating a kind of suprahuman human nature, and Habermas has attempted to install communicative norms in the same position. But no solution has been proposed that has not seemed to considerable numbers of critics naive or sinister or both.

The fact remains, however, that this is the position from which most people in industrialized countries and many people outside them now perceive the world, and the fact that it is so difficult to account for is perhaps, as Wittgenstein would have it, our best warrant that it is in fact our own. This invocation of Wittgenstein should also be taken as implying that it is also the position of the significant works, both famous and obscure, of 1922, and that this unsolved problem is the problem shared by Wittgenstein, Freud, Eliot, Joyce, Stein, Lippmann, Malinowski, and perhaps even Chaplin. The vantage point from which Wittgenstein recognizes the infinite relativity of language games, from which Malinowski perceives the variability of human culture, from which Freud discovers the power of the irrational, from which Chaplin discerns the ephemerality of his own image in the eyes of the audience is the vantage point of the twentieth century, and it is not in itself relative, variable, irrational, or ephemeral.[36] It is something else, and our inability to account for it or even describe it is the structural principle at the heart of the great literary works of this century, as it is the motive force behind most significant work in the human sciences. That it is somehow distinct from the world it describes as infinitely relative is what makes these works critical even as they remain part of the common culture around them.

If, as I have been suggesting here, beginning with Wittgenstein, the notion that truth is local and particular came into being as a reflex of the attempt to make it global and universal, then that notion still retains, as a kind of shadow, some of that original attempt, though in a diminished and subdued form, a little like the weakened virus that is used in a vaccine. Current notions of cultural and epistemological relativism do not imply that every point of view is relative, because such a wholly immersed point of view could not have conceived of the original notion of universal relativity. In fact, they imply a critical distance, one that largely defines the important intellectual and creative works of our time. The squabble between modernism and postmodernism is in fact a symptom of our inability to theorize that distance, which becomes, in turn, an inability to understand the important works that reflect on the twentieth century. To see those works in context, to see that putting them in context is not in fact to rob them of their critical power, as Adorno maintained, but rather to establish for the first time a basis for it, is perhaps the beginning of such an understanding.

Notes

Introduction

1. [Ezra Pound], "The Little Review Calendar," *The Little Review* 8 (Spring 1922): 2. Pound used the new numbering in at least one letter to Eliot. See *The Letters of T. S. Eliot*, ed. Valerie Eliot (New York: Harcourt Brace Jovanovich, 1988), p. 497. See also the discussions in Noel Stock, *The Life of Ezra Pound* (New York: Pantheon, 1970), p. 323, and Lawrence S. Rainey, *Ezra Pound and the Monument of Culture: Text, History, and the Malatesta Cantos* (Chicago: University of Chicago Press, 1991), pp. 42–43.

2. Gilbert Seldes, "Nineties—Twenties—Thirties," *The Dial* 73 (November 1922): 577.

3. For a number of instances, beginning with Pound, see Stanley Sultan, *Eliot, Joyce and Company* (New York: Oxford University Press, 1987), pp. 128–129. One of the most influential nominations of 1922 as annus mirabilis of modernism is Harry Levin's in "What Was Modernism?" See *Refractions: Essays in Comparative Literature* (New York: Oxford University Press, 1966), p. 283.

4. Willa Cather, *Not Under Forty* (New York: Alfred A. Knopf, 1936), p. v; Edmund Wilson, "Mr. Bell, Miss Cather and Others," *Vanity Fair* 19 (October 1922): 26–27. For a more complete discussion, see chapter 5.

5. F. Scott Fitzgerald, "Echoes of the Jazz Age," in *The Crack-Up*, ed. Edmund Wilson (New York: New Directions, 1945), p. 15; Ronald Berman, *The Great Gatsby and Modern Times* (Urbana: University of Illinois Press, 1994), pp. 15, 50.

6. F. Scott Fitzgerald, *The Great Gatsby*, ed. Matthew J. Bruccoli (Cambridge: Cambridge University Press, 1991), p. 22. For Eliot's influence on Fitzgerald, see Berman, *Great Gatsby and Modern Times*, p. 45. Fitzgerald was also indebted to Cather, or at least he feared

215

that he was. His letter to her about the possibility of unconscious plagiarism from *A Lost Lady* is discussed in a number of places, including Robert Roulston, "Something Borrowed, Something New: A Discussion of Literary Influences on *The Great Gatsby*," in *Critical Essays on The Great Gatsby*, ed. Scott Donaldson (Boston: G. K. Hall, 1984), pp. 57–58.

7. *Current Opinion*, March 1922, pp. 361–363.

8. *Vanity Fair* 19 (October 1922): 26. Benet's answer was a rather emphatic "no," but other novelists weren't so sure. See, for example, Dorothy Speare, *Dancers in the Dark* (New York: Burt, 1922).

9. Brander Matthews, *The Tocsin of Revolt* (New York: Scribner's, 1922); Lothrop Stoddard, *The Revolt Against Civilization: The Menace of the Under Man* (New York: Scribner's, 1922).

10. It was in fact reviewed twice in the *Times Literary Supplement*, on August 24, 1922 (p. 547) and again on September 21, 1922 (p. 590).

11. "Sapper" [pseud. Herman Cyril McNeile], *The Black Gang* (1922; rpt., London: Dent, 1983). John Buchan's contribution to the literature of the year, *Huntingtower* (London: Hodder and Stoughton, 1922), was also a conspiracy novel, but in this case the threat is more limited and more purely foreign.

12. Philip Gibbs, *The Middle of the Road* (New York: George H. Doran, 1923), pp. 55, 112–113.

13. G. A. Leask, "Changing London," in David Williamson, ed., *The Daily Mail Year Book for 1923* (London: Associated Newspapers Ltd., 1923), p. 77.

14. A. G. Gardiner, "Introduction," *England To-Day: A Social Study of Our Time*, by George A. Greenwood (London: Allan and Unwin, 1922), p. 7.

15. Charles F. G. Masterman, *England after War* (London: Hodder and Stoughton, 1922), p. 70.

16. There was a deep economic slump in 1921–1922, with unemployment reaching 18 percent, which was commonly said to have been the highest rate in a hundred years. By July 1922 there were over two million on Poor Law relief, almost two and a half times what there had been at the beginning of 1921. See Noreen Branson, *Britain in the Nineteen Twenties* (Minneapolis: University of Minnesota Press, 1976), pp. 13, 69, 76.

17. See Charles A. Beard, *Cross-Currents in Europe To-Day* (Boston: Marshall Jones, 1922), especially pp. 83–84, 95–97. Gibbs' novel is very largely taken up with the conflicts caused by differing European positions on the question of reparations.

18. John Maynard Keynes, *A Revision of the Treaty* (New York: Harcourt, Brace, 1922).

19. "Mr. Bennett and Mrs. Brown," in which Woolf delivered her famous pronouncement that "in or about December, 1910, human character changed," dates to 1924. Two years earlier Woolf had read "Old Bloomsbury" to the Memoir Club. In it she tries to describe and account for the changes in her own life and in society that she locates in 1910. See Virginia Woolf, *Moments of Being: Unpublished Autobiographical Writings*, ed. Jeanne Schulkind (New York: Harcourt Brace Jovanovich, 1976), pp. 157, 173.

20. D. H. Lawrence, *Kangaroo*, ed. Bruce Steele (Cambridge: Cambridge University Press, 1994), p. 216. Final revision of *Kangaroo* took place late in 1922. See Steele's introduction (p. xxxi).

21. Thus Michael Levenson's genealogy of modernism, which culminates in 1922. Michael H. Levenson, *A Genealogy of Modernism: A Study of English Literary Doctrine, 1908–1922* (Cambridge: Cambridge University Press, 1984). For a spirited nomination of 1900 as the all-important turning point, see Jay Dickson, "Surviving Victoria," in *High and Low Moderns: Literature and Culture, 1889–1939*, ed. Maria DiBattista and Lucy McDiarmid (New York: Oxford University Press, 1996), pp. 23–46.

22. Sanford Schwartz, *The Matrix of Modernism: Pound, Eliot, and Early Twentieth-Century Thought* (Princeton: Princeton University Press, 1985). The context in which Schwartz considers literary modernism includes Bergson, James, Bradley, Nietzsche, and Hulme. Even the excellent new study by Peter Nicholls, *Modernisms: A Literary Guide* (Berkeley: University of California Press, 1995), which sets out to expand the terms under which modernism is generally discussed, restricts its reconsideration to literary and artistic movements.

23. Thus, when Astradur Eysteinsson sets out in his admirable study to discover what "modernism" meant as a "sign," he considers only the opinions of critics and literary historians, not those of ordinary readers and consumers. See *The Concept of Modernism* (Ithaca: Cornell University Press, 1990), p. 51.

24. Beard, *Cross-Currents in Europe To-Day*, pp. 135, 251.

25. Ernest Hemingway, *Dateline Toronto: The Complete "Toronto Star" Dispatches, 1920–1924*, ed. William White (New York: Scribner's, 1985), pp. 127–168. Hemingway's stories provide an interesting look at what was a relatively new kind of journalism, one created at Versailles when the conferees were forced, against their will, to give daily press briefings. From the very beginning, the appetite for this kind of news exceeded the supply, and Hemingway is frequently reduced to reporting on the actions of other reporters and recording his inability to learn anything worthy of record.

26. Lord Lugard, *The Dual Mandate in British Tropical Africa* (1922; rpt., London: Cass, 1965). The quote is from Margery Perham's preface to the fifth edition. Lugard wrote his book in part as a response to Labour party pamphlets, one of them by Leonard Woolf. Labour announced its official commitment to freedom for India in 1918 and again in 1920. See Branson, *Britain in the Nineteen Twenties*, p. 68.

27. Henrika Kuklick, *The Savage Within: The Social History of British Anthropology, 1885–1945* (Cambridge: Cambridge University Press, 1991), p. 209.

28. Adam Kuper, *Anthropologists and Anthropology: The British School 1922–1972* (London: Lane, 1973), p. 9.

29. G. P. Baker and P. M. S. Hacker, *Language, Sense and Nonsense* (London: Blackwell, 1984), p. 2.

30. C. K. Ogden, I. A. Richards, and James Wood, *The Foundations of Aesthetics* (London: George Allen and Unwin, 1922). See also John Paul Russo, *I. A. Richards: His Life and Work* (Baltimore: Johns Hopkins University Press, 1989), p. 94.

31. See, for example, Jessie Fauset, "As to Books," *Crisis* 24 (June 1922): 66; Walter White, "The Negro's Contribution," *Bookman* 55 (July 1922): 530–531; and Robert Littell, "Negro Poets," *New Republic*, July 12, 1922, p. 196.

32. Carla Kaplan, *The Erotics of Talk* (New York: Oxford University Press, 1996), p. 108.

33. This is the way it is treated in Ernest Allen, Jr., "The New Negro: Explorations in Identity and Social Consciousness, 1910–1922," in *1915: The Cultural Moment*, ed. Adele Heller and Lois Rudnick (New Brunswick, NJ: Rutgers University Press, 1991), pp. 48–68.

34. Norman Edwards, "Broadcasting's Growth," in Williamson, ed., *Daily Mail Year Book*, p. 51.

35. David Robinson, *Hollywood in the Twenties* (New York: Barnes, 1968), p. 18.

36. The first movie biography was Louis Delluc's book on Chaplin: Louis Delluc, *Chaplin*, trans. Hamish Miles (New York: John Lane, 1922). The first use of the term "public relations" occurred, according to its inventor, Edward Bernays, when he described his profession to a reporter covering his wedding in 1922. See [Edward L. Bernays], *Biography*

of an Idea: Memoirs of Public Relations Counsel Edward L. Bernays (New York: Simon and Schuster, 1965), p. 290.

37. According to Edwin Ardener, Malinowski's functionalism is "the form that Modernism took at its developmental stage in social anthropology." See Edwin Ardener, "Social Anthropology and the Decline of Modernism," in *Reason and Morality*, ed. Joanna Overing (London: Tavistock, 1985), p. 49. Though Ardener sees Malinowski as the equivalent in anthropology of aesthetic modernism, he also emphasizes his isolation from other thinkers in England, apparently unaware of or unimpressed by his ties to Ogden. For a more complete discussion of these, see chapter 1.

38. The quoted phrase is taken from Lawrence Rainey, "The Price of Modernism: Publishing *The Waste Land*," in *T. S. Eliot: The Modernist in History*, ed. Ronald Bush (Cambridge: Cambridge University Press, 1991), p. 96. The relationship between Bernays and Liveright is discussed in chapter 2.

39. Charlie Chaplin, *My Trip Abroad* (New York: Harper and Brothers, 1922), pp. 32–33, 150. For earlier publications of "Tropics in New York," which Chaplin misquotes, see Claude McKay, *Spring in New Hampshire* (London: Grant Richards, 1920), and "Poems: Claude McKay," *Cambridge Magazine* 10 (Summer 1920): 55.

40. Hugh Kenner, *The Pound Era* (Berkeley: University of California Press, 1971), pp. 20–22.

41. As Kenner puts it in a very candid essay, "The Making of the Modernist Canon," *Mazes* (San Francisco: North Point Press, 1989), p. 34, "Via technology, science has shaped our century." Thus, when he says, "In the story I have been elaborating for thirty-five years, everything innovative in our century was response to something outside of literature" (p. 41), the outside has a fairly particular shape.

42. For Kenner's reasons for keeping Woolf outside the modernist canon, see "The Making of the Modernist Canon," p. 37.

43. See Michael Murphy, "'One Hundred Per Cent Bohemia': Pop Decadence and the Aestheticization of Commodity in the Rise of the Slicks," in *Marketing Modernisms: Self-Promotion, Canonization, Rereading*, ed. Kevin J. H. Dettmar and Stephen Watt (Ann Arbor: University of Michigan Press, 1996), pp. 64–65.

44. Andreas Huyssen, *After the Great Divide: Modernism, Mass Culture, Postmodernism* (Bloomington: Indiana University Press, 1986), pp. vii, 54, 57.

45. Houston Baker, Jr., *Modernism and the Harlem Renaissance* (Chicago: University of Chicago Press, 1987), p. xvi.

46. See Ann Douglas, *Terrible Honesty: Mongrel Manhattan in the 1920s* (New York: Farrar, Straus and Giroux, 1995), and Michael North, *The Dialect of Modernism: Race, Language, and Twentieth-Century Literature* (New York: Oxford University Press, 1994).

47. Sandra Gilbert and Susan Gubar, *No Man's Land*, 3 vols. (New Haven: Yale University Press, 1988), 1:156. This is an influential formulation that has been widely quoted, as, for example, in Bridget Elliott and Jo-Ann Wallace, *Women Artists and Writers: Modernist (Im)Positionings* (London: Routledge, 1994), p. 13. A similar idea is at the heart of Douglas' study.

48. Wayne Koestenbaum, *Double Talk: The Erotics of Male Literary Collaboration* (New York: Routledge, 1989).

49. Thus the foundational distinction between modernism and the avant-garde in Peter Bürger's *Theory of the Avant-Garde*, trans. Michael Shaw (Minneapolis: University of Minnesota Press, 1984). See especially the summary discussion and analysis in Jochen Schulte-Sasse's foreword (p. xv).

50. Raymond Williams, *The Politics of Modernism: Against the New Conformists* (London: Verso, 1989), p. 77.

51. For an account of this episode, see Wayne Cooper, *Claude McKay: Rebel Sojourner in the Harlem Renaissance* (New York: Schocken, 1987), p. 173.

52. Charlie Chaplin, *My Trip Abroad*, p. 23.

53. James Clifford, *Routes: Travel and Translation in the Late Twentieth Century* (Cambridge: Harvard University Press, 1997), pp. 4–5.

54. T. R. St.-Johnston, *South Sea Reminiscences* (London: Unwin, 1922), pp. 82, 96, 144.

55. Williams, *Politics of Modernism*, p. 45.

56. Alfred Viscount Northcliffe, *My Journey Round the World (16 July 1921–26 Feb. 1922)*, ed. Cecil and St. John Harmsworth (Philadelphia: J. B. Lippincott, 1923), p. 64.

57. Ibid., p. 200.

58. Ibid., p. 233.

59. Ibid., p. 72.

60. In "Instinct in Relation to Society," Rivers recounts an episode in which four Polynesians, after answering his questions for some time, fall to questioning him and are humorously astounded at his answers. "Their attitude toward my individualism was of just the same kind as that which we experience when we hear of such a custom as the couvade or of many examples of sympathetic magic." W. H. R. Rivers, *Psychology and Politics and Other Essays* (New York: Harcourt, Brace, 1923), p. 37. Pat Barker has given such an episode considerable importance in her fictionalized account of Rivers' life during the war: *Regeneration* (New York: Dutton, 1992); *The Eye in the Door* (New York: Dutton, 1994); and *The Ghost Road* (New York: Dutton, 1995).

61. Frank Worthington, *The Witch Doctor and Other Rhodesian Studies* (London: Field, n.d. [1922]), p. 34.

62. At least one story in this collection makes good on the title. It concerns a British colonial official in Egypt who becomes wildly popular, "a kind of fetish" in fact, because he is an exact replica in the flesh of the caricature Englishman the local clown has been forbidden to perform. The official believes that the authority he comes to enjoy in this town is the result of his strict methods, but it is in fact the result of the town's intense enjoyment of the perfection with which he confirms even the most exaggerated stereotypes of the British colonial official: "Though he was seen to be uncouth, devoid of manners as of understanding, and likely to prove dangerous at unawares, the people loved him and would crowd to gaze on him, hugging to their hearts the blest assurance that they saw his whole significance more truly than he did himself." See Marmaduke Pickthall, "The Kefr Ammeh Incident," in *As Others See Us* (London: Collins, 1922), pp. 1–29.

63. Simon Gikandi, *Maps of Englishness: Writing Identity in the Culture of Colonialism* (New York: Columbia University Press, 1996), p. 165.

64. Malinowski's infamous diary is full of confessions of resentment at having his scrutiny returned. See Bronislaw Malinowski, *A Diary in the Strict Sense of the Term*, trans. Norbert Guterman (New York: Harcourt, Brace and World, 1967).

65. See chapter 1.

66. Walter Lippmann, *Public Opinion* (New York: Harcourt, Brace, 1922), p. 79.

67. Ibid., p. 85.

68. Wallace Stevens, *Opus Posthumous*, ed. Samuel French Morse (New York: Knopf, 1957), p. 162.

69. This is, in fact, where Lippmann begins his analysis, with the ironic deaths of sol-

diers who continued to fight because the Armistice had been decided so far away it could not be communicated to them in time (p. 4).

70. Anthony Giddens, *The Consequences of Modernity* (Stanford: Stanford University Press, 1990), pp. 108–109.

71. Williams, *Politics of Modernism*, p. 45.

72. "Music by Wireless at a Range of 500 Miles," *Illustrated London News*, April 29, 1922, pp. 633–634.

73. William Le Queux, *Tracked by Wireless* (New York: Moffatt, Yard, 1922). Le Queux is listed on the inside front flap of the dust jacket and on the title page as a member of the Institute of Radio Engineers.

74. Northcliffe, *My Journey*, p. 91.

75. Edward S. Van Zile, *That Marvel—The Movie: A Glance at its Reckless Past, Its Promising Present, and Its Significant Future* (New York: Putnam's, 1923), p. 195.

76. W. G. Faulkner, "The Kinema in 1922," in Williamson, ed., *Daily Mail Yearbook*, p. 50.

77. Chaplin, *My Trip Abroad*, p. 114.

78. *Film Year Book 1922–1923* (Hollywood: Wid's Films and Film Folks, 1922), pp. 421–423.

79. "He is the first man in the history of the world of whom it can truly and literally be said that he is world-famous. Kings, prime ministers, and singers may be famous in the civilised world, but Charles is known in regions where Napoleon and Beethoven and Mussolini have never been heard of. He is known in the Solomon Islands, in the interior of New Guinea and the inner cities of Tibet, and in the recesses of Africa." Thomas Burke, *City of Encounters: A London Divertissement* (New York: Little, Brown, 1932), p. 138. Burke, a popular author of the time, escorted Chaplin during part of his London trip in 1922, and he is referring to this period of time in his statement.

80. Chaplin, *My Trip Abroad*, p. 56.

81. Ibid., p. 36.

82. *Illustrated London News*, April 15, 1922, p. 534.

83. Lippmann, *Drift and Mastery*, quoted in Ronald Steel, *Walter Lippmann and the American Century* (Boston: Little, Brown, 1980), p. 80.

84. Arjun Appadurai, *Modernity at Large: Cultural Dimensions of Globalization* (Minneapolis: University of Minnesota Press, 1996), p. 6.

85. Ibid., p. 4.

86. See John B. Thompson, *The Media and Modernity: A Social Theory of the Media* (Stanford: Stanford University Press, 1995), p. 100. Thompson takes from Daniel Lerner the idea that the media function as a "mobility multiplier" since they "enable individuals to experience vicariously events which take place in distant places, thereby stimulating their capacity to imagine alternatives to the ways of life characteristic of their immediate locales" (pp. 190–191).

87. Appadurai, *Modernity at Large*, p. 9.

88. Thompson, *Media and Modernity*, pp. 153–154.

89. Howard Carter and A. C. Mace, *The Discovery of the Tomb of King Tutankhamen* (1923; rpt., New York: Dover, 1977), p. 73.

90. Thomas Hoving, *Tutankhamun: The Untold Story* (New York: Simon and Schuster, 1978), p. 288.

91. Carter and Mace, *Discovery of the Tomb*, p. 97.

92. Ibid., pp. 106, 131.

93. *Illustrated London News*, December 9 (pp. 926–927) and 16, 1922 (p. 973). On December 23 the emphasis was still on "Objects That May Be Found" (pp. 1056–1057).

94. Hoving, *Tutankhamun*, pp. 154–157.

95. And yet even Carter eventually realized the strength of the affinity between Egyptology and the movies. A confirmed fan of Chaplin, Carter purposely mimicked the Little Tramp on camera and before the vast lecture audiences he entertained while in exile from the tomb. He had already made sure that a movie camera was on the spot when the sarcophagus lid was lifted. See H. V. F. Winstone, *Howard Carter and the Discovery of the Tomb of Tutankhamun* (London: Constable, 1991), pp. 193, 196, 207, 227–228.

96. *Egyptomania: Egypt in Western Art 1730–1930* (Ottawa: National Gallery of Canada, 1994), pp. 508–514.

97. Hoving, *Tutankhamun*, p. 183.

98. Ronny H. Cohen, "Tut and the '20s: 'The Egyptian Look,'" *Art in America* 67 (1979): 97.

99. Bernays, *Biography of an Idea*, p. 302.

100. *Egyptomania*, p. 509.

101. For a more complete discussion, see chapter 2.

102. Franco Moretti, *Modern Epic: The World System from Goethe to García Márquez* (London: Verso, 1996), p. 2.

103. Carter and Mace, *Discovery of the Tomb*, p. 115.

104. The articles collected in *Vers une architecture* (1923) had all appeared in *L'Esprit Nouveau* by January 1922. See Reyner Banham, *Theory and Design in the First Machine Age*, 2nd ed. (Cambridge: MIT Press, 1981), p. 220.

105. Jeffrey Weiss, *The Popular Culture of Modern Art: Picasso, Duchamp, and Avant-Gardism* (New Haven: Yale University Press, 1994). For a more detailed discussion, see chapter 2.

106. Clive Bell, *Since Cézanne* (London: Chatto and Windus, 1922), pp. 222–223.

107. Hoving, *Tutankhamun*, p. 200. For a picture of something called the Tutenkhamen Dance, see Maud Lavin, *Cut with the Kitchen Knife: The Weimar Photomontages of Hannah Höch* (New Haven: Yale University Press, 1993), p. 96.

108. For a discussion of this association, beginning with André Bazin's notion of a "mummy complex" behind film, see Antonia Lant, "The Curse of the Pharaoh, or How Cinema Contracted Egyptomania," *October* 59 (1992): 87–112. See also the excellent discussion by Melanie McAlister in "'The Common Heritage of Mankind': Race, Nation, and Masculinity in the King Tut Exhibit," *Representations* 54 (Spring 1996): 80–103.

109. James Joyce, *Ulysses*, ed. Hans Walter Gabler (New York: Random House, 1986), p. 93.

110. "Let Darbycord Photograph Your Voice," advertisement, *Illustrated London News*, April 29, 1922, p. 642.

111. See, for example, Cheryl Herr, *Joyce's Anatomy of Culture* (Urbana: University of Illinois Press, 1986); and David Chinitz, "T. S. Eliot and the Cultural Divide," *PMLA* 110 (March 1995): 236–247.

112. Appadurai, *Modernity at Large*, p. 64.

113. Ibid., p. 51.

114. Hans Robert Jauss, *Toward an Aesthetic of Reception*, trans. Timothy Bahti (Minneapolis: University of Minnesota Press, 1982), p. 28; Wlad Godzich, "Introduction," *Aesthetic Experience and Literary Hermeneutics*, by Hans-Robert Jauss, trans. Michael Shaw (Minneapolis: University of Minnesota Press, 1982), p. xii. Jauss attempts to provide a particular

example in "*La douceur du foyer*: Lyric Poetry of the Year 1857 as a Model for the Communication of Social Forms," pp. 263–293.

Chapter 1

1. Anonymous, "Language," *Times Literary Supplement*, April 6, 1922, p. 217. Hereafter the abbreviation *TLS* will be used to designate the *Times Literary Supplement*.

2. It is, of course, common to date the "linguistic turn" of twentieth-century philosophy from Wittgenstein's pronouncement "All philosophy is 'Critique of language'" made in *Tractatus Logico-Philosophicus* (London: Routledge and Kegan Paul, 1922), p. 63. See, for example, G. P. Baker and P. M. S. Hacker, *Language, Sense and Nonsense* (London: Blackwell, 1984), p. 2. All subsequent references to the *Tractatus* will be to this edition, except where specific comparison is to be made to the later Pears and McGuinness translation, and will be identified by *T* and the proposition number. For Malinowski's influence, see Jerzy Szymura, "Bronislaw Malinowski's 'Ethnographic Theory of Language,'" in *Linguistic Thought in England 1914–1945*, ed. Roy Harris (London: Duckworth, 1988).

3. C. K. Ogden and I. A. Richards, *The Meaning of Meaning: A Study of the Influence of Language upon Thought and of the Science of Symbolism* (New York: Harcourt, Brace, 1923), pp. xxviii, 454.

4. Ibid., pp. 394–395.

5. Bertrand Russell, *Essays on Language, Mind and Matter 1919–26*, vol. 9 of *The Collected Papers of Bertrand Russell*, ed. John G. Slater and Bernd Frohmann (London: Unwin Hyman, 1988), p. 42.

6. Rush Rhees, *Discussions of Wittgenstein* (London: Routledge and Kegan Paul, 1970), p. 51. See Ludwig Wittgenstein, *Culture and Value*, ed. G. H. von Wright, trans. Peter Winch (Oxford: Basil Blackwell, 1980), p. 37e.

7. Bronislaw Malinowski, "The Problem of Meaning in Primitive Languages," Supplement to Ogden and Richards, *The Meaning of Meaning*, p. 467.

8. The most complete account devoted solely to the composition and publication of the *Tractatus* is G. H. von Wright, "The Origin of the *Tractatus*," in G. H. von Wright, *Wittgenstein* (Oxford: Blackwell, 1982), pp. 63–109. See also Ray Monk, *Ludwig Wittgenstein: The Duty of Genius* (London: Cape, 1990), pp. 134, 162, 205.

9. *TLS*, p. 217. The article shifts attention from this army to the Englishman Sir William Jones and so restores priority to English thought in linguistics.

10. Ogden remarks that printing the two together, the standard practice for all of Wittgenstein's later works, is "somewhat unusual" (*T*, n.p. [p. 5]).

11. B. F. McGuinness and G. H. von Wright, "Unpublished Correspondence between Russell & Wittgenstein," *Russell* 10 (1990): 101–124. "The translation is being done by two young men at Cambridge who know mathematical logic, and I am telling them all that you and I agreed on as regards translations of terms" (Russell to Wittgenstein, December 24, 1921, p. 117). The letter is also available in Ludwig Wittgenstein, *Cambridge Letters: Correspondence with Russell, Keynes, Moore, Ramsey and Sraffa*, ed. Brian McGuinness and G. H. von Wright (Oxford: Blackwell, 1995), pp. 174–175. See also Monk, *The Duty of Genius*, pp. 38–39, 276. I. A. Richards later maintained that, at Ogden's suggestion, Ramsey taught himself German using a dictionary, a grammar, and Ernst Mach's *Analysis*. I. A. Richards, "Co-Author of the 'Meaning of Meaning,'" in *C. K. Ogden: A Collective Memoir*, ed. P. Sargant Florence and J. R. L. Anderson (London: Pemberton, 1977), p. 102.

12. G. E. M. Anscombe, *An Introduction to Wittgenstein's Tractatus* (London: Hutchinson University Library, 1959), p. 17. See also the series of open letters that ran in the *TLS*

signed by Wittgenstein's executors, Rush Rhees, G. H. von Wright, and Anscombe (February 18, 1965, p. 132; October 9, 1970, p. 1165).

13. Ludwig Wittgenstein, *Letters to C. K. Ogden with Comments on the English Translation of the Tractatus Logico-Philosophicus*, ed. G. H. von Wright (Oxford: Basil Blackwell, 1973). Note Russell's 1960 letter to Ogden giving his own recollections about Wittgenstein's collaboration in the translation (p. 10). The new translation, by D. F. Pears and B. F. McGuinness, first appeared in 1961.

14. David Pinsent, Wittgenstein's closest friend in his early Cambridge years, reported that he spoke English "fluently." G. H. von Wright, ed., *A Portrait of Wittgenstein as a Young Man: From the Diary of David Hume Pinsent 1912–1914* (Oxford: Basil Blackwell, 1990), p. 5. Nonetheless, others continued to find his English unidiomatic, at least. See, for example, Monk, *The Duty of Genius*, pp. 38–39, 434. For Wittgenstein's early training in English, which began at the age of six or seven, see ibid., p. 15.

15. Von Wright, *Wittgenstein*, p. 54; Monk, *The Duty of Genius*, pp. 102, 344–345, 363.

16. See, for examples, Monk, *The Duty of Genius*, pp. 183, 414.

17. "I have very often altered it such that now it doesn't seem to be a translation of the German at all. I've left out some words which occur in the German text or put in others which don't occur in the original etc. etc. But I al[l]ways did it in order to translate the *sense* (not the words)." Wittgenstein, *Letters to C. K. Ogden*, p. 19.

18. *Wittgenstein's Lectures: Cambridge, 1932–1935*, ed. Alice Ambrose (Oxford: Basil Blackwell, 1979), p. 54.

19. Russell, "Introduction," in Wittgenstein, *Tractatus*, p. 7.

20. Baker and Hacker, *Language, Sense, and Nonsense*, pp. 33, 37. See also P. M. S. Hacker, *Insight and Illusion: Themes in the Philosophy of Wittgenstein*, rev. ed. (Oxford: Clarendon Press, 1986), pp. 6–7; and Cora Diamond, *The Realistic Spirit: Wittgenstein, Philosophy, and the Mind* (Cambridge: MIT Press, 1991), pp. 115–144.

21. See Dinda L. Gorlée, "Wittgenstein, Translation, and Semiotics," *Target* 1 (1989): 71.

22. See Roy Harris, "Murray, Moore and the Myth," in Harris, ed., *Linguistic Thought*, p. 11.

23. Wittgenstein, *Letters to C. K. Ogden*, p. 25. Interestingly, Pears and McGuinness use "sign language," thus returning to Ogden and Ramsey's original translation and undoing Wittgenstein's own correction. Ludwig Wittgenstein, *Tractatus Logico-Philosophicus*, trans. D. F. Pears and B. F. McGuiness (Atlantic Highlands, NJ: Humanities Press International, 1961), p. 20.

24. Hacker, *Insight*, p. 102.

25. *T*, ed. Pears and McGuinness, p. 57.

26. That is to say, the "my" in 5.6 and 5.62 is not to be identified with any particular individual, nor is its relationship to language supposed to be an empirically contingent relationship. See Hacker, *Insight*, pp. 100–101. It is worth noting in this context that Hacker's subhead for this discussion conflates 5.6 and 5.62 in a very misleading way.

27. Wittgenstein, *Letters to C. K. Ogden*, p. 34.

28. Wittgenstein, *Lectures 1932–1935*, p. 32; *Wittgenstein's Lectures: Cambridge, 1930–1932*, ed. Desmond Lee (Oxford: Blackwell, 1980), p. 34.

29. Ludwig Wittgenstein, *Philosophical Investigations*, trans. G. E. M. Anscombe (Oxford: Blackwell, 1958), pp. 138e–139e. All subsequent references to *Philosophical Investigations* will be to this edition, identified in the text as *PI* and the proposition number.

30. Jeffrey Alexander, *Fin de Siècle Social Theory: Relativism, Reduction, and the Problem of Reason* (London: Verso, 1995), p. 69.

31. The articles collected in *Vers une architecture* (1923) had all appeared in *L'Esprit Nou-*

veau by January 1922. See Reyner Banham, *Theory and Design in the First Machine Age*, 2nd ed. (Cambridge: MIT Press, 1981), p. 220. For a discussion of Hemingway's early work, see chapter 5.

32. Wittgenstein, *Culture and Value*, p. 18e.

33. Rhees, *Discussions*, p. 51. See Wittgenstein, *Culture and Value*, p. 37e.

34. Wittgenstein, *Culture and Value*, p. 37e.

35. Rhees, *Discussions*, p. 50.

36. Monk, *The Duty of Genius*, p. 261.

37. Quoted in ibid., p. 268. The entire letter is available in Wittgenstein, *Cambridge Letters*, pp. 227–28.

38. Ludwig Wittgenstein, *Letters to Russell, Keynes and Moore*, ed. G. H. von Wright (Oxford: Basil Blackwell, 1974), p. 36. This letter is also available in the newer, more comprehensive collection of Wittgenstein's *Cambridge Letters*, p. 52.

39. Wittgenstein, *Letters to Russell, Keynes, and Moore*, p. 115. This letter is also available in Wittgenstein, *Cambridge Letters*, pp. 205–207.

40. Monk, *The Duty of Genius*, p. 530.

41. Wittgenstein, *Culture and Value*, p. 83e.

42. Ibid., p. 39e.

43. Monk, *The Duty of Genius*, pp. 380–381. See also Henry McDonald, *The Normative Basis of Culture: A Philosophical Inquiry* (Baton Rouge: Louisiana State University Press, 1986), pp. 66–67, where the tactic is called "fictitious natural history."

44. See, for examples, Wittgenstein, *Lectures 1932–1935*, pp. 93, 102, 105, 180; *PI*, 200, 282, 528; and Ludwig Wittgenstein, *Remarks on the Philosophy of Psychology*, vol. 1, ed. G. E. M. Anscombe and G. H. von Wright, trans. G. E. M. Anscombe (Chicago: University of Chicago Press, 1980), 65, 93, 96, 149, 662. One of the oddest of these thought-experiments is the one conducted in the *Remarks*, in which Wittgenstein imagines a tribe "that we want to enslave" (pp. 93–96).

45. Propositions in *Philosophical Investigations*, part II, are not numbered individually. See the excellent discussion and retranslation of this passage in Marjorie Perloff, "From Theory to Grammar: Wittgenstein and the Aesthetic of the Ordinary," *New Literary History* 25 (1994): 916–917, in the course of which she points out how much this passage "points directly to the author himself."

46. Ludwig Wittgenstein, *Remarks on Colour*, ed. G. E. M. Anscombe, trans. Linda L. McAlister and Margarete Schätte (Berkeley: University of California Press, nd), pp. 285, 345.

47. Wittgenstein, *Remarks on the Philosophy of Psychology*, p. 587.

48. Henrika Kuklick, *The Savage Within: The Social History of British Anthropology, 1885–1945* (Cambridge: Cambridge University Press, 1991), p. 53.

49. Ibid., p. 16.

50. Richard Slobodin, *W. H. R. Rivers* (New York: Columbia University Press, 1978), p. 74. Another Labour candidate in this election was Bertrand Russell, who had known Rivers for many years. See his review of *Instinct and the Unconscious*, published after Rivers' death, in Russell, *Essays on Language, Mind and Matter 1919–26*, p. 12.

51. Slobodin, *W. H. R. Rivers*, p. 72. For the effect of this death within the field, see Ian Langham, *The Building of British Social Anthropology: W. H. R. Rivers and His Cambridge Disciples in the Development of Kinship Studies, 1898–1931* (Dordrecht, Holland: D. Reidel, 1981), p. 160. Slobodin disputes the idea that Rivers' death cleared the way for Malinowski to assert his influence (p. 185), but he admits what many other observers have noted, that Malinowski felt an intense sense of rivalry with the older man. See also James

Urry, "*Notes and Queries on Anthropology* and the Development of Field Methods in British Anthropology, 1870–1920," *Proceedings of the Royal Anthropological Institute of Great Britain and Ireland* (1972): 52.

52. Adam Kuper, *Anthropologists and Anthropology: The British School 1922–1972* (London: Lane, 1973), p. 9. See also Langham, *Building of British Social Anthropology*, pp. xii, 245. What is apparently Ruth Benedict's first publication, "The Vision in Plains Culture," *American Anthropologist* 24 (1922): 1–25, also appeared in this year, but her real influence did not come until much later.

53. I have been unable to examine a first edition of the *Tractatus*, but the first edition of G. E. Moore's *Philosophical Studies*, which is early enough to list under "Volumes Already Arranged" a work by L. Wittgenstein entitled *Philosophical Logic*, also lists *Conflict and Dream*.

54. In a letter to Russell, Wittgenstein called *The Meaning of Meaning* "a miserable book" (Monk, *The Duty of Genius*, p. 214). He might perhaps have been influenced to some extent by its very critical attitude toward the *Tractatus*, which Ogden and his collaborator, I. A. Richards, had at their disposal while *The Meaning of Meaning* was in proof. Certainly, Richards at least reciprocated Wittgenstein's low opinion, calling the *Tractatus* "a magnificent specimen of the unintelligible" (*Ogden: A Collective Memoir*, p. 102). For a lengthier discussion of the intellectual relationship between Ogden's work and Wittgenstein's, see George Wolf, "C. K. Ogden," in Harris, ed., *Linguistic Thought*, pp. 91–94. Wolf's conclusion is that "the deeper aspects of the *Tractatus* do not seem to have had much importance for Ogden's work at this stage" (p. 94).

55. Malinowski, "Problem of Meaning," in Ogden and Richards, *The Meaning of Meaning*, p. 467.

56. Wittgenstein, *Culture and Value*, p. 37.

57. Brian McGuinness, *Wittgenstein: A Life* (Berkeley: University of California Press, 1988), p. 95.

58. George W. Stocking, Jr., *The Ethnographer's Magic and Other Essays in the History of Anthropology* (Madison: University of Wisconsin Press, 1992), pp. 22, 28.

59. See Myers' entry in *A History of Psychology in Autobiography*, ed. Carl Murchison (Worcester: Clark University Press, 1936), 3:218.

60. McGuiness, *Wittgenstein*, pp. 125–128. See also Monk, *The Duty of Genius*, pp. 49–50.

61. Charles S. Myers, "Individual differences in listening to music," *British Journal of Psychology* 13 (1922): 52–71.

62. Sooner or later, Wittgenstein seems to have dismissed as hopelessly benighted nearly everyone at Cambridge, and Myers was no exception. See McGuinness, *Wittgenstein*, p. 128.

63. Kuper, *Anthropologists and Anthropology*, pp. 25, 52; Urry, "*Notes and Queries*," p. 52.

64. Charles S. Myers, "Music," *Reports of the Cambridge Anthropological Expedition to Torres Straits* 4 (1912): 238–305. McGuinness suggests that "perhaps" Wittgenstein attended Myers' lecture (*Wittgenstein*, p. 127).

65. A. M. Hocart, "The 'Psychological Interpretation of Language,'" *British Journal of Psychology* 5 (November 1912): 267–279.

66. Langham, *Building of British Social Anthropology*, p. 327. Here, Langham suggests that 1912, and not 1922, be considered "the seminal year" for the discipline. See also ibid., pp. xix–xx, 173; and Stocking, *The Ethnographer's Magic*, pp. 36–40. For a good deal of information on the development of *Notes and Queries*, see Urry, "*Notes and Queries*."

67. Stocking, *The Ethnographer's Magic*, p. 39. For more on Malinowski's dependence on *Notes and Queries*, see p. 57 and Urry, "*Notes and Queries*," pp. 45, 53.

68. Barbara Freire-Marreco and John Linton Myres, *Notes and Queries on Anthropology*, 4th ed. (London: Royal Anthropological Institute, 1912), p. 221.

69. McGuinness, *Wittgenstein*, p. 128.

70. Wittgenstein, *Remarks on Colour*, p. 11e; Slobodin, *W. H. R. Rivers*, p. 271.

71. Wittgenstein, *Remarks on the Philosophy of Psychology*, p. 119e. The most complete bibliography of Myers' work apparently appears in the obituary contributed by F. C. Bartlett to *Obituary Notices of the Fellows of the Royal Society* 5 (1945–1948): 774–777.

72. Wittgenstein, *Remarks on the Philosophy of Psychology*, p. 169e.

73. Freire-Marreco and Myres, *Notes and Queries*, pp. 108–127.

74. Ibid., p. 125.

75. Ibid., pp. 258–259. See also Stocking, *The Ethnographer's Magic*, p. 38.

76. Kuper, *Anthropologists and Anthropology*, pp. 58–59; Urry, "*Notes and Queries*," p. 50; Stocking, *The Ethnographer's Magic*, p. 30.

77. A. R. Radcliffe-Brown, *The Andaman Islanders* (Cambridge: Cambridge University Press, 1922), p. 231.

78. Ibid., p. 266.

79. This comment is to be found in Radcliffe-Brown's 1932 preface to a reprint edition of *The Andaman Islanders*, identical to the first edition except for the preface and a few additions to the second appendix. See A. R. Radcliffe-Brown, *The Andaman Islanders* (New York: The Free Press of Glencoe, 1964), p. ix.

80. Ibid., p. 308.

81. Ibid., p. 303.

82. Ibid., pp. 306, 324.

83. Ibid., pp. 230, 188.

84. Ibid., p. 235.

85. Bronislaw Malinowski, *Argonauts of the Western Pacific* (New York: Dutton, 1922), p. xvi. This edition will be referred to hereafter in the text as *AWP*. See also Kuper, *Anthropologists and Anthropology*, pp. 20, 39.

86. After reading "The Problem of Meaning in Primitive Languages," Radcliffe-Brown wrote to Malinowski to say that he had attempted "a new linguistic method" of his own but had left it undeveloped in *The Andaman Islanders*. See George W. Stocking, Jr., "Radcliffe-Brown and British Social Anthropology," in *Functionalism Historicized: Essays on British Social Anthropology*, ed. George W. Stocking, Jr. (Madison: University of Wisconsin Press, 1984), p. 160.

87. Bronislaw Malinowski, "The Problem of Meaning in Primitive Languages," in Ogden and Richards, *The Meaning of Meaning*, p. 316.

88. Ibid., p. 472.

89. Ibid., pp. 495, 474.

90. See Szymura, "Malinowski's 'Ethnographic Theory,'" p. 118. One very brief comparison in the literature on Wittgenstein is to be found in John V. Canfield, "The Living Language: Wittgenstein and the Empirical Study of Communication," *Language Sciences* 15 (1993): 188. There is a more general comparison of Wittgenstein and anthropology in Roger Trigg, "Wittgenstein and Social Science," in *Wittgenstein Centenary Essays*, ed. A. Phillips Griffiths (Cambridge: Cambridge University Press, 1991). "This emphasis on context has coalesced with the concerns of social anthropology" (p. 213).

91. For an excellent discussion of these techniques, see Harry C. Payne, "Malinowski's

Style," *Proceedings of the American Philosophical Society* 125 (December 1981): 416–440. For an attack on the philosophical incoherence of the method, see D. Terence Langendoen, *The London School of Linguistics: A Study of the Linguistic Theories of B. Malinowski and J. R. Firth* (Cambridge: MIT Press, 1968), p. 22.

92. Such contradictions are the focus of much contemporary reconsideration of the status and role of anthropology. See James Clifford, *The Predicament of Culture: Twentieth-Century Ethnography, Literature, and Art* (Cambridge: Harvard University Press, 1988), especially "On Ethnographic Authority," pp. 21–54.

93. Charles Beadle, *Witch-Doctors* (Boston: Houghton Mifflin, 1922), pp. 242, 288.

94. Stocking, *The Ethnographer's Magic*, p. 52.

95. Beadle, *Witch-Doctors*, p. 318.

96. Radcliffe-Brown, *The Andaman Islanders*, p. 29. There is an interesting sidelight thrown on the Andamans by Edmund Candler's novel *Abdication*, in which an Indian political agitator is sentenced to prison there. Edmund Candler, *Abdication* (NY: Dutton, 1922), p. 279.

97. Payne, "Malinowski's Style," pp. 424–425.

98. Sir Everard Im Thurm, "Preface," *Essays on the Depopulation of Melanesia*, ed. W. H. R. Rivers (Cambridge: Cambridge University Press, 1922), p. xv. Some of the essays in the collection were actually written as early as 1912, according to Rivers' introduction (p. 2); Im Thurm's preface is dated April 23, 1922.

99. Im Thurm, "Preface," p. xvii. Specific examples are given throughout the essays in the collection.

100. Dr. Felix Speiser, "Decadence and Preservation in the New Hebrides," in Rivers, *Depopulation*, p. 37.

101. W. H. R. Rivers, "The Psychological Factor," in *Depopulation*, pp. 84–113.

102. See also Bronislaw Malinowski, "Ethnology and the Study of Society," *Economica* 2 (October 1922): 208–219.

103. Note how strongly Malinowski insists on this in ibid., p. 218.

104. Ibid., p. 209.

105. The analysis was also applied to areas outside the tropics. Edward Sapir echoes Rivers' analysis very closely when he describes in an article that appeared in the *Dial* in September of 1919 and in slightly different form in *The Dalhousie Review* in July of 1922 the "bewildered vacuity" that strikes the "typical American Indian tribe" when the "courage and joy" of its normal existence is destroyed by contact with European society. "Culture, Genuine and Spurious," *The Dalhousie Review* 2 (July 1922): 165–178.

106. Lord Lugard, *The Dual Mandate in British Tropical Africa* (1922; rpt., London: Cass, 1965), p. 209; Martin Johnson, *Cannibal-Land: Adventures with a Camera in the New Hebrides* (Boston: Houghton Mifflin, 1922), p. 4.

107. W. F. Adler, *The Isle of Vanishing Men: A Narrative of Adventure in Cannibal-Land* (New York: Century, 1922), p. 34.

108. Walter E. Traprock [George S. Chappell], *The Cruise of the Kawa: Wanderings in the South Seas* (New York: Putnam's, 1921), p. 128. Chappell published regularly in *Vanity Fair* throughout 1922.

109. T. S. Eliot, "Marie Lloyd," in *Selected Essays 1917–1932* (New York: Harcourt, Brace, 1932), p. 371. In the originally published form of this essay, as a "Letter from London," *The Dial* (December 1922): 661–663, Eliot seems more immediately aware of the recent death of Rivers, calling him "the great psychologist," and more depressed in general, going so far as to apologize for his mood at the end of the essay.

110. Beadle, *Witch-Doctors*, pp. 14, 313.

111. Kuklick, *The Savage Within*, pp. 294–295; and idem, "Tribal Exemplars," in *Functionalism Historicized*, ed. Stocking, pp. 70–71.

112. Bertrand Russell, *The Problem of China* (London: Allen and Unwin, 1922), p. 197. See also Sapir's articles (noted in n.105, this chapter) for further examples having to do with the United States.

113. For a survey of the controversy generally favorable to Rivers, see Slobodin, *W. H. R. Rivers*, pp. 173–179.

114. Charles F. G. Masterman, *England After War* (London: Hodder and Stoughton, 1922), p. 169. This was such a serious problem in Masterman's eyes that he devoted an entire chapter, entitled "Babies," to it.

115. Bertrand Russell, *Free Thought and Official Propaganda* (New York: B. W. Huebsch, 1922), p. 56.

116. C. E. Montague, *Disenchantment* (New York: Brentano's, 1922), p. 228.

117. Masterman, *England After War*, p. 70.

118. George A. Greenwood, *England To-Day: A Social Study of Our Time* (London: Allen and Unwin, 1922), p. 137.

119. Kuklick, *The Savage Within*, p. 179; Slobodin, *W. H. R. Rivers*, pp. 80–81.

120. Greenwood, in *England To-Day*, notes that England had changed from a creditor to a debtor nation (p. 122). The Washington Naval Conference of 1922 formally signified the end of England's domination of the oceans.

121. See also Noreen Branson, *Britain in the Nineteen Twenties* (Minneapolis: University of Minnesota Press, 1976), pp. 75–77.

122. Kuklick, *The Savage Within*, pp. 174–179.

123. Myers, *A History of Psychology in Autobiography*, 3: 225–227.

124. Greenwood, *England To-Day*, p. 123.

125. John Dewey, *Human Nature and Conduct: An Introduction to Social Psychology* (New York: Henry Holt, 1922), pp. 82–83.

126. John Cournos, *Babel* (New York: Boni and Liveright, 1922), p. 240. Further quotations will be identified in the text as *B*.

127. This experience is in fact the starting point for the conception and composition of *Babel* itself. See John Cournos, *Autobiography* (New York: G. P. Putnam's, 1935), p. 218.

128. C. K. Ogden, *Debabelization* (London: Kegan Paul, Trench, Trubner, 1931); Ezra Pound, "Debabelization and Ogden," *New English Weekly* 6 (February 28, 1935): 410–411.

129. Ezra Pound, *Literary Essays*, ed. T. S. Eliot (New York: New Directions, 1968), p. 50.

130. Hugh Kenner, *The Pound Era* (Berkeley: University of California Press, 1971), p. 96.

131. T. S. Eliot, *The Complete Poems and Plays 1909–1950* (New York: Harcourt, Brace and World, 1971), p. 55. This is, of course, the last of Eliot's notes to his poem. Quotations from *The Waste Land* itself will be taken from this edition and identified in the text as *WL* with the line number.

132. In his autobiography, Cournos regularly refers to London as Babylon.

133. Kenner, *The Pound Era*, p. 109.

134. Calvin Bedient, *He Do the Police in Different Voices* (Chicago: University of Chicago Press, 1986), p. 203.

135. James Joyce, *Ulysses*, ed. Hans Walter Gabler (New York: Vintage, 1985), p. 35. Subsequent quotations from this edition will be identified by *U*.

136. Malinowski, "The Problem of Meaning in Primitive Languages," in Ogden and Richards, *The Meaning of Meaning*, p. 307.

137. Marjorie Perloff, *Wittgenstein's Ladder: Poetic Language and the Strangeness of the Ordinary* (Chicago: University of Chicago Press, 1996), p. 76.

Chapter 2

1. D. H. Lawrence, *Psychoanalysis and the Unconscious* (London: Heinemann, 1923), p. 10.

2. Catherine Lucille Covert, *Freud on the Front Page: Transmission of Freudian Ideas in the American Newspapers of the 1920's* (Ph.D. diss., Syracuse University, 1975), pp. 274, 260.

3. Ibid., p. 264. See also Nathan G. Hale, Jr., *The Rise and Crisis of Psychoanalysis in the United States: Freud and the Americans, 1917–1945* (New York: Oxford University Press, 1995), pp. 71–72; and Ann Douglas, *Terrible Honesty: Mongrel Manhattan in the 1920s* (New York: Farrar, Straus and Giroux, 1995), p. 124.

4. Lawrence, *Psychoanalysis and the Unconscious*, p. 10.

5. Covert, *Freud on the Front Page*, p. 238.

6. Bronislaw Malinowski, *Sex and Repression in Savage Society* (1927; rpt., Chicago: University of Chicago Press, 1985), p. vii. Quoted in Elizabeth Abel, *Virginia Woolf and the Fictions of Psychoanalysis* (Chicago: University of Chicago Press, 1989), p. 16.

7. *Current Opinion*, January 1922; *Illustrated London News*, October 14, 1922, p. 607. See also Alfred Kuttner's chapter on "Nerves," in *Civilization in the United States*, ed. Harold E. Stearns (New York: Harcourt, Brace, 1922), pp. 427–442.

8. See, for example, the report in the *Illustrated London News*, April 15, 1922, p. 541.

9. James Oppenheim, *Your Hidden Powers* (New York: Knopf, 1923). These pieces originally ran in the *Los Angeles Times* in 1922. Oppenheim was actually only relatively orthodox; he had in fact been censured by the New York Psychoanalytic Society for practicing as a lay analyst. See Sanford Gifford, "The American Reception of Psychoanalysis, 1908–1922," in *1915, the Cultural Moment*, ed. Adele Heller and Louis Rudnick (New Brunswick: Rutgers University Press, 1991), p. 139.

10. A. A. Brill, *Psychoanalysis: Its Theories and Practical Application*, 3rd ed., (Philadelphia: W. B. Saunders, 1922); Smith Ely Jelliffe and Louise Brink, *Psychoanalysis and the Drama* (New York: Nervous and Mental Disease Publishing Company, 1922). For an encapsulation of Brill's career, see May E. Romm, "Abraham Arden Brill: First American Translator of Freud," in *Psychoanalytic Pioneers*, ed. Franz Alexander, Samuel Eisenstein, and Martin Grotjahn (New York: Basic Books, 1966), pp. 210–223. See also Joel Pfister, *Staging Depth: Eugene O'Neill and the Politics of Psychological Discourse* (Chapel Hill: University of North Carolina Press, 1995), p. 55; Hale, *The Rise and Crisis of Psychoanalysis*, pp. 68–69; and Gifford, "The American Reception of Psychoanalysis," pp. 133–140.

11. Charles Forcey, *The Crossroads of Liberalism: Croly, Weyl, Lippmann, and the Progressive Era 1900–1925* (New York: Oxford University Press, 1961), p. 109; D. Steven Blum, *Walter Lippmann: Cosmopolitanism in the Century of Total War* (Ithaca: Cornell University Press, 1984), p. 29; Hale, *The Rise and Crisis of Psychoanalysis*, pp. 60–61. There seems to be some dispute among these authorities as to whether it was Freud who reviewed Lippmann's *A Preface to Politics* or Ernest Jones. In either case, it met with official approval.

12. Perry Meisel and Walter Kendrick, eds., *Bloomsbury/Freud: The Letters of James and Alix Strachey* (New York: Basic Books, 1985), pp. x, 4, 40.

13. Hermione Lee, *Virginia Woolf* (New York: Knopf, 1997), pp. 449–450.

14. For a discussion of Virginia and Leonard Woolf's relationship to these developments, see Jan Ellen Goldstein, "The Woolfs' Response to Freud: Water Spiders, Singing

Canaries, and the Second Apple," in *Literature and Psychoanalysis*, ed. Edith Kurzweil and William Phillips (New York: Columbia University Press, 1983), pp. 232–255.

15. Anthony Giddens, *Modernity and Self-Identity: Self and Society in the Late Modern Age* (Stanford: Stanford University Press, 1991), p. 2. See also idem, *The Consequences of Modernity* (Stanford: Stanford University Press, 1990), pp. 35–45.

16. Joel Pfister, "Glamorizing the Psychological: The Politics of the Performances of Modern Psychological Identities," in *Inventing the Psychological: Toward a Cultural History of Emotional Life in America*, ed. Joel Pfister and Nancy Schnog (New Haven: Yale University Press, 1997), p. 174.

17. Jürgen Habermas, *The Structural Transformation of the Public Sphere: An Inquiry into a Category of Bourgeois Society*, trans. Thomas Burger (Cambridge: MIT Press, 1989), pp. 89–102.

18. Jelliffe and Brink, *Psychoanalysis and the Drama*, p. 5.

19. Walter Lippmann, *Public Opinion* (New York: Harcourt, Brace, 1922), p. 81.

20. Sigmund Freud, *Beyond the Pleasure Principle*, in *The Standard Edition of the Complete Psychological Works*, vol. 18, trans. James Strachey (London: Hogarth, 1955), pp. 27–28.

21. Ibid., p. 59.

22. Freud, *Group Psychology and the Analysis of the Ego*, in *Standard Works*, vol. 18, p. 117.

23. Brill, *Psychoanalysis*, p. 349.

24. Charles Platt, *The Psychology of Social Life: A Materialistic Study with an Idealistic Conclusion* (New York: Dodd, Mead, 1922).

25. Hale, *The Rise and Crisis of Psychoanalysis*, p. 22.

26. Matt K. Matsuda, *The Memory of the Modern* (New York: Oxford University Press, 1996), pp. 109–110.

27. For a sympathetic survey of the growth of crowd psychology and an application of its tenets to twentieth-century politics, see Serge Moscovici, *The Age of the Crowd: A Historical Treatise on Mass Psychology*, trans. J. C. Whitehouse (Cambridge: Cambridge University Press, 1985).

28. W. H. R. Rivers, *Instinct and the Unconscious*, 2nd ed. (1922; rpt., Cambridge: Cambridge University Press, 1924), p. 133. Rivers was active in a branch of British psychiatry quite distinct from Freudian psychoanalysis, with which he had a number of specific disagreements. Nonetheless, he was an associate member of the British Psycho-Analytical Society from its inception in 1919. See Edward Glover, "Psychoanalysis in England," in *Psychoanalytic Pioneers*, ed. Alexander, Eisenstein, and Grotjahn, p. 536.

29. Rivers, *Instinct and the Unconscious*, p. 252.

30. W. H. R. Rivers, *Psychology and Politics and Other Essays* (New York: Harcourt, Brace and Company, 1923), p. 51. That Rivers had some influence in the United States is suggested by the critical but respectful reading of his work given in John T. MacCurdy, *Problems in Dynamic Psychology* (New York: Macmillan, 1922), pp. 209–252.

31. Rivers, *Psychology and Politics and Other Essays*, pp. 15–17; Ronald Steel, *Walter Lippmann and the American Century* (Boston: Little, Brown, 1980), pp. 26–27. In fact, Lippmann had read Wallas even before he read Freud. Another prominent liberal of the time influenced by Wallas was R. H. Tawney. See R. H. Tawney, *Religion and the Rise of Capitalism*, Holland Memorial Lectures, 1922 (1926; rpt., London: Murray, 1936), p. 12.

32. Steel, *Walter Lippmann*, p. 26.

33. A contemporary account of this kind of liberalism is afforded by L. T. Hobhouse, *The Elements of Social Justice* (New York: Holt, 1922).

34. For a lengthy and detailed discussion of this shift, see Habermas, *Structural Transformation*, pp. 236–244.

35. Abbott Lawrence Lowell, *Public Opinion in War and Peace* (Cambridge: Harvard University Press, 1923), p. 7.

36. Ibid., p. 14.

37. Ibid., p. 212. See Habermas, *Structural Transformation*, pp. 94–95.

38. Nitza Rosovsky, *The Jewish Experience at Harvard and Radcliffe* (Cambridge: Harvard University Press, 1986), pp. 10, 15. This episode will be discussed in greater detail below.

39. Habermas, *Structural Transformation*, p. 124. See also W. J. T. Mitchell, "The Violence of Public Art: *Do the Right Thing*," in *Art and the Public Sphere*, ed. W. J. T. Mitchell (Chicago: University of Chicago Press, 1992), pp. 35–36.

40. Lowell, *Public Opinion in War*, p. 133.

41. Ibid., p. 131.

42. Hilaire Belloc, *The Jews* (Boston: Houghton Mifflin, 1922), p. 289.

43. Ibid., p. 145.

44. Steel, *Walter Lippmann*, pp. 46, 51–52, 54.

45. Forcey, *The Crossroads of Liberalism*, p. 109.

46. Lippmann, *Public Opinion*, p. 80. Subsequent citations in the text will be identified as *PO*.

47. Habermas, *Structural Transformation*, p. 102.

48. Another possible synonym is suggested by a chapter title in G. K. Chesterton's *What I Saw in America* (New York: Dodd, Mead, 1922). "Fads and Public Opinion" (p. 162).

49. See Lippmann, *Public Opinion*, pp. 27–29.

50. [Edward L. Bernays], *Biography of an Idea: Memoirs of Public Relations Counsel Edward L. Bernays* (New York: Simon and Schuster, 1965), p. 291.

51. Edward L. Bernays, *Crystallizing Public Opinion* (New York: Boni and Liveright, 1923), p. 41. Subsequent citations will be identified in the text as *CPO*.

52. Habermas, *Structural Transformation*, p. 194.

53. As Terry Smith puts its: "There is, in much advertising's address to its readers during the 1920s, an implicit invitation to complicity, to share in the sense that this particular statement, this type of imagery, is exaggeration. Truth is not the point; sharing illusion is the name of the game." *Making the Modern: Industry, Art, and Design in America* (Chicago: University of Chicago Press, 1993), p. 180.

54. See Pfister, "Glamorizing the Psychological," on glamor.

55. Clifford Geertz, *The Interpretation of Cultures* (New York: Basic Books, 1973), p. 194. See the discussion in Jeffrey Alexander, *Fin de Siècle Social Theory* (London: Verso, 1995), p. 181.

56. Henry John Welch, *Ten Years of Industrial Psychology* (London: Pitman, 1932); Stuart Ewen, *PR! A Social History of Spin* (New York: Basic Books, 1996), p. 183.

57. Ewen, *PR!*, p. 182.

58. John Peter Toohey, *Fresh Every Hour: Detailing the Adventures, Comic and Pathetic of One Jimmy Martin, Purveyor of Publicity, a Young Gentleman Possessing Sublime Nerve, Whimsical Imagination, Collosal Impudence, and Withal, the Heart of a Child* (New York: Boni and Liveright, 1922), p. 24.

59. Jill G. Morawski, "Educating the Emotions: Academic Psychology, Textbooks, and the Psychology Industry, 1890–1940," in *Inventing the Psychological*, ed. Pfister and Schnog, p. 236.

60. Classic thinking about the inwardness of modernism, its emphasis on psychological depth, is summed up in Charles Taylor, *Sources of the Self: The Making of Modern Identity* (Cambridge: Harvard University Press, 1989), p. 481.

61. Jeffrey Weiss, *The Popular Culture of Modern Art: Picasso, Duchamp, and Avant-Gardism* (New Haven: Yale University Press, 1994), p. 55.

62. Ibid., p. 66.

63. Émile Vuillermoz, quoted and paraphrased in Nancy Perloff, *Art and the Everyday: Popular Entertainment and the Circle of Erik Satie* (Oxford: Clarendon Press, 1991), p. 17.

64. For futurism, see Marjorie Perloff, *The Futurist Moment: Avant-Garde, Avant Guerre, and the Language of Rupture* (Chicago: University of Chicago Press, 1986), p. 100. For dada, see the photographs of the First International Dada Fair in Berlin in 1920 included in most histories of the movement. For example, see Marc Dachy, *The Dada Movement: 1915–1923*, trans. Michael Taylor (New York: Rizzoli, 1990), pp. 104–105. Edmund Wilson remarks on the appropriation by dada of American advertising strategies in "The Aesthetic Upheaval in France," *Vanity Fair* 18 (February 1922): 49.

65. See the illustrations in Weiss, *The Popular Culture of Modern Art*, pp. 63, 67.

66. Examples taken from America in the same time period would no doubt have been somewhat more sophisticated in their manipulativeness. See T. J. Jackson Lears, "From Salvation to Self-Realization: Advertising and the Therapeutic Roots of the Consumer Culture, 1880–1930," in *The Culture of Consumption: Critical Essays in American History, 1880–1980*, ed. Richard Wightman Fox and T. J. Jackson Lears (New York: Pantheon, 1983), pp. 1–38. According to Jennifer Wicke, what "we now recognize as the social and economic form of advertisement" came into being in the early 1920s. See her *Advertising Fictions: Literature, Advertisement, and Social Reading* (New York: Columbia University Press, 1988), p. 172.

67. Tom Dardis, *Firebrand: The Life of Horace Liveright* (New York: Random House, 1995), p. 116.

68. Lawrence Rainey, "The Price of Modernism: Publishing *The Waste Land*," in *T. S. Eliot: The Modernist in History*, ed. Ronald Bush, (Cambridge: Cambridge University Press, 1991), p. 96.

69. Dardis, *Firebrand*, p. 87; Rainey, "The Price of Modernism," pp. 96–97.

70. Bernays, *Biography*, pp. 112, 159.

71. Bernays maintained that the phrase "public relations" was first used in news reports of his marriage in 1922. See Bernays, *Biography of an Idea*, p. 290, and *Crystallizing Public Opinion*, pp. 11–12. The fact that he is still considered to be essentially synonymous with the practice of public relations is signified by the prominent place he occupies in Stuart Ewen, *PR!*, especially chapter 1, "Visiting Edward Bernays," pp. 3–18. See also Lears, "Salvation to Self-Realization," p. 20.

72. Bernays, *Biography of an Idea*, p. 287.

73. Ibid., p. 291; and idem, *Crystallizing Public Opinion*, pp. 177–178.

74. Bernays, *Biography of an Idea*, p. 277.

75. Ibid., p. 278.

76. Dardis, *Firebrand*, p. 120.

77. Ibid., p. 143.

78. Terry Eagleton, *Against the Grain: Selected Essays* (London: Verso, 1986), p. 140.

79. The term "consumerism" is taken from Peter Nicholls' survey *Modernisms* (Berkeley: University of California Press, 1995), p. 252.

80. Dardis, *Firebrand*, pp. 95, 98.

81. Rainey, "The Price of Modernism," p. 97; Dardis, *Firebrand*, p. 97. As Rainey reports, Liveright had doubled the usual publicity budget for *The Waste Land*, clearly sensing an opportunity to make a splash (p. 113).

82. That they are not alone in this is suggested by the analysis of *Vanity Fair* in Michael Murphy, "'One Hundred Per Cent Bohemia': Pop Decadence and the Aestheticization of Commodity in the Rise of the Slicks," in *Marketing Modernisms: Self-Promotion, Canonization, and Rereading*, ed. Kevin J. H. Dettmar and Stephen Watt (Ann Arbor: University of Michigan Press, 1996), pp. 61–89. According to Murphy, slick up-scale magazines like *Vanity Fair* made common cause between bohemianism and fashion, between avant-gardism and market savvy.

83. Dardis, *Firebrand*, pp. 116–118.

84. Bernays, *Biography of an Idea*, pp. 255, 261.

85. Bernays, *Biography of an Idea*, pp. 91–92. The possible application of the new science of psychology to advertising had, of course, been noticed much earlier. Walter Dill Scott published *The Psychology of Advertising* in 1908.

86. Bernays, *Biography of an Idea*, pp. 281–282.

87. Judith Ryan, *The Vanishing Subject: Early Psychology and Literary Modernism* (Chicago: University of Chicago Press, 1991), p. 1.

88. Pfister, *Staging Depth*, p. 71; see also idem, "Glamorizing the Psychological," pp. 167–213.

89. Lawrence, *Psychoanalysis and the Unconscious*, p. 24. See also the criticism of "crowd psychology" in *Kangaroo*: "But the only way to make any study of collective psychology is to study the isolated individual." D. H. Lawrence, *Kangaroo*, ed. Bruce Steele (Cambridge: Cambridge University Press, 1994), p. 294.

90. Pfister uses the same icon to represent this situation in both his book and the essay in the Pfister and Schnog collection. It is Carl Van Vechten's 1933 portrait of O'Neill in which his head seems to be suspended in a pool of darkness. See *Inventing the Psychological*, ed. Pfister and Schnog, p. 175.

91. Ronald Bush, "T. S. Eliot and Modernism at the Present Time: A Provocation," in *T. S. Eliot*, ed. Bush, p. 191. Bush is quoting from a letter by Edmund Wilson to John Peale Bishop.

92. Bernays, *Biography of an Idea*, p. 265. See Rainey, "The Price of Modernism," p. 103.

93. *The Diary of Virginia Woolf*, vol. 2, ed. Anne Olivier Bell (London: Hogarth, 1978), p. 211; David Williamson, ed., *The Daily Mail Year Book for 1923* (London: Associated Newspapers Ltd., 1923), p. 24. Woolf ultimately chose to set the novel in June 1923, but this event is clearly remembered from June of the year in which she began to write *Mrs. Dalloway* as a novel.

94. Virginia Woolf, *Mrs. Dalloway* (1925; rpt., New York: Harcourt Brace Jovanovich, 1981), p. 20. Subsequent citations will be identified in the text as *D*. In her essay "The Island and the Aeroplane," Gillian Beer includes a good deal of information about airplanes and Virginia Woolf in a discussion of this passage but does not make the connection to advertising. See Gillian Beer, "The Island and the Aeroplane: The Case of Virginia Woolf," in *Nation and Narration*, ed. Homi K. Bhabha (New York: Routledge, 1990), pp. 265–290.

95. *Illustrated London News*, June 10, 1922, p. 849.

96. *Daily Mail Yearbook*, p. 24.

97. Ibid., p. 24.

98. Jennifer Wicke, "Coterie Consumption: Bloomsbury, Keynes, and Modernism as Marketing," in *Marketing Modernisms*, ed. Dettmar and Watt, p. 117.

99. Wicke, "Coterie Consumption," p. 124.

100. Shoshana Felman, *Jacques Lacan and the Adventure of Insight: Psychoanalysis in Contemporary Culture* (Cambridge: Harvard University Press, 1987), pp. 56–61.

101. Lee, *Virginia Woolf*, pp. 449–450, 465; Abel, *Virginia Woolf*, p. 14, 139n.81.

102. Lee, *Virginia Woolf*, pp. 710–714. See also Abel, *Virginia Woolf*, p. 27; and Alex Zwerdling, *Virginia Woolf and the Real World* (Berkeley: University of California Press, 1986), pp. 295–296.

103. Felman, *Jacques Lacan*, p. 54.

104. There were a number of significant publications on immigration in this year, including Robert E. Park's *The Immigrant Press and Its Control* (New York: Harper's, 1922); Ludwig Lewisohn's *Up-Stream: An American Chronicle* (New York: Boni and Liveright, 1922); and Jerome Davis' *The Russian Immigrant* (New York: Macmillan, 1922); in addition to other works to be discussed in more detail below.

105. Paul Davis Chapman, *Schools as Sorters: Lewis M. Terman, Applied Psychology, and the Intelligence Testing Movement, 1890–1930* (New York: New York University Press, 1988), pp. 65–66.

106. Carl C. Brigham, *A Study of American Intelligence* (Princeton: Princeton University Press, 1923 [copyright date on verso given as 1922]), p. 155.

107. Allan Chase, *The Legacy of Malthus: The Social Costs of the New Scientific Racism* (New York: Knopf, 1977), p. 264. Events of 1922 were crucial in this process: in May, Congress extended the restrictions on immigration that had been passed into law the year before; at that time, the House Immigration Committee, advised by a number of influential nativists, formulated the strategy that led to a permanent law. See John Higham, *Strangers in the Land: Patterns of American Nativism 1860–1925* (New York: Atheneum, 1963), p. 314.

108. Chase, *The Legacy of Malthus*, pp. 227, 321–322.

109. For the first, see Rudolf Pintner, *Intelligence Testing: Methods and Results* (New York: Henry Holt, 1923); Philip Boswood Ballard, *Group Tests of Intelligence* (1922; 2nd ed., London: Hodder and Stoughton, 1925); Kimball Young, "Intelligence Tests of Certain Immigrant Groups," *Scientific Monthly* 15 (November 1922): 417–434; Lightner Witmer, "What Is Intelligence and Who Has It?" *Scientific Monthly* 15 (July 1922): 57–67; and C. C. Little, "The Relation between Research in Human Heredity and Experimental Genetics," *Scientific Monthly* 14 (May 1922): 401–414. Of these, only Little is skeptical about the genetic basis of intelligence. Charles Myers' *Mind and Work: The Psychological Factors in Industry and Commerce* (New York: Putnam's, 1921), which mentions the army tests quite approvingly (pp. 81–82), and Ballard's book, which acknowledges Myers' assistance (p. viii), show how the issue penetrated British psychological circles.

110. *New Republic*, October 25, 1922, p. 213.

111. Walter Lippmann, "The Mystery of the 'A' Men," *New Republic*, November 1, 1922, pp. 246–247.

112. Walter Lippmann, "The Abuse of the Tests," *New Republic*, November 15, 1922, p. 297.

113. Ibid., p. 298.

114. Alvin Johnson, "The End of the World," *New Republic*, November 22, 1922, pp. 331–333; W. McDougall, "Professor McDougall Protests," *New Republic*, May 23, 1923, p. 346; Lewis Terman, "The Great Conspiracy: The Impulse Imperious of Intelligence Testers, Psychoanalyzed and Exposed by Mr. Lippmann," *New Republic*, December 22, 1922, pp. 116–120; and Lippmann's reply, "The Great Confusion," *New Republic,* January 3, 1922, pp. 145–146, reprinted in N. J. Block and Gerald Dworkin, *The IQ Controversy: Critical Readings* (New York: Pantheon, 1976), pp. 30–38, 42–44. McDougall, like Charles Myers, had been associated with Rivers at Cambridge, and was a member of the Torres Straights expedition. See George W. Stocking, Jr., *The Ethnographer's Magic and*

Other Essays in the History of Anthropology (Madison: University of Wisconsin Press, 1992), p. 22.

115. Chapman, *Schools as Sorters*, pp. 99, 104–105, 138, 140–142.

116. See Block and Dworkin's collection, *The IQ Controversy*, which begins with a reprinting of the Lippmann-Terman exchange, and Stephen Jay Gould, *The Mismeasure of Man* (New York: Norton, 1981): "the era of mass testing had begun" (p. 195).

117. Brigham, *A Study of American Intelligence*, p. xvii. See Charles W. Gould, *America: A Family Matter* (New York: Charles Scribner's Sons, 1922), especially p. 163.

118. Brigham, *A Study of American Intelligence*, p. 210.

119. Roberts bases his authority entirely on eyewitness accounts of the "streams of humanity oozing slowly but ceaselessly out of Central Europe to America; streams of under-sized, peculiar, alien people." Kenneth L. Roberts, *Why Europe Leaves Home* (New York: Bobbs-Merrill, 1922), p. 35.

120. Lothrop Stoddard, *The Revolt Against Civilization: The Menace of the Under Man* (New York: Scribner's, 1923 [published May 1922]), p. 69.

121. Cornelia James Cannon, "American Misgivings," *The Atlantic Monthly* 129 (February 1922): 152–153.

122. George P. Cutten, "The Reconstruction of Democracy," *School and Society* 16 (October 28, 1922): 478.

123. Chase, *The Legacy of Malthus*, p. 273; Stephen Jay Gould, *The Mismeasure of Man*, pp. 224, 231.

124. Cannon, "American Misgivings," p. 154.

125. Edwin Grant Conklin, *The Direction of Human Evolution* (New York: Scribner's, 1922), p. 105.

126. Margaret Sanger, *The Pivot of Civilization* (New York: Brentano's, 1922), p. 102.

127. Terman, "The Great Conspiracy," p. 117.

128. McDougall, "Protests," p. 346; Walter Lippmann, "Mr. Lippmann Replies," *New Republic*, May 23, 1923, p. 347.

129. Lippmann, "The Great Confusion," p. 145.

130. Walter Lippmann, *The Phantom Public* (New York: Harcourt, Brace, 1925), p. 166.

131. See Edward A. Purcell, Jr., *The Crisis of Democratic Theory: Scientific Naturalism and the Problem of Value* (Lexington: University Press of Kentucky, 1973), in which Lippmann is considered a contributor to the general disbelief in "rational man" at the bottom of anti-democratic theories of the time.

132. Chapman, *Schools as Sorters*, p. 32.

133. Brigham, *A Study of American Intelligence*, p. 194.

134. Lewis M. Terman, "Adventures in Stupidity: A Partial Analysis of the Intellectual Inferiority of a College Student," *Scientific Monthly* 14 (January 1922): 37. How such a student was ever admitted to Stanford in the first place is a question that Terman dismisses, though the brief biographical sketch he provides reveals that the young man "belonged to one of the most prominent families in the small city where he lived" (p. 25).

135. Rosovksy, *The Jewish Experience*, p. 12.

136. Ibid., pp. 11–15.

137. Ibid., p. 15; Steel, *Walter Lippmann*, pp. 193–194.

138. Steel, *Walter Lippmann*, p. 194.

139. Lippmann, *Public Opinion*, p. 269; idem, *The Phantom Public*, p. 42.

140. Quoted in Steel, *Walter Lippmann*, p. 184.

141. Daniel Chauncey Brewer, *The Peril of the Republic: Are We Facing Revolution in the United States?* (New York: G. P. Putnam's Sons, 1922), p. 33.

142. Ibid., p. 23.

143. Robert B. Westbrook, *John Dewey and American Democracy* (Ithaca: Cornell University Press, 1991), p. 164.

144. James Mickel Williams, *Principles of Social Psychology* (New York: Knopf, 1922), p. 285.

145. William J. Fielding, *The Caveman Within Us* (New York: E. P. Dutton, 1922), p. 253.

146. Ibid., pp. 221–240.

147. Kuttner, "Nerves," pp. 440–442.

148. Stoddard, *Revolt Against Civilization*, p. 27.

149. See Morawski, "Educating the Emotions," p. 234.

150. Moscovici, *The Age of the Crowd*, p. 239.

151. Stoddard, *Revolt Against Civilization*, p. 27.

152. Cannon, "American Misgivings," p. 149, and Fielding, *The Caveman Within Us*, passim.

153. Stoddard, *Revolt Against Civilization*, p. 129.

154. Ibid., p. 138.

155. Ibid., p. 174.

156. Johnson, "The End of the World," p. 332.

157. Hans-Georg Gadamer, *Philosophical Hermeneutics*, trans. David E. Linge (Berkeley: University of California Press, 1976), pp. 22–23.

158. For a contemporary argument that diversity leads to greater intelligence, see Witmer, "What Is Intelligence?"

159. Giddens, *Consequences of Modernity*, pp. 176–177. See also idem, *Modernity and Self-Identity*, pp. 20–21.

160. Walter Lippmann, "Public Opinion and the American Jew," *American Hebrew*, April 14, 1922, p. 575. See also Heinz Eulau, "From Public Opinion to Public Philosophy: Walter Lippmann's Classic Reexamined," *American Journal of Economics and Sociology* 7 (1956): 439–451.

161. W. Adolphe Roberts, "My Ambitions at 21 and What Became of Them—Anzia Yezierska," *American Hebrew*, August 21, 1922, pp. 342, 358.

162. See Mary V. Dearborn, *Love in the Promised Land: The Story of Anzia Yezierska and John Dewey* (New York: Free Press, 1988).

163. Ibid., p. 109. For Dewey and Lippmann, see Steel, *Walter Lippmann*, pp. 47, 78.

164. Anzia Yezierska, *Salome of the Tenements* (1923; rpt., Urbana: University of Illinois Press, 195), p. 101. Though the copyright date of *Salome* is 1923, reviews make it clear that it was issued late in 1922. Subsequent citations in the text will be identified as *ST*.

165. Scott Nearing, in a review in the *Nation*, called Sonya "a devouring monster." Quoted in Louise Levitas Henriksen, *Anzia Yezierska: A Writer's Life* (New Brunswick: Rutgers University Press, 1988), p. 181; for other similar views, see ibid., pp. 181–182.

166. *Salome* was not much of a success, either with the critics or with the public, and it had in fact been turned down by Houghton Mifflin before Yezierska offered it to Liveright. See Henriksen, *Anzia Yezierska*, pp. 174–175, 181–182.

167. See Arjun Appadurai, *Modernity at Large: Cultural Dimensions of Globalization* (Minneapolis: University of Minnesota Press, 1996), p. 7. For a discussion of the ways in which Yezierska manufactures her own personality, see Mary V. Dearborn, "Anzia Yezierska and

the Making of an Ethnic American Self," in *The Invention of Ethnicity*, ed. Werner Sollors (New York: Oxford University Press, 1985), pp. 105–123.

168. Henriksen, *Anzia Yezierska*, pp. 170–171.

169. Dearborn, *Love*, pp. 114–115; Jo Ann Boydston, ed., *The Poems of John Dewey* (Carbondale: Southern Illinois University Press, 1977), pp. xxvi–xxvii.

170. Dearborn, *Love*, pp. 113–114, 165, Boydston, *Poems of John Dewey*, p. xli; and Anzia Yezierska, *Red Ribbon on a White Horse* (1950; rpt. New York: Persea, 1981), pp. 111–112.

171. John Dewey, *Human Nature and Conduct* (New York: Holt, 1922), p. 258; Boydston, *Poems of John Dewey*, p. lvii. Robert Westbrook also suggests that both participants in this relationship saw it as emblematic of a harmony of cultures and human faculties. See Westbrook, *John Dewey*, p. 220.

172. Yezierska, *Red Ribbon*, p. 37. See idem, *Salome*, p. 114.

173. Yezierska, *Red Ribbon*, p. 122.

174. Ibid., p. 79.

175. Ibid., p. 40.

176. In fact, *Salome of the Tenements* might be thought of as combining two 1922 films, *Flesh and Blood*, which starred Lon Chaney as the father of a young social worker who falls in love with a philanthropist, and Nazimova's celebrated screen version of Wilde's *Salome*, with sets and costumes based on illustrations by Aubrey Beardsley.

177. Yezierska, *Red Ribbon*, p. 124.

Chapter 3

1. See Otto Neurath, *International Picture Language: The First Rules of Isotype* (London: Kegan Paul, Trench, Trubner, 1936), and *Basic by Isotype* (London: Kegan Paul, 1937). For a discussion of the frequently vexed relationship between the Vienna Circle, which included Neurath, and Wittgenstein, see P. M. S. Hacker, *Wittgenstein's Place in Twentieth-Century Analytic Philosophy* (Oxford: Blackwell, 1996).

2. Ellen Lupton and J. Abbott Miller, "Modern Hieroglyphs," in *Design Writing Research: Writing on Graphic Design* (New York: Princeton University Architectural Press, 1996), p. 44.

3. Bertrand Russell, "Introduction," in Ludwig Wittgenstein, *Tractatus Logico-Philosophicus* (London: Routledge and Kegan Paul, 1922), p. 9.

4. Charles A. Beard, *Cross-Currents in Europe To-Day* (Boston: Marshall Jones, 1922), p. 2. The same point was made by Professor George Matthew Dutcher in the George Slocum Bennett Lectures delivered at Wesleyan University in February 1923. These lectures were a report on a world tour taken during 1922 and so have particular relevance to the tours discussed below, especially as Dutcher comments at length on the situation in India. George Matthew Dutcher, *The Political Awakening of the East* (New York: Abingdon [1925]).

5. Walter Lippmann, *Public Opinion* (New York: Harcourt, Brace, 1922), p. 66.

6. Ibid., p. 79.

7. Ibid., p. 92. As Chesterton put it, "Modern people put their trust in pictures, especially scientific pictures, as much as the most superstitious put it in religious pictures." *What I Saw in America* (New York: Dodd, Mead, 1922), p. 188. A rather pathetic instance of this quasi-religious faith in the photograph is provided by Arthur Conan Doyle's *The Coming of the Fairies*, which includes "a perfectly straight single-exposure photograph, taken in the open air under natural conditions" and showing a little girl with two "fairies," who are very obviously paper cutouts. See *Illustrated London News*, September 16, 1922, pp. 424, 444.

8. This association of modernity and photography may seem somewhat anachronistic, given that by the 1920s photography had already enjoyed a long history. But the rest of the discussion will make it clear that what is under discussion here is the mass-market photograph as published in popular magazines, which was not a common phenomenon before the war.

9. Sabine Hake, "Faces of Weimar Germany," in *The Image in Dispute: Art and Cinema in the Age of Photography*, ed. Dudley Andrew (Austin: University of Texas Press, 1997), p. 123. See also Allan Sekula, *Photography Against the Grain: Essays and Photo Works 1973–1983* (Halifax: Press of the Nova Scotia College of Art and Design, 1984), p. 95; and Jonathan Crary, *Techniques of the Observer: On Vision and Modernity in the Nineteenth Century* (Cambridge: MIT Press, 1990), p. 13.

10. Martin Heidegger, *The Question Concerning Technology and Other Essays*, trans. William Lovitt (New York: Garland, 1977), p. 134. For a discussion of modernity that begins with Heidegger's essay, see Anthony J. Cascardi, *The Subject of Modernity* (Cambridge: Cambridge University Press, 1992).

11. Heidegger, *The Question Concerning Technology*, p. 135.

12. See the discussion of Benjamin's ideas in Eduardo Cadava, *Words of Light: Theses on the Photography of History* (Princeton: Princeton University Press, 1997), especially p. xxiv.

13. Heidegger, *The Question Concerning Technology*, p. 134.

14. T. Alexander Barns, *The Wonderland of the Eastern Congo* (London: Putnam's, 1922), p. 258.

15. Alfred Viscount Northcliffe, *My Journey Round the World (16 July 1921–26 February 1922)*, ed. Cecil and St. John Harmsworth (Philadelphia: J. B. Lippincott, 1923), pp. 240–243.

16. Brenda Maddox, *The Married Man: A Life of D. H. Lawrence* (London: Sinclair-Stevenson, 1994), p. 293.

17. Our Indian Correspondent [E. M. Forster], "Reflections in India, II. The Prince's Progress," *The Nation and Athenaeum*, January 28, 1922, pp. 644–645.

18. Philip Ziegler, *King Edward VIII: The Official Biography* (London: Collins, 1990), p. 135. The Duke's own account is somewhat more guarded. See *A King's Story: The Memoirs of the Duke of Windsor* (New York: G. P. Putnam's Sons, 1951), pp. 164–166, 173.

19. Sir Harry Brittain, "Foreword," *Our Ambassador King: His Majesty King Edward VIII's Life of Devotion and Service as Prince of Wales*, by Basil Maine (London: Hutchinson, n.d.), p. 4.

20. Ibid., p. 76.

21. Ziegler, *King Edward VIII*, p. 138; Forster, "Reflections," p. 645.

22. Maine, *Our Ambassador King*, pp. 78–79.

23. Brittain, "Foreword," p. 7.

24. Similarly, in Isotype the "5 groups of men" are differentiated almost entirely by their headgear: a homburg for the European, a sombrero for the South American, a turban for the South Asian, a conical hat for the East Asian, and rather lumpish hair for the African. The latter four are black, except in those cases when two different colors of ink are available, when two of them become red. Otherwise, the silhouettes are essentially identical. See Neurath, *International Picture Language*, p. 47.

25. Mahatma Gandhi, *Freedom's Battle* (Madras: Ganesh, 1922), p. 186. For other Indian commentary on the situation, see S. M. Mitra, *Peace in India: How to Attain It* (London: Longmans, Green, 1922).

26. "The Unrest Among India's Teeming Millions: Types of Many Races and Creeds

in a Vast Country," *Illustrated London News*, February 4, 1922, p. 160. That England's relationship with India was at a crucial turning point is also the theme of more serious commentary as well. See, for example, Barbara Wingfield-Stratford, *India and the English* (London: Jonathan Cape, 1922).

27. *Illustrated London News*, February 4, 1922, p. 161. The phrase "teeming millions" was a popular and variously useful one in the British press of the time. *Peoples of All Nations*, to be discussed in more detail below, applies it to China (2:1290).

28. Lugard bases his analysis on Article 22 of the Covenant of the League of Nations, which set out the postwar rationale for continued European imperialism. Lord Lugard, *The Dual Mandate in British Tropical Africa* (1922; rpt., London: Cass, 1965), p. 61.

29. In other words, the category of the nation is contested where India is concerned. A common opinion of the time—"India is not a nation"—is voiced by Edmund Candler in *Abdication* (New York: Dutton, 1922), p. 217.

30. For contemporary official commentary on the situation in India, particularly on the notion of dyarchy, or shared governance, which was the particular Indian application of the principles of the dual mandate, see E. A. Horne, *The Political System of British India* (Oxford: Clarendon Press, 1922); and Sir Courtenay Ilbert, *The Government of India* (Oxford: Clarendon Press, 1922).

31. Harry Hervey, *Caravans by Night: A Romance of India* (New York: Century, 1922), pp. 378–379. The dynamics of disguise in this novel, in which every main character wears at one time or another one or two levels of false identity, deserve more discussion than is possible here.

32. Candler, *Abdication*, p. 270. See the discussion in Benita Parry's *Delusions and Discoveries: Studies on India in the British Imagination 1880–1930* (Berkeley: University of California Press, 1972), pp. 131–163.

33. Hervey's villain is actually physically deformed, a condition that reflects the "tragic anomaly" of his life. Educated in England though he may have been, "Civilization, with him, was a varnish; he did not possess its essence." Hervey, *Caravans by Night*, p. 178.

34. The photo originally appeared in *The Prince of Wales' Eastern Book: A Pictorial Record of the Voyages of the H. M. S. "Renown," 1921–1922* (London: Hodder and Stoughton, 1922). It is also available in Christopher Hibbert, *Edward: The Uncrowned King* (New York: St. Martin's Press, 1972), p. 75. There were a great many pictorial works published in commemoration of the Prince's travels. Among them were Sir Herbert Russell, *With the Prince in the East: A Record of the Royal Visit to India and Japan* (London: Methuen, 1922); W. Douglas Newton, *Westward with the Prince of Wales* (New York: Appleton, 1920); and Bernard C. Ellison, *H.R.H. The Prince of Wales's Sport in India* (London: Heinemann, 1925).

35. For a recent discussion of this trope, see Gail Ching-Liang Low, *White Skins/Black Masks: Representation and Colonialism* (London: Routledge, 1996).

36. *Peoples of All Nations*, ed. J. A. Hammerton, 7 vols. (London: Amalgamated Press, 1922), 1:514. Subsequent quotations from this encyclopedia will be identified in the text as *PAN*.

37. Roland Barthes, *Camera Lucida: Reflections on Photography*, trans. Richard Howard (New York: Hill and Wang), p. 4.

38. Cadava, *Words of Light*, p. 15.

39. *The Letters of D. H. Lawrence*, vol. 4, ed. Warren Roberts, James T. Boulton, and Elizabeth Mansfield (Cambridge: Cambridge University Press, 1987), p. 111. See also Maddox, *The Married Man*, pp. 294–295; and Mabel Dodge Luhan, *Lorenzo in Taos* (New York: Knopf, 1932), p. 12. Lawrence may not seem the most logical choice for such a project;

and yet, at this moment Middleton Murry also associated Lawrence with some sort of racial fusion. At any rate, he speaks quite sarcastically of "that dark, impenetrable blackness in which Mr. D. H. Lawrence tells us we must be bathed in order to renew our being." J. Middleton Murry, "Two French Novels," *The Nation and Athenaeum* 31 (July 1, 1922): 476.

40. See Ann Douglas, *Terrible Honesty: Mongrel Manhattan in the 20s* (New York: Columbia University Press, 1995); and Michael North, *The Dialect of Modernism: Race, Language, and Twentieth-Century Literature* (New York: Oxford University Press, 1994).

41. D. H. Lawrence, *Kangaroo*, ed. Bruce Steele (Cambridge: Cambridge University Press, 1994), p. 32. This is a relatively common phrase in *Kangaroo*; see also p. 332.

42. As Simon Gikandi puts it in a different context, "Travel is hence posited as a mechanism of totalization." *Maps of Englishness: Writing Identity in the Culture of Colonialism* (New York: Columbia University Press, 1996), p. 87.

43. Lawrence, *Letters*, pp. 215–216; see also ibid., pp. 221, 234; and Maddox, *The Married Man*, p. 302.

44. D. H. Lawrence, *The Complete Poems*, ed. Vivian de Sola Pinto and F. Warren Roberts (New York: Penguin, 1977), pp. 386–392. All subsequent quotations will be taken from this edition. The poem was originally published in the *English Review* in April 1923 and then in *Birds, Beasts, and Flowers*. The *English Review* text differs in minor respects, chiefly syntactical, from the text in *Complete Poems*.

45. Lawrence, *Kangaroo*, pp. 122–123.

46. Ibid., p. 238. This passage, interestingly, is about rural England and not Australia.

47. Linda Ruth Williams, *Sex in the Head: Visions of Femininity and Film in D. H. Lawrence* (Detroit: Wayne State University Press, 1993). For a more general discussion of anti-ocular thought in the twentieth century, see Martin Jay, *Downcast Eyes: The Denigration of Vision in Twentieth-Century French Thought* (Berkeley: University of California Press, 1993).

48. Lawrence, *Complete Poems*, pp. 443–446.

49. Quoted in Cadava, *Words of Light*, p. xxv.

50. Williams, *Sex in the Head*, pp. 80–96.

51. Williams calls it "a blind virtue." As she puts it in a description of *The Plumed Serpent*, the dark male "is 'invisible,' because, like the child who covers its eyes, he can see no one seeing him" (ibid., pp. 1, 37).

52. Barns, *Wonderland*, p. 171.

53. According to Brenda Maddox, Lawrence is credited with coining one of the most popular capsule descriptions of Australia: "Australia . . . a Sleeping Princess on whom the dust of ages has settled." But this is, in fact, a quote from the entry on Australia in *Peoples of All Nations*. Whether Lawrence read the entry on Australia before going there, whether this was a phrase so common it might crop up in a number of places, or whether this is simply a coincidence, it is not possible to determine. See Maddox, *The Married Man*, p. 318; and *PAN*, 1:248.

54. "A London Diary," *The Nation and Athenaeum* 31 (August 19, 1922): 677. For a current account of the Northcliffe press as an exemplification of the era, see Billie Melman, *Women and the Popular Imagination in the Twenties: Flapper and Nymphs* (London: Macmillan, 1988), especially pp. 7, 16.

55. Reginald Pound and Geoffrey Harmsworth, *Northcliffe* (London: Cassell, 1959), p. 78.

56. For a discussion of literary "fantasies about an empire united not by force but by information," see Thomas Richards, *The Imperial Archive: Knowledge and the Fantasy of Empire* (London: Verso, 1993).

57. J. A. Hammerton, *Books and Myself* (London: MacDonald, 1946), p. 175.

58. Pound and Harmsworth, *Northcliffe*, p. 275.

59. Northcliffe was providing, in other words, a vulgar version of the grand project of Neurath, which was to be known as *The Encyclopedia of Unified Science*. See Hacker, *Wittgenstein's Place*, p. 59.

60. Edmund Candler, *Youth and the East: An Unconventional Autobiography* (New York: Dutton, 1925).

61. Samuel Weber, *Mass Mediauras: Form, Technics, Media*, ed. Alan Cholodenko (Stanford: Stanford University Press, 1996), p. 79.

62. *Peoples of All Nations* was certainly not the first such pictorial project, but it was one of the first to be so widely and cheaply available. For a discussion of some earlier projects of global pictorialization, including H. J. Mackinder's *The Nations of the Modern World* (1912) and Robert Brown's *The Countries of the World* (1876–1881), see James R. Ryan, *Picturing Empire: Photography and the Visualization of the British Empire* (London: Reaktion, 1997), pp. 183–213. By the turn of the century, many such works were relying heavily on photographs, but Brown uses them only as the source material for engravings.

63. Etienne Balibar, "Paradoxes of Universality," in *Anatomy of Racism*, ed. David Theo Goldberg (Minneapolis: University of Minnesota Press, 1990), p. 285. See also Arjun Appadurai, *Modernity at Large: Cultural Dimensions of Globalization* (Minneapolis: University of Minnesota Press, 1996), p. 156.

64. Malek Alloula, *The Colonial Harem*, trans. Myrna Godzich and Wlad Godzich (Minneapolis: University of Minnesota Press, 1986). The picture on *PAN* 1:83, for example, is shown in Alloula's book as a postcard, complete with written message (p. 26).

65. This is, of course, a common practice in ethnographic writing of the time. Ivor N. H. Evans, fellow of the Royal Anthropological Institute and former colonial official in Borneo, writes in *Among Primitive Peoples in Borneo* (London: Seeley, Service, 1922): "Altogether the Mohammedan native is not usually a very attractive personage" (p. 30). Rev. John Roscoe, whose expedition to Central Africa was sponsored by Frazer and mentioned favorably by Malinowski, tended to rate the people he encountered by a similar system: "their features are good." See *The Soul of Central Africa: A General Account of the Mackie Ethnological Expedition* (London: Cassell, 1922), p. 56.

66. As Sara Suleri puts it in her illuminating discussion of *The People of India*, "The deployment of photographs for the classification of ostensibly unchanging racial types poses a peculiar interpretive problem, in that the specificity of each image begs to be read as illustrative only of itself rather than as a representative of an ahistorical racial type." *The Rhetoric of English India* (Chicago: University of Chicago Press, 1992), p. 106.

67. Weber, *Mass Mediauras*, p. 124.

68. The use of the photograph in anthropology was always based on faith in the type: a specific physical manifestation of some general category. See Elizabeth Edwards, "The Image as Anthropological Document: Photographic 'Types' and the Pursuit of Method," *Visual Anthropology* 3 (1990): 235–258. My argument about the encyclopedia is that the type comes apart into its constituent parts: the general category and its specific representation.

69. Lippmann, *Public Opinion*, p. 79.

70. As Chris Jenks puts it, "The programme set within modern culture for the supposed unification of seeing obviates the disruptive abrasion of conflict and the necessity for discussions of difference." Chris Jenks, ed., *Visual Culture* (London: Routledge, 1995), p. 7.

71. Hamilton Fyfe, author of this entry, was so taken with the idea of a "Third Sex" that he wrote a novel to illustrate it. For a discussion, see chapter 5.

72. Cadava, *Words of Light*, p. 57.

73. Hake, "Faces of Weimar Germany," p. 131.

74. Sekula, *Photography Against the Grain*, p. 96.

75. Appadurai, *Modernity at Large*, p. 161.

76. Quoted in Cadava, *Words of Light*, p. xxvi.

77. Maud Lavin, *Cut with the Kitchen Knife: The Weimar Photomontages of Hannah Höch* (New Haven: Yale University Press, 1993); and *The Photomontages of Hannah Höch*, exhibit org. Maria Mahela and Peter Boswell (Minneapolis: Walker Art Center, 1996).

78. Lavin, *Cut with the Kitchen Knife*, p. 220. For a discussion of the relationship between photomontage and the strategy usually called "defamiliarization," see Simon Watney, "Making Strange: The Shattered Mirror," in *Thinking Photography*, ed. Victor Burgin (London: Macmillan, 1982), pp. 154–176. Another important new kind of photographic process developed at this time was Man Ray's rayograph, in which objects cast their images directly onto photographic paper. See "A New Way of Realizing the Artistic Possibilities of Photography," *Vanity Fair* 19 (November 1922); and Francis M. Naumann, *New York Dada 1915–1923* (New York: Harry N. Abrams, 1994), pp. 216–217.

79. Dawn Ades, *Photomontage*, rev. ed. (London: Thames and Hudson, 1986), p. 42.

80. See Hake, "Faces of Weimar Germany," p. 136; and Rosalind Krauss, *The Optical Unconscious* (Cambridge: MIT Press, 1993), p. 53.

81. Selections from these are pictured in Lavin, *Cut with the Kitchen Knife*, pp. 71–121.

82. See, in particular, the "Paris Letter" that ran in *The Dial* in March 1923, reprinted in Harriet Zinnes, ed., *Ezra Pound and the Visual Arts* (New York: New Directions, 1980), pp. 175–177. Pound's general distrust of the photographic, which he tended to associate with Academy realism in painting, is tempered here by association with Cendrars and Man Ray, who saw artistic possibilities in film and photography that at least intrigued him.

83. *The Collected Poems of William Carlos Williams*, ed. A. Walton Litz and Christopher MacGowan (New York: New Directions, 1986), p. 240. See also MacGowan's note on p. 505, which dates this unpublished poem to 1922.

84. Franco Moretti, *Modern Epic: The World System from Goethe to Garcia Márquez*, trans. Quintin Hoare (London: Verso, 1996), pp. 167, 181, 219.

Chapter 4

1. As Seldes recalled it for the 1957 edition of *The Seven Lively Arts*, he announced his plans to John Peale Bishop and Edmund Wilson "on a late winter evening in 1922 at the corner of 54th street and Broadway" some time after those two men, as editors at *Vanity Fair*, had published the first of the articles that were to become chapters in the book. See Gilbert Seldes, *The Seven Lively Arts* (1924; rpt., New York: Sagamore, 1957), pp. 1–2; and Michael Kammen, *The Lively Arts: Gilbert Seldes and the Transformation of Cultural Criticism in the United States* (New York: Oxford University Press, 1996), pp. 85–86. Since the earliest of these essays, "Golla, Golla, the Comic Strip's Art!" was published in May, this meeting must have taken place in November or December, before Seldes' departure for Europe at the very end of the year. However, Bishop could not have been there at that time, because he was in Europe himself from the summer of 1922 until 1924. See Elizabeth Carroll Spindler, *John Peale Bishop* (Morganton: West Virginia Library, 1980), pp. 67–92.

2. Charles J. Maland, *Chaplin and American Culture: The Evolution of a Star Image* (Princeton: Princeton University Press, 1989), p. 88.

3. Kammen, *The Lively Arts*, pp. 59–61; Lawrence Rainey, "The Price of Modernism: Publishing *The Waste Land*," in *T. S. Eliot: The Modernist in History*, ed. Ronald Bush (Cambridge: Cambridge University Press, 1991), pp. 91–133. It is worth noting that Seldes resolutely denied to the end of his life that the *Dial* award was a quid pro quo for the right to publish *The Waste Land*. Kammen concludes in *The Lively Arts* that here Seldes' memory is in error (p. 59).

4. Gilbert Seldes, "Nineties—Twenties—Thirties," *The Dial* 73 (November 1922): 577.

5. Gilbert Seldes, "T. S. Eliot," *The Nation*, December 6, 1922, pp. 614–616. For Eliot's appreciative letter to Seldes, with unfavorable comments about Wilson's essay, see Kammen, *The Lively Arts*, p. 60.

6. For an account of the part played by Bishop and Wilson in this canonization, see Ronald Bush, "T. S. Eliot and Modernism at the Present Time: A Provocation," in Bush, *T. S. Eliot*, pp. 191–194. Bishop and Wilson, as editors at *Vanity Fair*, were also potential competitors for the poem, as Rainey shows ("Price of Modernism," p. 119), and they were also the two men to whom Seldes remembers having announced his intention to write *The Seven Lively Arts*.

7. Clement Greenberg, *Art and Culture: Selected Essays* (Boston: Beacon, 1961), p. 3. Elsewhere in the same volume, Greenberg talks about his critical indebtedness to Eliot. Adorno makes the same point with the same examples when he insists that to equate jazz with Eliot, Joyce, or cubism is the beginning of barbarism. "Perennial Fashion—Jazz," *Prisms*, trans. Samuel and Shierry Weber (Cambridge: MIT Press, 1981), p. 127.

8. Andreas Huyssen, *After the Great Divide: Modernism, Mass Culture, Postmodernism* (Bloomington: Indiana University Press, 1986), pp. 54, 57.

9. For a discussion of Eliot's interest in these popular arts, see David Chinitz, "T. S. Eliot and the Cultural Divide," *PMLA* 110 (March 1995): 236–247. There has been a fair amount of study of Joyce's sources in the popular arts. See, for example, Cheryl Herr, *Joyce's Anatomy of Culture* (Urbana: University of Illinois Press, 1986). Dan Schiff has suggested that Seldes was responsible for introducing Joyce to "Krazy Kat." See Dan Schiff, "Joyce and Cartoons," *Joyce in Context*, ed. Vincent J. Cheng and Timothy Martin (Cambridge: Cambridge University Press, 1992), p. 202.

10. Brander Matthews, "America and the Juvenile Highbrows," *New York Times Book Review*, January 29, 1922, p. 8.

11. See, for example, "The 'Young Intellectuals' Versus American Civilization," *Current Opinion*, March 1922, pp. 361–363, the very title of which indicates the direction the debate was taking.

12. J. E. Spingarn, "The Younger Generation: A New Manifesto," *The Freeman*, June 7, 1922, pp. 296–298.

13. Camille Mauclair, "Le Préjugé de la Nouveauté dans l'Art moderne," *La Revue*, April 1, 1909, p. 280; quoted in Jeffrey Weiss, *The Popular Culture of Modern Art: Picasso, Duchamp, and Avant-Gardism* (New Haven: Yale University Press, 1994), p. 53.

14. Spingarn had in fact contributed an essay to Stearns' collection *Civilization in the United States* and was close to the editors of *The Dial*. See Kammen, *The Lively Arts*, pp. 62–63.

15. Lothrop Stoddard, *The Revolt Against Civilization: The Menace of the Under Man* (New York: Scribner's, 1923 [published May 1922]), pp. 137–138. Stoddard's preface is dated March 30, 1922, about a week before Spingarn's manifesto appeared.

16. Ibid., pp. 137–138.

17. Royal Cortissoz, *American Artists* (New York: Scribner's, 1923), p. 18. For a paraphrase and a generally sympathetic response to the *New York Times* editorial, see [Albert Jay Nock], "A Reviewer's Notebook," *The Freeman*, June 28, 1922, pp. 382–383. For another racial critique of the younger writers, see "Applying the Anthropological Test to Our Fiction," *Current Opinion*, May, 1922, pp. 664–666, an account of Gertrude Atherton's claims that the low quality of current American fiction is attributable to the general lack of purely Nordic novelists.

18. Paul Rosenfeld, "The Younger Generation and its Critics," *Vanity Fair* 19 (September 1922): 53, 84, 106.

19. Gilbert Seldes, *The Seven Lively Arts* (New York: Harper and Brothers, 1924), p. 24.

20. Georges Braun, "Jazz," *Vanity Fair* 18 (May 1922): 65; Duncan M. Poole, "The Great Jazz Trial," *Vanity Fair* 18 (June 1922): 61–62. Braun mentions Manners by name; Poole alludes to him as "a celebrated playwright who has written a play . . . showing clearly that Jazz not only destroys the home but that its horrid example is corrupting the honest labouring man of the country."

21. J. Hartley Manners, *The National Anthem* (New York: George H. Doran, 1922), p. xi; Neil Leonard, *Jazz and the White Americans: The Acceptance of a New Art Form* (Chicago: University of Chicago Press, 1962), pp. 39–40.

22. Leonard, *Jazz and the White Americans*, pp. 44–45.

23. Morroe Berger, "Jazz: Resistance to the Diffusion of a Culture-Pattern," *The Journal of Negro History* 32 (1974): 464.

24. "Jazz, the impulse for wildness that has undoubtedly come over many things besides the music of this country, is traceable to the negro influence." Quoted in Leonard, *Jazz and the White Americans*, p. 38.

25. "The old are pushed into the back-ground.
    They have taken their places there without a murmur.
    Tired, world-weary, they wait for the final release.
    The Young rarely think of them. When they speak of them it is with some
         current, happy turn-of-phrase—'*Dumb-bells*'"
(Manners, *The National Anthem*, p. xi).

26. *New York Times*, October 8, 1924, p. 18; quoted in Berger, "Jazz," pp. 467–468.

27. Berger, "Jazz," p. 463. For a British example, see the passage from the *Daily Mail*, 1923, quoted as an extract in the OED under "jazz." See also Henry O. Osgood, *So This Is Jazz* (Boston: Little, Brown, 1926), pp. 245–246; and Sigmund Spaeth, "Jazz Is Not Music," *Forum* 80 (1928): 267–271.

28. Clive Bell, "'Plus de Jazz,'" in *Since Cézanne* (New York: Harcourt, Brace, 1922), pp. 214, 222–224. The essay originally appeared in the *New Republic* in September 1921. It is possible that Bell is reacting to an article published by Georges Auric in the May 1920 issue of *Le Coq*. Auric's article "Bonjour, Paris!" was meant to end the influence of American jazz on French composers, particularly the group, of which Auric was a member, known as Le Six, on whom the influence had been particularly strong. The failure of Auric's attempt is signified by the fact that another member of the group, Darius Milhaud, spent much of 1922 in the United States, soaking up jazz influences. See Nancy Perloff, *Art and the Everyday: Popular Entertainment and the Circle of Erik Satie* (Oxford: Clarendon Press, 1991), p. 175.

29. Paul Whiteman, *Jazz* (New York: J. H. Sears, 1926), p. 18. Wide reading in the literature of 1922 suggests that usage as a verb was nearly as common as usage as a noun.

In Seymour Hicks, *Difficulties: An Attempt to Help* (London: Duckworth, 1922) (p. 232), and Peter Blundell, *Princess of Yellow Moon* (London: Methuen, 1922) (p. 2), it is used as a verb meaning "to dance." In Harry Leon Wilson, *Merton of the Movies* (Garden City: Doubleday, Page, 1922), actors told to "jazz" up a scene are being encouraged to make it more violent (p. 76). Even Bertrand Russell got into the act, complaining that "modern philosophers have not the courage of their profession, and try to make their systems ape real life till they become indistinguishable from jazzing." Bertrand Russell, *Essays on Language, Mind and Matter 1919–26* (vol. 9 of *The Collected Papers of Bertrand Russell*), ed. John G. Slater and Bernd Frohmann (London: Unwin Hyman, 1988), p. 40. As Manners' play makes clear, to "jazz" in this sense meant either to dance or merely to move in a way that later became known as "jiving."

30. Whiteman, *Jazz*, p. 117.

31. Bell, "'Plus de Jazz,'" pp. 218, 222–224.

32. It is also possible that the motives behind this attack are personal rather than artistic. Bell and Eliot were involved in some rather spiteful intra-Bloomsbury gossip in the spring of 1919, and later, when two different funds for Eliot's support were announced, Bell was satirically dismissive. See Hermione Lee, *Virginia Woolf* (New York: Knopf, 1997), pp. 434, 440.

33. H. A. L. [Harold Loeb], "The Mysticism of Money," *Broom* 3 (September 1922): 124; advertisement, *Broom* 4 (December 1922).

34. Michael Grant, ed., *T. S. Eliot: The Critical Heritage*, vol. 1 (London: Routledge and Kegan Paul, 1982), pp. 141, 170; Malcolm Cowley, *Exile's Return* (New York: Viking, 1951), p. 176.

35. John Peale Bishop, "The Formal Translations of Jazz," *Vanity Fair* 23 (October 1924): 57, 90, 100.

36. Seldes, *The Seven Lively Arts*, p. 345; Kammen, *The Lively Arts*, p. 79.

37. A fact not lost on the African American press. See "Jazz," *Opportunity* 3 (May 1925): 132–133. This is also something for which Seldes makes profuse apology in the 1957 edition of *The Seven Lively Arts*.

38. Seldes, *The Seven Lively Arts*, p. 107.

39. Ibid., pp. 101–103, 106–107.

40. Ibid. [1957 ed.], p. 83.

41. W. G. Faulkner, "The Kinema in 1922," in *The Daily Mail Year Book for 1923*, ed. David Williamson (London: Associated Newspapers Ltd., 1923), p. 48. See also *Film Year Book 1922–1923* (Hollywood: Wid's Films and Film Folks, 1923), p. 377; and Robert E. Sherwood, *The Best Moving Pictures of 1922–23* (Boston: Small, Maynard, 1923), p. 38.

42. For accounts of the debate over the morals of the movies, see "An Arraignment and Defense of the Movies," *Current Opinion*, March 1922, pp. 353–354; and "Moving-Picture Morals Attacked and Defended," *Current Opinion*, April 1922, pp. 505–506. For a literary reflection of this outrage, see Edgar Rice Burroughs' *The Girl from Hollywood* (New York: Macauley, 1923), a good deal of which seems directly based on the Taylor case.

43. Those polled by the *Film Year Book* agreed almost unanimously that the appointment of Hays was the single most significant event in the movie industry in 1922 (p. 376). Hays himself provided an inspirational introduction for the *Year Book*, which representatively combines his two themes. See also *The Memoirs of Will H. Hays* (New York: Doubleday, 1955), pp. 328, 331, 353. And for public reaction, see "What Hays Can Do For the Movies," *Literary Digest*, January 28, 1922, pp. 12–13; "Public Demand for Risqué Movies,"

Literary Digest, July 15, 1922, pp. 33–34; and "The New $150,000 Boss of the Movies," *Current Opinion*, June 1922, pp. 759–761.

44. Sherwood, *The Best Moving Pictures*, pp. 134–147.

45. James C. Robertson, *The British Board of Film Censors: Film Censorship in Britain, 1896–1950* (London: Croom Helm, 1985), pp. 28, 31. O'Connor's book was written in 1922 and published at the beginning of 1923.

46. Ellis Paxson Oberholtzer, *The Morals of the Movie* (Philadelphia: Penn Publishing, 1922). For a supporting argument, see Donald Young, *Motion Pictures: A Study in Social Legislation* (Philadelphia: Westbrook, 1922).

47. *Film Year Book*, pp. 339–342.

48. William Lord Wright, *Photoplay Writing* (New York: Falk, 1922), pp. 106–107. See also Howard T. Dimick, *Modern Photoplay Writing: Its Craftsmanship* (Franklin, Ohio: James Knapp Reeve, 1922), especially chap. 26, entitled "Censorship, The Growing Menace" (pp. 373–379). *The Elinor Glyn System of Writing*, also published in this year, and John Emerson and Anita Loos' *How to Make It in the Movies*, published in 1921, contain no such concessions, perhaps because these were comfortably established screenwriters, or perhaps because they had become established by daring community standards.

49. *Film Year Book*, p. 340.

50. Rachel Low, *The History of the British Film 1918–1929* (London: George Allen and Unwin, 1971), p. 62.

51. Sherwood, *The Best Moving Pictures*, p. 146; Low, *History of British Film*, p. 60.

52. Oberholtzer, *Morals of the Movie*, pp. 78–79.

53. *Film Year Book*, p. 342; Low, *History of British Film*, pp. 63–64.

54. Low, *History of British Film*, pp. 63–64; M. Jackson Wrigley, *The Film: Its Use in Popular Education* (London: Grafton, 1922), p. 81.

55. Sherwood, *The Best Moving Pictures*, p. 137. In her study of British censorship in this period, Dorothy Knowles maintains that serious social criticism was almost the sole target of the censors. Dorothy Knowles, *The Censor, The Drama and the Film 1900–1934* (London: George Allen and Unwin, 1934).

56. See Adam Parkes, *Modernism and the Theater of Censorship* (New York: Oxford University Press, 1996). Parkes notes that the *Little Review* had first been prosecuted, for a story by Wyndham Lewis, under the same law that governed contraception and abortion (p. 66).

57. "Introduction," *Women in Love*, by D. H. Lawrence, ed. David Farmer, Lindeth Vasey, and John Worthen (Cambridge: Cambridge University Press, 1987), p. li; Edward De Grazia, *Girls Lean Back Everywhere: The Law of Obscenity and the Assault on Genius* (New York: Random House, 1992), p. 72. Parkes also discusses Lawrence's difficulties with the censors.

58. *Secession* 3 (August 1922): 31.

59. Tom Dardis, *Firebrand: The Life of Horace Liveright* (New York: Random House, 1995), pp. 156–170.

60. Ibid., pp. 158–161.

61. See, for example, *Poetica Erotica: A Collection of Rare and Curious Amatory Verse*, ed. T. R. Smith (New York: Boni and Liveright, 1922), which was actually identified on the title page as "Published for subscribers only by Boni and Liveright." The *Satyricon* was published "for private circulation only," but this did not apparently mollify Sumner.

62. Charles Norman, *E. E. Cummings: The Magic-Maker* (New York: Duell, Sloan and Pearce, 1964), p. 93.

63. Kammen, *The Lively Arts*, p. 27.

64. See John Dos Passos, "Off the Shoals," *The Dial* 73 (1922): 97–102; reprinted in *Critical Essays on E. E. Cummings*, ed. Guy Rotella (Boston: G. K. Hall, 1984), pp. 33–37.

65. Seldes, *The Seven Lively Arts*, p. 4.

66. Ibid., p. 249.

67. Gilbert Seldes, "Ulysses," *The Nation*, August 30, 1922, p. 211.

68. T. S. Eliot, "London Letter," *The Dial* 73 (September 1922): 329. The letter is date-lined August 1922, so it seems rather unlikely that Eliot would have seen Seldes' review. The two were in communication at the time, but the nature of their published correspondence does not suggest that Seldes would have shared a draft or typescript with Eliot.

69. Thus the title Wallace Stevens suggested for the six poems he published in *The Dial* in July was "Revue." J. M. Edelstein, *Wallace Stevens: A Descriptive Bibliography* (Pittsburgh: University of Pittsburgh Press, 1973), p. 203.

70. For a history of burlesque in America, see Robert C. Allen, *Horrible Prettiness: Burlesque and American Culture* (Chapel Hill: University of North Carolina Press, 1991). The most famous raid on the Winter Garden occurred in 1925 and was led by John Sumner, who had carried out a campaign against burlesque throughout the 1920s. Though partial nudity and suggestive dancing were perhaps the most outrageous aspects of burlesque in Sumner's view, the official complaint in this case was against obscene humor (p. 251). Allen's book ends with a thoughtful analysis of the "messy dialectics" involved in burlesque, especially where women are concerned.

71. In this sense, perhaps the purest version of "burlesque" to come out of the avant-garde of this period is the famous "Fountain" of Marcel Duchamp. Hung in a show of art-works (or at least presented to the jury of such a show, since "Fountain" was refused), a common urinal puts out in public something generally hidden, thus challenging common notions of decency. At the same time, however, it challenges the distinction between precious, sequestered works of art and common merchandise. That the whole thing was an elaborate joke, with references to the comic strip "Mutt and Jeff," also puts it within a tradition of subversive, semi-obscene humor, extending in France back to Le Chat Noir in the 1880s and forward to the 1920s in the United States, when comic strips like "Krazy Kat" would come to be idolized by the avant-garde.

72. Weiss, *The Popular Culture of Modern Art*, p. 195. For an excellent discussion of the influence of popular music and entertainment, French and American, on the composers who came to be grouped around Satie, see Perloff, *Art and the Everyday*. In fact, Perloff quotes from Milhaud the term "music-hall circus system of aesthetics" and uses the term "music-hall aesthetic" with reference to Henri Prunières (pp. 110, 190).

73. This history might be extended back to the early 1880s, to the French avant-garde groups that coalesced around cafes such as Le Chat Noir and the Café des Incohérents. See Phillip Dennis Cate and Mary Shaw, eds., *The Spirit of Montmartre: Cabarets, Humor, and the Avant-Garde, 1875–1905* (New Brunswick: Jane Voorhis Zimmerli Art Museum, Rutgers, 1996).

74. See T. S. Eliot, *The Waste Land: A Fascimile and Transcript of the Original Drafts including the Annotations of Ezra Pound*, ed. Valerie Eliot (New York: Harcourt Brace Jovanovich, 1971), p. 5.

75. For arguments to this effect, see Charles Sanders, "*The Waste Land*: The Last Minstrel Show?" *Journal of Modern Literature* 8 (1980): 23–38; and Michael North, *The Dialect of Modernism: Race, Language, and Twentieth-Century Literature* (New York: Oxford University Press, 1994), p. 85.

76. Quoted in Cheryl Herr, *Joyce's Anatomy of Culture* (Urbana: University of Illinois Press, 1986), p. 190.

77. Mary Powers, paraphrased from unpublished remarks, in ibid., p. 189.

78. Weiss, *The Popular Culture of Modern Art*, p. 65.

79. Ibid., p. 34. Here Weiss's argument is prefigured by Matei Calinescu's discussion of kitsch: "An extremely important 'strategic' advantage has been the tendency of kitsch to lend itself to irony. From Rimbaud's praise of 'poetic crap' and 'stupid paintings' through Dada and surrealism, the rebellious avant-garde has made use of a variety of techniques and elements directly borrowed from kitsch for their ironically disruptive purposes." Matei Calinescu, *Faces of Modernity: Avant-Garde, Decadence, Kitsch* (Bloomington: Indiana University Press, 1977), p. 230.

80. Michael Murphy, "'One Hundred Per Cent Bohemia': Pop Decadence and the Aestheticization of Commodity in the Rise of the Slicks," in *Marketing Modernisms: Self-Promotion, Canonization, Rereading*, ed. Kevin J. H. Dettmar and Stephen Watt (Ann Arbor: University of Michigan Press, 1996), p. 83.

81. For Flaherty, see *The London Illustrated News*, September 16, 1922, p. 433. For Johnson, see Martin Johnson, *Cannibal-Land: Adventures with a Camera in the New Hebrides* (Boston: Houghton Mifflin, 1922), especially pp. 26–27, 94.

82. Sherwood, *The Best Moving Pictures*, p. viii.

83. For a rigorous attempt to theorize this new public sphere, see John B. Thompson, *The Media and Modernity: A Social Theory of the Media* (Stanford: Stanford University Press, 1995).

84. *Film Year Book*, pp. 422–423.

85. Ibid., p. 423.

86. David Williamson, ed., *The Daily Mail Year Book for 1923* (London: Associated Newspapers Ltd., 1923), pp. 49–50.

87. *Film Year Book*, p. 423.

88. Samuel Goldwyn, *Behind the Screen* (New York: George H. Doran, 1923), p. 67; Edward S. Van Zile, *That Marvel—The Movie: A Glance at its Reckless Past, Its Promising Present, and Its Significant Future* (New York: Putnam's, 1923), p. 15. Van Zile in fact suggests that using this Esperanto of the eye at Versailles might have solved the international problems that arose there.

89. Allan Sekula, *Photography Against the Grain: Essays and Photo Works 1973–1983* (Halifax: Press of the Nova Scotia College of Art and Design, 1984), p. 82.

90. Miriam Hansen, *Babel and Babylon: Spectatorship in American Silent Film* (Cambridge: Harvard University Press, 1991), p. 76.

91. Vachel Lindsay, *The Art of the Moving Picture* (1922; rpt., New York: Liveright, 1970), p. 268.

92. Hansen, *Babel and Babylon*, pp. 76–77; Lindsay, *The Art of the Moving Picture*, pp. 93–94.

93. Sherwood, *The Best Moving Pictures*, p viii.

94. Van Zile, *That Marvel*, p. 128. He is explicitly referring here to arguments made by Hays, a version of which can be found in the *Film Year Book*, pp. 7–9.

95. Rupert Hughes, *Souls for Sale* (New York: Harper and Brothers, 1922), p. 35; John Amid [pseud. Myron Morris Stearns], *With the Movie Makers* (Boston: Lothrop, Lee and Shepard, 1923).

96. Amid, *With the Movie Makers*, pp. 161–162.

97. Oberholtzer, *Morals of the Movie*, p. 169.

98. Van Zile, *That Marvel*, p. 159.

99. See Oberholtzer, *Morals of the Movie*, p. 29.

100. Ibid., p. 169.

101. Ibid., pp. 62–63. Thompson's book *The Media and Modernity* is in part an attempt to deal with this sort of objection to the contemporary public sphere (see especially p. 202).

102. Walter Lippmann, *Public Opinion* (New York: Harcourt, Brace, 1922), p. 365. Note the objections of John Dewey to this rather illiberal solution, "Public Opinion," *New Republic*, May 3, 1922, pp. 286–288.

103. John Paul Russo, *I. A. Richards: His Life and Work* (Baltimore: Johns Hopkins University Press, 1989), pp. 114–115.

104. Hays, *Memoirs*, pp. 343, 347. James O. Kemm, *Rupert Hughes: A Hollywood Legend* (Beverly Hills, Cal.: Pomegranate Press, 1997), p. 135–136.

105. In *The Best Moving Pictures* Sherwood reports that *Gimme* was cut in unspecified ways (p. 146). William Lord Wright's example of an eye-catching title worthy of emulation by the young would-be screenwriter was Hughes' *Scratch My Back* (p. 45). But Hughes had, in fact, a rather complex relationship to the censorship issue. A noted opponent of screen censorship from the days of *Birth of a Nation*, he had also served during the war in the office of the chief military censor. There he collaborated with George Creel, of the Committee on Public Information, as did both Walter Lippmann and Edward Bernays. See Kemm, *Rupert Hughes*, pp. 66–67, 85–86, 93–94.

106. Oberholtzer, *Morals of the Movie*, p. 78; Sherwood, *The Best Moving Pictures*, pp. 84, 115; Kemm, *Rupert Hughes*, pp. 125–127.

107. Hughes, *Souls for Sale*, p. 35.

108. Ibid., pp. 20, 32.

109. Lary May, *Screening Out the Past: The Birth of Mass Culture and the Motion Picture Industry* (New York: Oxford University Press, 1980), pp. 96–146.

110. Walter Benjamin, "The Work of Art in the Age of Mechanical Reproduction," in *Illuminations*, trans. Harry Zohn (New York: Schocken, 1969), p. 223.

111. Hughes, *Souls for Sale*, p. 405.

112. Rudy Behlmer and Tony Thomas, *Hollywood's Hollywood* (Secaucus, NJ: Citadel Press, 1975), pp. 103–107.

113. Seldes, *The Seven Lively Arts*, p. 13; Sherwood, *The Best Moving Pictures*, p. ix. Seldes felt that Ben Turpin's *A Small Town Idol* was a funnier treatment of the same theme. See also Seldes' review, "A Trick of Memory," *The Dial*, July 1922, pp. 106–107.

114. Harry Leon Wilson, *Merton of the Movies* (Garden City, N.Y.: Doubleday, Page, 1922), pp. 76, 139. For a recent discussion of twenties fiction that includes *Merton*, see Chip Rhodes, "Twenties Fiction, Mass Culture, and the Modern Subject," *American Literature* 68 (1996): 385–404.

115. Rosalind E. Krauss, *The Optical Unconscious* (Cambridge: MIT Press, 1993), p. 209.

116. Amid, *With the Movie Makers*, p. 59.

117. Jean-Louis Comolli, "Machines of the Visible," in *The Cinematic Apparatus*, ed. Teresa de Lauretis and Stephen Heath (New York: St. Martin's, 1980), p. 140.

118. James R. Mellow, *Charmed Circle: Gertrude Stein & Company* (New York: Praeger, 1974), p. 408.

119. Seldes, *The Seven Lively Arts*, p. 41.

120. David Robinson, *Chaplin: The Mirror of Opinion* (Bloomington: Indiana University Press, 1983), p. 72; Dawn Ades, *Photomontage*, rev. ed. (London: Thames and Hudson,

1976), p. 34; Louis Delluc, *Chaplin*, trans. Hamish Miles (New York: John Lane, 1922); T. S. Eliot, "Dramatis Personae," *The Criterion* 1 (April 1923): 306.

121. *Illustrated London News*, November 25, 1922, p. 861.

122. Robinson, *The Mirror of Opinion*, p. 42.

123. Charlie Chaplin, *My Trip Abroad* (New York: Harper and Brothers, 1922), p. 77.

124. Ibid., p. 5; Robinson, *Mirror of Opinion*, p. 39; David Robinson, *Chaplin: His Life and Art* (New York: McGraw Hill, 1985), pp. 259–260. Apparently under the influence of Max Eastman, Chaplin did suggest that his ultimate destination might be the Soviet Union, and this caused predictable suspicion among a certain segment of the American populace. See Wes D. Gehring, *Charlie Chaplin: A Bio-Bibliography* (Westport, CT: Greenwood, 1983), p. 32.

125. Maland, *Chaplin and American Culture*, p. 48; "Charlie Chaplin, as a Comedian, Contemplates Suicide," *Current Opinion*, February 1922, pp. 209–210.

126. Charles Chaplin, "We Have Come to Stay," *Ladies' Home Journal*, October 1922, p. 12. Chaplin also appeared in *Photoplay* "With and Without a Necktie." The subtitle gushes "But What a Difference It Makes." *Photoplay* 22 (November 1922): 32.

127. Stark Young, "Dear Mr. Chaplin," *New Republic* 31 (August 23, 1922): 358–359; Maland, *Chaplin and American Culture*, p. 87; Seldes, *The Seven Lively Arts*, p. 52.

128. Charles Chaplin, "In Defense of Myself," *Collier's*, November 11, 1922; reprinted in Gehring, *Charlie Chaplin*, pp. 109–113. Another article that developed the same theme was "Why Is 'Charlie' So Funny When He Is So Sad?" *Literary Digest*, January 28, 1922, p. 48, which is based almost entirely on the reflections of Thomas Burke, author of *Limehouse Nights*, who had met Chaplin in London during his 1921 trip.

129. Seldes, *The Seven Lively Arts*, pp. 213–214.

130. Myron Osborn Lounsbury, *The Origins of American Film Criticism: 1909–1939* (New York: Arno, 1973), pp. 68–69. See Charlie Chaplin, "Making Fun," *Soil* 1 (1916): 6.

131. Seldes, *The Seven Lively Arts* (1957 ed.), pp. 52–53.

132. Maland, *Chaplin and American Culture*, p. 85. See Chaplin, *My Trip Abroad*, pp. 15–16.

133. Maland, *Chaplin and American Culture*, p. 85.

134. Chaplin, *My Trip Abroad*, pp. 6–7; Carl Sandburg, *Complete Poems* (New York: Harcourt, Brace and World, 1950), pp. 302–304.

135. Maland, *Chaplin and American Culture*, pp. 89–90, 385n.58.

136. Ibid., p. 385n.58.

137. Matthew Josephson, "Made in America," *Broom* 2 (June 1922): 270; H. A. L., "The Mysticism of Money," 130; Malcolm Cowley, "Valuta," *Broom* 3 (November 1922): 251.

138. Elie Faure, "The Art of Charlie Chaplin," *The Freeman*, March 22, 1922, p. 33.

139. Seldes, *The Seven Lively Arts* (1957 ed.), p. 49. It is true that Chaplin does a good deal less of this than some silent actors, but a look at *Pay Day*, the one original film he released in 1922, shows that he did not avoid it altogether, and he was certainly no more "silent" on screen than, say, Buster Keaton.

140. Seldes, *The Seven Lively Arts*, p. 41.

141. St. John Ervine, quoted in "Charlie Chaplin, as a Comedian, Contemplates Suicide," *Current Opinion*, February 1922, p. 210. See also Maland, *Chaplin and American Culture*, p. 102.

142. Gehring, *Charlie Chaplin*, p. 100.

143. An intriguing connection between Chaplin's work of this period and the general debate of this time over the effect of media representations on the public is sug-

gested by the alternate title for *A Woman of Paris*, which was distributed in France as *Public Opinion*.

144. For Fairbanks and Pickford, see May, *Screening Out the Past*, p. 198.

145. Chaplin, *My Trip Abroad*, pp. 29–30.

146. Ibid., p. 29.

147. Ibid., pp. 35–36.

148. Benjamin, "The Work of Art," p. 230.

149. Chaplin also appeared as himself in a number of movies made about the movies, including the film version of *Souls for Sale*, in which he is seen directing *A Woman of Paris*. See Behlmer and Thomas, *Hollywood's Hollywood*, pp. 111, 119.

150. Charles Musser, "Ethnicity, Role-Playing, and American Film Comedy: From *Chinese Laundry Scene* to *Whoopee* (1894–1930)," in Lester D. Friedman, *Unspeakable Images: Ethnicity and the American Cinema* (Urbana: University of Illinois, 1991), p. 55.

151. Krauss, *The Optical Unconscious*, p. 206.

152. Quoted in Susan Buck-Morss, "Dream World of Mass Culture: Walter Benjamin's Theory of Modernity and the Dialectics of Seeing," in *Modernity and the Hegemony of Vision*, ed. David Michael Levin (Berkeley: University of California Press, 1993), p. 322.

153. At about this time, Dziga Vertov was using reverse-action photography to investigate the nature of work in a more serious way. See P. Adams Sitney, *Modernist Montage: The Obscurity of Vision in Cinema and Literature* (New York: Columbia University Press, 1990), p. 41.

154. Benjamin, "The Work of Art," p. 250. In the fall of 1922, Duchamp told Paul Strand, "moving pictures are my dada now." Francis M. Naumann, *New York Dada 1915–1923* (New York: Harry N. Abrams, 1994), p. 209.

155. Ades, *Photomontage*, p. 34.

156. Weiss, *The Popular Culture of Modern Art*, p. 173.

157. Sitney, *Modernist Montage*, pp. 158–163.

158. Eliot, "Dramatis Personae," 306. A very similar comment appears in "The Beating of a Drum," *Nation and Athenaeum*, October 6, 1923, p. 12.

159. *The Collected Essays of John Peale Bishop*, ed. Edmund Wilson (New York: Charles Scribner's Sons, 1948), pp. 213–214.

160. Quoted in Christoper Butler, "Joyce, Modernism, and Postmodernism," in *The Cambridge Companion to Joyce*, ed. Derek Attridge (Cambridge: Cambridge University Press, 1990), p. 270.

161. F. Scott Fitzgerald, *The Great Gatsby*, ed. Matthew J. Bruccoli (Cambridge: Cambridge University Press, 1991), p. 46.

Chapter 5

1. Willa Cather, *Not Under Forty* (New York: Alfred A. Knopf, 1936), p. v.

2. This was such an uninviting strategy, in fact, that in later editions the title of the collection was changed to *Obscure Destinies and Literary Encounters*. This version did not include the preface.

3. Hermione Lee, *Willa Cather: A Life Saved Up* (London: Virago, 1989), pp. 183–185. Considerable difficulty has been caused for Cather scholars by their legal inability to quote directly from her letters.

4. Jo Ann Middleton, *Willa Cather's Modernism: A Study of Style and Technique* (Rutherford, N.J.: Fairleigh Dickinson University Press, 1990), pp. 36–37.

5. F. Scott Fitzgerald, "Echoes of the Jazz Age," in *The Crack-Up*, ed. Edmund Wilson

(New York: New Directions, 1945), p. 15. See also Ronald Berman, *The Great Gatsby and Modern Times* (Urbana: University of Illinois Press, 1994), pp. 15, 50. Fitzgerald himself was far from antagonistic toward Cather, going well out of his way to acknowledge a possible debt to her in an early draft of *The Great Gatsby*. For one of many descriptions of this episode, see Robert Roulston, "Something Borrowed, Something New: A Discussion of Literary Influences on *The Great Gatsby*," in *Critical Essays on F. Scott Fitzgerald's The Great Gatsby*, ed. Scott Donaldson (Boston: G. K. Hall, 1984), pp. 57–58.

6. In "Cather and the Academy," *New Yorker*, November 27, 1995, Joan Acocella attributes the pessimism of Cather's later work to this episode (p. 62).

7. This has become an almost obligatory quotation for the many recent discussions of gender bias and modernism. See the classic account by Sandra Gilbert and Susan Gubar, *No Man's Land: The Place of the Woman Writer in the Twentieth Century*, 3 vols. (New Haven: Yale University Press: 1988–1994), 1:156. For other useful discussions of masculinism in the creation and criticism of modern literature, see Bridget Elliott and Jo-Ann Wallace, *Women Artists and Writers: Modernist (Im)Positionings* (London: Routledge, 1994); and Bonnie Kime Scott, *Refiguring Modernism: The Women of 1928* (Bloomington: Indiana University Press, 1995).

8. Gilbert Seldes, "Claude Bovary," *The Dial* (October 1922): 343–345.

9. Edmund Wilson, *Shores of Light* (1952; rpt., Boston: Northeastern University Press, 1985), p. 118.

10. Otto Jespersen, *Language: Its Nature, Development, and Origin* (London: Allen and Unwin, 1922), p. 253.

11. To anyone who finds this term too harsh, I recommend a perusal of the methods by which Jespersen explains away the fact that women had been found to be more successful at reading tests than men (p. 252).

12. For the biographical details, see James Woodress, *Willa Cather: A Literary Life* (Lincoln: University of Nebraska Press, 1987), p. 475. Cather was bitterly disappointed by the lukewarm reception the story received from the editors of the *Woman's Home Companion*, to whom she had submitted it, and it was not published until after her death.

13. See ibid., p. 323, for the publication date. For a comment on the coincidence of names, see Robert J. Nelson, *Willa Cather and France: In Search of the Lost Language* (Urbana: University of Illinois Press, 1988), p. 99.

14. Willa Cather, *The Old Beauty and Others* (New York: Alfred A. Knopf, 1948), p. 44. "Naked," in this case, means with arms and legs exposed.

15. Lee, *Willa Cather*, p. 185.

16. Cather, *The Old Beauty*, p. 44.

17. Ibid., p. 66.

18. For example, see David Stouck, *Willa Cather's Imagination* (Lincoln: University of Nebraska Press, 1975), p. 47.

19. "I always did boy parts, you remember. They wouldn't have me in skirts" (Cather, *The Old Beauty*, p. 28).

20. These details are recounted in all of the biographical works but are given the greatest prominence in the work of Sharon O'Brien. See *Willa Cather: The Emerging Voice* (New York: Oxford University Press, 1987).

21. Cather, *The Old Beauty*, p. 39.

22. Ibid., p. 40.

23. See Elliot and Wallace, *Women Artists and Writers*, pp. 48–55. The androgynous Romaine Brooks self-portrait on the cover of this book was painted in 1923.

24. For the concept of lesbian panic, see Patricia Juliana Smith, *Lesbian Panic: Homoeroticism in Modern British Women's Fiction* (New York: Columbia University Press, 1997).

25. According to Woodress, *One of Ours* sold 54,000 copies the first year, and its financial success and the attendant demand for her other books was sufficient to make Cather comfortable for the rest of her life; "In many ways it was a turning point in her career" (*Willa Cather*, p. 334).

26. Mencken's review, which ran originally in the *Smart Set* in October 1922, is reprinted in *Willa Cather and Her Critics*, ed. James Schroeter (New York: Columbia University Press, 1967), pp. 10–12.

27. Seldes, "Claude Bovary," pp. 438–440. In the same spot in the September issue, Seldes delivered a very critical review of Edith Wharton's *Glimpses of the Moon*. As his title implies, the critical comparison in this case was to James: "The Altar of the Dead," *The Dial* (September 1922): 343–345.

28. Wilson, *Shores of Light*, pp. 40, 41.

29. Willa Cather, *Not Under Forty*, pp. 44, 48. The one modern writer mentioned explicitly here is D. H. Lawrence, and he is treated very harshly (pp. 50–51). This is ironic because Lawrence was perhaps the only modernist writer Cather knew at all well. See Woodress, *Willa Cather*, pp. 353–354.

30. Woodress, *Willa Cather*, p. 76. Also in *Not Under Forty* is "A Chance Meeting," a rather worshipful account of a meeting with Flaubert's niece.

31. Quoted in Frederick T. Griffiths, "The Woman Warrior: Willa Cather and *One of Ours*," *Women's Studies* 11 (1984): 262.

32. Quoted in Wilson, *Shores of Light*, p. 118. Hemingway repeated this accusation in *The Torrents of Spring* (1926; rpt., New York: Scribner's, 1998), p. 57. As late as the 1960s, this opposition between the idealistic account of the war supposedly given by women writers and the toughly realistic one given by the men was still a staple of academic literary criticism. See Frederick Hoffman, *The Twenties: American Writing in the Postwar Decade*, rev. ed. (New York: Free Press, 1962), pp. 67–77. To some extent, Hoffman bases his conclusions on accounts of wartime experiences, such as Faulkner's plane crash, now know to be apocryphal.

33. Rita Felski, *The Gender of Modernity* (Cambridge: Harvard University Press, 1995), p. 79.

34. See Woodress, *Willa Cather*, p. 329; and Nelson, *Willa Cather and France*, pp. 32–33.

35. Willa Cather, *One of Ours* (New York: Knopf, 1922), p. 103. Subsequent quotations will be identified parenthetically, marked with the abbreviation *OO*.

36. Harold Stearns, ed., *Civilization in the United States* (New York: Harcourt, Brace, 1922), p. vii.

37. E. E. Cummings, *The Enormous Room*, ed. George James Firmage (New York: Liveright, 1978), pp. 224, 227.

38. Ernest Hemingway, *In Our Time* (1925; rpt., New York: Scribner's, 1970), p. 70.

39. Billie Melman, *Women and the Popular Imagination in the Twenties* (London: Macmillan, 1988), pp. 52–53.

40. A. S. M. Hutchinson, *This Freedom* (Boston: Little, Brown, 1922), p. 144.

41. G. K. Chesterton, "Our Note Book," *Illustrated London News*, August 5, 1922, p. 198; "Can a Woman Run a Home and a Job, Too?" *Literary Digest*, November 11, 1922, pp. 40–63. In *The American Woman: Her Changing Social, Economic, and Political Roles, 1920–1970* (New York: Oxford University Press, 1972), William Henry Chafe takes *This Freedom* as paradigmatic of the controversy over the supposed conflict between work

and home. Chafe concludes that even for most women of the time the two roles were seen as incompatible (pp. 99–101). See also the discussion in Lynn Dumenil, *Modern Temper: American Culture and Society in the 1920s* (New York: Hill and Wang, 1995), pp. 122–123.

42. Hamilton Fyfe, *The Fruit of the Tree* (New York: Seltzer, 1922), p. 299. Fyfe's long entry on England in *Peoples of All Nations* throws an interesting light on this novel, since it tends to see the emancipation of British women primarily in terms of sports. See *Peoples of All Nations*, 3:1775–1776.

43. Fyfe, *The Fruit of the Tree*, pp. 105, 110; David Williamson, ed., *The Daily Mail Year Book for 1923* (London: Associated Newspapers Ltd., 1923), p. 30. A picture of Miss Ivy Williams in traditional wig and gown appears in the *Illustrated London News*, May 13, 1922, p. 693. Before this could happen the law specifically prohibiting women from practicing law had to be repealed.

44. Charles W. Wood, "Have You a Little Equality in Your Home?" *Collier's*, November 25, 1922, pp. 7–8.

45. *Illustrated London News*, January 28, 1922, pp. 124–125; Stanley Coben, *Rebellion Against Victorianism: The Impetus for Cultural Change in 1920s America* (New York: Oxford University Press, 1991), p. 98.

46. J. Stanley Lemon, *The Woman Citizen: Social Feminism in the 20's* (Urbana: University of Illinois Press, 1973), pp. 69, 66. Edward Bernays always maintained that he had played an important part in this transformation by insisting that his wife be able to travel under her own name and with her own passport. *Biography of an Idea: Memoirs of Public Relations Counsel Edward L. Bernays* (New York: Simon and Schuster, 1965), p. 218.

47. There were at least a few works published in this year that took a different view. The heroine of Margaret Ashmun's novel *Support* (New York: Macmillan, 1922), for example, takes a job because she cannot abide the dependency created in her when she lives on her ex-husband's alimony payments. The women workers in Cornelia Stratton Parker's *Working with the Working Woman* (New York: Harper and Brothers, 1922) have almost all taken their jobs from economic necessity. See also Winnifred D. Wandersee, *Women's Work and Family Values 1920–1940* (Cambridge: Harvard University Press, 1981).

48. Arnold Bennett, *Lilian* (London: Cassell, 1922).

49. Elinor Glyn, *Man and Maid* (Philadelphia: Lippincott, 1922), pp. 331–333.

50. Melman, *Women and the Popular Imagination*, chap. 1; Gilbert and Gubar, *No Man's Land*, 2:chap. 7. The notion that women had taken the opportunity afforded by the war to replace men in the work force was apparently fairly widespread, despite the results of the 1920 census, which were released in 1922. These showed that women made up a smaller part of the total work force than they had in 1910. See Patricia M. Hummer, *The Decade of Elusive Promise: Professional Women in the United States, 1920–1930* (Ann Arbor: UMI Research Press, 1979), p. 11. Hummer points out that most people probably did not draw their impressions from census studies (p. 13). In addition to these novels, there were also at least two films released in 1922 about wives abandoning their homes to go into business. See Mary P. Ryan, "The Projection of a New Womanhood: The Movie Moderns in the 1920's," in *Decades of Discontent: The Women's Movement, 1920–1940*, ed. Lois Scharf and Joan M. Jensen (Westport, Conn.: Greenwood Press, 1983), p. 125.

51. Fyfe, *Peoples of All Nations*, 3:1891.

52. That this is a particularly significant passage and not just a passing comment is suggested by its position at the very end of the first section of the novel, entitled "On Lovely Creek." The next section is rather bluntly titled "Enid."

53. Frances W. Kay, *Isolation and Masquerade: Willa Cather's Women* (New York: Lang, 1993), p. 125.

54. Maureen Ryan, "No Woman's Land: Gender in Willa Cather's *One of Ours*," *Studies in American Fiction* 18 (Spring 1990): 70.

55. Stearns, *Civilization in the United States*, p. 141. See also the discussion in Gilbert and Gubar, *No Man's Land*, 1:143.

56. Felski, *The Gender of Modernity*, p. 94.

57. Woodress, *Willa Cather*, p. 304.

58. Sinclair Lewis, *Babbitt* (New York: Harcourt, Brace, 1922), p. 3.

59. Havelock Ellis, *Little Essays of Love and Virtue* (New York: George H. Doran, 1922), pp. 98–99.

60. Hutchinson, *This Freedom*, p. 177.

61. Ann Douglas, *The Feminization of American Culture* (New York: Knopf, 1977), p. 46.

62. Felski, *The Gender of Modernity*, p. 41. A rather different look at "the maternal home" was provided in this year by Margaret Leonora Eyles' *The Woman in the Little House* (London: Grant Richards, 1922). Here, the average working-class home is depicted as an oppressive trap for the woman who does most, if not all, of the work in it. Yet even Eyles believed that making the home a happy haven would make capitalism a stable and secure system: "Those who seriously want to find the reason for revolutionary talk and action today must look into the little homes for it" (p. 20).

63. See Kay, *Isolation and Masquerade*, p. 120.

64. Lewis, *Babbitt*, p. 269.

65. Ibid., pp. 41, 273.

66. Cummings, *The Enormous Room*, p. 234.

67. *The Day of the Beast* was actually not as successful as the Western stories Grey published at this time: both *To the Last Man* and *The Wanderer of the Wasteland* appeared in the top ten, the former in 1922, the latter in 1923. See Alice Payne Hackett, *70 Years of Best Sellers* (New York: Bowker, 1967), pp. 125–127.

68. See Elaine Showalter, *The Female Malady: Women, Madness, and English Culture, 1830–1980* (New York: Pantheon, 1985), pp. 167–194.

69. Zane Grey, *The Day of the Beast* (New York: Grosset and Dunlap, 1922), p. 78.

70. "So once more Lane became a sufferer, burdened by pangs, a wanderer along the naked and lonely shore of grief" (p. 325). This is the same position occupied by the eponymous hero of *The Wanderer of the Wasteland*.

71. Sherwood Anderson, *Horses and Men* (New York: Huebsch, 1923), pp. 185–228. References to this story will be designated in the text by the abbreviation *HM*. For the dating of the composition of the story, apparently completed some time in the fall of 1922, see Judy Jo Small, *A Reader's Guide to the Short Fiction of Sherwood Anderson* (New York: G. K. Hall, 1994), p. 315. There is an interesting and suggestive relationship between this story and *Many Marriages* (New York: Huebsch, 1923), running at this time in serial form in *The Dial*. *Many Marriages* is another story of a cold, emotionless woman, but in this case her coldness is not related to modernity but rather to repressive tradition. When the husband breaks away from her, he also breaks from bourgeois society and becomes virtually insane.

72. I have found no direct evidence to establish that Anderson had read *My Antonia*. He and Cather were frequently compared at the time, as they are now. See "Editorial," *The Double Dealer* 1 (May 1921): 172; and Lee, *Willa Cather*, p. 38. In 1922 Cather and Anderson served together on the *Bookman* Committee of Contemporary American Fiction, along with Mary Austin, Zona Gale, Mary Roberts Rinehart, and William Allen White. See

James Schevill, *Sherwood Anderson: His Life and Work* (Denver: University of Denver Press, 1951), p. 176.

73. See Sharon O'Brien, "Combat Envy and Survivor Guilt: Willa Cather's 'Manly Battle Yarn,'" in *Arms and the Woman: War, Gender, and Literary Representation*, ed. Helen M. Cooper, Adrienne Auslander Munich, and Susan Merrill Squier (Chapel Hill: University of North Carolina Press, 1989), pp. 184–204.

74. Wayne Koestenbaum, *Double Talk: The Erotics of Male Literary Collaboration* (New York: Routledge, 1989).

75. James Joyce, *Ulysses*, ed. Hans Walter Gabler (New York: Random House, 1986), p. 277.

76. One might also add to this list the appearance, sometime in 1921, of Duchamp's female alter ego, Rose Sélavy. Nor was this sort of transsexual speculation confined to the avant-garde. In May the *Literary Digest* published some musings by Max McConn entitled "Mere Man Asks, How Should I Like to Be a Woman?" McConn imagines himself as female in quite specific detail. *Literary Digest*, May 20, 1922, pp. 59–62.

77. Wilson, *Shores of Light*, p. 119.

78. Marjorie Perloff, "'Ninety Percent Rotarian': Gertrude Stein's Hemingway," *American Literature* 62 (December 1990): 670.

79. Edward Burns, "Foreword," *Useful Knowledge*, by Gertrude Stein (Barrington, N.Y.: Station Hill, 1988), p. ix.

80. James R. Mellow, *Charmed Circle: Gertrude Stein & Company* (New York: Praeger, 1974), pp. 258–259.

81. Stein, *Useful Knowledge*, pp. ix–x.

82. Among the many other visitors Stein received at about this time was Anzia Yezierska, who spent part of 1923 traveling in Europe meeting other well-known authors. See Louise Levitas Henriksen, *Anzia Yezierska: A Writer's Life* (New Brunswick: Rutgers University Press, 1988), p. 195.

83. Wilson, *Shores of Light*, p. 118.

84. Gertrude Stein, *Geography and Plays* (1922; rpt., Madison: University of Wisconsin Press, 1993), p. 6.

85. Sherwood Anderson, "Four American Impressions," *New Republic*, October 11, 1922; reprinted in Mellow, *Charmed Circle*, p. 258. For a discussion of such attempts to domesticate Stein, see Catherine R. Stimpson, "The Somagrams of Gertrude Stein," in *Critical Essays on Gertrude Stein*, ed. Michael J. Hoffman (Boston: G. K. Hall, 1986), pp. 185–186.

86. Anderson, *Geography and Plays*, p. 7.

87. Ibid., p. 7.

88. Ibid., p. 5.

89. Mark Spilka, *Hemingway's Quarrel with Androgyny* (Lincoln: University of Nebraska Press, 1990), p. 298.

90. Ernest Hemingway, *Selected Letters*, ed. Carlos Baker (New York: Scribner's, 1981), p. 650. See the compilation of comments in Christopher Knight, *The Patient Particulars: American Modernism and the Technique of Originality* (Lewisburg: Bucknell University Press, 1995), pp. 117–118, for a number of other suggested relationships and an illuminating discussion of the influence of Stein on Hemingway.

91. Hemingway, *Selected Letters*, p. 62.

92. These have prompted a wholesale reconsideration of Hemingway's work. The biographical work that gives the most complete account is probably Kenneth Lynn's *Hem-*

ingway (New York: Simon and Schuster, 1987). Hemingway's uncertain gender position is also the subject of Spilka's book and of *Hemingway's Genders* (New Haven: Yale University Press, 1994), by Nancy Comley and Robert Scholes.

93. Gertrude Stein, *Portraits and Prayers* (New York: Random House, 1934), p. 193.

94. Lynn, *Hemingway*, p. 109.

95. Mellow, *Charmed Circle*, p. 263.

96. Ernest Hemingway, *Three Stories and Ten Poems* (Dijon: Contact Publishing, 1923), p. 3. This edition, now available in photoreprographic form, will be referred to in the text as *TS*.

97. Linda Ruth Williams, *Sex in the Head: Visions of Femininity and Film in D. H. Lawrence* (Detroit: Wayne State University Press, 1993), pp. 100–101. Williams also cites the question posed by Miriam Hansen about Valentino, which is pertinent here: "If a man is made to occupy the place of erotic object, how does this affect the organization of vision?" Miriam Hansen, *Babel and Babylon: Spectatorship in American Silent Film* (Cambridge: Harvard University Press, 1991), p. 252.

98. Alice Hall Petry, "Coming of Age in Horton's Bay: Hemingway's 'Up in Michigan,'" in *New Critical Approaches to the Short Stories of Ernest Hemingway*, ed. Jackson J. Benson (Durham: Duke University Press, 1990), p. 354.

99. Jespersen, *Language*, p. 246.

100. Glyn, *Man and Maid*, p. 125; see also p. 158.

101. Gertrude Stein, *Three Lives* (1909; rpt., New York: Penguin, 1990), p. 155. Knight places a passage from "Melanctha" next to one from "Up in Michigan" to demonstrate how much they resemble one another in sentence structure (*The Patient Particulars*, p. 121).

102. Perloff, "Ninety Percent Rotarian," pp. 678–680.

103. Stein, *Three Lives*, p. 147.

104. Lynn, *Hemingway*, pp. 109–110, 152–153.

105. Jespersen, *Language*, pp. 247–248.

106. Burns in Stein, *Useful Knowledge*, p. ix.

107. Marjorie Perloff applies to Stein Wittgenstein's question: "But isn't *the same* the same?" *Wittgenstein's Ladder: Poetic Language and the Strangeness of the Ordinary* (Chicago: University of Chicago Press, 1996), p. 92.

108. Burns in Stein, *Useful Knowledge*, p. x.

109. Stein, ibid., p. 91.

110. Ibid.

111. Jespersen, *Language*, p. 249.

112. See, for example, the account of Stein's proposal to Toklas in Linda Simon, *The Biography of Alice B. Toklas* (Garden City, N.Y.: Doubleday, 1977), p. 70.

113. Walter Benn Michaels, *Our America: Nativism, Modernism, and Pluralism* (Durham: Duke University Press, 1995), pp. 72–73.

114. Mellow, *Charmed Circle*, p. 273. Wayne Koestenbaum has also declared that "Stein Is Nice" (*Parnassus* 20 [1995]: 297–319), but in simplifying the term so that it contains none of its original meaning of "finely discriminating," he not only simplifies Stein but removes from her work the sense of linguistic irony and discontinuity that makes it so "nice." In this sense, he uses the word much as Hemingway did.

115. Ernest Hemingway, *The Sun Also Rises* (1926: rpt., New York: Scribner's, n.d.), p. 28.

Conclusion

1. Fredric Jameson, *Postmodernism, or, The Cultural Logic of Late Capitalism* (Durham: Duke University Press, 1991), pp. 2, 304. Though I am implying that the present study is an attempt to provide such a sociology by working from modern culture to modernism and vice versa, I am well aware that it says far too little about the structure of capitalism, late or otherwise, to meet Jameson's criteria.

2. Peter Nicholls, *Modernisms* (Berkeley: University of California Press, 1995), p. 5.

3. For the earliest examples of this practice, see Phillip Dennis Cate and Mary Shaw, eds., *The Spirit of Montmartre: Cabarets, Humor, and the Avant-Garde 1875–1905* (New Brunswick: Jane Voorhees Zimmerli Art Museum, Rutgers, 1996). For a description of such practices in France during the 1920s, see Nancy Perloff, *Art and the Everyday: Popular Entertainment and the Circle of Erik Satie* (Oxford: Clarendon Press, 1991).

4. Jeffrey Weiss, *The Popular Culture of Modern Art: Picasso, Duchamp, and Avant-Gardism* (New Haven: Yale University Press, 1994), p. 153.

5. Maud Lavin, *Cut with the Kitchen Knife: The Weimar Photomontages of Hannah Höch* (New Haven: Yale University Press, 1993), p. 67. According to Lavin, there was a decided shift in this direction in 1922, when Berlin dada ceased to function as a cohesive movement (p. 50).

6. Stephen E. Lewis, "The Modern Gallery and American Commodity Culture," *Modernism/Modernity* 4 (September 1997): 74.

7. Andreas Huyssen, *After the Great Divide: Modernism, Mass Culture, Postmodernism* (Bloomington: Indiana University Press, 1986), p. 60.

8. See Francis M. Naumann, *New York Dada 1915–1923* (New York: Harry N. Abrams, 1994), especially p. 209; and Perloff, *Art and the Everyday*, pp. 94–96.

9. Michael Kammen, *The Lively Arts: Gilbert Seldes and the Transformation of Cultural Criticism in the United States* (New York: Oxford University Press, 1996), pp. 89, 94.

10. For an excellent discussion of Pound's relationship to dada, centered on 1922, see Richard Sieburth, "Dada Pound," *South Atlantic Quarterly* 83 (Winter 1984): 44–68.

11. Ezra Pound, "On the Swings and Roustabouts: The Intellectual Somersaults of the Parisian vs. the Londoner's Efforts to Keep his Stuffed Figures Standing," *Vanity Fair* 18 (August 1922): 49; Edmund Wilson, "The Aesthetic Upheaval in France: The Influence of Jazz in Paris and Americanization of French Literature and Art," *Vanity Fair* 17 (February 1922): 49.

12. Huyssen, *After the Great Divide*, p. 58.

13. David Chinitz, "T. S. Eliot and the Cultural Divide," *PMLA* 110 (March 1995): 236–247.

14. Jameson, *Postmodernism*, p. 4.

15. Nicholls, *Modernisms*, pp. 5, 16.

16. John B. Thompson, *The Media and Modernity: A Social Theory of the Media* (Stanford: Stanford University Press, 1995), p. 175.

17. Jameson, *Postmodernism*, p. 412.

18. Thompson, *The Media and Modernity*, p. 43.

19. Arjun Appadurai, *Modernity at Large: Cultural Dimensions of Globalization* (Minneapolis: University of Minnesota Press, 1996), p. 63.

20. Ibid., p. 64.

21. Nicholls, *Modernisms*, p. 19.

22. François Bourricaud, "Modernity, 'Universal Reference' and the Process of Modernization," in *Patterns of Modernity*, vol. 1, ed. S. N. Eisenstadt (London: Frances Pinter, 1987), p. 18.

23. David Trotter, "A Horse Is Being Beaten: Modernism and Popular Fiction," in *Rereading the New: A Backward Glance at Modernism*, ed. Kevin J. H. Dettmar (Ann Arbor: University of Michigan Press, 1994), pp. 191–219; Billie Melman, *Women and the Popular Imagination in the Twenties: Flappers and Nymphs* (London: Macmillan, 1988).

24. Huyssen, *After the Great Divide*, p. 53. See also the skeptical discussion of this point of view in Astradur Eysteinsson, *The Concept of Modernism* (Ithaca: Cornell University Press, 1990), pp. 14–18.

25. Art Berman, *Preface to Modernism* (Urbana: University of Illinois Press, 1994), p. 28.

26. T. S. Eliot, *The Waste Land: A Facsimile and Transcript of the Original Drafts including the Annotations of Ezra Pound*, ed. Valerie Eliot (New York: Harcourt Brace Jovanovich, 1971), p. 31.

27. T. S. Eliot, *The Complete Poems and Plays, 1909–1950* (New York: Harcourt, Brace and World, 1971), p. 44.

28. Georg Lukács, *History and Class Consciousness*, trans. Rodney Livingstone (Cambridge: MIT Press, 1985), p. 131.

29. [Edward L. Bernays], *Biography of an Idea: Memoirs of Public Relations Counsel Edward L. Bernays* (New York: Simon and Schuster, 1965), pp. 206, 208–216.

30. Ibid., p. 247.

31. Edward L. Bernays, *Crystallizing Public Opinion* (New York: Boni and Liveright, 1923), p. 212.

32. Michael Murphy, "'One Hundred Per Cent Bohemia': Pop Decadence and the Aestheticization of Commodity in the Rise of the Slicks," in *Marketing Modernisms: Self-Promotion, Canonization, Rereading*, ed. Kevin J. H. Dettmar and Stephen Watt (Ann Arbor: University of Michigan Press, 1996), p. 79.

33. Jameson, *Postmodernism*, p. 4.

34. See Weiss, *The Popular Culture of Modern Art*, especially p. 66.

35. Jameson, *Postmodernism*, p. 5.

36. As Eysteinsson puts it in *The Concept of Modernism*, paraphrasing Habermas, "Our ability even to criticize reason and the 'rational order' . . . involved the Enlightenment's legacy of rationality, democracy, and critique" (p. 236).

Index